THE
INDIAN
ARMY

THE
INDIAN
ARMY
AND THE KING'S ENEMIES
1900-1947

CHARLES CHENEVIX TRENCH

With 70 illustrations,
including 20 maps and plans

THAMES AND HUDSON

Picture Research: Alla Weaver

Printed and bound in the German Democratic Republic.

Contents

Acknowledgments 6
Foreword 7
Maps and Plans 8
1 Soldiers of the Company, and of the Queen 9
2 Soldiers of the King 15
3 Their Mercenary Calling: Western Front, 1914–17 31
4 Gallipoli, 1915 50
5 East Africa, 1914–18 67
6 Mesopotamia, 1914–18 75
7 Palestine, 1918 91
8 Cloak and Dagger, 1917–19 101
9 Waziristan, 1919–21 104
10 Times of Peace, 1921–39 115
11 Getting Ready 134
12 The Second World War: Opening Bids, 1939–40 137
13 East Africa, 1939–41 142
14 The Arrival of Afrika Korps, 1941 150
15 Sideshows, 1941–42 158
16 Eighth Army Advances, 1941 162
17 Eighth Army Retreats, 1942 170
18 Eighth Army Defeated, 1942 175
19 Rising Sun, 1941–42 191
20 Eighth Army Triumphs, 1942–43 221
21 Italy: the Gustav Line, 1943–44 230
22 Burma: the Turning Tide, 1943–44 254
23 Italy: *Guerra è Finita*, 1945 270
24 Triumph of the Forgotten Army, 1945 277
25 Unfinished Business, 1945–46 290
26 Finis: 1946–47 293
Select Bibliography 297
Chronology 300
Glossary of Vernacular and Foreign Words 304
Indian Ranks and British Equivalents 305
Abbreviations 306
Index 307
Sources of Illustrations 312

Acknowledgments

I have received abundant and generous help in writing this book. Major General J. G. Elliott, who has told much of this story in *The Frontier* and *Roll of Honour*, and Mr Philip Mason whose book on the Indian Army, *A Matter of Honour*, is a classic, helped me with encouragement and general advice. On matters relating to artillery Major General B. P. Hughes and Lieutenant Colonel C. H. T. MacFetridge were my principal mentors, and the latter gave me permission to quote extensively from *Tales of the Mountain Gunners*. For engineering expertise I looked to Major General I. H. Lyall Grant, Colonel M. B. Adams and the officers whom they put in touch with me. Mrs Carmichael gave me a free hand with her late husband's book, *Mountain Battery*; and my former Adjutant, Brigadier Miles Smeeton, with his autobiography, *A Change of Jungles*. Mr James Leasor kindly allows me to quote from *Boarding Party*; Colonel R. C. Jackman and Major J. E. G. Lamond, representing the 2nd Goorkha Rifles, from the regimental history; and Brigadier D. F. Ryan, Secretary of the Royal Artillery Institution, from Lieutenant Colonel MacFetridge's article on Light AA in Burma in the *Royal Artillery Journal* for March 1982. A major source for the First World War is W. S. Thatcher's *History of the Fourth Battalion, DCO's Own, Tenth Baluch Regiment in the Great War*, to quote from which I was given permission by his daughter, Miss Mary Thatcher. Colonel J. H. Wakefield, Lieutenant Colonel C. J. M. Weippert and Miss Kathleen Grimshaw made available to me her father's diary before it was published under the title *Indian Cavalry Officer, 1914–1915*.

Of unpublished sources, I could not trace the copyright holders of Captain Bagot-Chester's diary in the Ministry of Defence Library, nor of Major R. S. Waters, Lieutenant Colonel P. M. MacDwyer, and Major C. J. L. Allanson in the library of the National Army Museum. For permission to quote from the papers of Lieutenant General Sir R. A. Savory and Captain T. C. Catty in the National Army Museum I am indebted to Major A. S. Savory and Mr R. H. Catty. I am also most grateful to Lady Bromhead and Lieutenant Colonel A. F. Harper for permission to quote from the papers of Lieutenant Colonel Sir Benjamin Bromhead, Bart, and Major T. Harper.

Finally I must thank the staff of the National Army Museum Library, the Ministry of Defence Library and the India Office Records for the great help they gave me; to all those who contributed letters, diaries and other material, whose names are listed under 'Unpublished Sources'; and to Lieutenant Colonel Patric Emerson, Secretary of the Indian Army Association, for his unstinted help in publishing my appeals for material and organizing the collection of it.

Foreword

This is not a history. It is a book about the British Indian Army, its officers and men, in peace and in war, in victory and in defeat, during its last forty years. It was an army of mercenaries, serving less for pay than for the prestige attached in India to the mercenary profession. It was composed of men of four main religions and a score of races speaking a dozen languages, all bound together by regimental pride and by the influence of officers at first all British, later increasingly Indians. It was the largest volunteer army the world has ever seen: not a man in it was conscripted.

Few would deny that the outstanding soldiers of the twentieth century were the Germans and the Japanese. They were defeated by sea- and air-power, overwhelming economic and military strength, and superior technology. But they had also to be defeated in battle, and in this the Indian Army took an honourable part. From 1914 to 1916 it was fighting a war for which it was neither trained, mentally prepared, organized nor equipped. Its performance was not always perfect. What army's is? But it came through the ordeal with great credit. For the Second World War it was far better prepared in every way, and its performance reflected this. The weakness so apparent twenty-five years earlier – over-reliance on regular British officers and going to pieces when these were killed – was corrected by a better system of officers' reserves, by more thorough replacement officers' training, and above all by thousands of young Indians holding the King's Commission, serving alongside British Officers with equal courage and efficiency, equally honoured by the men they commanded.

Maps and Plans

Cambrai, 1917   47
Gallipoli: Sari Bair, 6–10 August 1915   55
East Africa, 1914–18   69
Mesopotamia, 1914–18   76
Mesopotamia, March–April 1916   78
Mesopotamia, October 1918   88
Palestine, 1918   93
Waziristan, December 1919–January 1920   107
Waziristan (general)   113
Waziristan: Iblanke, 11–12 May 1937   129
East Africa: Keren, February–March 1941   145
North Africa   154–55
North Africa: Jebel Achdar, 1941   166–67
Burma   197
Burma: Sittang Bridge, 21–22 February 1942   201
North Africa: Wadi Akarit, April 1943   224
Italy: Monte Cassino, 1944   244
Italy: Monte Cassino area   248
Burma: Ngakyedauk, February 1944   257
Italy: February–May 1945   274

CHAPTER I

Soldiers of the Company,
and of the Queen

The French, who held the military in high esteem, were drilling and arming Indians to fight as early as 1674; while the English, whose memories of military rule under Cromwell's Major Generals made them suspicious of standing armies, were still by the 1740s arming Indians only to guard warehouses. But trade rivalry between the British and French East India Companies erupted into war, in which the British were worsted. After this they took more seriously the organizing of Indian sepoys under European officers in regular units. These proved to be greatly superior to the armies of native potentates. They were no braver, no better armed: their advantage was in superior 'bundobust', a portmanteau term embracing administration, supply, regular pay and rations, discipline and tactical training. The British had greater resources than the French and, generally, command of the sea; and by 1764 the Honourable East India Company was on its way to becoming master of the sub-continent.

The influence and territory of the Company expanded from its three main 'factories' (trading centres) at Calcutta, Madras and Bombay. Its administrative structure was therefore divided into the three Presidencies of Bengal, Madras and Bombay, each with its Governor and Council. Because Bengal expanded faster and had more economic potential than the others, it became *primus inter pares*. Military organization followed suit.

Crucial to the Company's victories were Indian sepoys under British officers. At first these were Madrassis, organized only in companies. But shortly after the battle of Plassey (1757) the first Indian regiment was raised in the British service. It was called the 1st Bengal Native Infantry because it was raised in Bengal Presidency, but its rank-and-file were men from northern India. This was the beginning of the Bengal Army which during the next hundred years overran India, smashed the Mahrattas, suffered catastrophic defeat in Afghanistan, and in the hardest fought battles yet seen in India, demolished the empire of the Sikhs. It contained seventy-four regular infantry battalions, besides cavalry and field artillery; and had more prestige, because it saw more active service, than the Madras and Bombay Armies.

If a man is to risk his life and endure great hardship, he needs a strong motive. Cromwell's 'lovely company' fought for the 'Good Old Cause' of Dissent against bishops, and republicanism against the King. The armies of the French Revolution and Napoleon were inspired by patriotism and hatred of kings. Germans fought for Kaiser and Fatherland, or Hitler and National Socialism, Japanese for the Emperor, Boers for Independence.

For centuries Moslem armies roared into battle for the One God and his Holy Prophet.

The British soldier was rather different. To a degree unknown in other armies (except in the French Foreign Legion) his strongest motive was pride in and loyalty to his regiment. Compare the *Marseillaise*, a hymn to patriotism, with *The British Grenadier*, a regimental rant.

What, then, made the Indian soldier fight? Until well into the twentieth century he had no concept of India as his country. Men of at least four religions fought side by side. If his sovereign was not some Rajah or Nawab, until 1857 it was a trading company, and he looked down on trade; after 1857 it was a dumpy little widow whom he never saw. He was a mercenary, but although a man might join up for eight rupees (about twelve shillings) a month, he was not likely to risk his life for it. However, the Indian soldier's was a highly esteemed calling, he was respected in his village. The mercenary profession was an honourable one: Rajputs had commanded the armies of the Moghul, Pathans served every Maharajah and Nawab from Lahore to Mysore. Serving the Company Bahadur was, therefore, an honourable service.

Naturally, British officers in sepoy regiments grafted onto the Indian concept of an honourable profession the British concept of pride in one's regiment. If it was honourable to be a soldier, it was thrice honourable to be one in Skinner's Horse or the 1st Bengal Native Infantry. Even sepoys who mutinied in 1857 retained pride in their regiments, and went into battle against the British wearing their scarlet uniforms, behind their regimental colours.

The causes of the Mutiny of 1857 are sufficiently well known not to be detailed in this book, which is more concerned with its consequences. Briefly, they amounted to a loss of contact with and confidence in the officers; a feeling that the sepoys' special, privileged position was being eroded by unsympathetic, 'levelling' Commissioners and Collectors; and a suspicion, not entirely groundless, that some officers wished to turn them, willy-nilly, into Christians. Through an administrative blunder the bullets of the new cartridges, which the soldier bit as part of the loading process, were greased with tallow made from pig's fat, abhorrent to Moslems, and cow's fat, sacred to Hindus. This was the spark which set off the explosion. It was a mutiny only of the Bengal Army, and an uprising in the areas where the Bengal Army was most recruited: the Madras and Bombay Armies, and the irregular forces raised in the Punjab, helped suppress it.

The Mutiny produced the most appalling atrocities, with officers, their wives and children mercilessly butchered. There is no evidence that the women were raped, but stories to this effect roused British soldiers to berserk frenzies of revenge and wholesale executions of guilty and innocent alike. When it was all over, and the victors emerged reeking from the shambles, a very different army was created.

There were several lessons from the Mutiny. The proportion of British to Indian troops should never fall below one to three, and the field artillery should all be in British hands. Proselytizing was out: indeed British Officers insisted on the tenets of their men's religions being most strictly observed, for instance in discharging from the regiment any Sikh soldier who, for whatever reason, cut or trimmed his hair or beard. (It was said that, but for the Army, Sikhs would have merged back into the Hindu community from which they came.) Except in certain classes which were considered completely reliable, it was considered safer to have regiments of mixed classes, rather than all of one class: they would be less likely to be infected simultaneously by the same grievance. Irregular cavalry regiments were more reliable than regular: they had fewer British Officers, the Native Officers had more responsibility, and they attracted a better class of man. The government of India was taken over by the Crown: Indian soldiers were no longer soldiers of the Company but of the Queen.

Of the seventy-four regular regiments of the Bengal Army, eighteen had stayed loyal and these were re-numbered 1–18th Bengal Native Infantry. To complete the infantry complement of the Bengal Army, twenty-seven regiments raised recently, mainly to suppress the Mutiny, were taken in. The Bengal regular cavalry regiments were replaced by eight pre-Mutiny irregular regiments, and eleven which had been raised to suppress the Mutiny. Both in infantry and cavalry, the number of British Officers was small, varying from time to time between seven and twelve to a regiment. It was a deliberate policy to build up the prestige and responsibility of Native Officers – Subadars and Jemadars of infantry, Risaldars, Ressaidars and Jemadars of cavalry.

Since the Madras and Bombay Armies had remained loyal, it might have been expected that the classes enlisted in them would thereafter be favoured. This was not so. Madrassi regiments were gradually phased out. Mahrattas were not regarded with great favour. The favoured classes were from the Punjab and the North-West Frontier – Sikhs, Punjabi Mussulmans, Dogras, Jats, Pathans; and, of course, Gurkhas. Very few of these had mutinied; they had enlisted in large numbers, and vied with men of the Island Race in slaughtering 'Pandies'.

Reasons for preferring northerners were largely racial. To Kipling's contemporaries, the taller and fairer a native, the better man he was likely to be. He looked more impressive on parade, he might be physically stronger, he would surely be braver and more 'loyal' than the down-countryman. There was a general preference for the wild over the 'half-educated' native, as being less addicted to unwholesome political thinking. Although themselves, in Brahmin eyes, untouchables, the British acquired from Indians a sort of caste-snobbery. Soldiers should be of the warrior or at least cultivator class if Hindus, and their social equivalent if Moslems – but not of too high caste: Brahmins had been prominent in the Mutiny, and their diet and prejudices made difficulties on active service. The ideal soldier was the sturdy, independent yeoman farmer, be he Rajput, Jat, Sikh or Moslem. The Madrassi soldier was smallish, blackish and rather low-caste. The Mahratta was also in origin of no very high caste, and smallish to boot. The fact that his grandfathers had held India to ransom did not make him more acceptable to the Indian Army.

A typical Punjab regiment might consist of four classes – Sikhs, Jats, Dogras and Pathans, each for administrative convenience grouped in its own class-company. This made for healthy rivalry, but also a brotherhood of the regiment, besides the brotherhood of one's own class.

Someone unfamiliar with the Indian Army might assume that between British Officers and Indian soldiers the Mutiny would be a closed subject. On the contrary: it was recalled on appropriate anniversaries and reunions, depicted in photographs and drawings in officers' messes. It was to most Indian regiments as the Peninsular and Waterloo were to British regiments. Broadly speaking, units who formed the post-1857 army were either those who had remained loyal during the Mutiny, or those who had been raised to suppress it. Both were proud of the part they had played.

In the half-century after 1857 the Bengal Army found a new role which was wholly satisfying: mountain warfare against the independent Pathan tribes along the North-West Frontier.

The 'Frontier Problem' was a legacy of the Sikhs. Essentially it was: how to protect the comparatively law-abiding tribes, Pathan and Punjabi, cultivating the fertile Indus valley from the lawless and predatory Pathan tribes who inhabited the tangle of mountains between the Indus valley and Afghanistan? There were two rival policies, the merits of which were heatedly argued: the 'Forward Policy' of administering and disarming the tribes right up to the Afghan border, and the 'Close Border Policy' of holding back the army in the Indus valley and India itself and allowing the denizens of 'Tribal Territory' to stew in their own juice. Only when their raids and other outrages became too intolerable did a military force advance ponderously into the territory of the guilty tribe, kill a few of the men, blow up a few tribal forts, extract a fine in cash and rifles – and then withdraw. This policy was also known as 'butcher and bolt'. It had its drawbacks, but the experience of fifty years and thirty punitive expeditions seemed to show that the Forward Policy for the whole length of the Frontier was impracticable with the resources at India's disposal.

The essence of mountain tactics is to protect the main body by holding all hilltops within sniping range of its advance, withdrawal or encampment. The tribes were well armed, knew every inch of the country and had been practising this sort of thing for generations. Soldiers had to be tough, and very agile uphill and down; junior officers and NCOs, half a mile from the company commander, had to display great initiative. These skills were developed by the Bengal Army, and to a lesser degree, in Baluchistan, by the Bombay Army. The Madras Army never went to the Frontier. The greatest experts, not part of the Bengal Army, were the Punjab Irregular Frontier Force ('Piffers') consisting of nine infantry battalions, five cavalry regiments and four mountain batteries, all Indian. They were always on the Frontier, and took part in every frontier expedition: other units of the Bengal Army only took their turns.

SOLDIERS OF THE COMPANY

There was a Russian dimension to Frontier policy. It was the intention of British government to check, or at least divert from India, the inexorable advance of Russia over the landmass of Asia. To this end the Khyber and Bolan Passes were held, and strong forces kept in the Punjab and Quetta. It was a top military and diplomatic priority to keep the barbarous kingdom of Afghanistan neutral but well-disposed. This resulted in the signal catastrophe of the First Afghan War (1839–42) and the somewhat better managed Second Afghan War (1878–80) in which Sir Frederick Roberts marched from Kabul to Kandahar and won the last battle. He loved Indian troops – or at least some of them. But with the 'brilliant exception of the Madras Sappers and Miners, a most useful, efficient body of men', he had no use for Madrassi soldiers. Most of his Bengal Army contemporaries agreed with him: to them it was axiomatic that soldiers who were small, black and low-caste were also cowardly and 'effeminate'. So the northward drift of recruitment continued, leaving only four battalions of the Madras line and the Sappers and Miners to carry on a tradition of unspectacular but steady, faithful, meritorious service.

The object of recruiting from fewer 'martial classes' was simply to obtain the best soldiers. There was no deeper or more sinister motive. But it did distance the Indian soldier from the population as a whole, and insulate him from nationalist politics. There was thus an element, never formulated or authoritatively expressed, of 'Divide and Rule'.

In 1885 Roberts became C-in-C of the Bengal Army, with supervisory powers over the other two. He was not a great innovator, but he set new standards for the three armies: they must be able not merely to fight Pathan tribesmen, to suppress another mutiny and maintain law and order, but to hold a Russian attack until help came from England. Individual training was greatly improved, particularly in shooting straight, a martial art strangely neglected in many armies.

In 1895 the posts of C-in-C Madras and Bombay were abolished: there was to be only one Indian Army, in which was merged the Punjab Irregular Frontier Force. Every unit was now liable for service on the Frontier, though some served there more than others.

From about 1900 frontier campaigns became more serious and more prolonged. As the British and colonial armies were re-armed with the Lee-Metford magazine rifle, their discarded Martinis, bought up by dealers, passed in large numbers through the Persian Gulf to the tribesmen of the North-West Frontier. The Martini, although not a magazine rifle, is a very good weapon, accurate to a thousand yards. It was no longer enough to piquet every height within three hundred yards of a column; piquets had to go much further, slowing down every advance and infinitely complicating the problems of withdrawal. The tribesmen castrated any wounded man left behind: rather than leave a single wounded sepoy, a company, even a battalion, might have to counter-attack.

Lord Curzon, Viceroy from 1899 to 1905, devised a compromise frontier policy: he decreed an Administered Border of British India, enclosing the

13

plains and lower foothills, to the east of which would be all the blessings of civilization; while to the west of it, up to the Afghan border, was an area known as Tribal Territory. The Army was held back in cantonments in British India; in Tribal Territory Political Agents would, without actually administering the tribes, do what could be done to wean them from their wicked ways. Each Political Agent would have at his disposal a local, irregular Militia, led by British Officers seconded from the regular army but not part of the army or under military command. These included the North and the South Waziristan Militias, each of about brigade strength, employed on such tasks as convoy escorts, road protection, the pursuit and interception of raiders. Recruited entirely from Pathans and largely from *local* Pathans, they were a calculated risk, an attempt to turn poachers into gamekeepers. Just how reliable they would prove was a matter of doubt.

In 1903 Kitchener became C-in-C, dourly determined that the Indian Army should profit by the lessons painfully learnt by the British Army from the Boers, the first enemy it had encountered armed with high-velocity magazine rifles and quick-firing artillery. With the details of his quarrel with Curzon we are not concerned: it was about control of the army at the top, military administration and supplies, and Kitchener won. This gave him a free hand in reorganizing the Indian Army. He knew nothing about India, but he was a master of military administration.

The army in India, which included British units, was divided into three categories, in any of which any regiment might be placed. These were: 1, covering troops; 2, field army; 3, internal security troops. The responsibilities of the covering troops were the suppression of minor troubles on the Frontier, and to cover the mobilization and concentration of the field army.

The Indian Army must be organized and equipped for a minor and a major danger. The minor was a Frontier uprising escalating perhaps into a Third Afghan War; the major, a war against Russia, in which the Indian Army must hold the Russian invader until help came from England. For this task it must be armed not with slightly obsolescent weapons, but with the very latest, subject only to the prior claim of the British Army. The Mutiny must be forgotten; the army must be stationed and prepared for its major task. It must be organized in peacetime in the brigades and divisions in which it would go to war, trained in peacetime by the officers who would command it in war, served by staff officers taught at the Staff College in Camberley and a similar staff college to be set up in Quetta.

For half a century the Royal Navy and the Indian Army – with the British Army intervening on special occasions – defended and advanced British interests east of Suez. The Indian Army fought in Egypt, the Sudan, Abyssinia, British Somaliland, Jubaland, British East Africa, Aden, the Persian Gulf, Persia, Afghanistan, the North-West Frontier, the North-East Frontier, Tibet, Burma, Malaya and China. Refashioned by Lord Kitchener to fight the Russians, it fought Turks and Germans. So it merits a closer look.

CHAPTER 2

Soldiers of the King

The private soldier in infantry was either a sepoy or a rifleman; in cavalry a sowar (rider). He looked upon even a subaltern as his *mām-bāp*, mother-and-father, who would not only command him in battle and go in front to get shot first, but would see that he was trained, clothed, fed, paid and received preferential treatment from the civil authorities in his village. Nothing was thought more important than to preserve that relationship.

An army in which the soldiers spoke at least nine languages and the officers a tenth needed a lingua franca. This was Urdu, the camp-language of the Moghul armies, an amalgam of Persian and Hindu, written in the Roman script for use with the Morse code. It was always used in official matters between officers and men in Indian regiments: in Gurkha regiments Gurkhali was used. English was *never* used. Most soldiers had to learn Urdu as recruits, but it was close enough to the languages of northern India to be fairly easy for them. For British Officers it was more difficult. But learn it they must: until they had passed the Higher Standard examination they could neither take home leave nor be confirmed in the Indian Army. Furthermore, an officer had to learn at least one of the languages the men in his regiment spoke in their villages – Pushtu, Punjabi, Mahratti or whatever. So perhaps the most important factor in the officer-man relationship was that the officer came more than half way, linguistically, to meet the man.

In 1907, fifty years on from the Mutiny, it would have been inconceivable for an officer to refer to his men as 'niggers', as his grandfather would have done, or even 'natives'. And if he grudged time spent in their company, he had better transfer to the British Army. He was expected to spend a good deal of his off-duty hours with them – taking them shooting, acquiring a couple of Salukis and joining the regimental coursing club, playing hockey with them in Indian infantry or football in Gurkha regiments, in cavalry competing with them in jumping and tent-pegging. He probably spent more than one period of ten days' leave touring round the district from which his men were recruited, meeting the regimental pensioners and listening to their tales of '57 and '78.

The sepoy or sowar was, to be sure, a soldier of the King, but it is unlikely he gave much thought to that except on royal occasions, which meant a lot of ceremonial parades. As for the King's Birthday Parade, he would have been more emotionally moved by the Colonel Sahib's birthday. What made the Indian Army tick was the sepoy's pride in his profession and in his regiment, and complete, unquestioning trust between officer and man. But there was a reverse side to this coin: it was a *personal* relationship between the sepoy and the officers whom he knew. If too many of these officers were killed, and replaced by strangers who might not speak his language or know his name, then the Indian soldier might be utterly lost.

'Native Officers' as they were called in the nineteenth century, or 'Indian Officers' in the twentieth, were links between British Officers and sepoys, advisers in matters relating to sepoys, examples to sepoys of what men of their race could become and achieve. The Subadar Major in infantry, the Risaldar Major in cavalry, was the Colonel's confidential adviser in matters relating to the men. A Subadar in infantry, a Risaldar in cavalry, might command a platoon or troop, or be second-in-command of a company or squadron. Jemadars commanded platoons and troops. In 1907 they were unlikely to be educated, and might have difficulty with a map. But they knew everything about the men in their own classes, and about company and squadron administration. They had a prestige far greater than their official disciplinary powers and were expected to sort out all kinds of troubles without the British Officers knowing. They were good men at arms, and in cavalry horsemen and horsemasters; but the years 1900 to 1914 were in general years of peace for the Indian Army, so some of the Indian Officers were rather too old for rigorous active service. They were *officers*, saluted by the men, on easy social terms with British Officers, who invariably called them 'Sahib'. One could have a drink or a meal with an Indian Officer as his host or guest. The extraordinary thing was that these formidable veterans would cheerfully take orders from a junior subaltern who was far less experienced, albeit far better educated and more technically instructed than they. But he would be very unwise not to ask the Subadar Sahib's advice.

W. G. Raw of Rattray's Sikhs (in 1907 the 45th Sikhs, in 1922 the 3rd Battallion of the 11th Sikh Regiment) tells a story which illustrates the relations between the Subadar Major and the latest joined subaltern. The incident occurred in 1931: it could equally well have occurred twenty-five years earlier.

'I was . . . shortly to go on the young officers' rifle course at the Small Arms School at Pachmarhi. The regiment was ultra-smart, and I used to think myself pretty smart, having quite recently been an Under-Officer at Sandhurst. One day . . . I was being polished up in bayonet-fighting by the top regimental instructor, and thought I really was pretty good at it. When the period was finished the Subadar Major, who had been looking on, asked to speak to me. He was a very fine man, and very tough, on this occasion dressed impeccably in our white muslin mufti, with a beautifully tied safa [turban] and a faultlessly rolled-up beard. Standing stiffly to attention with his cane under his arm, he said in a very quiet voice, "Huzoor, I hope you will forgive my mentioning it, but your bayonet-fighting leaves more than a little to be desired. I know you will find it possible to put in *considerably* more practice before you go to Pachmarhi. When you are there, you must never forget that you represent the 45th Sikhs. It is quite immaterial if you personally suffer in

1 Captain George Jolland (1743–73), 7th Coast Sepoys, later 2/1st Punjab Regiment.
The sepoy is a Madrassi, a class which had a record of faithful, steady service.

2 *(above)* Irregular Indian Cavalry Regiment, possibly Skinner's Horse; mid-nineteenth century. Tent-pegging was a favourite sport.

3 *(below)* 'Tom Raw plays billiards', watercolour by Sir Charles D'Oyly Bt, *c.* 1815–20. It was reproduced by R. Ackerman in 1828 in *Tom Raw, the Griffin*, a poem by the artist.

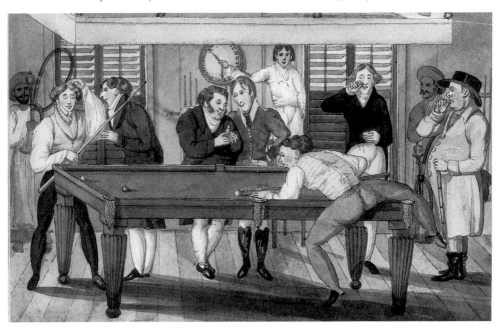

4 *(above)* Indian sepoy of 36th Native Infantry (raised August 1794), carrying musket – with wife.

5 *(below)* Sepoys of Bengal Native Infantry at rifle practice, *c.* 1857. Most of such men mutinied.

6 (above) Mutiny veterans, 53rd Sikhs (later 3rd/12th Frontier Force Regiment): very proud of the part they had played in suppressing the Mutiny.

7 (below) Officers and men of the 19th Lancers. c. 1870. A typical 'Silladar' cavalry regiment.

8 *(above)* Scouts of the 10th Bengal Lancers (Field Service Kit), *c.* 1910. A somewhat idealized picture: it wasn't really so neat and tidy – or so dust-free.

9 *(below)* Indian Artillery, No. 31 Mountain Battery Gunner (Punjab Mussulman), *c.* 1910.

Sikhs au cantonnement. P. Sarrut
15ᵉ Sikhs (Allouagne)

10 *(above)* 15th Sikhs in France, 1915. Drawing by P. Sarrut.

11 *(below)* Gobind Singh, 2nd Lancers, winning the VC, Cambrai 1917. He carried vital messages three times over 2½ miles of ground swept by artillery and machine-gun fire.

12 Indian cavalry on the Western Front, 1917. They seem to be wearing their steel helmets on top of their pagris.

13 Naik Darwan Sing Negi, of the Garhwal Rifles, leading round the traverses at Festubert, November 1914, and thereby winning the second Indian VC.

any way, but it must *never* happen that the name of the Paltan [regiment] should suffer in any way whatsoever, such as if your bayonet-fighting is not up to standard. Please never forget this, Huzoor." With a beautiful salute and about-turn, he marched off, leaving me feeling like a minute speck of droppings from a baggage-camel. I am glad to be able to say that I got a "Distinguished" at Pachmarhi, and the Subadar Major said when I got back that he was "pleased with me". They were a *very* fine regiment, incredibly smart and efficient, all the men being Jat Sikhs. Waves of nostalgia smother me!'

The British Officer – there were twelve per battalion – would be of the upper or upper-middle class, product of a public school – Rugby or Wellington rather than Eton. He probably had a father or an uncle in the Indian service. In the cavalry he would need a little private money, £50 or £100 a year. His pay was slightly more than the British Army subaltern's ten shillings a day. As a subaltern he ran up debts which he hoped to pay off as a captain. Because British Army subalterns needed considerably more private means, and because the best chance of active service was in India, there was strong competition to get into the Indian Army. In 1913, for instance, of the cadets who passed out of Sandhurst, twenty out of the top twenty-five chose Indian Army. (It may be relevant to their future relations that Montgomery failed for the Indian Army, Auchinleck – at about the same time – succeeded.)

The average officer's spare-time interests were sporting rather than intellectual. He believed that vigorous exercise was necessary to health, and conducive to that sexual abstinence which was the general lot of young officers in India at that time. (But not of all young officers. There was a famous Everest climber, a great character, named Bruce. Years after his retirement, a subaltern asked the Subadar Major of his Gurkha battalion what Bruce Sahib was like. 'What do you want to know about him, Sahib?' 'Well, anything.' 'I can tell you this, then. He was the only officer who screwed every Gurkha wife in the battalion.') In cavalry and some infantry regiments the young officer spent a lot of time and more money than he could afford on horses. Infantry officers were entitled to one government charger, cavalry officers to two; and they could hire troop-horses for about ten shillings a month insurance premium. In some districts there was pig-sticking, by far the most exciting and dangerous of all horse-sports; in others hunting (the Peshawur Vale Hunt gave wonderful sport); and polo almost everywhere. Most officers were keen on *shikar*, shooting. They could get good bird-shooting (duck, snipe and various partridges) near most cantonments; tiger, bear, panther, bison, buffalo and several kinds of stag in the jungles. The cream of sport, in the opinion of aficionados, was the pursuit of the wild goats and sheep of the Himalayas, ibex, markhor and ovis ammon, two or three weeks' march from roadhead.

Cavalry officers used to say that, although they took a more relaxed view of life, they worked harder than infantry officers because they had horses to look after. But no one was exactly overburdened with labour. The day's work started at about 6.30 a.m. and ended at lunchtime; the afternoon was given over to a siesta, or language-study; the evening to games and sports. But they probably worked harder than their contemporaries in the British Army: having less money, their outlook was more professional.

Every British and Indian Officer had his orderly, who was not a domestic servant carrying out menial tasks, but was expected to keep his officer's weapons in good order, and on manoeuvres and active service to see that the best arrangements were made for his officer's shelter and bedding while the officer was performing a similar service for the men under his command. Above all, an orderly was his officer's runner (or galloper), and bodyguard. The idea was that the less time an officer spent on looking after himself, the more time he spent on looking after his men.

There was an informal, well-understood pecking order of regiments. Naturally one's own was at the top. After that, northern-recruited regiments were generally seen as 'better' than some 'down-country' regiments; but neither braver nor more efficient, as events in two World Wars were to show.

The Indian cavalry, even more than the British cavalry, found it difficult to swallow the main lesson of South Africa – that the horse's job was not 'shock-action' but to carry riflemen and machine-gunners to the point where they could dismount and use their weapons to the best effect. They longed for the charge with lances and the new, straight, thin-bladed cavalry thrusting sword, with no cutting-edge, the most lethal cavalry-sword ever devised, thirty years too late.

Nearly all the cavalry regiments were 'irregular', a term defined by three characteristics: 1, an attitude of mind, an emphasis on regimental differences and idiosyncrasies, a slight disdain for excessive enthusiasm and parade-ground precision; 2, a loose, practical khaki uniform for service, and for ceremonial occasions the most splendid Indian-style uniforms, scarlet, dark blue, light blue, rifle-green, primrose yellow, stiff with gold lace, with tight Kashmir-shawl cummerbund and safa streaming in the wind of the gallop-past; and 3, the 'silladar system' whereby each sowar owned the horse he rode and the equipment he wore, paying for it by monthly stoppages from his pay. A silladar regiment cost the government much less than a regular regiment; the sowar had a direct, financial interest in looking after his horses and equipment; and it attracted to cavalry a type of yeoman farmer who joined for other than financial motives.

A feature of the silladar regiment was the Darbar, a periodic assembly with the British and Indian Officers on chairs, the rank-and-file sitting cross-legged on the ground in front of them, all in plain clothes, at which any man could raise any point in the regiment's administration or internal economy. He was, after all, a sort of shareholder in a joint-stock company. Why were the regimental bunniah's prices so high? Could not two more syces be engaged to help look after the remounts? Was it not time for the night stable-guard to start wearing greatcoats? How was the regimental co-operative bank's money invested? A commandant's reputation depended in part on his readiness in answering impromptu awkward questions. At an anniversary Darbar of the Tenth Bengal Lancers (Hodson's Horse) a lot of pensioners were present, as was their right. One aged Mussulman rose shakily to his feet to say that because of his services in the Mutiny, the benign government allowed him to travel at half price on the railways. He now wanted to make the pilgrimage to Mecca. Would the Colonel Sahib kindly arrange for the shipping company and the Turkish authorities to grant him similar facilities? Colonel Cowper rose to the occasion. 'Certainly,' he said. 'No problem. But,' he added with impeccable logic, 'if you do your pilgrimage at half price, you can expect only half the benefit.' No more was heard of the matter.

Infantry did not hanker after the weapons and tactics of a bygone age. All they wanted was the latest weapons and plenty of them. They were extremely well trained, especially for frontier warfare. In Kipling's India the British battalion in every Indian brigade, keeping the one-to-three proportion, was considered to be the pace-setter, the example for the natives to follow, taking on the difficult and dangerous jobs with the natives in support. No longer. Any good Indian battalion was confident that it could give points to any British battalion in mountain warfare, being more mobile on the hillside, more alert, less liable to lose its rifles or leave its wounded to be mutilated. They may have been flattering themselves, but this is what they believed. And British battalions probably would not argue the point: mountain war was not their forte. Infantry weapons were the rifle, the bayonet, the kukri in Gurkha and Garhwali regiments, and two Maxim machine-guns to a battalion. Grenades and mortars were folk-memories, almost as remote as pike and longbow. Musketry was taken seriously and the standard was very high: a man's pay, and his prestige, depended on his annual musketry classification.

Alongside the Indian Army, there were the Indian State Forces, armies of the semi-independent Maharajahs and Nawabs. Selected units of the State Forces were upgraded in equipment, training and by the attachment of one or two British Officers to take their place in war in Indian Army brigades.

In Indian regiments there was very little 'crime' in the military sense: where every man wants to stay in the army as long as possible, discipline presents no great problem. There was much debate among officers about the virtues and defects of various classes. Sikhs were given to intrigue and trouble-making under weak officers, but made splendid soldiers if worked really hard. Pathans were much the same, with an added complication: about 5,000 Pathan soldiers hailed from Tribal Territory, outside British India and some even from Afghanistan. The civil authorities had therefore no authority over them, they could desert with impunity and could not be arrested in their villages. A soldier's rifle was worth across the border three or four years' pay, and the temptation to desert with it was not always resisted. Many Afridis and Mahsuds were enlisted in Piffer, Baluchi and Punjab regiments because they were magnificent fighters: but they were also the most prone to desertion and the occasional fanatical murder of an officer. Mahsuds were a byword for unreliability, which the Mahsud himself would not deny: 'We are a very untrustworthy people', he would say with a sly grin and not without pride. The Punjabi Mussulman was the backbone of the Indian Army, solid and reliable but not flashy. The Dogra was thought to be quiet, reliable, well-behaved, courageous, but lacked the Pathan's native cunning, and was apt to get killed unnecessarily. The Rajput was much the same. Jats were worthy and slightly dull. No one thought much of Mahrattas before 1914; everyone thought a great deal of them after 1918. Their own officers proclaimed *ad nauseam* that Gurkhas were the best infantry in the world because of their phenomenal speed in mountainous country and their total lack of imagination. In Gurkha messes the merits and demerits of Magars and Gurungs, Limbus and Rais were hotly argued; but to other people they seemed very much alike – nice little fellows, excellent, aggressive infantry though a trifle thick, liable (like everyone else) to have their off-days.

Indian soldiers were at least as well trained as British soldiers for war against Afghans, but they had not enlarged their knowledge and brought it up to date by fighting against the Boers. In armament they were half a step behind the British Army, using in 1907 the Lee-Metford or long Lee-Enfield which the British had used in South Africa.

There was no set period of colour and reserve service. A man could take his discharge after three years, or soldier on for eighteen years if a sepoy, longer if an Indian Officer or NCO, to qualify for a pension. There was no obligation for reserve service, only a modest financial inducement. These arrangements produced an efficient, long-service professional army; but many, such as subadars with twenty-five years service, were too old for modern war, and all the goods were in the shop window. In 1911 battalions with a war establishment of 745 had on average only 300 reservists on their books, although experience in South Africa had shown that in modern conditions (even apart from casualties) there could be a wastage of 80 per cent in a year's active service. Most of the reservists were too old, and too much family men, to be eager for the fray. It is strange that Kitchener did not remedy these defects, which were to have disastrous consequences in 1914–18.

As for officers, there was an Indian Army Reserve of Officers, in which young men did a month's training every year with the unit of their choice. But there were only forty of them in July, 1914.

Recruits were generally brought in very young, by friends or relations already in the regiment. They would be vetted by the Indian Officers, the Adjutant, and Medical Officer, for physical, social and general suitability: the regiment was very much a family affair. If, as was usual, there was no immediate vacancy, the accepted recruit would be placed on the *umedwar* ('hopeful') list until his turn came to be sent for. There were no training depots: recruits' training was the responsibility of the Adjutant and the Woordie Major or Jemadar Adjutant of the regiment. This was a grave flaw in the Indian Army's organization, which was to have painful consequences.

Pioneer battalions were trained to fight as infantry and to work as road-makers, trench-diggers, dock labourers, or on any other job which needed doing. Generally they were of a lower caste than infantry: the Sikh Pioneers, for instance, were Sikhs by religion but Untouchables by descent, and not acceptable in units which recruited only Jat Sikhs of the farmer class. But they had a fine fighting record.

The only artillery manned by Indians since the Mutiny were the mountain-guns, carried dismantled by big, strong mules which could climb any slope a man could negotiate without pulling himself up by his hands. In 1907 the Mountain Batteries were armed with a breech-loading gun firing a 10lb shell to a maximum range of 6,000 yards. It made five mule-loads. It fired shrapnel, either over open sights or laid indirectly, or case-shot in dire, close-range emergency. Whatever their rivalries, no cavalry or infantry officer would dispute the supreme excellence of the Mountain Batteries: the Indian Army was very proud of them. The mules were magnificent, and far more sure-footed over rocks or across the steepest shale-slope than any horse. The men had to be bigger and stronger than the average to manhandle the guns. The officers were not regular Indian Army, but were seconded for a period of years from the Royal Artillery. Many became hooked on the mules and the screw-guns, and returned to them again and again.

A mountain battery going into action was one of the sights of the Frontier – the gun position officer galloping up to the selected gun position; the mounted surveyors with flapping artillery boards on their backs, the signallers with drums of cable on either side of the saddle and field telephone on the back, moving at top speed to their positions; the gun mules with their leaders pounding into action, halting in a circle round the gun position, each in his exact place, while the stalwart gunners heaved the gun parts off their backs, assembled them, off-loaded the ammunition. It was a supreme example of 'time and motion' work practised hundreds of times, so that within three minutes the first shell fell on target.

The engineers of the Indian Army were called Sappers and Miners – Madras, Bombay and Bengal. They were officered by volunteers from the Royal Engineers. They were artificers, blacksmiths, builders, surveyors, road-makers, experts in demolitions, wiring, the layout and construction of trenches and fortifications. They were the men who bridged rivers under fire. The Queen Victoria's Own Madras Sappers and Miners were mainly low-caste men, but they had their pride: they formed their own caste, 'Quinsap', whose daughters might marry only men who had served in the corps.

Every unit had its own signallers, trained to communicate by field telephone and in the Morse code by helio, lamp and flag, according to the light, the terrain and the distance. Signallers tended to be better educated than the average, but few had any English. It was an advantage in working with Morse that they could not understand a word they were sending or receiving: they did not guess or try to anticipate a group.

No one doubted that the Indian Army could cope with the minor danger of a general Frontier uprising and an Afghan war. The major danger, of Russian invasion, would be more serious. But from the Russian point of view, an advance of five hundred miles through the roadless, often waterless, mountains of Afghanistan, carrying every bullet, biscuit and bale of forage they would need, harassed by hostile tribes every yard of the way, to meet on the Indian frontier nine field divisions with excellent road and rail communications, would be a most hazardous operation.

But with the Anglo-Russian agreement of 1907 Britain and Russia became potential allies rather than potential enemies. The major danger suddenly receded: the enemy the Indian Army had to face seven years later was far more formidable.

Despite what Kitchener had done, not all their training was best calculated to meet it. Reggie Savory, newly joined, was present when the 14th Ferozepur Sikhs were being exercised by their Brigadier General. He was astonished to hear the order, 'Prepare to receive cavalry, half right!' Whereupon each company formed half-right, front rank kneeling, rear rank standing, just as at Waterloo, and fired a volley of blank at the imaginary cuirassiers. Seven months later they were in Gallipoli.

CHAPTER 3

Their Mercenary Calling: Western Front, 1914–17

At the outbreak of war against Germany, the Indian Army consisted of about 155,000 men. The Government of India immediately offered a corps of two infantry divisions and two cavalry divisions for service wherever required. The infantry divisions each consisted of three brigades, each of one British and three Indian or Gurkha battalions, plus divisional troops; the cavalry divisions likewise had three brigades, each brigade consisting of one British and two Indian regiments. The Field Artillery was entirely British.

The place where reinforcements were most needed was France, where the British Expeditionary Force, the Old Contemptibles who had been out since the beginning, were shattered and exhausted after two months' fighting against overwhelming numbers. But there was some doubt whether Indian troops should be pitted against Germans.

It must have been a surprise, even a shock, to the average Indian soldier to learn that he was to go to Europe to fight against Germans, a people of whom he had hardly heard except, perhaps, as allies in China at the relief of the Legations in 1900. He was psychologically prepared to fight Russians. He could envisage Russians pouring down through the passes, killing the men, raping the women, burning the villages, carrying off the cattle. But there was no likelihood of Germans perpetrating any of these outrages in India. He was to fight the Germans because the King of England was at war with them. Well, that was all right. That was what he was paid fifteen rupees (about twenty-three shillings) a month to do: he had eaten the King's salt and must now keep faith. But his motivation was less than that of the British soldier, who could well imagine a victorious German army behaving in England as it behaved in Belgium and France.

There was a further factor deeply troubling to Moslem troops. In October, Turkey, hitherto always a friend to Britain, came into the war on Germany's side. The Sultan of Turkey was Khalif of Islam, Commander of the Faithful, Shadow of God on earth. To ask Moslems to fight against him was like asking Catholics to take arms against the Pope. The strain on loyalty was greatest for trans-Frontier Pathans, notably Afridis and Mahsuds, for whom desertion was so easy: once in their villages, they were safe from arrest. There was immediate trouble from the Mahsuds recruited in Baluchi battalions – a triumph of hope over experience. In one battalion a subadar and twenty-two men failed to return from embarcation leave; in another, a recruiting party in Mahsud territory obtained two recruits but lost five recruiters. An officer of the 130th Baluchis was bayoneted by a

Mahsud on embarcation at Karachi. There were other unfortunate incidents, and a trickle of Moslem deserters in Mesopotamia. A faint question-mark hung over trans-Frontier Pathans in particular throughout the war. But once they got to France, Mahsuds 'seemed to revel in the fighting', and officers commanding them in East Africa were lyrical in their praise. The vast majority of Moslem soldiers, Pathans and others, whatever their scruples about fighting Turks, did their duty.

A Russian army in the Khyber Pass would have been at the end of a very long and bad line of communications. The German army in Flanders was close to the armament factories in the Ruhr, and could draw food and forage from the most productive farmlands in Europe. Defending the Khyber, the Indian Army would have been in a familiar climate and environment. They could go home on short leave, and at all times keep in touch with their families. If they were wounded, their relatives could visit them in hospital. None of these conditions applied in France, where they would suffer from what modern psychiatrists call the 'culture shock syndrome' which has a numbing effect on some people working in a strange environment.

Finally, the German Army was the best in the world. (The BEF, with only five divisions in France, hardly counted as an army.) It had *more* of everything – more machine-guns, more artillery, more trained staff officers and apparently unlimited reserves of men.

Nevertheless, it was decided to take the risk of sending Indian troops to France. No other decision was possible. The British Second Corps, at its last gasp in the First Battle of Ypres, *had* to be relieved; and there were no trained British or Canadian divisions to do the job.

The Indian Corps, consisting of Lahore and Meerut divisions, landed at Marseille in mid-October, practised for a day or two with the short Lee-Enfield rifle which was new to them, and were entrained for the front.

On 21 October the first two battalions, the 129th Baluchis and the 57th (Wilde's) Rifles, were rushed in buses from the railhead to the trenches south of Ypres, split up into companies and used to plug gaps in the line held by dismounted British cavalry. The latter's situation was desperate. The only wire they had was what they could take off farm fences, and their only artillery support came from the 13-pounders of their horse-batteries. Even with the 57th and the Baluchis, they could muster only a thousand rifles to a mile, including supports and reserves. It was here that the Germans came nearest to breaking through to the Channel ports.

The heaviest attack was against a company and two machine-guns of the Baluchis, on 22 October. They occupied a salient and lost many men from an artillery bombardment, including their company commander. The company officer, Lieutenant Lewis, took over:

'The trenches in the salient were being very heavily bombarded: many were obliterated. Captain Dill with his machine-guns and most of his men were, however, still in action. I brought up two platoons . . . but could not find a yard of trench for them to occupy. . . . The men lay down in the open near the farm . . . in which were some men of the machine-gun sections filling belts. The farm was cut in half by a shell and caught fire and the occupants burnt before our eyes. Wounded were numerous and as, owing to casualties, stretchers had not arrived . . . I ran back to fetch some. Coming up again . . . I saw English, Indian and German troops together coming out from the salient. . . . Each man extricated himself as best he could from the mêlée and fell back on a position 600 yards behind.'

But the machine-guns stayed in the ruined farm, and fought with great determination. One was wrecked by a direct hit, most of its crew killed or wounded. The survivors served the other gun. Dill was wounded but his men kept the gun in action, mowing down in swathes the Germans who were now right on top of them. Then they were overrun and shot or bayoneted. There was only one survivor, Sepoy Khuda Dad Khan, a Punjabi Mussulman, left for dead by the Germans. He made his way back to the battalion that night and was the first Indian to be awarded the VC.

The 57th Rifles were split up into several detachments spread over five or six miles of front. The Dogra and Afridi companies bore the brunt of it. The Dogra company was wiped out, the last man on his feet, Jemadar Kapur Singh, shooting himself with his last round rather than surrender – a typical Dogra. Havildar Gagna, a famous gymnast, killed five Germans and, when his bayonet broke, snatched up a German officer's sword and went on fighting. When the trench was retaken in a counter-attack, he was still alive, with six wounds. The battalion went into action with eleven British Officers and 729 Indian Other Ranks: it came out seventy-two hours later with five British Officers and 274 Indians.

In desperate fighting the village of Neuve Chapelle was lost. The 20th and 21st Field Companies, Bengal Sappers and Miners, fighting in this emergency as infantry, lost all their officers, and 119 out of 300 Indian Other Ranks. It was a wicked waste, for they were specialists who should not have been used as infantry – but there was no one else.

The 39th Garhwal Rifles were a new regiment, formed from the Hindu hillmen of Garhwal, who had previously served in Gurkha regiments. They wore Gurkha-type uniforms and carried the kukri. The Germans had driven the 57th Rifles out of some 300 yards of their front-line trenches, but the 57th still held the trenches on either side of the gap. The 1st Battalion of the Garhwalis were ordered to re-take the trench by a frontal attack, but this did not commend itself to the commanding officer, Lieutenant Colonel E. R. R. Swiney, who chose instead to take his men into the part of the trench which was still held by the 57th and then, from the left, clear the enemy-held trench traverse by traverse. Naik Darwan Singh Negi was the first round each traverse, facing bombs and bullets at a few feet range. He was twice wounded, but went on to finish the job and become the second Indian to win the VC.

The most useful weapon was the bomb, of which the Garhwalis had plenty, having found a store of German bombs and worked out by trial and error how to use them. Thereafter the Sappers and Miners of the Indian Corps took a lead in the manufacture of bombs, trench mortars, periscopes and other special equipment. They had already invented the Bangalore Torpedo, a tube filled with explosives to be pushed under barbed-wire entanglements to blow a gap. They copied the German 'hairbrush' bombs, and made 'jampot bombs', tins filled with guncotton and nails with detonator and fuse pushed through the lid. These had to be activated by a cigarette applied to the fuse, and thrown in haste: practice was unpopular. The first trench-mortars were tubes wrapped round with wire. The first trench searchlights were powered by the enemy electrical system in La Bassée, until the enemy cut them off.

All these heroics and boy scout contrivances are the stuff of legend and regimental history. They are all true – but for the whole truth one must read also diaries and letters written not for publication.

Captain 'Roly' Grimshaw of the Poona Horse kept such a diary, which conveys the fog and the beastliness of war. He had the regimental reputation of a perfectionist, and was the sort of rider for whom even the most sluggish horse livens up. This should be borne in mind in reading his strictures on almost everyone except his own D Squadron of the Poona Horse. The regiment was fighting on foot, rushed up to meet crisis after crisis as there was no infantry available. It was not the war for which they had been trained, and they had not had an hour's instruction in bayonet-fighting. Otherwise his story might be that of any officer of any battalion in the line in those early days.

On 1 November the 2/2nd Goorkhas* were heavily attacked in trenches deep in water. The Poona Horse was ordered up to reinforce them.

'The moment the advance commenced we came under a hail of heavy howitzer, shrapnel, machine-gun and rifle-fire. Casualties came quickly, increased by many of our men refusing to lie down and thus avail themselves of what cover existed – very little. When about 150 yards from the objective, the leading squadron, B, reached a road with a ditch on either side of it and the colonel [C. O. Swanston] halted to allow the other two squadrons to come up, his intention being to rush the last 150 yards with all available men. At this juncture there appeared some uncertainty as to whether the trenches we were to succour were in the hands of the Gurkhas or the enemy. Swanston therefore raised himself above the cover to . . . ascertain the situation. Whilst thus occupied with his glasses he was shot dead.

It soon became obvious that the trenches were in occupation by the Germans. The 2nd Gurkha Adjutant strongly advised us to rush them. . . Colonel Norie [commanding 2/2] arrived on the scene and decided that no attack should be made until darkness, so we continued to hold the road . . . until 11.00 p.m. After a conference among the powers that be, we were withdrawn and the salient abandoned *in toto*. Owing to the

*Others spelt it 'Gurkhas'.

darkness many men got left behind or straggled in. My own belief about the entire affair is that it was carried out to save the face of the 2nd Gurkhas. There is ample evidence that the latter quitted their trenches. Colonel Norie gave everyone to understand that his battalion had been almost annihilated and that if we could succour the remainder it might save the situation. Whether he was aware of this abandonment of the trenches by his battalion at the time he asked Swanston to undertake this succour, I cannot say. . . . His Adjutant was certainly aware of what had taken place, and several artillery officers round about saw many 2nd Gurkha riflemen sneaking about when they ought to have been in the trenches. If Norie did not know, he ought to have known. His Adjutant told me the next day that his men were all over the place and like myself he was trying to round up stragglers. On this search I found 2nd Gurkha men in all kinds of places, ditches, ruins and even under the culverts, and I regret to say one or two men of C Squadron amongst them. . . .
3 Nov. Got my squadron into new billets and made off to try and find our stragglers. . . . After collecting a few, all C Squadron men, I returned to my headquarters. . . . I felt rather surprised that Gray, who returned with only a handful of his men the day before, did not offer to come and look for his own men. However, I dare say he wanted a rest and thought that a fanatic like myself would do it just as well. Again most of the men I brought in were C Squadron. There was something very wrong here.'

On 24 November the Poona Horse were ordered back into the line to relieve the 58th (Vaughan's) Rifles. All the tricks of trench warfare, such as one unit relieving another, they had to learn the hard way. There was dreadful congestion in the communication trenches with the 58th coming down and the Poona Horse going up. The 58th were

'trying to pass out the wounded and the groans and shrieks of the latter were enough to make one's blood run cold, especially when they bumped up against us. . . . It was a stupid thing to try to pass out wounded on stretchers at the same time that the reliefs were coming up. . . . There seemed to be about a foot of muddy slush in the trench and what I thought were filled sandbags to give us a footing in the mire. I switched on my electric torch. To my horror I saw I was standing on the corpse of a human being. I was very nearly sick, but I bent down and extricating the man's hand from the mud I felt his pulse to see if by any chance he was still alive. I could see no trace of life, which is not extraordinary seeing that at least two hundred men had trampled over him. There he was, almost submerged in the mud and slush. His face had hardly been injured, and I could see he was a young Pathan. . . . Moving on, I tried to blot the hideous picture from my brain, but could not.

We arrived in the trenches proper at 5.30 a.m. and took over the loopholes of the 58th Rifles. . . . The sight which met my eyes at daybreak was perfectly revolting. Dozens of corpses choked the trenches. . . . Fragments of human beings everywhere. Most of the dead seemed to have been bayoneted, but some had their heads blown clean off. . .

About 8 a.m. the Germans started bombing us and before long I had one man killed and four wounded. The killed was Ashraf Khan, one of the nicest fellows. . . . Both his legs were blown off below the knee, and one arm, and half his face. . . . Poor Ashraf Khan, an only son, and his mother a widow. He lived for forty minutes. . . . I had him carefully put on one side where he would not be flung about or trampled on, till I had time to bury him. I moved him myself and was astounded at his extraordinary lightness. . . .

My men complained terribly of their feet. Mine were bad enough, so I knew what theirs must be like. I had no waterproofs, rugs or braziers. . . . The cold was intense. . . .

25 Nov. De Pass volunteered to go down to the enemy sap and destroy the loopholed sandbag traverse, from behind which all these bombs were coming. . . . I told him he could take two volunteers, and he selected Fateh Khan and Firman Shah. They entered the sap carrying the charge for destroying the traverse. They found a German at his loophole with his rifle. Fortunately he did not fire but threw a bomb at the party which by good luck exploded behind them, doing no damage. De Pass then placed the charge and blew up the traverse. A very gallant exploit [for which De Pass, who was killed a few days later, was awarded a posthumous VC]. I had no more casualties that day from bombs.

26 Nov. Another ghastly night. I could not sleep, . . . so I tramped up and down the line cheering up our men who really were in a pitiable condition. . . . Their almost dumb suffering was infinitely worse than if they had complained openly. I think they recognized that I was doing my best for them and their perpetual exhortations to me to rest and that they would keep on the qui vive were, I am sure, quite sincere. Here and there I sat down beside a sowar and chatted to him. It is curious how suffering draws one together. These simple-minded men had hearts of pure gold. Never a complaint that they were half-frozen to death, or that they were being called upon to fight as they had never in their wildest transports of imagination pictured, armed with a weapon they had never handled before they set foot in France. I was disappointed with all the Indian Officers. They sat huddled up and never thought of a single useful idea. . . .

When it was dark I got Fateh Hyder Shah to organize a little rescue party under my direction. We got in a young Sikh lad of the 58th Rifles. He had been shot through the temple with a shrapnel bullet and was almost dead from exposure. I gave him some hot rum and water and we chafed his frozen limbs and by degrees he came to. It was quite a neat piece of work getting him in. Firstly a man crept out (Fateh Hyder Shah) and made a round of the bodies grouped together some 150 yards off. He had carefully to feel each to see if any life existed. After about twenty minutes I heard a long, low, faint whistle followed by a single short note. This was the signal, pre-arranged, that told me that only one survivor existed amidst that group. I therefore sent out four men to bring him in.

They were in full view of the German trenches and stood out vividly against the snow. I saw them arrive, seize the man and begin dragging him towards the shelter of our trench. The Germans opened a brisk fire on them snaking their way towards me. . . . By degrees they got closer and closer and were soon in with the wounded man. It was an anxious half-hour as I did not want to lose sound men for wounded ones.'

Major Molloy, commanding the Poona Horse after Swanston's death, would not have agreed with Grimshaw's strictures on Indian Officers: 'Ressaidar Badan Singh was put in charge of the bombing. He proved a tower of strength; and whenever an unpleasant situation called for my attention, I was sure to find Badanjee already in the thick of it, his dour face stretched into a huge grin.'

The Poona Horse had no winter clothing, and by 20 November were still clad in the khaki cotton drill uniforms designed for the Indian autumn. Their only mackintoshes had been bought by officers' wives in England. They were ordered to attack and recover lost trenches.

'Streams of wounded poured past us. . . . The state of the wounded beggars all description. Little Gurkhas slopping through the freezing mud barefooted, Tommies with no caps on and plastered with blood and mud from head to foot, Sikhs with their hair all down and looking more wild and weird than I have ever seen them, Pathans more dirty and untidy than usual, all limping or reeling along like drunken men . . . misery depicted on their faces. . . . I stopped some Gurkhas and asked why they walked in bare feet. Those that replied said, "Sahib, our feet hurt terribly, but in boots they hurt worse."'

The support trenches to which they were posted were

'half-full of icy water. I would not allow my men into them but foraging round got some straw and put it down behind the trenches and made them sit on it. I decided that only a whirlwind of shell-fire would make me occupy those trenches. My own belief is that frostbite is infinitely more deadly than "bullet bite". . . . About 9 p.m. I moved up to support trenches . . . infinitely worse than the ones we had quitted, being sited in a marsh. They were brimful of water and positively dangerous. . . . However, I was ordered to occupy these miniature canals and so I did. . . The 8th Gurkhas on my immediate left had two men drowned.

About midnight we were ordered up to Festubert. . . . It was obvious we were about to be launched in one of those deadly counter-attacks, and as far as I could see this one promised to be a greater fiasco than usual.'

Grimshaw's fears were well founded. Having been ordered by Molloy to support A Squadron, commanded by Ressaidar Badan Singh, he was ordered by a senior infantry officer to change direction and fill a gap to the left of the 2/8th Gurkhas. Unable to communicate with Molloy, he could only obey, under protest.

Molloy was directing the regiment's attack from the right of the leading squadron, C, commanded by Major Loring.

'When we reached to within about 150 yards of the enemy's position, I gave the word "Charge" and dashed forward, but as I did so I saw most of the men simply swept away. It was probably at this moment that Major Loring was killed and his Indian Officers wounded. As we got nearer to the trench the Germans climbed out at the back and made off, and when I reached it I found it empty, and that I had now with me only Daffadar Sharaf Khan of C Squadron and a sower of A. I sent the former to the right and the latter to the left, and after some time both returned saying that the trench was empty for several hundred yards and that there was no sign of any more of our men. Further, by the light of the dawn now breaking, I could see nothing of [Grimshaw's] D Squadron, while the enemy was becoming unpleasantly active in the second line not far in our front. An immediate return was indicated.'

Grimshaw, having been sent off to the left of the Gurkhas instead of supporting A and C Squadrons, made the best of a bad job.

'The order came from the Gurkhas to advance, and we all rose and forged ahead. The fire was hellish and my own men began to drop quickly. The rattle tattle of the enemy's machine-guns was nerve-racking: we seemed to be walking straight into dozens of them. . . . After about three or four hundred yards the Gurkhas lay down, which was contrary to orders. My men seeing them do so lay down also. . . . After five minutes during which the firing grew hotter and hotter I saw it was no use waiting for the Gurkhas to move. I could see no British Officers and I fancy all had been hit by this time. I got up and ordered the men to do so, which they did at once, and again we advanced. . . . A second later I felt a fearful blow on my left side and fell over.'

That was the end of the war for Roly Grimshaw.

Some were less squeamish than he. In his progress along a trench near Givenchy Captain Davies of the 129th Baluchis was advised, 'You can walk on him, Sahib. He's dead – No, not on him, he's not dead yet.' They were ordered to attack two German saps. A Mahsud company took the first by surprise, but machine-guns in enfilade barred the way to all support until a trench could be dug through so that they could advance under cover. A message had to be sent to the Mahsud company, and Captain Lewis called for volunteers.

'Two Mohmands step forward and one climbs the parapet. He pauses for a moment and then rushes forward and dies. His comrade sees this. "Now," he says, "it's my turn." Thank God I was at hand to stop him.'

In the captured sap a desperate struggle lasted all day. When the company commander was killed, command devolved on a young Mahsud Jemadar, Mir Badshah. They hurled back German bombs; they made repeated bayonet charges; at one end of the sap a Mahsud kept his machine-gun firing even after the Germans had jumped in behind him. After dark Mir Badshah got them back to the remnants of the battalion in the trench behind.

On Christmas Day, recalled Captain W. G. Bagot-Chester of the 2/3rd

Gurkhas in the Garhwali Brigade:

'One German from his trench raised the butt of his rifle. No fire from our side. He then put his helmet on the butt. No fire. He then commenced to climb out of the trench. Still no fire from our side. So he began to advance towards the 2/39th Garhwali trenches, carrying a bottle of beer in one hand and a box of cigarettes in the other. One from our side went out to meet him and he pointed to the dead lying about. The first arrivals were followed by others from each side until there was quite a collection of Germans, or rather Saxons, and Garhwalis in No Man's Land. The burial of the dead proceeded, meanwhile the remainder fraternized, each giving the other cigarettes etc. After this had been going on for some time the 39th thought the informal armistice had lasted long enough, so they fired two shots in the air, whereupon the Germans retired and fired a shot and the armistice ended. Some of the Garhwalis went into the Hun trench and said they were very comfortable, with Christmas trees burning with candles.'

A cosy, heart-warming scene indeed; but the next entry in Bagot-Chester's diary is less heart-warming: 'Yesterday we had the unpleasant duty of being present at the corporal punishment of a rifleman with thirty lashes for sleeping at his post while on sentry duty.'

After Christmas the fighting was less intense, both sides finding it all they could do to keep warm and more or less dry. The Indian Corps had time to train methodically in what they had hitherto picked up as they went along, by trial and error – bombing, wiring, the construction of proper trenches and dugouts, the routine of trench reliefs, the use of telephones. They were even issued with winter clothing.

Contributing to the culture shock syndrome was the experience of buying refreshments at canteens from memsahibs – indeed, did they but know it, from veritable Lady Sahibs: Lady Egerton, Lady Hicks Beach and others at Rouen. Captain R. S. Waters of the 40th Pathans noted:

'The Dogras are the politest and gravest in the matter. . . . It was odd to see all these memsahibs behind the counter giving out cake, butter, coffee, bread, oranges, cigarettes, bootlaces to Tommies and our own men who swarmed in. The Mussulmans bought the shop out nearly. The Pathan especially is falling into European ways very quickly. He is an adaptable blighter, the Dogra the reverse. The Punjabis are all nuts on French bread and butter.'

In March, 1915, there was a black day for the 58th (Vaughan's) Rifles. Jemadar Mir Mast deserted with fourteen other Afridis. He was lionized by the Germans and presented with the Iron Cross by the Kaiser. But Ayub Khan, a Mahsud of 129th Baluchis, 'deserted' to obtain information about the enemy. He reported:

'I arrived near Point 62 about an hour before dawn. I waited till it was light and then stood up and held up my arms saying, "Germani, I am Indian Mussulman." An officer signalled me to put down my rifle. I climbed over the barricade. . . . There were many Germans in the trench, all wearing 15 on their shoulders. . . . The trench was very deep and strong, the parapet about 9 foot high. It was revetted with boards held up by stakes. The firing-step was about 4 foot high covered with boards, as was the floor. The bottom of the trench was wide enough to allow two men to pass without difficulty. In the parados were well built shelters for about eight men, the officers' dugouts having boards and windows. . . . I saw four machine-guns on this front. They were placed in dugouts roofed with beams, very strong uncut trees meeting one another. Above these beams was corrugated iron about as thick as three of our sheets, and above this about four feet of sandbags. The guns were about one to two feet above ground level and fired through an iron loophole. . . .

I left the fire-trench about 8 a.m. . . . The course I followed was . . . Points 65, 130, 131, 133, then by a communication trench back to a wood. . . . A trolley line ran along behind the wood and turned to the right by two bungalows. . . . I started off along the trolley to a main road. On the road . . . I saw three companies of infantry dressed like those I saw in the trenches. I could not see the number. I was taken to . . . a large house. While I was there . . . I saw about eight men with No 55 on their shoulders and about ten men with No 13 on their shoulders. An officer who spoke a little Hindustani came out with a General whose shoulder-strap carried thick silver braid, as thick as my finger. The interpreter brought a map and asked me what trenches I knew. I said I could not read. . . . The senior officer then said that if I would come over to the Germans I would get very good pay, and that he would give me three hundred rupees if I would bring over twenty men. . . .

At about 9.00 p.m. one of the officers and I returned to the same trenches in a motor-car. It was arranged that at dawn I would bring over the twenty men. I then left them and returned to my own trenches.'

In January 1915 the cold was such that the 2/3rd Gurkhas had to vaseline themselves to the waist before going into trenches deep in mud and water. Then came the spring and, with it, winter clothing in such profusion that a man could hardly move for extra woollen underclothes, greatcoat, sheepskin overcoat, thigh-high waders. They had all the special equipment which had hitherto been a German monopoly – bombs, rifle-grenades, periscopes, mortars.

Confidence was high. Waters wrote: 'We are top-dogs, I can see that. The Indian Army is good. It has pulled its weight and I never saw a better demeanour than I did last night among the men. They are recovering from adverse winter conditions and most of the tales one heard in the past must be heavily discounted.'

The little village of Neuve Chapelle, a natural redoubt with walled gardens and strongly built houses, had changed hands four times during the previous October, remaining finally with the Germans who greatly strengthened it, with machine-guns enfilading the approaches. In front were fields intersected with hedges and deep waterlogged ditches; and in front of these, the Des Layes stream, ten foot wide and nearly Gurkha-deep.

The Indian Corps attacked it on 10 March. It was the first recital of a story which was to become familiar: an artillery preparation, puny by later standards, which neither cut the wire proplerly nor destroyed the machine-guns; the enemy front line overrun, but the second wave of the attack inexplicably delayed for hours; then well organized counter-attacks.

The Garhwali Brigade were given as their objective Neuve Chapelle village and the trenches on either side of it. At 7.30 a.m. Bagot-Chester was awed by the artillery preparation: 'Never before in history has there been such a one. I should think for a full half-hour our guns, all 480 of them, fired without a fraction of a second's break. You could not hear yourself speak for the noise.'

His 2/3rd Gurkhas carried the village and first-line trenches, took three hundred prisoners and dug in. But the Garhwalis lost direction, inclined too much to the right, and came up against a belt of wire in which they tore gaps with bare hands. Eventually, having lost all their British Officers, they took about two hundred yards of enemy trench, but were separated from the rest of the brigade.

It was the first time on the Western Front that the German line was broken. But the follow-up was a problem never solved. It was largely a matter of communications: telephone cables were cut, runners shot and carrier pigeons unreliable. The Garhwali Brigade was in Neuve Chapelle by 9.30 a.m., but the Dehra Dun Brigade in support did not come forward until 4.00 p.m., and by that time the impetus of the attack was lost. They crossed the Des Layes stream, but had barely made contact with the enemy when they were withdrawn behind it.

The Dehra Dun Brigade was then assailed by an avalanche of men in field grey, tramping forward without firing a shot and singing *Deutschland über Alles*. 'Such a moving multitude seemed almost impossible to stop.' But the little Gurkhas, stolid and unimaginative, were not impressed.

'The fire of our lines, withheld until the enemy were barely two hundred yards away, now broke out in a furious tornado of shells, machine-guns and rifle fire. In a short time their solid formations broke up and left our front littered with dead and dying.'

For the next two days Bagot-Chester had

'absolute hell from enemy shelling. The men behaved excellently. It would fail me to express my admiration for their behaviour. At 5.00 p.m. we got news that we were to be relieved. Oh, how pleased we were! And all my men bucked up and started chattering away.'

But they had hardly reached their billeting area when the order was cancelled: back they had to go to the trenches. 'I explained the situation to the men and almost cried with pity for their disappointment. They took it very well, turned about without a word and marched back.'

Despite local successes, Neuve Chapelle was a strategic failure, the first of many such. There was no breakthrough.

On 24 April the Germans attacked at Ypres, using poison gas for the first time and breaking the line where French colonial troops bolted. They were barely checked by the Canadians, and the Lahore Division moved up in support. The leading brigades were given as their objective an 'enemy' trench about four hundred yards away, and dashed forward with great élan thinking they had only a short distance to go. But the position they were assaulting was an empty trench abandoned by the French three months before. The real enemy position was 1,100 yards further on. The 'furious rush' of the 40th Pathans and 47th Sikhs, pounded by shells and machine-guns, ran out of steam, petering out in scattered groups hanging on in shell-holes and ditches, one only forty yards from the enemy.

Then a fog of greyish-yellow gas billowed down towards the Ferozepur Brigade. The French on their right again bolted, as did some Indians, screaming, 'We have come to hell!' They had no gas-masks, and could only hold turbans over mouth, nose and streaming eyes, many rolling on the ground in agony. Jemadar Mir Dast, attached to the 57th Rifles, stopped the rot. Pulling and pushing, cursing and cajoling, he made the runaways halt and the more lightly gassed stand and fight. He organized the defence until he could withdraw in good order, bringing with him eight wounded and gassed. For this he was presented by the King with the VC, to match the Iron Cross which the Kaiser had presented to his brother, Mir Mast.

In May Bagot-Chester's 2/3rd Gurkhas took over trenches from a battalion of the London Regiment.

'We worked all night at it, first of all getting dead bodies from the neighbourhood of our parapet and putting them in a ditch in front. Then we put up our wire entanglements and started building up the parapet and generally clearing up the mess left by the Londons. Some say Indian troops are dirty and have dirty habits compared to Europeans, but my experience is the reverse. I would much rather take over a trench which had been occupied by an Indian regiment, Gurkha or native, than one occupied by a British regiment. The filth and smell in my trench when we took over was awful. The Londons had done nothing to get rid of the swollen corpses in front. The actual trench was littered with rubbish, paper, bones, biscuits and tins. No work seems to have been done over the actual strengthening of the trench. Some British regiments do not work at all in the trenches.'

Bagot-Chester's orderly, who had been in hospital, amused him 'with tales of fearful shamming sick of Indians in Boulogne'. There were also, the Secretary of State informed the Viceroy, far too many cases of self-inflicted wounds, men shooting themselves in the hand or foot in order to get away from it all: nearly half the wounds in October 1914, before discipline was tightened up, were of this type.* In this, Indian troops were not unique. Among the soldiers of every nation in every war there have been outbreaks of malingering and self-inflicted wounds.

But it cannot be denied that the Indian Army was not at its best in the dreadful conditions of winter on the Western Front. Nor was any other

*J. Greenhut in *Journal of Imperial and Commonwealth History*, October 1983

army: British, German, French metropolitan and French colonial troops, Belgians and Portuguese all knew from time to time confusion, demoralization, panic. The original British Expeditionary Force, which fought at Mons and Le Cateau and was destroyed at Ypres, was of the highest quality: the Kaiser acknowledged that 'the First Corps under Douglas Haig is the best in Europe'. Yet at the very time when the first Indian units were arriving in the line to take over from them, Haig was 'astounded at the terror-stricken men' of his Corps retreating. He told the King, who naively believed that all British soldiers were invariably brave, 'of the crowds of fugitives who came back down the Menin Road from time to time during the Ypres battle having thrown away everything they could, including their rifles and packs, in order to escape, with a look of absolute terror on their faces such as I have never before seen on any human being's face'. It is in this context that judgment should be passed on the stragglers whom Grimshaw found hiding in ditches and under culverts when they should have been in the trenches; and on three hundred men whom another observer met, 'mostly 129th Baluchis, retiring from Givenchy. Many had thrown their rifles away and said their officers had been killed.' * The Indian soldier was neither better nor worse than British and Germans, and a great deal better than most of the French and all the Belgians. But more was expected of him, thanks largely to Kipling and his ilk who had depicted him as a superman. He wasn't, so many people in England felt he had failed to live up to the Kipling legend.

Three factors told more against Indian than European troops. In the first place, the bitter cold, in trenches deep in mud and water, was worse for them than for northern Europeans, and until Christmas they had only tropical uniforms.

Secondly, the slaughter of their regular British Officers on whom they had been taught, perhaps too much, to rely. Replacement officers did not know the men, who did not know them; and in many cases they spoke no word of any Indian language.

Thirdly, the dilution of regiments through the failure of the reserve system meant that units in France had to be kept up to strength by drafts from units in India; where possible these were of the same class as the companies to which they were sent, but often this was not possible. The Indian soldier's morale depended as much on esprit de corps as on trust in British Officers whom he knew. But how could a man of the 57th Rifles have much esprit de corps when the battalion consisted of men from six different regiments; or a man of the Baluchis when his battalion, its strength reduced to 263, included men from thirteen other units?

Officer casualties and the mix-up of regiments had a dire effect. No one could have been more devoted to Indian troops than the Corps commander, General Sir J. Willcocks, but even he conceded that the British battalions in the Corps, not suffering nearly so much from officer

*Ibid.

shortages (at least their new officers spoke the same language) and regimental dilution, were carrying more than their fair share. More divisions were arriving, trained, from Britain and Canada; so it was decided that by the end of 1915 all the Indian infantry would be moved to Egypt, East Africa and Mesopotamia, where the climate and general conditions would be more familiar to them, and contacts with India much easier.

Despite all the stresses to which they were subjected, they had done vital work. The 21st October, 1914, was perhaps the most critical day of the whole war. If the Germans had broken through the wafer-thin screen of British cavalry to the Channel ports, the war would have been lost. It was the Indian Corps which showed at Neuve Chapelle that the Germans *could* be driven from their formidable trenches.

A German soldier wrote to the *Frankfurter Zeitung*:

'Today for the first time we had to fight against the Indians and the devil knows these brown rascals are not to be under-rated. At first we spoke with contempt of them. Today we look on them in a different light. The devil knows what the English had put into those fellows. With a fearful shouting thousands of those brown forms rushed upon us. At a hundred metres we opened a destructive fire and mowed down hundreds, but in spite of that the others advanced. In no time they were in our trenches and truly these brown enemies are not to be despised. With butt ends, bayonets, swords and daggers we fought each other and we had bitter hard work.'

Housman's 'Epitaph on an Army of Mercenaries', written for the British regulars of 1914, could apply equally to the Indian Corps. Their shoulders, too,

> held the sky suspended;
> They stayed, and earth's foundations stay.
> What God abandoned, these defended,
> And saved the scheme of things – for pay.

Two divisions of Indian cavalry, designated the 4th and 5th (which included the Canadian Cavalry Brigade), remained in France until the spring of 1918, part of the Cavalry Corps of five divisions, to exploit the breakthrough which never came. They dug, wired, took their turns in the trenches, did their quotas of trench-raids, groomed and exercised their horses, waited and hoped.

At dawn on 20 November 1917, Third Army attacked south-west of Cambrai, led by 380 tanks, the first big tank battle in history. There was no preliminary bombardment. The enemy was taken by surprise and a hole five miles deep by nine miles wide was driven through the first two systems of the immensely strong Hindenburg Line. Behind them was the cavalry, to go through the gap, bypass Cambrai and exploit north-eastward. Cambrai, an important base, headquarters and communications centre, would thus be isolated, and the Germans would be rolled up from the south.

The infantry were through by 9 a.m. There were no more sounds of battle. The cavalry moved up to the Hindenberg Line. The morning wore on. There were no more orders. They watered and fed their horses; investigated the mysteries of the Line; sampled the half-cooked meals which the enemy had left – and waited. At mid-morning the 1st Cavalry Division moved forward, but not very far.

It was not until 12.15 that the 5th Cavalry Division, commanded by Major General H. J. M. MacAndrew, was ordered to move. The Secunderabad Cavalry Brigade was directed on Marcoing, the Canadian Cavalry Brigade at Masnières: at both places, it was reported, the infantry were across the St Quentin Canal. Very efficient arrangements had been made, and many times practised, for horses to cross the trenches in the Hindenburg Line by temporary bridges, but it was still a slow business negotiating the chasms and threading a way through the wire; and it was not until 2.15 that Marcoing was reached.

Over the bridge at Marcoing the fog of war descends, all the thicker for the passage of seventy years. According to the *Official History*, the leading squadron of the 7th Dragoon Guards was stopped there by machine-gun fire. But the Poona Horse, halted just short of Marcoing, had successive messages dropped by a contact plane that the bridge had a hole in the middle but was quite passable by cavalry; and that there were only about fifty enemy with one machine-gun on the far side. These messages did not mention the 7th Dragoon Guards or the infantry across the canal, and the CO, Lieutenant Colonel Cooper, prepared to gallop the bridge in column of half-sections (two-by-two).

Lieutenant D. S. E. MacNeill was called to regimental headquarters and told to make ready a patrol to ride north to the Sensée river, six miles away, contact a patrol of the 1st Cavalry Division, and send back reports of any enemy found; but not actually to move until given the go-ahead. While he was waiting for this, his orderly thoughtfully handed him a flask of whisky, but this the Colonel appropriated: 'Give it to me. You'll lose your way if you drink it.' He never got the go-ahead, and remained at regimental headquarters all day. But it was widely reported that a patrol of the 1st Cavalry Division, which he was supposed to meet, did reach the Sensée, and returned, through open country almost empty of Germans.

Three thousand yards to the right of the Poona Horse the Canadians found the bridge at Masnières blocked by a stranded tank. But there were on the front of the two cavalry brigades twelve bridges still intact, of which eight were passable by horses. To Brigadier Gregory, commanding the Secunderabad Brigade, it seemed that the enemy beyond the canal were few and could be dislodged by mounted action. Brigadier Seely, commanding the Canadians, believed likewise, but preferred dismounted action. Both were, however, told firmly by division that the cavalry were not to get involved in the infantry fight, that their work began only when the infantry had broken through. Gregory literally begged MacAndrew to let him go; but the latter, an irascible individual, probably under orders which he furiously resented, stamped his foot and roared, 'God damn it, Gregory, I said you were NOT to go.'

So the fleeting opportunity was lost. By next day the Germans were resisting strongly. There were no more British infantry divisions to complete the breakthrough: they had been squandered at Paschendaele, or sent to prop up the Italians. The Cavalry Corps, disappointed and disconsolate, rode back to the billets they had left in such high hopes thirty-six hours earlier.

When it was clear that the Cambrai offensive, like all the others, had petered out, the cavalry prepared to take their turns again in the trenches. Hodson's Horse was ordered to move up during the night of 30 November, so in the morning they stripped and packed their saddles, sent the horses out on exercise and prepared for dismounted action. But all morning continuous 'drumfire' was heard from the north, so it was no surprise to be ordered suddenly to prepare for mounted action. The enemy had counter-attacked south of Cambrai in tremendous strength, driving deep into the side of the British salient and taking Gauzeaucourt at the base of it.

The Ambala Brigade (Hodson's Horse, the 18th Lancers and the 8th Hussars) was ordered to concentrate near Epéhy, eleven miles north of their billets, and four miles south of Gauzeaucourt.

In haste the horses were called back, saddlery was unpacked and re-assembled and, cheerfully shouting their warcries, the squadrons trotted off, arriving at Epéhy about 11 a.m. There they heard more details of the debacle, and that the Guards Division was counter-attacking at Gauzeaucourt. At 1 p.m. the Divisional Commander gave verbal orders to the Brigade to push on to Gauche Wood, about two thousand yards south-east of Gauzeaucourt which the Guards by then had re-taken.

With the 8th Hussars in the lead, the brigade rode forward. The 8th were held up in the wire of the British second-line trenches: one squadron found a way through and advanced to the shelter of a sunken road four hundred yards west of Gauche Wood, where they dismounted. Hodson's was then ordered up on the left of the Hussar squadron, filling the gap between them and the Guards.

The two leading squadrons, C (Punjabi Mussulmans) commanded by Major A. I. Fraser, and D (Pathans) commanded by Captain M. D. Vigors, trotted briskly forward, weaving their way between the barbed wire and trenches, to approach Gauche Wood from the west. They reached a trench held by a party of clerks and ordnance corps personnel, who were putting a brave face on things but were much relieved at the arrival of somebody else. There a gap was found in the wire, through which C Squadron passed and, breaking into a gallop, rode straight for the sunken road a mile away. They were just in time: German infantry were coming out of Gauche Wood and advancing towards the sunken road, where there was only the squadron of Hussars. Seeing Fraser's squadron galloping towards them, they ran back to the wood, covered by machine-gun fire. C Squadron dismounted alongside the 8th Hussars and formed a front facing

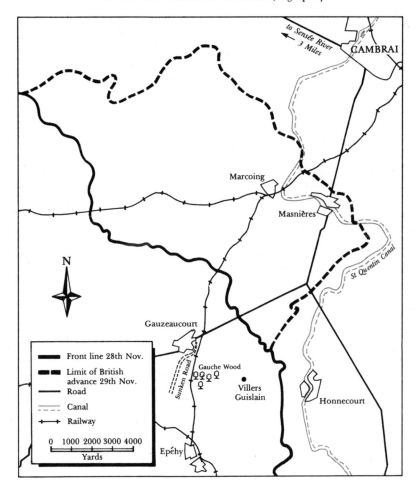

Cambrai, 1917

Gauche Wood. There Fraser was killed, trying to rush a machine-gun firing at them from the railway embankment to their front.

They had got through with surprisingly few casualties; but by the time D Squadron reached the gap in the wire, the enemy artillery had ranged on it and the leading troop, closed up to pass through, lost many horses and men. However, the others never wavered or changed their pace until they opened out in diamond formation and galloped hard for the sunken road. Following them A Squadron (Sikhs) also lost heavily coming through the wire, and their squadron commander, Major F. St J. Atkinson, was killed.

47

It was a classic example of cavalry tactics in the post-Boer War era, the horses being used to carry riflemen and machine-gunners at speed to the point where they could with advantage dismount and fight on foot.

During the night the 18th Lancers arrived and took over from the 8th Hussars. This was the open warfare they had hopefully practised but never experienced. The sunken road, unwired, undug, was the British front line, held by squadrons and companies of seven units, and four machine-guns from the brigade machine-gun squadron.

Next morning the 18th Lancers, with the Grenadiers on their left, were to attack Gauche Wood dismounted, supported by fourteen tanks. By zero-hour no tanks had arrived. The Grenadiers attacked without them and lost heavily. Lieutenant Colonel E. C. Corbyn, commanding the 18th, decided to give them a little longer and was rewarded by their arriving twenty minutes late and immediately firing on his regiment.

The 18th attacked at 7.15. There was enough enemy fire 'to make you want to put up your coat-collar and pick up your feet'; but with no barbed wire to negotiate, they were not held up. They captured the wood, prisoners, twelve machine-guns and a whole battery of howitzers. The Grenadiers also got there, but with so many casualties that they asked the 18th to lend them some officers, an unusual incident in the history of both regiments.

The Medical Officer of Hodson's Horse, Captain S. Dutt, a Bengali, won the MC in the sunken road for gallantry in attending wounded under fire. It was not his only decoration. A German colonel, whom he treated in circumstances of great danger, took the Iron Cross from his tunic and pinned it on Dutt's.

The German counter-attack also caught off balance the 2nd Lancers in the Mhow Cavalry Brigade in 4th Cavalry Division. They had already sent forward a large 'trench party' on horseback which, with horseholders to bring back the horses when they reached the trenches, accounted for most of the regiment. The main body, left behind in their bivouac fifteen miles south of Gauzeaucourt, consisted of little but regimental headquarters, farriers and veterinary personnel. At 11 a.m. they were ordered to turn out mounted, with every available man. This they did, sending gallopers to recall the trench party whose swords and lances were loaded into wagons. They rode to the brigade rendezvous, then fourteen miles further to their night bivouac where they were joined by the trench party who had spent a frustrating day marching and counter-marching. But the sword and lance wagon did not arrive.

In the morning the brigade rode to Epéhy where they were ordered to take Villers Guislain, three miles to the north-north-east, by a mounted attack timed to coincide with the Grenadiers' and 18th Lancers' attack on Gauche Wood. While the Inniskilling Dragoons went for Villers Guislain, the 2nd Lancers were to gallop forward and form a defensive front facing south-east. The swords and lances arrived just in time to be tossed up to the men as they rode past the wagon to the attack.

The 2nd Lancers trotted forward, about 440 all ranks, passing some British infantry who could hardly believe their eyes. They extended and attacked with C Squadron leading.

'Before us lay a shallow valley averaging about four hundred yards wide, covered with rank, dead grass and pitted here and there with shell-holes. C Squadron had barely started when there was a tremendous outburst of machine-gun fire from both sides and the pace was increased to a gallop. The deserted landscape became alive with running grey figures. Although the air seemed to be full of bullets and the flying turf showed they were not all going over our heads, very few casualties were noticeable. Except for the shell-holes, the going was splendid and the pace must have been at least fifteen miles an hour.'

C Squadron were checked by wire protecting a fortified sunken road named Kildare Lane, formerly part of the British front line. Two gaps were found, through which they passed, and scrambled down into the road. Risaldar Mukand Singh and his troop, pursuing some enemy, jumped a wire fence and got in with the lance. A German officer made to surrender, produced a pistol and shot Lieutenant Broadway. He was promptly spitted by Broadway's orderly with a hogspear. Other squadrons galloped up, dismounted and took up positions in and around Kildare Lane. Colonel Turner was killed by machine-gun bullets. As there was not cover enough for all the led horses, those not in the lane were sent back to Epéhy, losing heavily on the way. The 2nd Lancers, with the brigade machine-gun squadron, were now in position as ordered, forming a front to the south-east. There they stayed, beating off sundry probing attacks by the enemy who seemed uncertain of their strength.

About mid-day volunteers were called for to carry a message to brigade headquarters at Epéhy. Of those who came forward, Lance Daffadar Gobind Singh and Sowar Jot Ram were selected. They were given duplicate messages and set off at a gallop on their two-mile ride, running the gauntlet of machine-gun fire from both sides of the valley. Jot Ram was killed almost at once. Gobind Singh's horse was shot after about a mile. For some time he lay still, then he started to run. When fired at, he pretended to be hit and lay as though dead. Running, sometimes crawling, he reached brigade and delivered his message. A return message had to be sent, and he volunteered to take this too. Again his horse was shot, but he made his way, running and falling, to the sunken road. Another message had to be sent, and Gobind Singh insisted on taking it, saying that by now he knew the best way. This time his horse was cut in half by a shell behind the saddle, but Gobind Singh again got through on foot. He was, of course, awarded the VC. No lesser decoration would match his valour that day.

CHAPTER 4

Gallipoli,

1915

The grand strategy of the Gallipoli venture is not for this book. But the unsuccessful attempt in February and March 1915 to force the Dardanelles with warships alone warned the Turks of what was to come. On 25 April British, Australian and New Zealand divisions landed with shocking losses and managed to force their way from the beach into the tangle of deeply-eroded ravines and knife-edged ridges; but they never looked like breaking through to the Straits and letting the fleet through to Constantinople.

Two Indian Mountain Batteries, the 21st (Kohat) and the 26th (Jacob's), landed with the Anzac Corps. Both were composed of Sikhs and Punjabi Mussulmans, and armed with 10-pounder breech-loading guns. On 1 May they were joined by the 29th Indian Infantry Brigade which, after some changes, was composed of the 14th Sikhs, and the 1/5th Royal, 1/6th and 2/10th Gurkha Rifles. It held the left of the line at Helles where the smell of corpses was so awful that men stuffed their noses with 'four-by-two', the flannelette patches used to clean rifles.

The Mountain Batteries had their heaviest day's fighting on 19 May, described by Major A. C. Fergusson, commanding the 21st Battery, who in the morning visited his sections in action:

'One progressed in a series of dashes from one funk-hole to another. . . . In the early dawn Rawson had been called upon to blow up a wagon which the Turks were dragging up to a salient in our lines: we never discovered what it was. He put a gun on the parapet under heavy fire and did it in. While this was going on, Subadar Mit Singh with the other gun engaged . . . a 4-inch Turkish field battery at 2,000 yards, and made it move off. Not a bad effort for a very old pattern mountain gun. . . .

After leaving Rawson, I went round to Thom's section. His usual job was supporting Quinn's Post where our firing line practically touched the Turks. . . . The battery on this day fired 613 rounds, heavy going for a slow-firing gun. . . .

The drivers were also wonderful. The senior Havildar sat in the telephone-room and when a message was received, would shout, "Three mule loads of ammunition for Right Section," and the next drivers for duty started off right away. Now leading a mule was very different from proceeding by bounds as I did. A mule does not take cover when he hears a shell, but probably stops to bray . . . yet not a man jibbed nor a mule broke loose from its driver. . . .

Two little Turkish mountain guns in a place called "German Officer's Trench" used to knock Quinn's Post about a lot, and I was asked to do something about it. I went and selected a place for a tunnel emplacement in Quinn's Post and got it made so that the front would only be opened at the moment of firing. . . . Thom waited till he was sure the [enemy] guns were in their emplacements before he opened out. He told the gunlayer, Jan Mohamad, to carry on pumping shell into one or other of the guns till he was told to stop. The range was only 350 yards. Before the second round could be got off, an HE came straight at Thom's OP and knocked him out. Jan Mohamad carried on, in spite of part of the emplacement being knocked down by HE and had loosed off 22 rounds, 17 of which went into one or another of the enemy gun-ports, before Thom came round again. Jan Mohamad got an IOM for this, and the enemy guns never spoke again. . . .

The Australians were always hanging around chatting to our fellows, though how they communicated was a marvel. They were a nuisance at times, sitting in the open when the guns were firing and giving the show away, and we had on occasion to have armed sentries to keep them out. Our shellfusing depot on the beach was exactly like a bunniah's shop in an Indian bazaar. During the first three months our men were out every night and all night carrying stores for the Anzacs. . . . The Australians . . . would take orders from our NCOs probably better than from their own. . . . We had one linesman who . . . was always out repairing lines in dangerous places and two or three times brought back chits from Australian officers to say they had seen him repairing lines under heavy fire.'

Water was short, and a water-expert told Fergusson that he must water his mules only once a day. Fergusson replied that they would then be unable to hump stores every night for the Australians, and was told to dig his own well. This he did, in a spot chosen by the Havildar Major who had done this in the Punjab. It watered 200 mules twice a day, and the expert was understandably cross.

The mountain gunners were served by a section of Indian Field Ambulance which did wonderful work, not least in setting an example to the more happy-go-lucky Australian medicos on sanitation to prevent a cholera outbreak. Australians suffering from diarrhoea and dysentery, as most did, used to patronize this establishment in preference to their own. From their doctors all they got was bully-beef, biscuits and Number 9 which the heaving stomach rejected, but the Indians gave them dhal and chupattis, which was fair dinkum, and dried them up.

On 28 June the 14th Sikhs took part in an attack on Gully Spur. Reggie Savory, a young subaltern, waited to go over the top 'with a void in the pit of his stomach'.

'And then . . . twelve noon . . . blow the whistle . . . scramble over the top . . . off you go. I waited a second to see the men up and then popped over myself. The roar of the musketry was so intense as to drown all other sound, except that of the guns. To try to give an order was useless. The nearest man to me was a yard away, and I could not see him. Soon I found myself running on alone, except for my little bugler, a young handsome boy just out of his teens who came padding along behind me and whose duty it was to act as runner and carry messages. Poor little chap. Before I could realize it I found myself standing on the parapet of a Turkish trench and looking down at a Turk inside it. He seemed an ordinary person. There was nothing of the "Terrible Turk" about him. He was not even firing, but was leaning against the back of the trench. Yet if I had given him time he would have shot me, and there were others on either side of him. I jumped in and skewered him to the back of the trench with my bayonet. Poor devil! I can see his grimace to this day. I then went a bit along the trench. . . .

My next recollection is of lying on my back on the parapet, with two Turks using my body as a rest over which to shoot at our second line coming forward. I must have been knocked out. It was not pleasant being used as an aiming-rest. I suppose I must have passed out again. When I came to there was silence. The Turks seemed to have gone. I began to look around me and saw my little bugler lying nearby, brutally mutilated. No one else was near. My head was bleeding and I was dazed. I could find none of my men. I walked back to the trench we had started from.'

The 29th Brigade felt for the first few weeks that the Turks were having the best of it. But on 2 July the enemy staged one of those mass attacks, in close order, which (as the British had learned in South Africa) were suicidal for the attacker and gave the defence the chance to win a resounding victory at very little cost. In the late evening, after a heavy artillery bombardment, from the Turkish trenches only 150 yards away close-packed ranks advanced, calling on Allah. The 1/5 Gurkhas opened a murderous rapid fire at a target which a third-class shot could hardly miss, and the artillery joined in the slaughter. No troops in the world could have persisted against such a fire, and the attack melted away.

It was renewed three days later, this time before first light. The Turks came on again and again in dense masses, pounding forward like lemmings to destruction, helpless targets for rifles, machine-guns and artillery. They were mown down in heaps, annihilated, whole battalions blotted out. The Indian trenches were so packed with riflemen pumping fifteen rounds a minute into the helpless masses in front, that many men climbed out of the trenches and sat on the parados, firing over the heads of their comrades. This went on for four hours, and served the enemy no purpose whatsoever: a whole Turkish division was thus destroyed before they saw the futility of it.

But although the Turks could not, by such suicidal heroism, drive the allies back into the sea, neither could the British, Anzacs and Indians prevail against men who were as skilful and stubborn in defence as they were heroically incompetent in attack.

In July Major C. J. L. Allanson arrived to take command of the 1/6th Gurkhas.

'The conditions are pretty bad. Flies terrible, mosquitoes bad, heat great, stench appalling and never any rest from fire. Masses of troops in a crowded space. Everyone is unanimous that the Indian Brigade has done well, but it depreciates ten per cent for the loss of each British Officer and twenty per cent when the CO goes. The Indian Officer on whom we rely in peace becomes nearly valueless outside India. No troops could be at a higher level of peace training, but nothing can compete with the disastrous effect of the loss of BOs. It appears to paralyse a unit completely.'

No doubt some Subadars were too old and set in their ways. But there is abundant evidence that most behaved not merely bravely but competently. Perhaps those who didn't are not mentioned in the regimental histories.

An ambitious plan was made to capture the highest peaks of the Sari Bair, the spine along the peninsular, by two columns moving out by night from the Anzac enclave at Anzac Cove, marching along the shore and then turning inland to storm the heights at dawn. At the same time there would be a new landing in Suvla Bay, five miles north of Anzac Cove, by the 10th and 11th British 'New Army' Divisions to make good the left flank of the attack on the heights. The more Allanson examined the country through binoculars, the less he liked it.

'When the plan of attack was disclosed to me confidentially I gasped. No one has been able to reconnoitre the ground and no one can guarantee the map. The whole country seemed to be stiff with sharp rocky cliffs covered with thick scrub. I have a few ideas about night marches, and their great difficulty, and the need for careful reconnaissance; but when I was told that we were to break through the opposing outpost lines at 10 p.m., march along the sea coast for three miles, then turn at right angles and attempt to get under the big ridge about two miles inland by dawn, I felt, what would one have done to a subaltern at a promotion exam who made any such proposition? In my own regiment there were four officers out of seven who had never done a night march in their lives.'

Two officers going sick left him with only five. 'No quartermaster, no signalling officer, no machine-gun officer, and yet these services were maintained, and very well maintained too.'

By whom? By the Gurkha Officers.

The Brigade was brought over from Imbros to Anzac Cove after dark on 5 August to rest for twenty-four hours, but the Movement Staff made a nonsense.

'Which means that the night before their great ordeal my poor little fellows will not get a night in bed. Bad staff work. . . . At 4.30 a.m. they rolled up. Many had been sea-sick, and as best I could I fitted them into their dugouts. Terribly crowded, frightfully hot and we were shelled all day. . . . Then a shell burst the fresh water tank . . . and I had great difficulty in getting my men's water-bottles filled. I was told this must do for 48 hours, perhaps longer, and the temperature by day is near 100 degrees. It turned out to be 96 hours, not 48. I went round all the men and impressed on them the immense necessity of husbanding food, water and ammunition. They are lovable little fellows and quite bright and cheery, but my heart could not help bleeding for what I knew they must go through.'

The assault force consisted of a Right Assaulting Column (a New Zealand brigade) and a Left Assaulting Column (4th Australian and 29th Indian Brigades), each with a battery of Indian mountain artillery. The Left Column was commanded by Major General H. V. Cox who had arrived only five days previously. The Right Column was to turn inland a mile north of the Anzac Cove defence line, ascend Rhododendron Spur and storm Chunuk Bair, a mile and a half from the coast. The Left Column was to march along the shore for two miles before turning inland for two or three miles, the Australians to storm Koja Chemen Tepe and the Indians, Hill Q.

If these heights could be captured and held, all the Turkish forces to the south would be cut off, the Dardanelles forts taken from the rear and the campaign as good as won. But an approach march of that length across unknown country, rocky, scrub-covered ridges and deep, eroded winding nullahs, was an exercise which must have failed even in peacetime.

The Left Assaulting Column were to form up on the beach and pass through the Anzac front line at 10.30 p.m. on the 6th, Australians leading. But the leading half of the column moved off too soon and Allanson

'had to go off on my own. After half an hour of deadly funk as to where I was, I ran into the rest of the column halted. It was now 12.15 midnight and we were two hours behind our programme time. There was a feeling of panic and doubt in the air as to where we were and where we were going; it was a pitch black night.'

Like most cross-country night marches, it was a succession of long unexplained halts, short shuffling moves forward, and doubling to catch up. The Australians rushed the Turkish outposts, but were then interminably delayed taking a 'short cut' recommended by their Greek guide. Allanson

'suddenly heard a rush in front. I thought it was the Turks and drew my revolver, and was almost knocked down. Dallas behind me fixed bayonets and stopped the rush; it was only a panic of a few men of the regiment in front. Later an order was passed down to turn about and go back. I refused to take it, and went up the line to find out whose order it was. The CO in front had not had it or given it. By this time I knew the state of everyone's nerves. We were supposed to be at the foot of the hills two hours before dawn, but were still on the edge of the sea.'

The Australian brigade bore off to the left and Allanson was ordered to support them; the remainder of the column bore half-right.

'I followed up the Australians and found them hopelessly stopped by a big precipice in front, so I swung to the lower ground on the right and let the GOC [Cox] know that the best support I thought I could give was to

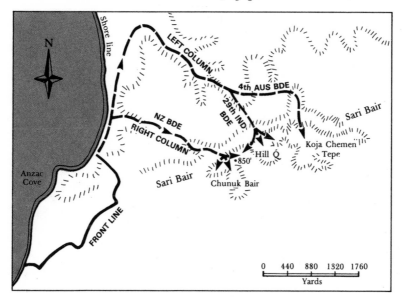

Gallipoli: Sari Bair, 6–10 August 1915

make a frontal attack, making full use of the hilly country. On my way I found quite a big Turkish camp deserted, with lots of rifles, ammunition, bombs, horses, tents etc, which made me feel very hopeful. We had had great luck. The great thing now was to push on everyone at all costs.'

If Allanson felt very hopeful, no one else did. The Australian brigade spent all day trying to discover where it was, where its battalions were and whether the guides had the slightest idea of their position. (They hadn't.) Far down and to the left they could see Suvla Bay where the 10th and 11th Divisions were coming ashore – but only in the sense that a stranded whale comes ashore. They seemed to make no attempt to move inland, though there was nothing to stop them.

29 Brigade, less Allanson's 1/6th Gurkhas, took up a position below the crest of the Sari Bair. The 14th Sikhs, like every other unit, was short of officers; so Savory, having gone forward with them in his capacity of Adjutant, returned in his capacity of quartermaster to bring up machine-gun and ammunition mules.

'An intense fire had broken out along the top of Sari Bair, and it was clear that another crisis had come. I clambered slowly up with my string of mules, led by Sikh drivers. There was no danger. The branch of the Aghyl Dere along which we were wending our way was narrow and deep; only stray or spent bullets could reach it. Suddenly a panic-stricken crowd of soldiers, led by an officer with ginger hair and without a hat, came streaming round the corner. He and his men seemed to have thrown away their arms. They were a terrible sight. Screaming and shouting, "Go back! The Turks are after us!" they tried to pass. My Sikhs with the stubbornness of their mules stood firm and edged into the side of the ravine. I shouted to the officer to stop. He only yelled the louder, "The Turks are coming! Go back, go back!" Panic is infectious. I had seen it before. Something had to be done. I pulled out my pistol and threatened him. He took not the slightest notice but rushed on. I fired at him, and missed. He and his men swept on, down towards the beach. Thank God my own men stood staunch.'

(That evening the 14th Sikhs' CO, Colonel Palin, took Savory on a liaison visit to the neighbouring British battalion. They were offered a tot of rum: Savory was brought his by the officer he had tried to shoot that morning. They recognized one another. It was not a cordial occasion.)

Allanson pushed on, heading to the right (south) of Hill Q. When over half way up, he received orders to stop and take up a covering position for the night to protect others coming up behind him. 'Far better have let me go on.' There they spent the night, their third without sleep.

By moving to the right when the Australians were held up by the precipice, the 1/6th Gurkhas had crossed in front of a brigade consisting of the 7th North Staffordshire, 6th South Lancashire and 9th Warwickshire Regiments, which was following the assaulting columns. The heights would now have to be stormed twenty-four hours later than originally planned, and Allanson received orders for this at 1.30 in the morning of the 8th.

'We had been heavily shelled that evening and I had been much frightened. We had no blankets and no coats and when I got the orders I was so shivering with cold (fright!) that I could only with difficulty read them. My regiment was ordered to make a frontal attack, leaving at 2.45 a.m., supported by two British battalions. . . . The officer who issued the orders had never seen the country, and the point of assembly was the junction of two nullahs, each two feet wide. The confusion was, of course, awful, and as I could not get in touch with the British battalions, I started off on the attack on my own, asking the others by note to follow. We were then two and a half hours behind the scheduled time. The ground was covered by a horrible scrub.'

Leading from in front, with the double companies commanded by Dallas, Le Marchand and Underhill in the front line and the reserve under Cornish behind, he got to within two hundred yards of the objective, Hill 971. Then in a few minutes Dallas was wounded and Underhill killed; and Allanson saw that he must get help from the British brigade.

'I went down to find the nullahs all full of men, but the moment one got out, down he went, and that did not encourage the others. The regiments should have moved up in open formation. I got hold of an officer, North Staffords, . . . and said I must get more men up, and managed to push 50 or 60 on. We got the regiment and these men another fifty yards on when casualties . . . stopped us. I went back again to try to get some more men, and got . . . about 50 Warwicks, and again we got on another fifty yards.

14 Gurkhas: 'Charing Cross', Gallipoli 1915.

15 (above) Indians with AT carts carrying forage for mules, Gallipoli 1915: the carts were instruments of torture for any wounded carried in them.

16 (below) Indian sepoys crossing the Diala River, Mesopotamia.

17 *(above)* Jat Regiment Lewis-gun firing at enemy aircraft, Mesopotamia 1918.

18 *(below)* Palestine: the Pathan squadron of 9th Hodson's Horse leads the 5th Cavalry Division through the gap in the Turkish line, September 1918. Painting by J. A. Stewart.

19 *(above)* 9th Hodson's Horse entering Damascus, 2 October 1918: the climax of the last great cavalry campaign in history.

20 *(below left)* Daffadar Kalbi Mohamad and Havildar Awal Nur of the Guides disguised as merchants in Bokhara, 1919. Between them is Lieutenant Colonel F. M. Bailey disguised as a Hungarian prisoner-of-war.

21 *(right)* Kalbi Mohamad and Awal Nur at Kashgar, 1919.

22 Equitation, Hodson's Horse, 1939: Jemadar Atta Mohamad negotiating an almost perpendicular slide.

23 Hodson's Horse loading camels on a frontier column, 1938.

24 Trumpeters of Hodson's Horse, 1938.

25 Risaldar Zalim Singh, Poona Horse, 1912–39: a Rathor Rajput. From the portrait by
Lance Cattermole at the Cavalry and Guards Club.

I then got forward right under the final crest with Le Marchand, about 10 Gurkhas, and 30 Britishers, with all the rest of the regiment just below.

Further movement was impossible. It was now 9.30 a.m. and blazing hot. I lay there without moving till 6 p.m. with every conceivable shot flying in the air about one, shrapnel, our own maxims, rifles, and our own high explosive bursting extremely close, which told me how near we were to the top. I lay between two British soldiers; the man on my left had a Bible and read it the whole day; the man on my right I found was a corpse. . . .

Immediately it got dark I got all the men up another fifty yards, and then we dug in like hell. . . . We got quite a good line, but above us, at an angle of about 35 degrees and only 100 yards away, were the Turks. I sent a message down to the General and told him how precarious my position was, and asked for pistol flares, but there were none available. I was terribly afraid of a bomb attack, as they only had to roll them down the hill.'

Again he went down to ask the British battalions to give him some men as a reserve, for all his Gurkhas were in the firing line. He managed to get three companies: 'the entire three regiments should . . . have pushed up and joined me.' He got written orders from General Cox to attack Hill 971 at 5.15 a.m. An essential element of the plan was a brigade of four British 'New Army' battalions, commanded by Brigadier General Baldwin, who would 'come up on my right, it was hoped, for certain'. But Baldwin lost his way: he never arrived.

'Throughout the night there was a perfectly terrific fire; my wee dugout was a mass of dust flying about. Phipson, our doctor, slept beside me and Cornish next with the telephone glued to his ear. The men fired over 120 rounds on an average each that night. The roar was incessant. I was rather weak from want of food and I trembled for most of the night. The Navy helped us greatly by keeping their searchlight on the hill, which enabled my fellows to keep the Turks from getting up to rush us. At 4.30 a.m. [9th] I telephoned to Le Marchand my plans for the attack. . . . He telephoned back, "Right, Major, everything is quite clear," and we compared watches. As I could only get three companies of British troops, I had to be satisfied with this. All the company commanders regarded the plan as hopeless and the cliff too steep to get up and asked if my regiment would lead. I said, "No, we must all go up together, in one line; it makes our strength appear greater, and the attack must take place at all costs," and that those were my orders.

I had only fifteen minutes left; the roar of the artillery preparation was enormous; the hill was almost leaping underneath one. I recognized that if we flew up the hill the moment it stopped, we ought to get to the top. I put the three companies into the trenches among my men, and said the moment they saw me go forward carrying a red flag, everyone was to start. I had my watch out, 5.15. I never saw such artillery preparation; the trenches were being torn to pieces; the accuracy was marvellous, as we were only just below. 5.18, it had not stopped, and I wondered if my watch was wrong. 5.20, silence. I waited three minutes to be certain, great as the risk was. Then off we dashed, all hand in hand, a most perfect advance and a wonderful sight. I left Cornish with fifty men to hold the line in case we were pushed back and to watch me if I signalled for reinforcements. At the top we met the Turks. Le Marchand was down, a bayonet through the heart. I got one through the leg, and then, for about ten minutes, we fought hand to hand, we bit and fisted and used rifles and pistols as clubs; blood was flying about like spray from a hairwash bottle. And then the Turks turned and fled, and I felt a very proud man. The key of the whole peninsular was ours. . . . Below I saw the Straits, motors and wheeled transport on the roads leading to Achi Baba.

As I looked round, I saw we were not being supported, and thought I could help best by going after those who had retreated in front of us. We dashed down towards Maidos, but had only got about three hundred feet down when I saw a flash in the bay and suddenly our own Navy put six 12-inch monitor shells into us, and all was terrible confusion. . . . The first hit a Gurkha in the face; the place was a mass of blood and limbs and screams, and we all flew back to the summit and to our old position just below. I remained on the crest with about fifteen men. It was a wonderful view; below were the Straits, reinforcements coming over from the Asia Minor side, motor cars. We commanded Kila Bahr, and the rear of Achi Baba and the communications to all their army there.

A message came up to say that Cornish had been very badly hit, and had gone, and I was now left much crippled by the pain of my wound, which was stiffening, and loss of blood. I saw the advance at Suvla Bay had failed, though I could not detect more than one or two thousand Turks against them. . . . Victory was slipping from our grasp.'

If only – if only Allanson had been better supported; if only the corps landing at Suvla Bay had shown more dash; if only the Navy had not fired that fatal salvo; above all, if only Brigadier General Baldwin had not lost his way. If only one of these things had gone right, what might the results not have been? The Turkish forts guarding the Straits rushed from the rear; the great grey battleships steaming up to Constantinople; Turkey, cut off from Germany, suing for peace; supplies moving freely through the Straits to Russia; even, perhaps, no battle of the Somme, no Paschendaele, no Russian Revolution. . . .

The whole Gallipoli campaign was a litany of 'if onlys' and lost opportunities, but this was surely the most poignant of them all. And the last. There were no more great efforts to break through to the Straits; and on 19 December the British evacuated Gallipoli, leaving behind many thousands of dead.

But there was one momentous result of Allanson's battle. A subaltern of the Warwicks, Bill Slim, was there. Before being badly wounded, he saw enough of the Gurkhas to determine that one day he would be one of them.

CHAPTER 5

East Africa,
1914–18

In Egypt there continued a desultory campaign with Indian troops, notably the Bikanir Camel Corps, defending the Suez Canal against a Turkish army which never seemed likely to master the administrative problems of crossing the Sinai desert with a force large enough to trouble the Canal's defenders. The 129th Baluchis and the 40th Pathans, after leaving France, passed through the Canal and went on to take part in the East African campaign where there were no Turks, so Islamic consciences were not troubled.

The British, based on Nairobi and from time to time quite competently commanded, were opposed by a military genius, General von Lettow Vorbeck. With no hope of reinforcements from Germany, short of food, boots, clothing, medical supplies, arms and ammunition; with only some 16,000 askaris led by German planters, civil servants and businessmen, Von Lettow fought a brilliant rearguard action for four years, containing many times his own numbers of allied troops.

To offset his difficulties, he had some advantages. The theatre of operations was vast: from Mount Kilimanjaro in the north to the River Zambezi in the south, as far as from Paris to Leningrad; and from the Indian Ocean in the east to the great lakes in the west, as far as from Paris to Naples. In this huge area it was almost impossible to corner him, or to bring him to battle except on ground of his own choice. His askaris were well trained in bush warfare; knew the country, the tracks through the bush and the waterholes; and through all vicissitudes showed exemplary courage and fidelity to their German officers. There were virtually no roads in German East Africa: transport was by porters, donkeys and rail. Von Lettow, until he was driven off them, had excellent lateral communications by two east-west railways, one from Tanga to Moshi, the other from Dar-es-Salaam to Lake Tanganyika. These enabled him to use heavy guns, taken from scuttled German warships, on railway mountings. Retreating slowly south, imposing on the British endless delays, depending for his news from Germany on captured newspapers, he was still fighting after the Armistice, and became, like Rommel, a sort of hero to the British as well as to the Germans. But in the end the British mastered the difficulties of the campaign, and won it. No war could have been more different from that from which the 40th Pathans and 129th Baluchis had come; but Von Lettow noted in his diary that the Indian battalions who had fought in Flanders 'are without a doubt very good' – by implication the best on the British side.

They arrived when the reputation of the Indian Army stank. A brigade from India, badly commanded and badly staffed, sea-sick and without an hour's training in beach-landings, had tried in November 1914 to take the port of Tanga in German East Africa. They were seen off by a smaller force of German-led askaris who, not wishing to be burdened with prisoners, allowed them to depart with their tails between their legs. Only a State Forces battalion, the Kashmir Rifles, came out of Tanga with any credit, having taken two trenches, reached the suburbs of Tanga and covered the withdrawal. Their next job was to patrol against German raids the Mombasa-Nairobi railway, which was also patrolled nightly by man-eating lions, progeny of the 'maneaters of Tsavo'.

The 40th Pathans and Baluchis were soon able to restore the Indian Army's repute. General Smuts started his offensive to drive the Germans out of Africa by an attack on Salaita Hill, near Taveta on the British-German border, in February 1916. The main attacking force was the South African Mounted Brigade, rough and tough, mainly Boers, equally scornful of the 'Kaffirs' against whom they would be fighting and the 'Coolies' who were on their side. Unfortunately, they had omitted to train for bush country so different from their open veldt; and by the time they were half way up Salaita they were desperate with thirst and exhausted from forcing their way through thorn-scrub. The German machine-guns opened up, unseen but deadly. Then hundreds of shrieking blacks, Von Lettow's *Schutztruppe*, charged down on them. They bolted, leaving six hundred dead and wounded. On their flanks the 2nd Rhodesians and the 129th Baluchis stood firm and covered their rout. Next day the Rhodesians and Baluchis exchanged compliments. To the South Africans the Baluchis returned the machine-guns they had lost, together with a request 'that you do not refer to our sepoys as coolies'.

The country was ideal for the defenders, very difficult for the attackers. Most of it was covered with thorn-scrub, with a visibility from five to two hundred yards. The thorns were the hooked 'wait-a-bit' thorns of acacia bushes, which cling to the clothes and flesh of anyone who tries to force his way through. For most of the year there was far too little water, and men suffered tortures from thirst. In the rains the whole land was a quagmire between rivers which could be miles wide; normally the rains are from April to June, but in 1917 they started in January. It was as hot as the Punjab in May; malaria, blackwater fever, tick-typhus, dysentery and all kinds of intestinal diseases were rife. Mounted troops – of which India provided the 17th Cavalry and South Africa a Mounted Brigade of Boer commandos – were at a discount, for over most of the country African horse-sickness, for which there was no cure, slew tens of thousands of horses.

Making as much use as possible of lorries for transport, the British had to cut roads as they advanced. Smuts was well served by his engineers, including a State Forces unit, the Faridkote Field Company, officered entirely by Sikhs at a time when the only Indians holding the King's Commission were medical officers. They had to improvise, and learned

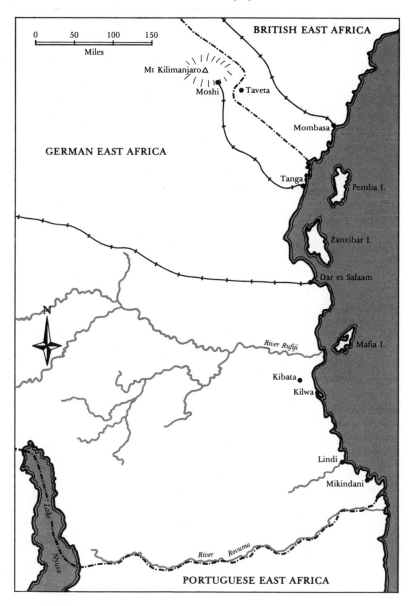

East Africa, 1914–18

through experience that papyrus reeds laid in thick transverse layers make a tough road-surface; and that ebony makes the best scantlings on corduroy roads during the rains. They acquired a grey parrot which screeched 'Hoch der Kaiser!' and 'Gott straffe England'. But when it began to whistle the 'Fall in' at inappropriate moments, it had to be suppressed.

Much of the engineers' work consisted of making and maintaining roads through the bush by toil and sweat, panga and machete, pick and shovel. The alignment and organization was the responsibility of the Sappers, the muscle was provided by Pioneers and infantry. During the standard ten minutes' halt in the hour, every man cut the bush to right and left for three minutes, and rested for seven minutes. The result could be used by lorries and guns. But not, of course, during the rains, when they were bogged to the axles. Then recourse was had to porters or donkeys. The braying of amorous donkeys at night was an intolerable nuisance, until some genius discovered that a donkey cannot bray without cocking his tail. Thereafter to each donkey's tail at night was attached a gunny-bag filled with earth, and sleep was undisturbed.

The Railway Companies, Sappers and Miners, were recruited mainly from men who worked on Indian railways in peacetime. In the early days, when the Mombasa-Uganda railway was vulnerable to enemy raiders, they guarded bridges and developed a keen eye for signs of mines laid under the rails. They were then provided with ox-carts for transport and acted as Field Companies. In 1917 they came into their own when the British gained control of the railway from Dar-es-Salaam to Lake Tanganyika and innumerable blown bridges and culverts had to be repaired. Then the little German ports of Kilwa, Lindi and Mikindani were captured, and light railways had to be laid from them inland, using material found on German sisal plantations, the traction provided by Ford vans mounted on tramway axles.

But (like almost every war in history) it was mainly an infantry war. The machine-gun was king, impossible to detect in thick bush and deadly even when nothing could be seen of the enemy but dust-clouds or the shaking of acacia bushes. It was a nerve-racking war: a man twenty yards from his mates felt he was alone in Africa.

Laboriously, with little of the dash associated with the reputation of the Boer War commando leader, Smuts's forces pushed the Germans back to Dar-es-Salaam. He then speeded up the advance on land by outflanking the enemy by sea, in a series of left hooks from one small port to another. In October 1916, Kilwa was captured by two battalions of the King's African Rifles (KAR), the 40th Pathans and the Baluchis, who then moved inland to take the high ground dominating the port. The key to their position was Kibata, a village with German administrative buildings and an old fort surrounded by rocky hills.

Von Lettow could not permit this build-up, and from the shady verandah of a German planter's bungalow further inland directed a formidable attack on Kibata, supported by two heavy guns brought up with long and arduous labour. The defenders had no proper trenches with dugouts and overhead cover, and the high-explosive shells bursting on rock were extraordinarily unpleasant even to men accustomed to bombardments on the Western Front. The enemy worked from hilltop to hilltop, closer and closer, almost surrounding Kibata.

'The Lodgement', at the end of a rocky ridge, was a German strongpoint, trenches and weapon-pits all surrounded by thickets of sharpened stakes and a dense thorn 'boma'. (A thorn boma was the African equivalent of barbed wire and almost as impenetrable. It consisted of a tangle of interlocking branches of the acacia tree. The stumps of the branches, which could be gripped with relative impunity, were on the defender's side, so that he could easily make a gap by pulling out a few branches. But the attacker had nothing to grip except the thorny extremities of the branches, and the harder he pulled on one branch, the more stubbornly it clung to its neighbours.) In enemy hands the Lodgement was a menace to Kibata. The KAR had tried to capture it and failed, so the job was given to the Baluchis. Major Lewis planned the attack for 11 p.m., when there would be some light from a quarter-moon. A covering fire plan for machine-guns and mountain artillery was arranged. A hundred Mills bombs, a novelty in East Africa, had just arrived. Lewis's plan was that ten 'pioneers', old soldiers, Mahsuds and Punjabi Mussulmans, under the same Jemadar Ayub Khan who in France had collected valuable information by pretending to desert, would drag out the thorn-branches and sharpened stakes while machine-guns and bombs kept the enemy's heads down. Behind the pioneers, waiting until the gap was made and they could charge in, were the storm-troops, newly arrived Mahsud recruits, selected perhaps on the principle that ignorance is bliss. These had never seen Mills bombs before, and there was no time to do more than explain, 'This is a Mills bomb. Right? You pull out this ring and throw it.' They thought it quite a good idea for a night attack, better than the rifles and daggers they had handled since boyhood.

There was a light breeze, enough to muffle the small sounds of men moving barefoot. They climbed out of their own trench, gently pulled out branches to make a gap in their own boma, and crept along a razor-backed ridge towards the faint, recurrent glow of a cigarette smoked by an enemy sentry. The pioneers reached the enemy boma, threw their bombs and tore frantically at the thorns. Behind them, yelling like fiends, the recruits closed up and hurled their bombs too. With the rattle of machine-guns, the crash and blinding explosions of the shells from the mountain guns, the excited yells and warcries of the Mahsuds, it was pandemonium. The pioneers flattened themselves to the ground while machine-gun bullets streamed over them, tugging with lacerated hands at the thorns, shaking loose and pulling out the stakes. It took them fifteen minutes, and as they pulled out the last stake, a well-aimed bomb silenced the machine-gun and the storming party dashed in, shooting and stabbing and screaming, led by Jemadar Ayub Khan – though he had been shot in the face – and 'an astonishingly brave youth named Sahib Jan'. It was soon over, and as they

71

counted the prisoners they noticed that the machine-gun which had so troubled them was fired through a loophole in a steel shield, and could not be depressed enough to harm them. *Al Hamdulillah!* As so often in night operations, there was more noise than damage, and casualties were few.

This spirited little action removed the threat to Kilwa and the build-up of supplies continued.

The East African campaign was the Mahsuds' finest hour in the Indian Army. (In 1919–20 they had some pretty fine hours *against* the Indian Army – see Chapter 9.) There was a premium on fieldcraft and quick snap-shooting. One who excelled at the game was Havildar Zardad, nicknamed Qalaband, who led a band of Mahsud lads calling themselves the *jangian*, warriors. Lewis sent them to reconnoitre down the railway to the German position. Qalaband returned and reported:

'I moved down the railway until I reached a ridge covering the station where I judged the enemy would have a piquet, and on scouting forward I saw one. I placed the *jangian* in cover with orders to open fire if I was fired on, and proceeded down the railway alone. A black sentry saw me and brought up his rifle to the present, covering me. He shouted out "*Kwenda*" [Go away]. I replied "*Hapana piga*" [Don't shoot]. But as I got quite close he shot and missed. So I fired and the *jangian* fired and the piquet ran away. From the piquet position we saw many Germans leave their huts and occupy such-and-such positions. I could do no more, so I returned.'

Qalaband saw that Lewis did not believe him and, nettled, went out again the following morning. At dusk he returned and made his report.

'I placed my *jangian* as before in the grass by the road. This time I did not advance in the open on the road, but moved stealthily through the grass. As I expected there was a piquet on the ridge. A white officer was inspecting it. So I crept up quite close behind a fig tree. First I shot the officer, then the sentry, then the Lance-Naik and then a bugler.'

Qalaband paused for a moment and then said, 'Here is the officer's revolver, the sentry's rifle, the Lance Naik's stripe and the bugler's bugle. And now, Sahib, do you believe my first story?'

By the standards of Flanders, there was not much blood shed in this campaign, but a great deal of tears, toil and sweat. Take, for instance, Captain Gover's march from Kibata with two companies of Baluchis.

They came to a flooded river, out of a man's depth. As they could not get the baggage across, carried by porters, there was nothing for it but to make a bridge. But where? And how? The stream ran through swamp and jungle, and the first difficulty was to locate the banks. They had no rope, wire, nails or planks. There were plenty of trees, but when one was felled, it was extremely difficult to extract it from the undergrowth and haul it to where it was needed. There was no open space in which to assemble material and put things together.

'The men, who had never done such a thing before, were bored with the whole business. At last I got them to get a move on and they spread out into the jungle to cut wood, but without any hope that it would be the slightest use if they did cut it. I had other men pulling down creepers and twisting them into ropes.

The first pier I built almost entirely with my own hands, when suddenly a hawk-faced Afridi officer realized that there was something in it after all and plunged into the water at my side to help. Then the men began to get interested; at first they had all denied they could swim, now some realized that they could. It was a perilous time as the material was of necessity very light and they would crowd round and get in each other's way and nearly bring the whole thing down into the torrent ten feet deep. However, by nightfall we were half-way across, and next day we finished it and took the baggage across at four in the afternoon.'

The bush and its denizens were neutral, that is to say, equally hostile to both sides – particularly rhinos, short-sighted and shorter-tempered. One of these truculent creatures interrupted a patrol action by charging and scattering first the Indians, then the Germans, and finally killing a Masai herdsman who was watching the conflict. Hippos sometimes disrupted river crossings, attacking boats and having to be fended off with bayonets. Once when the 40th Pathans' mules were watering, a large crocodile surged across the river like a speedboat and grabbed a mule by the leg. There ensued a grim tug-o'-war, men on one side, croc on the other, mule in the middle. The men won; and the mule, after trembling all night, characteristically made a complete recovery. Lions stampeded baggage animals, and sometimes devoured the wounded. (Subadar Mehrab Din, 40th Pathans, shot a maneater.) Giraffes often galloped off with overhead telephone cables trailing round their necks.

Then there were the bees. . . . In one of the Baluchis' actions a bullet hit a bee-hive hanging from a tree. In a moment bees were everywhere, and so were the machine-gun mules. Officers and men flung themselves on the ground, faces in the grass. A South African cyclist rode up with a message from Brigade asking, 'Why the delay?' He handed his message to the scarcely recognizable CO; then he too buried his face in Mother Earth. The only two men to escape were the Mahsud Subadar, Mir Badshah, who stood stockstill muttering prayers through motionless lips, and his company commander, Lewis, who followed his prudent and pious example.

By far the worst enemy in this campaign was disease – malaria, blackwater fever, bilharzia, jaundice, sleeping sickness, hookworm, tick-fever, intestinal diseases of all kinds. Especially malaria, for which there were none of the prophylactics available in World War II. At one time the Baluchis had more than three hundred officers and men on the sick list.

East Africa was not a country that favoured the artillery arm. It was difficult in the bush to identify targets and to spot the fall of shells; even more difficult, before the days of wireless, to communicate from OP to gun position; and not easy to find positions where guns, with relatively flat trajectories, could find positions with clearance enough to fire without endangering their own detachments. What was wanted was a light howitzer, but there was none. Then, in April 1918, Major J. H. M. Stevenson, commanding No 2 (Derajat) Mountain Battery, heard through the grapevine an interesting rumour from the base at Dar-es-Salaam. He hastened there, and was privileged to be one of the first artillerymen to see the 3.7-inch howitzer, a wonderful little gun, still in service fifty years later. It fired a 19lb HE shell with extreme accuracy, to a range of 6,750 yards, and required eight mules to carry it.

By dint of wining and dining the Assistant Director of Ordnance Stores, Stevenson was allowed to exchange two 3.7-inch howitzers for two of his old 2.75-inch guns. There were no spares, range tables, handbooks or gun-drill books, so he found plenty of scope for improvisation; he carried out a comparative calibration, invented a drill for unlimbering and limbering up, and fired some practice rounds. On 11 April the gun was fired against an enemy for the first time, and blasted them out of a strong hilltop position.

Von Lettow's indomitable little army, hungry, in rags, riddled with malaria, replenished their arms, ammunition, clothing, boots and medical supplies from the Portuguese, and then invaded Northern Rhodesia. Hunted by half a dozen columns, but still full of fight, they laid down their arms only when told of the Armistice and the Kaiser's abdication.

CHAPTER 6

Mesopotamia,
1914–18

For a campaign generally regarded as governed from start to finish by Murphy's Law ('Anything which can go wrong, will.'), the war in Mesopotamia got off to a singularly auspicious start. The object was simple and sensible: to safeguard the Anglo-Persian Oil Company's installations at Mohammerah and on Abadan Island, without which the British Empire could not have continued the war for a week. They were forty miles up the left bank of the Shatt-el-Arab which flows into the head of the Persian Gulf, and on Persian territory. Persia was neutral but pro-German in sympathy, and full of German consuls, merchants, geologists, archaeologists and advisers of all kinds who were up to no good. Across the Shatt-el-Arab, which is formed by the rivers Tigris and Euphrates, was Turkish territory. Sixty miles from the mouth of the Shatt-el-Arab, twenty miles above Abadan, was the fly-blown, pestilential port of Basra, modest in its facilities but the only one in Mesopotamia.

The campaign was eventually to suck in 600,000 British and Indian troops, but it achieved its essential object with an admirable economy of force. From 23 October 1914 a small British and Indian force had been waiting at Bahrein, poised to steam up the Shatt-el-Arab when Turkey came down off the fence on the German side. As soon as this happened, Basra was occupied on 31 October by the 16th and 18th Indian brigades against very weak opposition; and on 9 December, Qurna was taken, fifty miles further upstream, where the Tigris and Euphrates join. A detachment occupied Ahwaz, in neutral Persia, to protect the oil pipeline to Mohammerah.

By April 1915, the Expeditionary Force had grown to a weak corps consisting of the original 6th Indian Division, the newly arrived 12th Indian Division (very short of artillery) and a cavalry brigade, the whole under General Sir John Nixon. So far, so good. The climate of Basra in winter is clement but bracing; there were no great problems of administration or enemy action. The campaign seemed to justify envious references to 'the Mesopotamia picnic'.

By holding Qurna, Basra could be defended against an attack down the river. But fifteen miles south-west of Basra the Turks were in considerable force, some 12,000 regulars and 10,000 Arab tribesmen. The regulars were not the cream of the Turkish army, which was in Gallipoli, and were routed in an action known euphorically as 'The Miracle of Shaiba'. It was the last miracle the Mesopotamia Expeditionary Force was to see for many a long day, and it enabled the British to gain more depth for the defence of Basra,

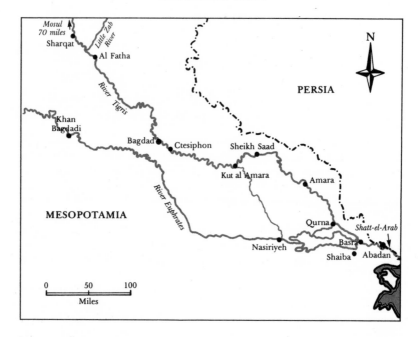

Mesopotamia, 1914–18

advancing to Amara, seventy-five miles up the Tigris, and Nasiriyeh, seventy-five miles up the Euphrates. It seemed appropriate to occupy also a small town named Kut-al-Amara, 130 miles further upstream of Amara. Kut was taken in September 1915 by the 6th Indian Division (16th, 17th and 18th Brigades) and the Cavalry Brigade, all commanded by Major General C. V. F. Townshend.

He had made his name twenty-four years earlier by the defence of Chitral Fort against Pathan tribesmen. He was reputed to be a brainy soldier, apt at tricks and dodges, and a good tactician. Above all he was a 'card'. He had a way with British troops who called him 'Charlie'; but not with Indians, of whom he had no very high opinion, nor they of him. The King disliked him as an 'advertising sort of fellow' and Haig thought him a 'semi-lunatic'.

There was no military reason to go further than Kut. The object of the expedition was to safeguard the oil installations. They were now safe. There was only the political reason that the capture of Bagdad would balance the loss in prestige of failure in Gallipoli. This was argued by the Prime Minister, Mr Asquith; the Viceroy, Lord Hardinge; the commander of the Expeditionary Force, Sir John Nixon; and the C-in-C India, aptly named Sir Beauchamp Duff. The two last doubtless believed that their military talents were worthy of more than the passive defence of a horrible country.

They did not appreciate the difficulties of capturing Bagdad. From April to September Mesopotamia is one of the hottest countries in the world. From January (sometimes earlier) to March there is heavy rainfall, turning the desert into a quagmire. Very little was known about water-supplies away from the rivers; so an army using animal transport and cavalry must stay close to the rivers. They must use gunboats as artillery, and barges as baggage carts. The rivers were torrents during the rains, with shifting shoals and sandbanks at other times, and always a succession of U-bends, each a hazard to navigation. Hitherto the best divisions of the Turkish Army, tough Anatolians, had not been encountered, but soon they would be arriving from Gallipoli. Casualties front gunshot wounds would be multiplied many times over by malaria, jaundice, scurvy, dysentery, typhoid, cholera. Last but most important, the administrative back-up for mobile operations 500 miles upstream from Basra were ludicrously inadequate. And with every mile Townshend advanced, his supply problems would increase and the enemy's would be simplified. Townshend saw the difficulties, but was over-ruled. The decision was made – Forward to Bagdad!

Neatly out-manoeuvring the Turkish rearguard, Townshend bumped into their main position astride the great Arch of Ctesiphon, thirty miles south of Bagdad, on 21 November. The defences were immensely strong: deep, narrow trenches, impossible to locate in a mirage, approachable only over a dead-flat plain without a scrap of cover, and manned by 19,000 Anatolian Turks who had seen off the British and Anzacs from Gallipoli. In retrospect it seems that Townshend was crazy to attack it with only 12,000 men. But morale was high and Bagdad almost within reach. The key point was stormed by the 24th and 66th Punjabis, the 2/7 Gurkhas and the 117th Mahrattas. They found the wire uncut and, while the 66th hacked down the posts with dahs brought from Burma, the champion long-jumper of the 24th, more spectacularly if less usefully, took a run at the wire, jumped clean over it and charged on alone, berserk, into the enemy trench. He was killed, but his comrades took the front line, broke through the second and beat off a counter-attack by a whole Turkish division. So it was in a way a victory, but it cost 4,500 casualties. As another such victory would ruin him, Townshend withdrew to Kut.

In pouring rain, sploshing through mud, with the knowledge that anyone left behind would be castrated by the Arabs, the troops trudged on, and on, and on. They were hungry because their supply barges stuck on sandbanks; they were bitterly disappointed and utterly exhausted. The final forced march of 44 miles in 36 hours was a nightmare. On 3 December 1915 they reached Kut.

Townshend must have been aware that a retreating army is doomed which surrenders its mobility to take refuge in a fortress. But the idea of himself as the heroic commander of a besieged garrison seems to have fascinated him. That is how, at Chitral, he had first won fame. Did he fantasize over history repeating itself on a much larger scale before the eyes

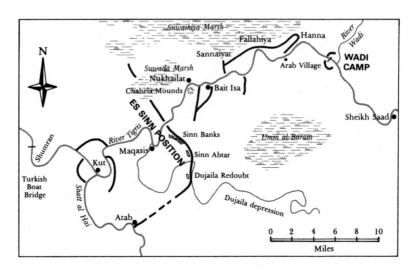

Mesopotamia, March April 1916

of the world? Kut seemed strong, situated on a peninsular two miles long and a mile wide with the Tigris on three sides. He was sure he would soon be relieved: the 7th (Meerut) and 3rd (Lahore) Divisions, battle-hardened in France and rested in Egypt, were on their way to Basra. His decision to stand at Kut was approved by Nixon, who promised that relief would come by early February at the latest. But Kut was not a good place to go to ground. A relieving force would have to fight its way through strong defensive positions at Hanna and Sannaiyat. He might have done better to go on to Amara, 130 miles closer to Basra. But could his exhausted division have got there?

The Hanna and Sannaiyat defences, their flanks protected by the river and by marshes, could be overcome only by a strong, well-organized, well-supplied attack. But Townshend, without taking stock of his supplies in Kut, greatly under-estimated the time he could hold out. Had it been known in December that Kut could stand a siege until late April, a proper attack could have been laid on. As it was, Nixon was under the impression that Kut must be relieved immediately; and the Tigris Corps of the 3rd, 7th and 14th Divisions were sent up-river piecemeal. The 7th Division was really only a scratch formation, brought up to strength by regiments already in the country; short of artillery, transport and equipment, it was hurried forward long before it was ready.

For three weeks Tigris Corps hammered at the Turkish defences at Hanna, suffering dreadful casualties. By the end of January it had shot its bolt and could not try again for six weeks. On 22 January Townshend signalled that he could carry on another month on half-rations; and, later, that by eating horses and mules, he could hold out until April. So all the makeshifts, the hurried improvisations, the terrible losses of the January attacks had been unnecessary.

While Townshend was advancing triumphantly to Ctesiphon, the shortcomings of the medical services were hardly noticed. But during the winter of discontent, with tens of thousands more sick and wounded to be sent down to Basra, these services broke down completely and occasioned an outcry comparable to that which sent Florence Nightingale to the Crimea. It is this, if anything, that is remembered of Mesopotamia, and blame for it rests fair and square on the bureaucratic cheeseparing, the inefficiency, procrastination and inertia of the Government of India.

A wounded man first suffered a torture worse than being drawn on a hurdle through the cobbled streets of London to Tyburn. The only transport for him was the AT (Animal Transport) cart, an iron-framed box without springs jolting across the desert on iron-shod wheels behind two mules, its occupants screaming in agony whenever the mules shied or the driver had to rush them up the steep bank of a nullah. Having arrived at the river bank, only a few of the worst cases could be crammed into the hospital ships: most were dumped onto the open decks of barges in pouring rain, without even mattresses, men with stomach wounds and fractured thighs sandwiched between men with amoebic dysentery. 'When you went aboard,' wrote Captain T. C. Catty, a staff officer in 3rd Division, 'the stench almost knocked you down. I fear many poor devils died – of wounds officially – really of neglect.' With luck they might reach Basra in five days, having their wounds dressed once en route. By that time the decks were slippery with blood and faeces, and the sides of the ship festooned, as though with ropes, with dried stalactites of human shit. Wounds festered, turned gangrenous and maggoty; the least of a wounded man's suffering was the unbearable irritation of ants getting under the dressing and feeding on the blood and pus. Even the lightly wounded developed huge, festering bed-sores.

All this resulted in deteriorating morale, an ominous sign of which, noted by Catty, was that 48 per cent of the gunshot wounds were in the hand or the foot, probably self-inflicted. Another bad sign was that medical comforts, parcels, cases of whisky, cigarettes sent up by river transport seldom reached the troops at the front because they were stolen by soldiers on board.

Meanwhile Townshend announced that he would defend Kut 'like Chitral'. Protected on three sides by the 400-yard wide, fast flowing Tigris, Kut would have been eminently defendible against Pathans. But against an enemy well supplied with artillery and machine-guns, it was a death-trap made worse by being constantly flooded, since the Tigris, swollen by the rains, was higher than the surrounding country and held back only by embankments and earthworks thrown up and maintained by the overworked Sappers and Miners of Sirmur State Forces. Townshend, always prejudiced against Indians, alleged, and others vehemently denied, that for the first day or two only the British troops were capable of any digging. Thereafter everyone dug like badgers into the waterlogged soil. All day they had to crouch in these trenches: only at night could they move round with comparative safety.

In addition to his 10,000 fighting men, Townshend had to feed up to 2,000 sick and wounded, 3,500 Indian non-combatants and 6,000 Arab inhabitants. He had a better teeth-to-tail ratio than another Charlie, at Khartoum, but could have done with a few of Gordon's paddle-steamer gunboats. He was all right for ammunition and had enough food (no vegetables) for, he calculated, two months on full rations. Belated checks and the requisitioning of civilian supplies revealed a lot more. He was very short of medical supplies and tobacco. Upholding his reputation as a 'card', he sent by wireless such signals to Tigris Corps as, 'You seem to be in difficulties. Can I be of any assistance?' The answer should have been that, while his men were still capable of the effort, he could indeed be of assistance by sorties or mere demonstrations timed to coincide with attacks by the relief force. But he did nothing of the sort: his defence was purely passive.

On 20 January the garrison was put on half-rations. This was gradually reduced until by April the day's ration consisted of four ounces of barley meal plus nine ounces of horse or mule for those who would eat it. Famished as they were, many Indians considered themselves forbidden by their caste rules to do so. Indian Officers of the 103rd Mahrattas set an example by consuming it publicly. But men often fainted while trench-digging, and some died of hunger. Eventually sentries had to sit at their posts, and men spent as much time as possible lying down.

By March the relief force, now known as III (Tigris) Corps, consisted of the 3rd, 7th and 14th Indian Divisions, the all-British, New Army, 13th Division, and the 6th Indian Cavalry Brigade, all commanded by Lieutenant General G. F. Gorringe, an unpopular and not over-able martinet whose orders were absurdly over-detailed because he would not trust his divisional commanders. 'Such is the fear of Gorringe,' wrote Catty, 'that unless you have £1,000 a year of your own and are a prize-fighter, you can't stand up to him.' Always one to find criticism easier than praise, Catty added:

'Returns and correspondence are of the first importance; you can kill as many men as you like and make the most awful tactical blunders; but as long as you send in your returns punctually and properly filled in, nothing else matters.'

For good measure Gorringe should send half the staff officers forward to the trenches, and all the divisional and brigade commanders, old, incompetent and 'a danger to the State', back to India.

With battalions down to 250 men, the Corps took six weeks preparing for another attack at Hanna. This took place on 8 March, and failed. On 13 April the 13th British Division, newly arrived and up to strength, pushed the Turkish rearguard from Hanna to an even stronger position nine miles back at Sannaiyat, where their attack failed – largely, it was alleged, because they did not try.

The 3rd Division then had a go on the right bank. On the night of 17 April the 1/1 and 1/9 Gurkha Rifles in the 9th Brigade rushed the Turks with bomb, bayonet and kukri, captured 400 prisoners, six machine-guns and two field guns. It was a brilliant exploit. But next evening the Turks counter-attacked in mass, thousands behind thousands, as they had done in Gallipoli. The Gurkhas killed and killed, but could not stop them and at last ran. Catty was there.

'Once started, there was a regular rout. Why they broke, it is impossible to say. The Gurkhas themselves say it was due to want of ammunition and bombs, but the Brigade Major says they had plenty. Highland Light Infantry and 93rd Punjabis, coming up in support, were caught in the maelstrom and carried back. In the dark the confusion was terrible, and it was only in the former Turkish front-line trenches that it stopped. Here Egerton [commanding the division] brought up other units and parts of units, started bombing back, and the Turks were held. Old Egerton was the hero of the hour, and all say it was he who stopped the rout.'

A sign of the prevailing disappointment and frustration was ill-feeling between the Indian Divisions and the 13th British Division, though never between Indians and the British battalions who formed part of every Indian brigade. This was, characteristically, voiced by Catty.

'Great things were expected of 13th Division, but alas they did nothing, even losing a bit of trench we handed over. They seem very sticky, and have by no means wiped out the Sannaiyat failure. They don't seem to have any discipline or go, and are not a good advertisement for K 1*. At Sannaiyat one battalion had 23 officers and only 20 men killed: it speaks for itself.'

The relief force could do no more. On 29 April, its last handful of barley flour eaten, the garrison of Kut surrendered. It was the worst disaster to British arms between Yorktown and Singapore. Townshend had his sword chivalrously returned to him, was lionized by the Turks and departed to comfortable captivity in a fully staffed villa overlooking the Bosphorus. Turkish chivalry did not extend to his officers and men. Verminous, ragged and starving, they were goaded through Mesopotamia in a death-march to prison camps in the windswept uplands of Anatolia, suffering more than any prisoners-of-war before 1942.

After the fall of Kut, the military reasons for going on to Bagdad were no stronger than they had been a year earlier, but the political imperative was overwhelming. Nothing but the capture of Bagdad would wipe out the shame of Kut.

Already an attack was being made on the administrative shambles. The British Government, not before time, took over the running of the campaign and replaced Nixon by General Sir Percy Lake, a competent

*K 1: The First Hundred Thousand volunteers in Kitchener's New Army.

administrator who did good work before being invalided out in July. After a general post of corps and divisional commanders, the final arrangement left General F. S. Maude in overall command and Lieutenant General A. S. Cobbe in charge of Tigris Corps. In a war in which British military genius was in short supply, Maude was a sound commander in the Montgomery pattern, all system, balance and caution. Also he was lucky, taking over just when the army was being provided with everything it had hitherto lacked – more field and medium artillery, enough planes to command the air, efficient supply services, and vastly improved arrangements for the sick and wounded.

They spent the summer of 1916 resting, re-organizing, training. There was not much fun that summer. Major Davson of the 82nd Punjabis noted in his diary:

'30th April. Heat is appalling and only just begun. Flies bite hard and are in thousands. . . . We lie and gasp all day. . . . Food is disgusting: we live on bully-beef, fly-blown, and stale bread. . . . 20–22nd May. The most awful march. . . . One water-bottle per officer and man was the allowance. En route men fell like flies. More than a thousand collapsed from heat and lack of water . . . men simply crumpled up. They looked as if they had been shot. The last two or three miles I was carrying one man's rifle and pulling another along by the arm. I collected my strongest men and we kicked, cajoled and pulled men along. Anything to get them in. One felt an awful brute, letting a man have it in the ribs as hard as one could, but it was a case of getting them in or leaving them out to have their throats cut by Arabs, to mutilation. Young sepoys were stumbling along blindly, calling out, *"Mai! Mai"* ["Mummy! Mummy!"]. . . . 1st July. There is enormous wastage through sickness, scurvy and jaundice. We have sent 175 to hospital in 19 days.'

Major Tom Harper of the 62nd Punjabis succumbed not to jaundice or scurvy but to measles, and was evacuated to Basra, a hell-hole of unclean air and savage heat, 'sixty miles up the world's arsehole'. While regiments at the front were short of officers, Basra was full of them, waiting for passages upriver. 'Thompson belongs to the 62nd Punjabis, but may go to any old regiment.' Ice, beer, whisky, goodies of all kinds were obtainable, at a price, from Arab shops. There were European tailoring and outfitting emporiums from Bombay, charging ruinous prices although they got all their stuff out free in government transports. 'It is sickening to see Englishmen piling up fortunes at the expense of officers and men who are making it possible for them to carry on business at all.' Harper almost died of boredom, and got into trouble with the censor for his observations on some units sent to this God-forsaken army, notably a Bengali battalion, unfit for any exertion and regarded apparently by terrorists as a refuge from the police. It disappeared from the scene, as did the 1st and 3rd Brahmins, fine strong men but so meticulous about caste that each had to cook his own vegetarian food, and throw it away if the shadow of a non-Brahmin fell on it.

No one had anything but praise for the Mahrattas, of whom there were five battalions in Mesopotamia. Before the war they had not been highly regarded by those who did not know them. They were lowish in caste, and in stature, but well built, a tribute to their favourite sport, wrestling. Cyril Hancock, a newly joined subaltern, found that most of the Deccani Moslems in the 114th Mahrattas were Bombay tongawallahs (cab-drivers). 'It was hard to believe that under Shivaji Mahrattas controlled most of India. . . . But whatever was said to them and wherever they found themselves, they were always happy and smiling. Never did I see a sullen Mahratta.'

By December 1916, Maude was ready to advance on Kut and Bagdad. His Striking Force D was composed of I Corps (3rd and 7th Divisions) under General Cobbe, III Corps (13th and 14th Divisions) under General W. R. Marshall, and the Cavalry Division under Major General Crocker. All were up to strength, re-trained, re-equipped and at peak form. '13 Division', noted Catty, 'are reported to be 20,000 strong and talk loudly about showing Indian troops the way. Let us hope they do. At present they are called the Scrap Iron Division, and no one has any confidence in them.'

The tactical situation was untidy. The Turks were still strongly established on the left bank at Sannaiyat, in Kut itself and in the Shumran Bend of the river some six miles above Kut. On the right bank they held two salients, the smaller, Khaidora, north-east of Kut; and the larger, Hai Salient, some two miles square, south of Kut. Anyone could see that they could best be prised out of these positions by crossing the Tigris from the right to the left bank well above Kut and cutting their road and river communications with Bagdad. But first the right bank salients must be cleared.

The 3rd Division cleared Khaidora. The Hai Salient was a tougher nut. 13th British Division took the front line trenches, but then lost them. The job was given to the 26th and 82nd Punjabis.

The 82nd, wrote Major Davson, having marched from 4.00 the previous evening until 4.30 a.m., was told it was to attack that morning. 'We hopped the parapet at 10.40 and they say we looked as though on parade. We didn't run but walked in quick time up to the enemy trench which we took and kept.'

On 1 February 1917, the 37th Brigade of the 14th Indian Division stormed on a two-battalion front the main Turkish position in the Hai Salient. The 36th and 45th Sikhs showed what a reckless fighting man the Sikh can be. The 45th (Rattray's) Sikhs was commanded by Lieutenant Colonel H. B. Rattray, whose father had raised them in 1856: 'The orders for the attack were carefully explained to all ranks who were exceedingly happy and cheerful. They had their food and tied their safas afresh as though for a guard mounting parade.'

They went over the top just after noon, 45th on the right, 36th on the left, moving steadily forward. They lay down in front of the wire until the barrage lifted, then moved in and killed the few Turks still alive in the front-line trench. The 36th, enfiladed by several machine-guns, could go no further. But the 45th went on, flayed by machine-gun fire, to their next objective, 'the Bank', a deep nullah packed with Turks, whom they attacked with bomb and bayonet. There they lost three British Officers, and were driven back by a strong counter-attack. Sixty Sikhs, with the Colonel and the Adjutant, were cut off and surrounded in the Bank: all were killed or wounded. Eventually both battalions were back where they started, having lost 16 out of 17 British Officers, 28 out of 30 Indian Officers and 988 out of the 1,180 men who went over the top. In its valour, its slaughter and its futility it matched any frontal attack between 1914 and 1918. Two days later the attack was renewed by the 1/4th Devons and the 1/2nd Goorkhas, who swept the enemy out of their trenches. But they did not have to attack across a flat plain devoid of cover: there was ample cover behind and between the heaped carnage of Sikh corpses.

The way was now clear for the crossing of the Tigris, the greatest feat of arms in this campaign. Maude selected as his crossing place the Shumran Bend, six miles above Kut; and by sundry feints drew the enemy's attention and reserves away from that point. The crossing was by Egerton's 14th Division. The river there was about 300 yards wide with a five-knot current. Below the bridging point, at intervals of 500 yards, three ferries would each take across a battalion to secure a bridgehead on the left bank. The crossing would be supported by the divisional machine-guns firing across the river and enfilading the Turkish positions. The ferrying would be organized and controlled by 12 Company, Madras Sappers and Miners, under Major S. Pemberton; the bridging would be by Number 2 (Mobile) Bridging Train, Bengal Sappers and Miners commanded by Captain F. V. B. Witts.

During the night of 22/23 February the bridging train moved up to within a mile of the bank; and a company of the Welch Pioneers prepared ramps through the high embankment down which the pontoons and anchor-laying motor-boats would be launched. Three battalions of the 37th Brigade – the 2nd Norfolks, the 2/9 Gurkhas and the 1/2 Goorkhas were detailed for the ferry crossing, one for each crossing place. To each battalion was allocated thirteen wood-and-canvas pontoons, rowing-boats with a crew of five, each carrying ten passengers. A total of 735 rowers were needed, to give three reliefs of rowers and a reserve. For the first flight they were expert watermen from the Norfolks and Hampshires, with Sappers and Miners to replace casualties.

Every man had been practised time and time again at his duties; the wheel axles of the carts carrying the pontoons had been greased to prevent noise; the boats' crews carried wooden plugs to stop bullet holes. Nothing was omitted to ensure success.

They marched across the desert for five miles in the dark, their routes marked by small piles of earth, and halted at 1.00 a.m. a little back from the river while the boats were carried to the bank. All was silence: from the enemy came no shot, no Very light, no shouted challenge.

The crossing began just before dawn and by 5.30 all the boats were in the water, and the crews were rowing like mad. At Number 1 the Norfolks met little opposition: the first flight was soon ashore, making good a line three hundred yards inland, and the boats were returning for the next flight.

The Gurkhas had no such luck: they were hardly half way over when rifle and machine-gun fire lashed the water like hail. Of the 2/9th Gurkhas at Number 2, ten out of thirteen boats got across, three drifted downstream with their cargo of wounded and dead. Major G. C. Wheeler and half a dozen men leapt from the first boat and rushed the nearest Turkish trench, fifteen yards away; the remainder of D Company, as they landed, extended their hold on it. A Lewis-gun jammed, the Turks counter-attacked, one of them hurling a bayoneted rifle like a javelin at Wheeler, cutting his head to the bone. But he rallied his men and led them on to take the next trench, 150 yards inland. The ten boats set off back to the right bank, but only six reached it. Five of these crossed again, bringing Wheeler's force up to about 150 including the regimental bombers and six Lewis-guns. After that there were no more boats, or rowers, and the rest of the battalion were directed to Number 1 (Norfolk) crossing, from which by 10.00 a.m. they managed to link up with Wheeler.

At Number 3 (1/2nd Goorkhas) all thirteen boats got across, but only fifty-six unwounded men. The surviving Hampshire rowers were enough to take only three boats back. The small party of Gurkhas were too few to press inland against strong opposition, and Lieutenant Toogood lit a bullseye lantern to guide the second wave. But there was no second wave. Of the four boats rowed by Madras Sappers which put off again from the right bank, only one made the crossing, bringing Toogood a reinforcement of one unwounded man. Three went down in midstream. In the last afloat, the rowers were reduced to two. One was killed, and his oar drifted away. The last rower paddled on until his oar was smashed. He then tied a line round his waist, jumped overboard and tried to tow the boat by swimming. For a while his head was seen among the bullet-splashes, then it disappeared. If ever a deed deserved the VC, it was his: but there was no survivor to tell his name. He was just an anonymous, little, blackish, low-caste Madrassi.

Meanwhile, to hold Turkish reserves away from the crossing, the 7th Division tried once again at Sannaiyat. The attack by the 82nd Punjabis was, wrote Major Davson,

'the most magnificent thing I have ever seen. We advanced in quick time, no rushing, over 3,000 yards of flat ground with no cover. It took us 35 minutes and we had the enemy's main position in our hands. We went through three belts [of machine-gun fire]. Whole platoons dropped, but we went on steadily. . . . I am awfully proud of my company. . . . My greatcoat changed hands four times. My orderly was carrying it first. He was hit and threw it to another man, and so on. My Mahomedans made it a point of honour that my greatcoat must get in.'

The most magnificent thing Davson ever saw cost the 82nd Punjabis six out of eight British Officers, twelve out of fifteen Indian Officers, and 240 out of 500 rank-and-file.

Back at the Shumran Bend the position at 8.00 a.m. was that at Number 3 ferry about fifty of the 1/2nd Goorkhas under Toogood were hanging on but unable to influence the battle. At Number 2 Wheeler's party of about 150 held a shallow but fairly firm bridgehead. With a signalling-lamp they gave the artillery and machine-guns on the right bank many good targets. They could see, quite close, an enemy machine-gun, dug into a nullah, giving great trouble to the Norfolks. Creeping up behind the Turks who were all unconscious of their fate, the fierce little men charged in with bomb and kukri and shouts of 'Ayo Gurkhali!', killed the machine-gunners and gave the Norfolks much relief when they most needed it. (For his work that day, Wheeler was awarded the VC. He had arrived the previous evening; left, badly wounded, the next day, and saw no more active service.) The Norfolks were across in strength, with two companies of the 2/9th Gurkhas and some of the 1/2nd. They had not yet extended their bridgehead to the site selected for the pontoon bridge, but were moving that way. Major General Egerton made the bold decision not to wait any longer, but to start on the construction of the bridge, albeit under fire.

The bridging train was parked in the desert about a mile away. It consisted of bi-partite pontoons carried by two hundred AT carts; the trestles and superstructure on fifty-six GS wagons; and two motor-boats, required for laying anchors for the bridge. The carts and wagons came up at a gallop, dumped their loads all in the proper places, and galloped back. By 8.30 the shore transoms were in position on the sites prepared by 71st Field Company, RE, and the Welch Pioneers; the land anchors were fixed. But it proved impossible to lay the anchors from boats rowed across the swirling current. So the motor-boats were ordered up. If they were damaged, the crossing would have failed. Perched eleven feet high on their bullock-carts, lurching and swaying as they were drawn forward through the shell-bursts, they seemed appallingly vulnerable. But by a miracle they arrived at the bank and were launched; the engines were started, and the anchors were laid across the river, for every second pontoon a 1cwt anchor with a ½cwt kedge, at the end of 400 feet of rope. Work proceeded all day under fire and with the constant threat of floating mines. By 4.30 p.m. a 295-yard bridge was ready for traffic and the 14th Division started to cross. By midnight the whole of the 14th Division and leading elements of the 13th Division were over, and the Turks were streaming back from Sannaiyat and Kut.

It was a great victory, but hardly a famous one. Who, seventy years later, has heard of the Shumran Bend? And not for the first or last time in British military history, it was not completed by a determined pursuit. For this the cavalry was blamed. Why had they not ridden across the desert to cut off the retreating enemy? Harper, commanding his divisional machine-guns, wrote: 'The Turks have vanished into the blue. The victory is a good one but just failed to be complete, owing to lack of energy of the cavalry division.'

Catty put it more brutally: 'Their efforts were puerile, and that night Crocker's Travelling Circus returned behind the infantry outposts having done nothing.'

'Bagdad at last!' exulted Catty on 13 March. 'Who'd have thought it three weeks ago?' They marched in through the cheering populace which had cursed and spat on the prisoners from Kut. The hot months were spent resting, refitting and training. In November Maude died of cholera and was succeeded by Marshall.

The Turks, still full of fight, had to be pushed back a safe distance from Bagdad. At Khan Bagdadi on 26 March 1918, the 11th Cavalry Brigade had a dashing and ambitious commander, R. A. Cassells. While 15th Division attacked frontally, he led his brigade on a detour through the desert to cut the enemy's line of retreat to Aleppo. Looking nervously over their shoulders, the Turks put up little resistance to the infantry and retreated until, six miles back, they bumped into the cavalry brigade. Five thousand surrendered, with a dozen field guns and forty-seven machine-guns. The horsemen watched all the rout of a beaten army – long queues of prisoners, stray horses, wrecked wagons, guns and gun-carriages abandoned. At last the 'cavalry spirit' had inspired the cavalry leadership, and the mounted arm had redeemed its reputation.

The last battle of the campaign was fought in October 1918. I Corps (General Cobbe), with 7th and 11th Cavalry Brigades under command, were poised to deliver the *coup de grâce* to the enemy ensconced in an extremely strong position, between Bagdad and Mosul, astride the Fatha gorge where the Tigris cuts through the Jebel Hamrin, with a second line fifteen miles behind. Although their war was lost, the Turks were still fighting indomitably, and Cobbe had no taste for frontal assaults against almost impregnable mountain defences.

On the right (west) bank of the Tigris the 17th Division confronted the enemy. During 24/25 October Cassells led his 11th Cavalry Brigade (7th Hussars, Guides and 23rd Cavalry) on a wide detour through the desert to the east, to attack the left flank of the enemy second line, along the Little Zab River. Leaving all weak men and horses behind, carrying two days' rations for horses and men, they covered seventy miles in thirty-nine hours to the Little Zab. There they were joined by the 7th Cavalry Brigade, who had made a shorter detour, and together they cleared all the enemy from the left bank of the Tigris. A convoy of Ford vans carrying a third day's rations met them on the 26th.

Cassells then made another great detour, striking the Tigris twenty-five miles further upstream. After some hours' search, his patrols found an unmapped ford. It was a difficult one, over three branches of the Tigris, crossing the third by a narrow rock ledge four-and-a-half feet under water with much deeper water on either hand. 11th Brigade negotiated this without loss in daylight, but following troops lost twenty men and horses drowned.

As soon as the leading regiment, the Guides, were over, Cassells led them at a gallop to Huwaish, five miles downstream, reconnoitred a suitable position running back from the river across the enemy's line of retreat to Mosul, and deployed his brigade as it arrived. There was no waiting, no hesitation. The Turks acted as might be expected of such stout fighters, pulling out of the Fatha position to smash a way through to Mosul. By the morning of the 28th Cassells was in a critical position, with 3,000 Turks and twenty-four guns attacking his thinly stretched line from the south, and more coming down from Mosul. Then the 7th Cavalry Brigade arrived to

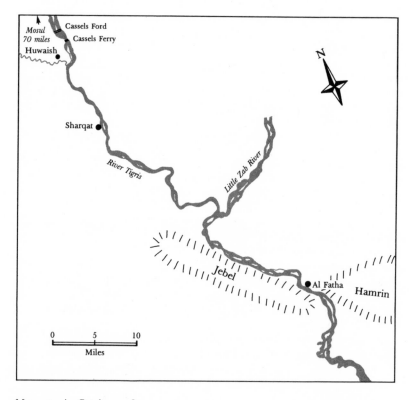

Mesopotamia, October 1918

strengthen his line, crossing the river by 'Cassells' Ford', and the 1/7th Gurkhas, after a forced march of thirty-three miles, crossed by 'Cassells' Ferry', a couple of boats discovered two miles downstream. His artillery, 18-pounders, unable to cross the river, supported him from the left bank; and some armoured cars arrived after making a long detour to the west. The 17th Division, coming up from Fatha, pressed hard on the Turks' heels.

So hard that they outpaced their rations. Cyril Hancock, now Adjutant of the 114th Mahrattas, recalls:

'We came upon a miserable little field of winter wheat and with a whoop descended upon it like so many locusts. The CO [Lt Col C. H. Wintle] was shocked to the core and sent me off to restore order, but everyone was laughing so much that discipline restored itself, and the troops rubbed the grain between their hands and got something to fill their empty bellies.'

The Turks were brought to bay at Sharqat, and 34th Brigade attacked, the 45th Sikhs leading, followed by the Mahrattas who had only three British Officers, the Colonel, the Adjutant, and Captain Reed commanding A Company. Other companies were commanded by the Subadar Major and Subadars. It was some 3,000 yards to the enemy trenches, and the Mahrattas were still in column of fours when shells started bursting and machine-gun bullets, fired at long range, dropping round them.

Then they were ordered forward to attack and Hancock gave the signal to deploy into artillery formation, well dispersed, one company behind the other. Apart from skirmishes against Arabs, it was his first battle. The men, realizing that this was the supreme moment, all shouted the Mahratta warcry, 'Shivaji Maharaj ki Jai!'

'Battalion headquarters was between the second and third companies, in diamond formation with signallers, clerks, stretcher-bearers etc, the Jemadar Adjutant leading one section. [The machine-guns were under brigade control.] I said as the bullets fell like manna all around us, "Sir, would one of these bullets go through us at this range?" All I got in reply from the CO was a snort indicating that I should stop asking damned silly questions. . . .

Next came a shell which pitched at the feet of the Jemadar Adjutant who, without changing pace, came huffing and puffing, waving a hand to disperse the dust. I asked the CO whether this battle fighting business got better or worse the more one had of it. This time he condescended to answer, "Worse." Next came a shrapnel shell, perfectly timed to burst 20 feet above the CO and myself. The shrapnel bullets fell in a circle, leaving a blank space where the CO and I happened to be. I took off my topi, annoyed to think it had been discoloured by the burning gunpowder, but it hadn't, so I stopped asking questions'.

Visibility was very bad. As the Sikhs, already under machine-gun fire, topped a ridge, out of thick dust there charged at least a thousand Turks in close order. The Sikhs, widely extended, were forced back, as were the two leading companies of the Mahrattas, Captain Reed and Subadar Major Mahadeorao Khanvilkar both being killed. Having established, like a nanny her charges, his Commanding Officer and Battalion headquarters in a comparatively safe place, Hancock went forward to see what all the noise was about. The Turkish counter-attack was in full swing, and in the front line he found a Mahratta sepoy with, so he said, an unserviceable Lewis-gun. Actually only the foresight was missing. With no foresight, and no backdrop to show where his bullets were striking, Hancock opened speculative fire, by guess and by God, on a group of Turks. God, or his guess aided by a shikari's instinct, was good, and the Turks disappeared. In the growing darkness there was some confusion, but Wintle brought up the two reserve companies and restored the situation. By the time he had done so, it was dark. The brigade was ordered to consolidate during the night.

Four days' fighting had cost the 114th 360 casualties, 'but we gained glory for the good name of the Mahrattas, and next morning the white flags appeared all along the Turkish trenches'. It was the end of the war in Mesopotamia.

The last battle produced, among other decorations, a DSO awarded, most unusually, to a battalion Medical Officer, Captain H. M. M. Cursetjee, a Parsee. He was to become one of the best-known figures in the Indian Army, a major general and a knight. A small man, but fierce, he was an ardent horseman, spending his furloughs hunting in Ireland, playing polo and pig-sticking at every opportunity; and hounding on his juniors, by no means as keen as he, to prodigies of equestrian activity. When inspecting a hospital, he was a terror, his white-gloved finger running along all the places where dust might collect unnoticed.

CHAPTER 7

Palestine, 1918

It is a relief to turn from the mismanagement and carnage of frontal attacks in 'Mespot' to Allenby's campaign in Palestine, the last great cavalry campaign in history. Although it was, of course, the infantry – mainly Indian – who broke the Turkish line, it was the cavalry pouring through who turned defeat into rout. Moreover, never was such a victory won with so little loss of life on both sides. The Turks were not what they had been in Gallipoli, but their Yilderim (Lightning) Army, commanded by General Liman von Sanders, staffed and stiffened by Germans, was a good one.

In 1914 and 1915 British forces in Egypt had been concerned mainly with guarding the Suez Canal. Then, to give depth to the defence, they moved forward into Sinai. These operations were not attended with marked success until, in July 1917, General Sir Edmund Allenby, 'the Bull', took over and 'gave the British people Jerusalem as a Christmas present'. His first push took his army to a line about twenty miles north of Jerusalem, from Arsuf on the sea-shore eastward across Jordan to the Wilderness of Moab. Then, to stem the German March offensive, his British and Australian infantry were sent to France, and replaced by raw battalions from India, the 7th (Meerut) Division from Mesopotamia and the Indian Cavalry Corps from France. Needing to train new formations, he made no major move during the summer.

But he made his plans. In the Desert Mounted Corps he had the 4th and 5th Indian Cavalry Divisions and two Australian and New Zealand divisions. The obvious course was to use these in a wide sweep round the enemy's open desert flank, and this was the impression he intended to give. Instead, he would break the enemy line near the sea and send the cavalry through.

The deception plan required of the Desert Mounted Corps a filthy summer, in and beyond the Jordan valley, hundreds of feet below sea-level, malaria-ridden and stifling hot. The men suffered severely, the horses not so much: they became lean and hard, and were trained to do without water for long periods. The Indians and Anzacs were mounted mainly on English thoroughbreds and on the thoroughbred's cousin, the Waler, which stood up to the conditions much better than half-bred horses or the Arabs of the French contingent.

Operations in the Jordan valley were on a small scale, patrols and raids, generally dismounted. Moslem soldiers were sent on leave to Jerusalem, their holy city. They left boots and spurs outside the Mosque of Omar and entered to pray, many wearing white robes brought for this occasion. It was with enormous relief that in late August they were moved out of the pestilential Jordan valley.

The Indian Cavalry Divisions were composed as follows:

4th Cav. Division (Major General G. de S. Barrow.)

10th Cav. Bde.	11th Cav. Bde.	12th Cav. Bde.
Dorset Yeo.	1 City of London Yeo.	1 Staffs Yeo.
2nd Lancers	29th Lancers	6th Cavalry
38th Central India Horse	36th Jacob's Horse	19th Lancers

5th Cav. Division (Major General H. J. M. MacAndrew.)

13th Cav. Bde.	14th Cav. Bde.	15th (Imperial Service) Cav. Bde.
1 Gloucester Yeo.	1 Sherwood Rangers	Jodhpur Lancers
9th Hodson's Horse	20th Deccan Horse	Mysore Lancers
18th Lancers	34th Poona Horse	Hyderabad Lancers

They went into bivouacs in orange groves south-east of Jaffa. Elaborate measures were taken to conceal their presence, and 15,000 dummy horses, wood and canvas, were left in 'horse-lines' in the Jordan Valley. The cover-plan succeeded: enemy Intelligence summaries in September reported an increase of twenty-three squadrons there, and forecast, 'They will use most of their attack troops, cavalry, in the country nearest the Jordan.'

The enemy consisted of the Eighth Army near the coast, the Seventh Army on its left, and the Fourth Army east of the Jordan. They numbered about 4,000 sabres, 26,000 rifles and 370 guns actually confronting our 12,000 sabres, 57,000 rifles and 540 guns. Overall, this did not give Allenby the three-to-one superiority in numbers which was considered necessary for a breakthrough; but his cover-plan ensured that he would have a far greater superiority at the point chosen for his attack.

His plan was for XXI Corps to break the enemy line near the coast and wheel right, pushing the enemy into the hills, to let the cavalry through. The 5th Cavalry Division was to ride due north for about twenty miles and then north-east to the Yilderim headquarters at Nazareth. Allenby half-jokingly suggested that they bag Liman von Sanders himself. The 4th Division, on the right of the 5th, was directed first on the rail junction at Afule, then down the valley of Jezreel to Beisan in the Jordan valley. The Australian Mounted Division would follow the 4th, in reserve; and the

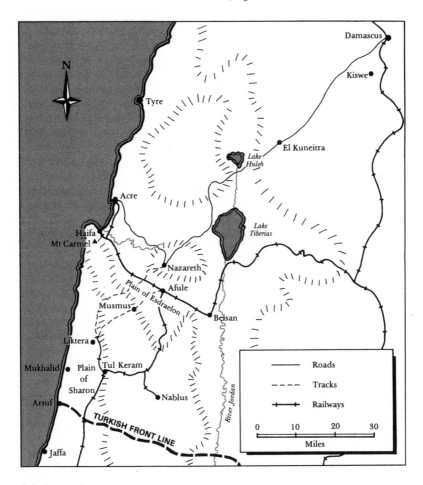

Palestine, 1918

Australian and New Zealand Mounted Division would operate beyond Jordan, as part of the cover-plan. The Turkish Seventh and Eighth Armies would thus be surrounded on three sides, their only way of escape eastward into the desert which was buzzing with very hostile, if not very effective, Arab forces of the Sharif of Mecca.

Unhappy experience in France had taught the need to have the cavalry close up to the line, but not so close as to obstruct the infantry; and to have accident-proof arrangements to let slip the cavalry the instant the gap was made, before the fleeting moment was lost by the enemy recovering his balance. To this end each cavalry division had a staff-officer at the headquarters of the 7th and 60th Divisions of XXI Corps. Both these infantry divisions were commanded by cavalry officers, so the horsemen felt they would have a run for their money.

On the night of 17/18 September they moved to their concentration area, in orange-groves east of Jaffa. The following night they moved up closer to the line, riding along the level sands by the sea, with no noise but the occasional faint clink of curb-chain or stirrup-iron. This was it! This was what they had been waiting for all these disappointing years. They halted and off-saddled where the sappers had drilled artesian wells and provided water-troughs for the last water-and-feed. Then they lay down, heads on saddles, beside their horses in long lines, and tried to sleep. All was silence.

At 4.30 in the morning of 19 September the barrage came down with a rolling crash on the enemy trenches. At 5.15 it lifted and the infantry of XXI Corps went over the top. By a quarter to six the Guides were through by the beach, and had four hundred prisoners. Further to their right the Rajputana Rifles were through also, and captured three of a four-gun Turkish field battery. The fourth gun was being driven rapidly away when the diminutive Captain Pete Rees jumped onto a captured horse, galloped after it and peremptorily ordered the drivers to return, which they duly did. XXI Corps began its right wheel.

Close on the heels of their old friends, the Guides (they had served together at the siege of Delhi and Hodson had been the Guides' Adjutant), rode the 9th Hodson's Horse, led by Major Mervyn Vigors's D (Pathan) Squadron, followed by the remainder of the 13th Cavalry Brigade.

They trotted along the shore, shielded by a line of low cliffs; and although it was heavy going, they rode so fast that General MacAndrew galloping to slow them down, could not catch them. It was not until 8 o'clock that they were fired on by some dismounted Turkish cavalry which D Squadron outflanked through the dunes while C Squadron charged direct. A plane dropped warning of some two hundred enemy with two field guns in an orchard four hundred yards to the right front. Without hesitation Vigors charged, capturing the guns, a dozen wagons and sixty Turks. Across the open plain were streaming parties of enemy in retreat. These they generally ignored, unless they were directly obstructive: charges by individual troops accounted for another machine-gun and more prisoners. By the time they reached the village of Mukhalid, some thirteen miles from the start, D Squadron horses were beginning to flag, so the lead was taken by B, across the plain of Sharon into Liktera where, just before noon, white flags fluttered above the Turkish and German garrison, a lorry park and a sumptuously equipped hospital. There they halted, off-saddled, watered and fed the horses and rested for six hours, having ridden since dawn twenty-six miles, the first part over heavy going.

The gap in front of the 4th Cavalry Division was not opened so expeditiously. Fretting with impatience, General Barrow himself rode up to 7th Division headquarters, and was at last given the go-ahead. Jacob's Horse, leading the 11th Cavalry Brigade, crossed the front line, following routes cleared and marked through the wire at 8.58.

'As we cleared the Turkish trenches [recalled Captain Davidson, commanding the 2nd Lancers] and rode through the debris of defeat, we felt that the G in GAP for which we had waited patiently for years had at last been reached. Far over the undulating Plain of Sharon rode the division; to our left and along the sea-shore rode the 5th Cavalry Division; while on our right could be seen and heard the din of the infantry battle as XXI Corps drove the Turks farther into the hills.'

Meeting even less opposition than the 5th, by ten o'clock at night they were watering and feeding at the mouth of the Musmus Pass leading to Afule.

Moving parallel to the 5th Division some five miles to their left, they negotiated the rocky track, sometimes mounted, sometimes leading their horses, losing their way and finding it again. As day broke they emerged into the plain of Esdraelon, on the very field of Armageddon, and were fired on by a body of Turks astride the road leading to El Afule. Captain Davidson rode forward to reconnoitre and estimated the opposition to be a hundred or more, with machine-guns. It was, of course, very wrong for cavalry to charge unbroken infantry, but to Davidson this did not seem to be an occasion for playing it by the book.

'The soil was black cotton and not so bad as to stop horses galloping. The enemy's flank could be distinguished and, as there seemed to be no obstacle to hold us up, I decided to turn his flank and gallop the position. I accordingly directed the OC D Squadron (Captain Vaughan) to left shoulder, pointed out the enemy's position and ordered him to go slow for five minutes to enable me to get the machine-guns into action, and then to turn the enemy's flank and charge. . . . By the time I had got the machine-guns into action I could see that D Squadron was well round the enemy's flank in column of troops, and almost immediately they wheeled head left, formed squadron and charged in open order, rolling up the Turkish front line.'

Davidson's intention had been that B Squadron should form a defensive flank to the right while D charged. But Captain Whitworth, commanding B Squadron, had other ideas. His story is:

'As we debouched from the pass dawn was breaking, and we saw a broad plain covered with low mists. . . . Hardly had the regiment begun to move forward when heavy rifle and machine-gun fire broke out from the direction of the road. Bullets were coming unpleasantly close and I increased the pace to a hand gallop and edged towards the right with the intention of locating the enemy's left flank. Almost immediately I saw the reserve Squadron (D) moving out in my direction, and I guessed that the CO intended making an enveloping movement from the right. There was no time to receive orders, so I decided to co-operate with D. Just then B Squadron ran into a wire fence hidden in the *jowar* [a tall crop] which covered that part of the plain. I was on ahead and left it to my second-in-command (Ressaidar Jang Bahadur Singh) to reform the squadron, which he did with great celerity.

Bullets were coming thick and fast now, and I imagined that the squadron had had pretty heavy casualties; added to this, I was in a blue funk of striking an uncrossable nullah, for the map showed a tributary of the Kishon between me and the enemy. . . . I became obsessed with the fear of sharing the fate of Sisera's host on the same field, and the words 'the mighty river Kishon' kept ringing through my head.

We were moving at a good fifteen miles an hour by now. It was just then that I caught a glimpse of the Turks. They were formed in two lines . . . with a distance of two hundred yards [between the lines]. The men saw the enemy at the same moment, and I was just able to direct the leading troop on the rear line of the enemy before they all saw red and broke into a hell for leather gallop. . . . I was still in mortal terror that the Turks' determined stand might be fortified by the knowledge that a deep nullah lay between themselves and us. We had overtaken our ground scouts long ago. However, I need not have worried, we were in for it now. I could hear yells from D in my left rear.

Before I realized it we were right on top of the enemy, and it was only when I saw a young Turk deliberately aiming at me that I realized I was still holding my map in my right hand and had forgotten to draw my sword. The little brute missed me and ran under my horse's neck and tried to jab his rifle in my stomach. I had just time to draw and thrust over my left knee. The point got him somewhere in the neck and he went down like a house of cards. My next opponent was a moustachioed warrior, probably an NCO, who was hopping about with a fixed bayonet and bloodthirsty expression. I suppose he had never met an opponent going at fifteen miles an hour: at any rate he had not begun to point when I poked him in the ribs.

All the Turks on the left flank had now had enough of it, but a few ran out of the line on the right and fired down the line at us. It did not take long to polish them off. I made for one who had murderous intentions but changed his mind at the last moment. My point caught him plumb between the shoulders and the shock nearly dislocated my arm. During this time I was naturally preoccupied with saving my own skin and saw little of what was going on around me. I only remember my orderly, Lal Chand, on my second horse, Advocate, who had the regimental flag furled round his lance, dragging along the ground a Turk who had stuck on the point; and I distinctly remember Jemadar Gobind Singh, VC, deliver a magnificent cut at an opponent, but as his sword was not made for this sort of thing, the Turk was not damaged.*

The men stopped killing directly all resistance ceased, but rallying them was an awful business. . . . While we were rounding up the prisoners

---

*It is human instinct to cut rather than thrust in moments of excitement; but it is far harder to kill a man with a cut than with a thrust. The cavalry sword of that period was, therefore, designed *only* for thrusting: it had no cutting edge. Jemadar Gobind Singh had let his excitement get the better of his training.

I became aware of a fat officer doubling about in circles. He finally fetched up in front of me and fell on his knees, shouting, "Spare my life. I am a Syrian." To which I answered, "All right, old cock, go and join your pals over there." . . . We found to our immense astonishment that although about half-a-dozen horses had been hit, not a single man was wounded. One horse which had been hit by a bullet which passed between the tendons of his off hind did not even go lame.'

The Turkish force was found to consist of a battalion with three machine-guns. Of these, between forty and fifty were speared and 470 taken prisoner.

El Afule was seven miles on, and as they arrived on the airfield two German planes landed. One was chased along the runway and caught by an armoured car: the other tried to take off and was shot down, with the latest mail from Berlin. The bag at Afule included three more planes, ten railway engines, hundreds more prisoners and large quantities of grain which came in very useful for the horses. Vaughan of the 2nd Lancers spent there one of the happiest hours of his life, in a deckchair, smoking an excellent German cigar and drinking a magnificent bottle of Hock.

The 19th Lancers led the brigade along the railway to Beisan, where the leading squadron was well rewarded for its efforts by finding a German canteen full of champagne and Hock. They liberated a camel and loaded it with two dozen of each for the squadron mess. From Beisan the brigade went on down into the Jordan valley, clocking up a hundred miles in forty-eight hours. Some of the men slept as they rode, fell to the ground still asleep, and were prodded awake and lifted into the saddle – only to fall asleep again.

At six in the evening of the 19th the 5th Cavalry Division, 13th Brigade leading, set off on the second stage of its great ride, a thirty-mile night march through difficult hill country to Nazareth. The track could hardly have been more rough, and they often had to dismount and lead. Behind the leading troop of the 18th Lancers rode, or walked, Brigadier General P. V. Kelly, a fluent Arabic speaker, who picked up a couple of guides. These were slightly better than useless, and only once took a wrong road, through narrow, winding, rocky valleys, up and down steep hills with the brigade strung out in single file over five miles. It was lucky there was no enemy about.

As the 18th debouched at 1.00 a.m. into the Esdraelon plain, it became clear – well, fairly clear – that they had lost the brigadier, the CO and the guides. At 2.30 the Brook Kishon was reached. There they halted, watered and fed until the situation clarified itself. Patrols were sent on to look for the Haifa-Afule railway. The troop which had been leading the brigade now loomed through the dark, coming back with orders from the brigadier to move on. This they did, coming upon Kelly and his headquarters actually sitting on the line an hour before dawn.

It was full steam ahead for Nazareth. While it was still dark they reached a village. 'Nazareth,' said the guide. But could it be? The *Palestine Handbook* said that Nazareth was in a cup between hills, but this seemed to be on a hillside. Revolver in hand, Kelly and a couple of officers approached the nearest house, pushed open the door and roused from his slumbers the village night watchman.

'Where is the German general?'

'What German general?'

'The big one with his headquarters here in Nazareth.'

'How should I know? This is Mejdel.'

A Turkish officer appeared and very politely in German asked what they wanted. They told him.

The home-town of Jesus was three miles on, and by the time they reached the outskirts it was broad daylight and the gaff was blown. The streets were full of running, shouting Turks and Germans in every stage of deshabille, horses being saddled, horses being backed between shafts, cars and lorries being cranked up. It was now the turn of the Gloucestershire Hussars, who sent squadrons round to left and right and galloped one straight down the main street. Unfortunately, they leaped from their horses to search the Hotel Germania, the Yilderim headquarters; and while they were doing so Liman von Sanders emerged from the Hotel Casanova, two hundred yards down the street, still in his pyjamas, jumped into a staff car and escaped.

The loot was fantastic, and included a Turkish treasure chest stuffed with currency notes and gold coins. But how to get it away? Every lorry had been drained of petrol. There was, however, one full of petrol cans, but to it was chained a large bear who seemed to be emotionally disturbed. A sowar of the 18th misguidedly undid the chain and the bear jumped onto the top of the petrol cans and defied all until he met a soldier's death. The treasure was driven away and handed over to the proper authority. The 18th confidently expected the reward of virtue. Should it be invested in the Followers' Benevolent Fund? Or the Polo Fund? Or, more prudently, in the Regimental Co-operative Bank? After some months it arrived: five Turkish sovereigns.

Scores of cars and lorries were put out of action; some 1,200 prisoners, mainly German, were rounded up; enough documents were collected from their headquarters to keep the intelligence experts happy for weeks. But Nazareth was getting distinctly unhealthy with the staff and pupils of a machine-gun school firing into the streets from the hillsides. There was no intention of holding Nazareth: this had just been a raid, the main object of which had been missed by the narrowest of margins. The 13th Brigade, with its prisoners, withdrew to rejoin the division at Afule.

Next day Nazareth was re-occupied, unopposed. The 13th Brigade spent the night there and in the morning set off for Acre, the coastal fortress which had caused Richard Coeur de Lion and Napoleon no end of trouble.

Brigadier General Kelly's spirited order, 'Gallop the town!', was received coldly by the 18th Lancers, for the town appeared to be walled, and surrounded by thick cactus hedges. But while officers peered through their binoculars, seeking the best approach, the unmistakable figure of their Commanding Officer, Lieutenant Colonel Keighley, appeared on top of Napoleon's Mound. Acre had fallen.

There, in the orange groves and bathing in the sea, they enjoyed three days' rest.

Meanwhile, the 15th (Imperial Service) Cavalry Brigade had kept close to the sea, directed on the fortified town of Haifa. It was difficult to approach, on a cape tucked between the steep slopes of Mount Carmel and the sea. The road and railway entered the town from the south-east, through a defile between the mountain on the left and the Nahr-el-Muqata, the brook Kishon, on the right. The Jodhpur Lancers led the brigade, commanded by Major Thakur Dalpat Singh, who had won the MC in a charge in the Jordan valley, riding down single-handed a machine-gun and its crew. He had as his adviser, as was usual in Imperial Service units, a British Officer, Major Holden.

It was decided to cross the Kishon and attack the town from the north-east, avoiding the dangerous defile. But when the two ground scouts spurred their horses down the bank, they were engulfed in quicksands. Immediately the order was given to change direction left, the leading squadron to charge several machine-guns on the lower slopes of Mount Carmel. While they did so, supported by fire from some Mysore Lancers, two squadrons galloped straight through the defile into the town. With the loss of 3 killed and 34 wounded they captured 689 Turks, 16 field guns and 10 machine-guns. It was perhaps the most extraordinary feat of cavalry, on that scale, in that or any other war. Probably no regiment but the 'Jo Hukums'* would have been crazy enough to try it. Sadly, among the dead was the gallant Thakur Dalpat Singh.

With the capture of Haifa, Nazareth and the east-west railway, the first stage of Allenby's advance was completed. The Turkish Seventh and Eighth Armies were no more. There remained the pursuit to Damascus and beyond. Unlike most pursuits by the British Army, this was pressed to the uttermost limits of endurance of horse and man, as though Alexander or Napoleon were in command. All wheeled transport was left behind; only two days' rations and forage were taken: when this was finished, they must live off the land. It was a hundred miles by the most direct route from Nazareth to Damascus, much of it over rough ground and blown bridges disputed by enemy rearguards. Hodson's Horse reached Damascus in four days, including a seventeen-hour halt to rest and graze the horses at Kuneitra. On the fourth day Risaldar Nur Ahmed, accompanied only by his orderly, rode into Kiswe village which was packed with Turks. One fired at him and missed; Nur Ahmed fired back and did not miss. Hundreds of Turks then surrendered to him.

Just short of Damascus a squadron of the Poona Horse charged in error a body of Arabs who proved too elusive for them. They did, however, bag a

* 'Jo hukum' – 'Whatever the order' – was the nickname of the Jodhpur Lancers.

large motor-car containing a European splendidly Arab-garbed. Suspecting a German spy, Risaldar Major Hamir Singh demanded his surrender, and there ensued a heated altercation, neither understanding one word the other said. It transpired that this individual's name was Lawrence, and that he had something to do with the Sharif of Mecca's forces. The incident may account for T. E. Lawrence's antipathy to the Indian Army. But not for all Indian soldiers. A machine-gun section of Hodson's Horse, Pathans commanded by Risaldar Hassan Shah, took part in many of Lawrence's raids. Although they were not as good camel-riders as the Bedouin, Lawrence thought highly of them, especially of Hassan Shah, 'a firm and experienced man', 'their officer and greatest-hearted man'. Years later Hassan Shah, a pensioner with henna-dyed beard, came to visit his old regiment, in which I was a subaltern. We spent an enthralling hour poring over Eric Kennington's portraits of Auda abu Tayi and the rest in *The Seven Pillars of Wisdom*, while Hassan Shah talked about them. I asked what Lawrence was like. His reply was worth recording. 'Lawrence Sahib,' he said, 'was a great snob. Unless you were of good family, he had no use for you. He thought the world of me, but only because I am a Qureshi, descended from the Prophet's own tribe.'

But there must have been more to it than that, for Hassan Shah was awarded the MC and a high Sharifian decoration.

While the Indian cavalry surrounded Damascus, Australians and Arabs disputed the honour of being first in. What did it matter? The war was reduced to the pursuit of the remnant of the Turks by the remnants of the 5th Cavalry Division, decimated by malaria and Spanish influenza, past Baalbek, Homs and Aleppo until 31 October when the Armistice with Turkey was signed.

CHAPTER 8

Cloak and Dagger,
1917–19

In October 1917, the Bolshevik Revolution took Russia out of the war. The British Government tried both to prevent the Bolsheviks helping the Germans, and to persuade them to help the British. To the first end, a British-Indian force under General Malleson was sent to Meshed in north-east Persia where it tried to persuade White Russians to stand up to the Reds, and itself fought the Reds on the Merv front. At the same time a mission was sent through Kashgar in Chinese Turkestan to Tashkent in Russian Turkestan to persuade the Bolsheviks in control there to go on fighting the Germans and Turks.

The mission consisted of Lieutenant Colonel F. M. Bailey of the Indian Foreign and Political Department, a Russian speaker, and Captain L. V. S. Blacker of the Guides. With them went sixteen Indian soldiers, all but two of them Guides, intended as instructors for a Turcoman and Kirghiz army raised, with or without Bolshevik approval, to make the world safe for democracy. These men from a multi-talented corps included speakers of Russian, Arabic, Turkish and French, a machine-gunner, a bombing specialist, a signaller, a carrier pigeon fancier, a first-aid man, a vet, and a topographical artist. Marching up from Kashmir, they crossed the Pamirs on yaks (a photograph suggests that yakmanship was not one of their accomplishments) and stayed in Kashgar while Bailey went on to tackle the Commissars in Tashkent.

His hand was weak. Since it was not British policy to recognize the Bolshevik regime, he carried no diplomatic credentials. The Commissars asked, 'Why should we help you fight the Germans, while you are helping counter-revolutionaries to fight us?' They suspected he was a spy, which he was.

After the Armistice with Germany, the original purpose of his mission was no more. But the Commissars were convinced now that he was a spy, so he had to disappear. This was not difficult. Bailey spoke German, as well as Russian, and Tashkent was full of former soldiers of the Austro-Hungarian Army released from prisoner-of-war camps, forlornly waiting for someone, anyone, to send them home. Bailey was able to obtain the uniform and identity papers of an Albanian serving in a Hungarian regiment. He thought it improbable that there could be any genuine Albanians in Tashkent to blow his cover. Thus disguised, he stayed for many months in peril of arrest and execution, collecting butterflies and sending, by intrepid couriers, long reports of the political and military situation to the Consul-General in Kashgar and to General Malleson at Meshed, who, Bailey assumed, must soon advance on Tashkent to take advantage of the strongly anti-Russian sentiments of the Turcoman tribes.

But his position was hazardous, not least because his beloved bull-terrier, looked after by Russian friends secretly White in sympathy, might at any minute meet him in the street and come up grinning and tail-wagging. He decided he must depart. How?

The eastward route to Kashgar would be watched. West of Tashkent, however, was the Emirate of Bokhara, fanatically Moslem, feudatory of Tsarist Russia but hostile to the Bolsheviks. Bailey gained entry into the Bolshevik Secret Service and volunteered to go to Bokhara to seek news of an English spy reported to be there, named Bailey. The Commissars accepted his offer with alacrity. Several of their agents had been caught by the Bokharan authorities, tortured and strangled, and there was a dearth of volunteers. So, still in his Austro-Hungarian uniform with a red star on the cap, Bailey travelled prosaically by train to the Bokhara border and then, discarding his red star, to Bokhara on foot. The authorities regarded with suspicion this individual claiming membership both of the Bolshevik Secret Service and of the Indian Foreign and Political Department, wearing the uniform and carrying the papers of an Albanian in the Austro-Hungarian army. But the Emir did not actually have him strangled. Nor would he allow him to depart to Meshed. So Bailey had to kick his heels in Bokhara, still butterfly-hunting and awaiting either permission to depart or the arrival, inevitable sooner or later, of the Red Army. However, his bull-terrier had been brought to him by his Russian friends.

One day two men in the robes of Bokharan merchants presented themselves to him with smart salutes. They were two of the Guides whom he had last seen in Kashgar. Awal Nur, a Havildar of the Guides Infantry, was a Pathan, wounded and decorated in France and East Africa, holder also of the MacGregor Memorial Medal for geographical exploration. The other, a Daffadar of the Guides Cavalry, was of the Hazara tribe, of Mongol origin, settled in Western Afghanistan. The Hazaras are Shiahs, and this man, who looked rather like an outsize Gurkha, had twice made the pilgrimage to the Shiah Holy Place, Kerbela, hence his name, Kalbi (Kerbali) Mohamad. They were very fine men.

Their story was a strange one. When it became obvious that there would be no Kirghiz-Turcoman army for them to instruct, the Guides with Blacker had travelled through Yarkand, over the Kuen Lun mountains, then over the fearsome Mustagh Pass into Baltistan, and so to India. After a short sojourn there, Awal Nur and Kalbi Mohamad had been sent to Meshed to offer their Central Asian expertise to General Malleson, who was still engaged on the forlorn task of trying to build some sort of resistance to the Bolsheviks from White Russians whose one ambition was to get away safely to India. Malleson had sent them in charge of a hundred camel-loads of rifles to the Emir of Bokhara, across the Kara Kum desert where any armed party they saw might be Red Russian, White Russian or Turcoman bandit. Just as they reached the Bokhara border, the river Oxus, they were joined by three Russians who they thought must be Reds, and would report them to the nearest Red patrol. Awal Nur was equal to the occasion, informing the Bokharan frontier officer that these were very dangerous characters who should be arrested. This the Bokharan officer did, and asked Awal Nur what should be done with them. 'None of my business,' said Awal Nur. So, to avoid any more questions and difficulties, all three were shot.

Bailey and the two Guides were overjoyed to meet, embracing and pumping hands up and down. 'There can't be much wrong with the British in India,' remarked a Bokharan who was present. Together they planned how to get away, and after much diplomacy and the distribution of presents, obtained not merely permission to depart but seven Russian rifles. Their party was to have consisted only of Bailey, Awal Nur, Kalbi Mohamad, Mr and Mrs Manditch, Bailey's friends from Tashkent, and the bull-terrier. Now the Bokharan authorities added seven White Russian officers to the party, which made it far too unwieldy and conspicuous. However, off they set, riding small, wiry horses, wearing Turcoman clothes and huge sheepskin hats, on their hazardous three weeks' journey.

It was a terrible desert crossing. Their guide confessed, half way over, that he had not the slightest idea where the next well was. Unless they found it, they would all die of thirst. When, by pure luck, it was found, it proved to be over 700 feet deep; but by another stroke of luck they encountered some shepherds who lent them a rope long enough to draw water. On 6 January 1919 they reached the Persian border and galloped across, Awal Nur and Kalbi Mohamad keeping at bay a party of Bolshevik soldiers who tried to stop them. Their only loss was a saddlebag full of Mrs Manditch's silk gowns.

CHAPTER 9

Waziristan,
1919–21

The Amir Habibullah of Afghanistan had prevaricated and procrastinated when Germans and Turks urged him to declare the Holy War on Britain. But he was murdered, and his successor, Amanullah, sent his regular army across the Indian border in May 1919. The Afghan regulars were soon bundled back into their own country, loudly proclaiming themselves victorious. But the tribes in Waziristan and north Baluchistan rose in Islamic frenzy; nearly all the Wazirs and most of the Afridis in the Waziristan Militias defected, with their rifles; and by the end of the year the British were faced with a frontier war harder than any they had experienced.

Between 1914 and 1918 the Mahsuds, who were fighting so well in Flanders and East Africa, were also fighting extremely well at home, but on the wrong side. They perpetrated hundreds of raids, murders, kidnappings; they killed 246 soldiers, wounded over 300 and captured some 400 rifles; and the Wazirs had been almost as bad. But during the war they got away with it. By November 1919, the cup of their iniquity was full, and it was formally announced that:

1. Afghan propaganda that the British were on their way out was rubbish.
2. On the contrary, the British intended to make roads and station troops wherever they wished in Tribal Territory.
3. They would have to pay the penalty for their misdeeds, including (indeed, especially) the surrender of several hundred modern rifles.

The Utmanzai (northern) Wazirs accepted these terms; the Ahmedzai (southern) Wazirs havered. The Mahsuds replied in effect, 'If you want our rifles, come and get them.'

Accordingly the Derajat Column, consisting of the 43rd and 67th Infantry Brigades, with three batteries of mountain artillery and other attached troops, entered Mahsud territory and by 13 December 1919 was concentrated in a perimeter camp a mile and a half north of Jandola, prepared to advance into the Mahsud heartland and exact retribution from the groups of fortified villages of Makin and Kaniguram. The column included no British infantry, which was perhaps just as well in 1919.

It was unthinkable that the great British Empire should not in the end prevail against a few thousand ragged desperadoes owning nothing more valuable than their Lee-Enfield rifles. Everyone knew this. But the tribesmen hoped to make victory so expensive for the British that the government would interfere with them no more. In this they were never closer to success than in 1919–20.

The Indian Army was fed up with fighting. They had been doing it for four years and it seemed a bit hard that, a year after the Armistice, they should be at it again. Most of the battalions in India were wartime units, hastily trained and inexperienced. From regular battalions most of the veterans had been demobilized, and the quality of the few that remained had been diluted by young soldiers who had barely completed their recruits' training. In four years of trench warfare the infantry of all nations had come to regard the bomb, the machine-gun and the shovel as their most useful weapons, the rifle as little more than an encumbrance; and the standard of rifle-shooting was abysmal. Fieldcraft was at a discount. What was the use of it when defence meant sitting in an eight-foot-deep trench, and attack meant walking forward in a long line across a dead-flat plain? Far better rely on an artillery barrage in attack, and machine-guns in defence. But in the Derajat Column there was very little artillery and no Vickers machine-guns. On the frontier, fieldcraft and quick, first-shot accuracy were the vital skills, and at these Mahsuds excelled. Even men who had walked through artillery barrages and machine-gun fire found it extremely disconcerting that in Waziristan every shot seemed to be aimed at oneself, personally; and there was nothing to be seen of the man who fired it except, perhaps, a flicker of grey rags among brownish rocks and grey-green gurgura bushes. Finally, most of the natives of India were plainsmen to whom these mountains were almost as harsh and hostile as the men who inhabited them. Time and training are needed to make a plainsman feel at home in the hills and teach him the tactics of mountain warfare, the essence of which is holding the hilltops. Almost the only new advantage of the British was a squadron of Bristol fighters, invaluable for reconnaissance and for straffing and bombing the reverse slopes, but becoming less so as the tribesmen learned that if they kept still and did not look up, they would probably not be spotted.

On the Mahsud-Wazir side morale was high. The young men were spoiling for a fight. Never had they been so well armed. From Mesopotamia (which had been flooded with modern rifles for four years), from Afghanistan, from Militia deserters and by capture from regular troops, they had so many high-velocity magazine rifles that the lashkar leaders forbad them to use in daytime the ten thousand or so Martinis which they also possessed. When a Martini was fired, a puff of smoke gave away the sniper's position, but the new rifles were smokeless, and accurate over much longer ranges.

Mahsuds and Wazirs had always been very skilful guerrilla fighters, adept at concealment and ambuscade, quick to seize any chance of a knife-rush, in pursuit of a withdrawing piquet bounding like falling boulders down the steepest hill. Now the lashkars included several thousand men who had defected from the Militias or been disbanded from the regular army, who knew British military methods inside out and were well trained in the principles of 'fire and movement'. So there was never a knife-rush which was not supported by accurate rifle-fire.

The Derajat Column commander, General Sir Andrew Skeen, a very experienced frontier officer, had pointed all this out to the government, and had been told to get on with the job.

Information came in of lashkars gathering. The perennial problem of guerrilla war, bringing the enemy to battle, seemed about to solve itself, and there was quiet jubilation in the staff. On 18 December 1919 the column advanced three and a half miles to Palosina Plain, north-west of Jandola, with only seventy-eight casualties. (Only!)

The only practicable route to Makin and Kaniguram was up the narrow valley of the Tank Zam river. This was dominated by the steep Mandanna feature, on the west bank, a mile and a half from Palosina. So before there could be any advance, Mandanna must be strongly piqueted. But Mandanna was in its turn dominated by a long ridge known as Broken Hill, six hundred yards to the west of it; so while the Mandanna piquet post was being constructed, that must be held too.

On the morning of 19 December the 55th (Coke's) Rifles, 'Cookies', an experienced 'Piffer' battalion, and the 103rd Mahrattas, occupied the southern end of Broken Hill. For an hour the Mahrattas made repeated attempts on the higher, northern end, losing their Commanding Officer and four other British Officers. Then they were rushed by Mahsuds who had crept close in dead ground. All their companies were in the firing line, they had no supports on which to fall back. They were outflanked, outfought and chased helter-skelter down the hill, across the Tank Zam and back to camp with the loss of 95 killed, 140 wounded, 131 rifles and 10 Lewis-guns. It was a shocking defeat.

On their left Coke's Rifles, although not themselves attacked, had to retreat down the mountain too, in a hurry. Their Commanding Officer, Lieutenant Colonel H. Herdon, later used to dine out on this story against himself. He was a very dark man, as dark as many Indians, and as he was 'withdrawing' with unseemly haste, he was sent sprawling by a terrific kick up the arse. Looking round, he saw a large tribesman grinning down at him. 'Get a move on, Babu!' said the Mahsud – undoubtedly an ex-soldier – in Urdu and bounded off in search of worthier prey with a rifle to snatch.

More than once during these operations proceedings were interrupted by the arrival in camp, under flag of truce, of parties of bemedalled Mahsuds come to shake hands with their old officers and exchange memories of Givenchy and Kibata. Lewis's old orderly was brought in, blindfold, to have a chat with him. No doubt they asked news of one of their fellow-tribesmen who managed to keep his nose clean during these difficult times, Subadar Mir Badshah, IOM, soon to be Honorary Lieutenant and Subadar Major, aide-de-camp to His Royal Highness the Duke of Connaught and member of the Royal Victorian Order.

On the 20th another attempt was made to establish a piquet on Mandanna, this time by four battalions, the 2/19th Punjabis, 'Cookies', the 109th Infantry and the 2/112th Infantry. Supported by the mountain batteries firing from the camp, and by RAF planes, they occupied with

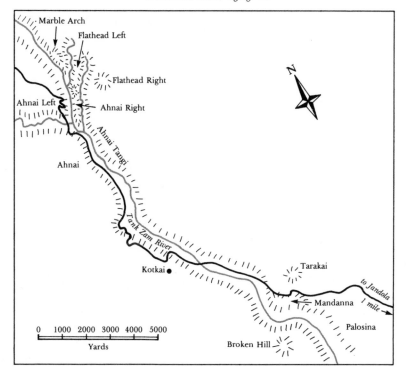

Waziristan, December 1919–January 1920

suspicious ease Mandanna and the whole of the Broken Hill feature. Work started on building a sangar (strongpoint) on Mandanna, and by mid-afternoon it was decided that it would give sufficient protection during the night to the piquet garrison, a company of the 2/19th Punjabis. The covering troops then withdrew to camp.

Back in Palosina Camp the 7th (Bengal) Mountain Battery were watering, feeding and grooming their mules, and cleaning their guns. Suddenly there was a shout, 'They're attacking Mandanna!'

'Within minutes the Battery was in action in the gun-park, pouring shrapnel and high explosive shell into the piquet. Through binoculars we could see amid the dust and smoke tribesmen coolly handing out cases of small arms ammunition and bombs. The defenders, disarmed by their fellow-Moslems, were literally kicked down the steep hillside.'*

Having twice failed to establish a piquet on the far side of the Tank Zam, Skeen decided that morale must be restored by an easier operation on the near side. A piquet would be established on Tarakai, a tangled mass of

*R. A. Curties in *Tales of the Mountain Gunners.*

107

rocks, peaks and ridges towering up to the north-west, about 1,700 yards from the camp. Again the objective was taken quite easily, by the 2/82nd Punjabis and the 104th Infantry. Two companies of the 3/34th Sikh Pioneers started constructing the piquet position, building walls, putting up wire, under the protection of those two battalions.

Pioneers, it will be recalled, were infantry trained also in simple engineering tasks. The Sikh Pioneers were low-caste Sikhs, not the lordly Jat Sikhs who alone were considered worthy of enlistment into cavalry, infantry and mountain batteries. But they had built up a reputation as dour, dogged fighters. They piled arms fifty yards below the work-site, rolled up their sleeves and started collecting boulders for the sangar-wall.

The first hour's work was interrupted only by sporadic sniping. Then there was a heavier burst of fire and a solid mass of several hundred tribesmen emerged from dead ground and dashed towards the piquet, yelling, shooting, brandishing swords and knives. The covering parties lost their nerve and fled. A British Officer of the 2/82nd tried to shame his men into holding fast and advancing again on top of the hill. 'If you won't follow me,' he shouted, 'I'll go alone.' They let him go alone.

The Pioneers also ran – but only as far as their piled rifles. Grabbing these, they dashed back to the sangar, just in time. The walls were only two feet high and there was but one strand of barbed wire stretched across the front, but these were better than nothing. The four British Officers in the post, with a Lewis-gun each, were the mainstay of the defence. Charge after charge, its momentum checked by the puny strand of wire, withered away under fire from these guns and the Pioneers' rifles.

With ammunition running low, a Jemadar and a seventeen-year-old bugler, Sangat Singh, who had no rifle, went down to organize a working party to bring more from a dump at the bottom of the hill. On their way back, a tribesman in ambush fired at the Jemadar at point-blank range, and missed: the Jemadar fired back, and missed. Sangat Singh then went for him with a pick-axe, and did not miss. He arrived back at the sangar gleefully carrying his victim's rifle and ammunition.

There they found the most savage hand-to-hand fight raging. The post was designed to hold 120 men, and there must have been at least 300 packed into it, hacking and thrusting, slashing and stabbing as a century's hatred between Sikh and Pathan exploded. Then the Regimental Havildar Major roared out with a drill instructor's voice the Sikh warcry. They all took it up and with a concerted heave expelled the Mahsuds from the sangar.

The firefight was resumed. All the British Officers were down, and ammunition was again running short. The fall of the post was only a matter of time; but 'Cookies' had been sent up the hill to a fall-back position on which the Pioneers could withdraw. It was half a mile away, down a track so narrow that for much of it men had to move in single file. They had four British Officers and many more wounded who could in no circumstances be left behind to be cut up by the Mahsud women. But the Indian Officers organized the withdrawal with practised skill. First a party of riflemen and Lewis-gunners were sent down to an intermediate fall-back position; then stretcher-bearers and wounded, escorted by more riflemen to act as flank-guards where the path was wide enough. From the camp Mahsuds could be seen rushing them with sword and knife, to be driven off with bullet and bayonet. Finally, when the wounded were safe, the rear party came bounding down the hill. At the very last moment, just as the tribesmen were swarming up to the crest, a Naik named Labh Singh, who on leave was well known to supplement his pay by highway robbery (I have hinted that the Sikh Pioneers were not socially acceptable), attracted the attention of a dozen men by blowing a whistle and led them back to the crest, in a desperate counter-attack which would give time for their comrades to get away.

Of the 250 Sikh Pioneers in that action, 189 were killed or wounded. But not one wounded man was left behind.

Battalions which had been found wanting were relegated to rear duties and replaced. The column advanced four miles to Kotkai.

On 2 January 1920 Lieutenant Kenny of the Garhwalis won a posthumous VC, leading one of those desperate counter-attacks to give time for the rest of his company to withdraw to a fall-back position. The column made camp at Ahnai and prepared for the hardest fight of all, forcing the Ahnai Tangi. It had to be forced: there was no way round.

Tangi means a gorge. The Ahnai Tangi consisted of walls of stratified limestone, heaved up on end, 300 foot high, and slit by a 30-foot-wide gap through which boiled the pent-up waters of the Tank Zam. An unsuccessful attack on 7 January had shown that the problem was not so much the tangi itself as debouching from its north end, commanded by Ahnai Right, a long steep ridge, running parallel and close to the Tank Zam, and rising at its north end to a flat-topped mountain named Flathead Left* which towered 800 feet above the river. So precipitously did the side of this ridge rise from the river-bank that it could not be piqueted in the usual way by sending piquets up in succession from the column's axis of advance. Right-flank protection to the column would be provided by the 2/5th Royal Gurkhas climbing onto the ridge at its lower, southern end and moving along it, keeping pace with the advanced guard, dropping off piquets as it went and finally occupying Flathead Left.

What turned out to be the fiercest battle in Frontier history was fought on 14 January, 1920. The second-in-command of the 103rd Mahrattas was

---

*The nomenclature is confusing since Flathead Left and Ahnai Right are both on the true left bank of the Tank Zam, i.e. the left bank looking downstream. But the column viewed them from below, looking upstream; Ahnai Right was thus called because viewed from below it was to the right of the Tank Zam. And Flathead Left was so called because about 800 yards to the right of it was a higher hill of similar shape dubbed Flathead Right.

commanding two companies as baggage-guard, and had from the floor of the tangi a worm's-eye view of the battle when once he had got his baggage animals moving. This was easier said than done.

'I climbed onto Lady Nan's back and rode into the river, where various transport officers were busy assembling camels of which the river-bed was full, a great dense mass. Presently I let them go and they headed upstream four and five strings abreast, reinforced after a mile or so by long strings of dark mules and tawny camels spat out unceasingly by Derajat Column camp as an ant-heap vomits forth ants. Where the two flows coalesced sulphurous-mouthed transport personnel tried to keep their flocks together, each his own. The ammunition column fouled the RE Park and the Supply crowd cut diagonally across both, while into the resultant whirlpool swirled Cookies' second-line camels under a joyously Bolshevik baggage-guard caring naught for any man so their Sahibs' kit headed the procession.

The brigade Transport Officer on a tall, bead-bedecked riding camel swept into the melee with a stock-whip, restoring order, and the whirlpool flattened out again into a smooth-flowing stream until the hills closed in to form the Ahnai Tangi.'

The advanced and rearguards were provided, respectively, by two famous battalions of Frontier Force Rifles, the 55th, 'Cookies', and the 57th, Wilde's. The 2/5th Gurkhas were scrambling up Ahnai Right as right flank guard, and the 2/9th Gurkhas were piqueting the less formidable Ahnai Left on the other (western) side of the river.

B Company of the 2/5th Gurkhas was dropped half-way along the ridge, while Battalion Headquarters and A Company went on to the top of Flathead Left. There they were joined by two platoons from B, while Lieutenant Colonel Crowdy selected a piquet-site. This was never easy. Lest it be overlooked from higher ground it should preferably be on the crest of a hill; but when, with lungs bursting and every muscle aching one reached what looked like the true crest, there was another three hundred yards ahead, and another beyond that.

While Crowdy was engaged on this tricky task, bullets were cracking past him and kicking up stones from a half-moon shaped cliff with a cave-hollowed base called Marble Arch, half a mile to the north; and also from the higher feature, Flathead Right, half a mile to the east across a steep-sided, deep couloir. Since the construction of the piquet would be much interrupted by this fire, Crowdy ordered Captain Maconchy with two platoons of A Company to capture Flathead Right. They dropped over the edge into the couloir and disappeared as though the ground had engulfed them. One man survived, dragging himself into camp that night with a tale of being overwhelmed by hundreds of Mahsuds.

That left on Flathead Left only Battalion Headquarters with two platoons of A Company and two of B, with two more of B several hundred yards down the ridge – a thoroughly unsatisfactory situation. Covered by accurate, long-range fire, parties of tribesmen crept up the gullies to rush this little party. When ammunition was nearly expended, Crowdy led a charge against them, and on the rocky slopes Gurkha and Mahsud hacked with kukris, thrust with bayonet and knife and hurled jagged rocks at one another. The Gurkhas were pushed back up the hill, leaving Crowdy's body, and that of B Company's Commander, thrust through and through with knives. The remnants of the two companies re-grouped on the bullet-swept summit of Flathead Left where it was a feat merely to survive.

Far below 'Cookies', the Advanced Guard, emerged from the tangi, and mountain guns came into action, firing over open sights at glimpses of grey-clad figures among the caves and boulders of Marble Arch. Cookies came up level with Flathead Left, passed it and were set upon by swarms of tribesmen emerging from the nullah on their right, supported by covering fire from Marble Arch. There Cookies stuck.

To the Gurkhas on Flathead Left could now be sent grenades and ammunition; but this vital feature, overlooking at close range the mainguard with its closely packed men, mules, horses and camels, was now held by only seventy or eighty men under constant fire. Nor could they be given any support except from the air, for the ridge was so high and steep that even the howitzer battery could not clear the crest. So the 2/76th Punjabis were sent on to reinforce the Gurkhas and pass through them to take Flathead Right.

This was a wartime second battalion of very young soldiers, Sikh, Jat and Punjabi Mussulman. They had never been in action and perhaps not much was expected of them. They scrambled up onto the ridge and followed their Colonel Sahib, Chamberlayne, over the crest and into that ill-omened couloir, crammed with Mahsuds waiting for them to come down and be cut up. The first hundred and fifty yards cost them some sixty casualties, so Chamberlayne withdrew them to a position just below the crest of Flathead Left where the Gurkhas, flat on their stomachs, were trying to pile up stones first into headcover, then into sangars. There they stuck it out all afternoon, flayed by snipers, beating off five knife-rushes which erupted from the gullies below them. The little rocky hollow between them and the veterans of the 2/5th Gurkhas reeked with blood and cordite and was cluttered up with dead and dying. The pitiless bullets smacked into bodies, sent stones flying and ricocheted whining off rocks. Chamberlayne died under a little thorn-bush below the crest; two company commanders were killed; and the second-in-command was slid down the precipice into the Tank Zam with a dumdum bullet through his thigh.

A company of Mahrattas came up to join them, and with Flathead Left secured, Skeen called it a day. The road into Mahsudland lay open, cleared by common-or-garden Indian Infantry, Punjabis and Mahrattas, Frontier Force Rifles and Gurkhas and Sikh Pioneers.

Derajat Column went on to Makin and Kaniguram to blow up the fortified towers, pull down the terraces of the fields, break the irrigation channels and generally give the Mahsuds weeks of backbreaking work to repair the damage. The Mahsuds then sued for peace, handed over the required rifles and promised to be good as gold for ever and ever – or at least until the next time. The whole show cost Derajat Column 639 dead and 1,683 wounded. Quite a lot for peacetime.

Increasingly the RAF acted to back up the Political authorities and the army. They gave direct support, bombing and straffing, in military operations. More important, they often obviated the need for a punitive column by bombing the towers of recalcitrant clans; and, after an area had been 'proscribed', shooting up and bombing any livestock found grazing in it. It was one of the rules of the game, strictly observed, that no action should be taken until the tribe had been given fair warning by notices dropped on them. Plenty of time was then given for them to move out of a village or an area about to be bombed. The idea was not to kill anyone – it was very rare for anyone to be hurt – but to cause the maximum inconvenience and trouble. The tribesmen would have to shelter in caves where myriads of fleas made life unendurable, graze their cattle only at night, and laboriously repair the fortified towers which had been knocked down. Air action was a useful adjunct to, but not a substitute for, military action.

A modified forward policy was applied to Waziristan in the early 1920s. It would be dominated from within by two brigade groups garrisoned at Razmak and Wana. The Militia corps were disbanded and in their place were raised the Tochi Scouts and the South Waziristan Scouts, each of about brigade strength, not under army command but at the disposal of the Political Agents of North and South Waziristan. They were similar to the Militia except that not more than a third of their strength were trans-Frontier Pathans, the remainder being recruited from more reliable Pathan tribes in British India; and they had very few Mahsuds or Wazirs. The third element of the security forces were tribal levies known as Khassadars, armed with their own rifles, undisciplined, un-uniformed and unreliable; but useful for low-grade jobs such as piqueting roads when not much was happening. So to tribal outrages there was a graduated scale of response: first the Khassadars, then the Scouts, and only in the last resort would the Razmak or Wana column trundle into action with infantry, artillery and armoured cars.

An essential feature of the new frontier policy was the opening up of Waziristan by motorable roads. The tribesmen, well understanding that the main purpose of these roads was to facilitate troop movements, much resented them, although they were to bring great economic benefits. The work was put out to contract to deserving Maliks, who employed their fellow-tribesmen – an economic alternative to raiding and highway robbery. The roads were surveyed, aligned and the work supervised by officers of the Royal Engineers. Theirs was a dangerous task. It was axiomatic in Waziristan that if you wanted to stay alive you must never develop habits of which unfriendly persons could take advantage. But the road engineer had to be a creature of habit: he must every day inspect the

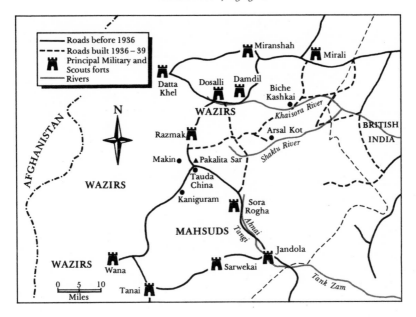

Waziristan (general)

work at roadhead, and mark the subsequent alignment. It got some of them down, including Captain Dixon. So in 1922 Lieutenant B. G. D. Bromhead of the Sikh Pioneers volunteered to help and keep him company.

'Dixon lived at Tamre Oba. A rough stone wall enclosed the camp with the tents of the road labourers huddled within its shelter. Dixon's hut, a windowless, flat-roofed affair of mud and stone, was in the centre. It was an ill-favoured camp, swarming with flies; protected by Khassadars, some of whom slept on our roof at night, making the birch-pole supports creak and sag, and keeping us awake with their hawking and spitting.

There was a vague threat of danger, and living with danger over a period of time brought awareness, of which I being fresh was unaware.

The 12th December was a day with a threat of snow. We set out, walking along the track past the labourers. My bodyguard commander pointed to a figure seated on a heap of spoil beside the road and remarked, "He's one of the gang that will shoot you." The man had a dirty blanket flung over one shoulder, and expressionless eyes, and he certainly did not look friendly.

Like all good sappers Dixon became absorbed in his work. At length he finished his task and we started back to camp. I said, "We'll soon be home." Dixon replied, "No, they'll get us at that corner." He spoke quite casually, and neither of us noticed that our bodyguard had hung back a few paces.

A minute or so later a burst of fire, at short range, came suddenly from our right and Dixon, who was walking on my right, fell. We took shelter behind a boulder with a bush growing out of it. The whiplash of the bullets cracked past, snicking twigs from the bush by our heads. Dixon's intestines had spilt out where an expanding bullet had hit him, but he seemed in no pain, and turned and smiled, "I see you've been hit too." A bullet had broken the little finger of my right hand, and I hadn't noticed it. Dixon lifted his head and turned to speak, and a bullet struck him in the mouth and he fell forward dead. I was trying to ease my revolver from my holster with my left hand. The fire slackened and I looked incautiously over the boulder. A bullet hit the rock close to me, splashing splinters of stone and bullet-casing into my face, so I lay still and then heard voices. Our escort was coming towards us and one of them slapped his headcloth on my head where I felt it warm and greasy. It was a friendly action, and they spoke kind words to me.

We started back to camp. Before we had walked far, I saw my Sikh orderly running to see if I was alright. It was a very brave thing for a Sikh to have exposed himself alone in Tribal Territory. His name was Bir Singh, and he lived near the village of Jawalamukhi in the Punjab, and I remember him with very great gratitude.'

CHAPTER 10

Times of Peace,

1921–39

The growth of the Indian Army from 155,000 in August 1914, to 573,000, all volunteers, in November 1918, was a triumph of improvisation in a system so riddled with defects that nothing but expense was spared in remedying them. New weapons cost money, so none were obtained except the 3.7-inch howitzer, ideal for mountain batteries because of its high trajectory, accuracy and heavy shell. But organizational reforms which cost little were brought in quite promptly, by Indian standards.

First, there had to be a proper reserve. After the war men enlisted for seven years with the Colours – which could, of course, be extended for Indian Officers and NCOs – and eight with the Reserve. Thereafter reserves would be sufficient and not too old. Nor were the Subadars and Risaldars too old, as many had proved in 1914–18. Before the war promotion from NCO to Jemadar, a giant step, had been by a combination of seniority and merit, with the emphasis on seniority. After the war it was by a combination of seniority and merit with the emphasis on merit. But the Commanding Officer who made merit the only criterion, ignoring seniority and a rough balance between the different classes in his regiment, would soon find himself commanding a regiment riddled with intrigue and ripe for trouble. Nothing was harder than to strike the right balance between seniority, merit and giving each class a fair share of promotions.

There was a wholesale re-organization of infantry regiments. Instead of 131 separate regiments (plus Gurkhas) in 1913, there were after 1922 nineteen infantry regiments, each of five active battalions, one training battalion for recruits and reservists, and one territorial battalion – all, so far as possible, of the same class composition. To take one example, the 14th Punjab Regiment was composed of:

Titles 1903–21	Titles of 1922
19th Punjabis	1st Battalion, 14th Punjab Regiment
20th Punjabis	2nd Battalion, 14th Punjab Regiment
22nd Punjabis	3rd Battalion, 14th Punjab Regiment
24th Punjabis	4th Battalion, 14th Punjab Regiment
40th Pathans	5th Battalion, 14th Punjab Regiment
21st Punjabis	10th (Training) Bn, 14th Punjab Regiment
	11th (Territorial) Bn, 14th Punjab Regiment

The organization of the Gurkhas was unchanged: ten regiments each of two battalions.

In 1931 the Pioneer battalions were disbanded as an economy measure deplored by all. It was a great loss to the army.

The thirty-nine prewar cavalry regiments were reduced, mainly by amalgamation, to twenty-one. In 1937, three of these were converted into training regiments, each to provide recruits and reservists for six active regiments. The 'silladar' system was abolished as impracticable where heavy horse casualties were expected, because one could hardly expect wartime volunteers to produce the money to buy their own horses.

There were also changes in class composition. Because they had proved unreliable – though magnificent fighters – against their fellow-Moslems, the enlistment into the regular army of trans-frontier Mahsuds, Wazirs and Mohmands was stopped, and Afridi enlistment greatly reduced. Other classes were phased out because they had not done well during the war. Some down-country regiments were disbanded, others were Punjabi-ized.

Before the war there had been very keen competition among Sandhurst cadets to get into the Indian Army. After 1918 that was no longer so. A young Briton who took the most cursory interest in public affairs might not feel confident that the Indian Army would offer him a career until the age of fifty-five. Nevertheless, for all sorts of reasons – family, quicker promotion, higher pay, greater chances of active service – many still preferred the Indian to the British Army.

During the war nearly seven hundred Indians had been granted King's Commissions in the Indian Medical Service. None were commissioned into combatant corps. In 1918 it was announced that in future Indians would be commissioned into all arms of the service, and that ten places a year would be reserved for them at the Royal Military College, Sandhurst. A drop in the ocean, said Indian nationalists: the thin end of the wedge, said English conservatives. There were doubts even – especially – in high places: would Indian soldiers follow Indian captains and subalterns into danger? Would Indian captains and subalterns lead them?

The Indian Officer Cadets had a tough time at Sandhurst. Their upbringing had been far softer than that for which the Sandhurst system was devised. They then had to serve a year (as did newly commissioned British officers) in a British battalion in India, commanding platoons from London, Glasgow, Birmingham. Any Indian who came through these ordeals had to be pretty good. In 1931 there was established at Dehra Dun the Indian Military Academy, where eventually all Indian Officer Cadets would be trained. This was far more satisfactory. In 1938 its output was fifty-six subalterns – still, said Indian nationalists, a drop in the ocean. Had there been no Second World War, by 1945 half the officer intake to the Indian Army would have been Indians, and the senior ones would have been commanding regiments and battalions.

There remained the unmentionable reluctance of subalterns of the Island Race to take orders from 'natives' (though they would never have used a term which had illogically acquired pejorative implications). To circumvent this, three cavalry regiments and twelve battalions were

'Indianized', i.e. no more British subalterns would be taken into them, so that soon all the subalterns, then all the captains and majors, finally the colonel would be Indian. Some Indians, such as Rajendrasinhji of the 2nd Royal Lancers, flatly refused to transfer to an Indianized regiment, and the 2nd Lancers refused to let him go. (He was to end his career as Commander-in-Chief.) This invidious system did not last long in war: the concept of Indianized units was dropped; soon all regiments and battalions (except Gurkhas) had both British and Indian officers, the former serving quite happily under the latter if the chances of seniority ordained it thus.

Indianization of the officer ranks of the army ended one of the most objectionable features of British India, the ban on Indians joining local clubs. It was such obvious nonsense to claim that a man fit to hold the King's Commission was unfit to join the Shittipur Gymkhana Club that club after club expunged this odious rule. The last to do so was the Peshawur Club, when the (British) colonel of an Indianized cavalry regiment informed the club committee that unless *all* his officers could join the club, none would, and he could not see his way to hiring out cavalry horses for hunting with the Peshawur Vale.

Indian captains and lieutenants necessitated a change in nomenclature. To call Risaldars, Subadars and Jemadars 'Indian Officers' would be confusing, so they were called Viceroy's Commissioned Officers (VCOs); and the Indian products of Sandhurst and Dehra Dun were known as King's Commissioned Indian Officers (KCIOs).

In the Second World War Indianization was of enormous value to the Indian Army. No longer did the loss of half a dozen British Officers paralyse a battalion.

The Indian Army Reserve of Officers expanded from forty in July 1914, to over a thousand in July 1939. The Auxiliary Force (India), AF(I), raised from European civilians on a part-time basis, was another source of British Officers and NCOs. It consisted of ten units of cavalry, thirty-eight of infantry, six of artillery, and signals, varying greatly in strength and quality. Its original purpose was to preserve internal security when the regular army was over-stretched. It was never used for that purpose. Annual camps were not, to be sure, dedicated entirely to military training: the Calcutta Light Horse notably served Venus and Bacchus as well as Mars. But they were a good source in war of officers who spoke at least some Urdu.

The two biggest postwar changes in the life of British subalterns and captains were the arrival of Indian subalterns and captains, and the motor-car. Few officers could afford a car of their own, but most officers' messes owned one which could be hired out at a reasonable price. This was of enormous benefit to a life of – let us face it – abundant leisure: a duck shoot or a pig-sticking meet, a dance or a tennis tournament, forty miles away was within easy reach.

And leisure was abundant. Thursday and Sunday were both holidays. An officer could expect at least one period of ten days' local leave in a year, which could be extended by adroit use of Thursday and Sunday to nearly a fortnight; he had two months' Privilege Leave (three if he were on the Frontier) every year; and about six months' Home Leave after about three and a half years. In addition he enjoyed Hindu, Moslem, Sikh and Christian religious holidays. Not for nothing was his life-style described as 'half a day's work for half a day's pay'. The subaltern's pay was about fifteen shillings a day.

An officer might marry young, but could not draw a marriage allowance until he was thirty. I am not qualified to discuss the marital problems of Kings' Commissioned Indian Officers, which must have been considerable because Indians usually marry young. The British Officer who married prematurely was viewed with disfavour by his colonel, on the grounds that marriage would distract him from his duties and he would not carry his weight in the regiment. It might be put to him that subalterns in, say, the Poona Horse were expected to spend their money on polo ponies, not on wives; so would it not be a good idea for him to take his talents and his wife elsewhere?

Sexual mores were more relaxed than before 1914, but not nearly so relaxed as they were to become during and after the Second World War. It would still be unthinkable, and arouse the colonel's wrath, for an officer to have a liaison with an Indian woman, or with the slightly dusky hairdresser or hotel receptionist, however beautiful, well educated and charming she might be. The 'Fishing Fleet' of socially acceptable girls who came out to India every cold season were equally tabu, or at least ninety-nine per cent were: they came to get *married*, not to set up as 'station hacks'. The philanderer's best bet was a brother officer's wife, summering in Kashmir – regarded by some as a Saturnalia where the ordinary rules did not apply – while her husband sweltered in the plains. When the lady's husband came up, the boyfriend would go off trout-fishing, and all her friends would forget he ever existed. His colonel would be unlikely to make a fuss unless the injured husband was in the regiment, in which case Don Juan would be invited to transfer to another. But divorce was deprecated: a named co-respondent might have to resign his commission. This is not to imply that many officers were rams, or many officers' wives available; but some were – as in other walks of life.

Within its limitations, an Indian Army officer's life was a pretty agreeable one. His day started before dawn, when his bearer brought him a cup of tea. I never actually knew anyone who was shaved in bed or dressed by his bearer, but perhaps such sybarites existed. Soon after dawn he would be on parade for PT, riding school, range-duty, weapon training, dummy thrusting, bayonet practice, close-order drill, or whatever. Then to the mess for breakfast, and after breakfast more parades, stables, office work, until luncheon. The two hours after luncheon would be spent working with the munshi for a language exam, or for a promotion exam, or 'studying for the Staff College' (which during the hot weather was also a euphemism for 'Persian PT' or an afternoon kip). Then, after a cup of tea, some sort of exercise: polo or schooling polo ponies, tennis or golf or squash at the club, hockey or football or tent-pegging with the men. Bachelor officers normally dined formally in mess, resplendent in mess-kit; married officers generally dined in mess only on the weekly guest-night, when a toast was drunk to the King-Emperor. After dinner there might be a visit to the cinema, or perhaps a hop at the club, for which one did not wear mess-kit but a dinner jacket, or in some clubs white tie and tails. The latest joined subaltern was probably made Mess Secretary. On my first day in office the Mess Clerk came to me with a delicate problem, 'Sir, what to do? Mess cook wishes to marry bazaar pros.'

Married officers lived, of course, in their own bungalows with their families. Bachelors shared, two or three to a bungalow, each with his bedroom, sitting-room and bathroom (no mod. cons.) Each had his own syce or syces if he kept horses, but they shared the services of a sweeper, a bhistee (water carrier) and a gardener. It was an agreeable custom in cavalry regiments for any NCO or VCO who had been promoted to come in full uniform to each officer's bungalow to be congratulated, and to half-draw his sword to be touched by the officer, a sign of homage. On such occasions, and indeed other occasions, the VCO would be invited in for a drink (three inches of neat whisky if a Sikh) or a cigarette if he were a Moslem.

That was the routine, in the station, five days a week. (The Orderly Officer for the day would also have other duties, including making a round of sentries, turning out the guard and walking round the horse-lines at different and unexpected times.)

The hot weather was given over to leave and individual training. Collective training started in early autumn, first at the troop/platoon level, then the squadron/company level, working up to brigade and perhaps divisional training by February. Then, of course, one was away from the station, working remarkably hard, day and night: the image of war without the danger, but with much of the fatigue.

The two months' leave a year was taken in the hot weather, so as not to interfere with collective training. The Indian soldier, having a farm to look after, invariably took his at home. Some officers still went after big game in mountain or jungle, but already the ethics of shooting animals for sport was being questioned, and few cameras were as yet capable of good game photographs. So one went up to the hills to get cool, to play tennis, golf or polo, to trek and camp up to the snowline, troutfish in Kashmir, sail at Naini Tal, or just 'poodlefake' with young women on Kashmir houseboats.

It is significant that by the 1930s the term 'sepoys' was seldom used. An infantry private might be 'Sepoy Lal Singh', but one did not refer collectively to 'the sepoys', a term which raised unwelcome memories of 1857. Instead, in Indian (but not in Gurkha) regiments, one referred, affectionately if perhaps paternally, to 'the jawans', the young men: 'See that the jawans get a hot meal when they come in'. The postwar Indian soldier was not as helplessly dependent on his British Officer as his father had been. He was better educated, and encouraged more to think for himself. One heard nothing of VCOs too old and set in their ways.

In the 1920s and early 1930s hardly anyone expected that the Indian Army, or for that matter the British Army, would ever again fight a 'first class enemy'. Hopes of active service were limited to the Frontier. But there was another preoccupation, infinitely distasteful, with no medals to be won and every prospect of disgrace if one acted too soon or too late, too little or too much: that was Aid to the Civil Power, a euphemism for riot control.

A code of practice was drawn up so as to preclude any repetition of the 'Amritsar massacre' of 1919.

1. Troops should never be in physical contact with a mob, because their only weapons were lethal. Physical contact was the job of the police.

2. With every body of troops there should be a magistrate, British or Indian.

3. If the situation got out of control by the police, the magistrate would, by loud hailer or written notice prominently displayed, declare the mob to be an unlawful assembly and order it to disperse.

4. If the mob failed to disperse, the magistrate would instruct the senior military officer present to disperse it, confirming the order in writing.

5. It was up to that officer to use the minimum force necessary for that purpose, and he was the sole judge of the minimum. If shots had to be fired, they should never be aimed over the rioters' heads, which would enrage but not deter them. Soldiers who had to shoot must shoot to kill. But the response to the magistrate's order must be gradual, nothing like Amritsar. The officer should select one or two steady men, good shots, and order them to fire one shot each 'At *that* man', indicating a ringleader. Only if this failed would a section fire a volley. Automatic weapons should never be used.

6. The only other occasion on which soldiers could fire on a mob was in self-defence.

It was effective: it controlled riots, with no more Amritsars. But there were a few occasions when soldiers were breast-to-breast with furious rioters snatching at their rifles because an officer, remembering Amritsar, hesitated too long.

In the 1930s urban riots were less likely to be anti-government than communal, Moslems against Hindus and Sikhs. Since Indian soldiers, however well disciplined, could hardly be emotionally detached in such situations, the authorities preferred to use British or Gurkha troops. There was a tacit assumption that the Indian Army must continue to be insulated from politics. No British Officer would dream of discussing politics with Indian ranks, other than making an occasional derisive reference to Congress as a bunch of bunniahs and failed BAs – a view which, it was assumed, the Indian soldier would share. So he did – except, perhaps, in technical corps and in one or two regiments with Sikhs.

After 1919 the Indian Army trained very seriously for frontier warfare, and by the mid-1920s it was an extremely efficient instrument for that purpose, if, perhaps, for nothing else.

There were certain features peculiar to frontier campaigns. In the end the government must win: everyone knew that. The tribes' objective was to make the government's victory so expensive in lives and money that in future they would be left alone. 'We want,' they said, 'neither your stings nor your honey.' On the whole the Afridis, Mahsuds and Mohmands achieved this: they were left largely to manage their own affairs. The butcher's bill must be low. British public opinion would not accept a lot of casualties. So methods were adopted which saved lives but were very time-consuming.

Frontier tactics were based on piqueting. A brigade 'column' had generally to move along a valley, accompanied by hundreds of baggage mules and camels carrying artillery and machine guns, ammunition and barbed wire, picks and shovels, tents and blankets, rations and fodder, telephone wire and canvas watering-troughs. They made a target no sniper could miss, even at twelve hundred yards. So every hill within range of a column's route had to be crowned by a piquet varying in strength from a couple of sections to a company. The method of posting, occupying and withdrawing a piquet was laid down in exact detail, so that the thickest Lance Naik, after his officer had been killed, could make no mistake.

Piquets were posted by the Advanced Guard commander, fanning out to their hilltops as the column moved slowly down the valley. The piquet commander carried prominently a small canvas piqueting screen, khaki on the side facing the enemy, orange on the side facing the column, so that his friends could see how far he had got. Having reached his piquet position, he positioned his men for all-round defence, built from rocks a bullet-proof sangar, and stayed there, keeping his eyes skinned, until he was recalled by the rear-guard commander waving a huge red flag and the piquet's serial number. This meant, 'Pull out as soon as you like but as quickly as you can.'

Now came the most dangerous part of the operation. The enemy found it far more rewarding, in terms of captured rifles, to attack a withdrawing piquet in the afternoon than an advancing piquet in the morning. Moreover, it was the first rule in frontier war that no wounded man, if possible no dead man, and no rifle should be left to the tribesmen. First, men named by the piquet commander crawled back from the crest and ran down the hill to a fall-back position. Then the Lewis-gun went down. Finally the commander and the rest of his men came bounding down twice as fast as they thought they ever could, because the enemy would be on top shooting as soon as they left. If a man was wounded, the withdrawal must be halted while he was carried down; and perhaps a platoon, a company, a whole battalion would have to counter-attack to save that one man from mutilation.

Early in the afternoon the column halted. Protected by piquets on the surrounding hilltops, the brigade settled into a perimeter camp inside a bullet-proof drystone wall, each man dug into his own funkhole.

Opinions differed on the value of this in training for modern war. But the experience of taking cover and moving at speed when real bullets cracked past, and of shooting back, was thought to be of great value to the Indian Army. Probably it was.

There were only three important post-1919 innovations: the 3.7-inch mountain howitzer, the restricted use of aircraft, and, where possible, lorry convoys, escorted by armoured cars, instead of the long vulnerable lines of laden camels.

So quiet was the Frontier between 1925 and 1930 that many soldiers began to think that the poor old Pathan had had it. A pity, really, but Progress – Progress. This assessment was to be sharply corrected in the 1930s.

The trouble started in April 1930 with fierce riots in Peshawur, sparked off by the arrest of a dozen leaders of the dangerous and subversive Redshirt movement. Troops went in to support the police. The mob set fire to an armoured car, beat to death a dispatch-rider and knocked the Deputy Commissioner senseless with a brick. Inhibited from shooting by memories of Amritsar, a company of Garhwalis was embroiled in a savage struggle with men battering them with staves and axes, trying to snatch their rifles.

Seven thousand Afridis, draped with rifles, daggers and cartridge-belts, descended from the Tirah to free their Hindu brethren from atrocious British oppression, mine roads, rampage through the environs of Peshawur and loot Hindu shops. Some invaded the Supply Depot, but were seen off by a Jemadar with no inhibitions about using a Lewis-gun. European women and children were evacuated and Government House was put in a state of defence with rifles and revolvers laid out on the billiards-table.

There ensued a strange combination of aid to the civil power inside the city and warlike operations against the tribesmen outside it, among canals, orchards and head-high crops. In that country the Poona Horse were at a disadvantage. They had several casualties trying to swim horses across a canal to get at the tribesmen and had to withdraw to more open country. The withdrawal was followed up by the Afridis, who were checked by a mounted attack led by the Adjutant, Captain Newill. In the evening things quietened down, and three men captured by the tribesmen as they struggled out of the canal were returned unharmed in a tonga. Eventually the city was restored to quiet and the Afridis were pushed back to their mountain fastnesses.

In 1935 there were two frontier campaigns north of Peshawur. The second and larger, against the Mohmands, drew in four brigade groups, a medium battery, a cavalry regiment, a light tank company and two little-known brigadiers named Alexander and Auchinleck. Its object was to open up the Mohmand country by a road over the Nahakki Pass and to break up hostile lashkars.

The Nahakki Pass was duly crossed and the Nowshera and Peshawur brigades were established in perimeter camps on the far side of it. But there was the usual difficulty in bringing the enemy to battle in circumstances in which they would not slip away. They were known to be in force on a precipitous mountain marked on the map as Pt 4080. The ridge leading to this had on it three lower features, known from their appearance as Teeth, Nipple and Pimple. The whole country was very 'big', and the route from Teeth to Pt 4080, past Nipple and Pimple, was along the narrowest of ridges, with precipitous slopes on either hand.

The task of occupying Pt 4080 and giving the lashkar there a good drubbing was given to one of the best-trained Piffer battalions, the 5/12th Frontier Force, famous as 'the Guides'. Their advance was to be by night, silent. The plan was for B Company to lead and occupy Teeth; C to pass below B and occupy Nipple; A to pass through C and, with two of C's platoons, go on to Pt 4080. B Company was composed of two platoons of Pathans (Orakzais and Khattaks), one of Sikhs and one of Dogras (the Guides were unusual in having companies of mixed classes). It was commanded by Lieutenant G. J. Hamilton, three years out of Sandhurst.

They reached Teeth with no difficulty except for the atrocious going, clambering in the dark over huge boulders and lumps of shale which sometimes shifted and trundled noisily down the hill through those following below. Hamilton

'was immensely relieved when at long last we found ourselves intact among the vast cathedral-like outcrops that were Teeth. As it became light I pulled out my field-glasses and strained my eyes towards Nipple. ... I could just make out C Company toiling towards the higher crags. A shot rang out. So much for surprise, I thought. ...

I could see that Shadi Khan [Subadar Major, commanding C] had got his first two platoons in position on Nipple. I could see the two Vickers machine-guns being lugged up the last few hundred feet of almost perpendicular cliff. ... They were being caught up by battalion headquarters, Syd [Good, the C.O.], Godfrey [Meynell, the Adjutant] and Tony [Rendall, commanding A Company]; gunner FOOs and the British wireless operator from Brigade.

To the north and south of Pt 4080 ran long spurs forming the cross of a T. Enemy on the spurs could bring cross-fire to bear from two directions on troops advancing along the ridge. ... The summit of Nipple seemed to get more and more crowded as Shadi Khan's two platoons and A Company prepared to advance on Pt 4080. I could just make out the small red cross flag denoting Frank's [Doherty, Medical Officer] Regimental Aid Post.

I saw the leading platoon moving out, closely followed by the second. ... The top of the ridge was very narrow with steep sides dropping to the plain below. As the leading sections got out on the ridge the hidden tribesmen on Pt 4080 started firing. ...

In reply the two machine-guns opened fire with their familiar rattle. ... I could just make out Syd and Godfrey now on the way to Pt 4080 behind the two leading platoons. As the fire increased they quickened their pace until they reached a small outcrop of rock [Pimple] about 400 yards from Pt 4080 where the leading platoons had been halted.'

The enemy fire grew in intensity and accuracy. Rendall and two of his platoons managed to reach the highest point on the eastern side of Pt 4080 where they were held up by heavy fire from the broken ground all around. The next two platoons of A Company to arrive, with Good and Meynell, took up positions to protect the left and rear of the front platoons, whom Meynell now joined. Finding that Rendall had been killed, he took command. Good then ordered up the two platoons of C Company. But under very heavy, close-range fire from numerous tribesmen concealed in caves and boulders, they could not scale the cliffs of Pt 4080, and took up positions below A Company. There were thus on the lower slopes of Pt 4080 the survivors of A Company, two platoons of C, and Battalion Headquarters, all pinned to the ground under very heavy fire.

If ever infantry needed artillery support it was now. FOOs from a medium and a mountain battery had been with Battalion Headquarters, but both were wounded and the telephone was lost. At the gun position it was not known who held Pt 4080. Good, however, was able to contact Hamilton with a signal-shutter.

'I saw the white shutter twitching on the lower slopes of Pt 4080 and my signaller read it.... 'Send two platoons'.... I yelled to the Khattak and Dogra platoons to follow me, and to Subadar Rur Singh to hold Teeth with the Sikh and Orakzai platoons until further notice.

We went like hunted chamois over the rocks, sliding down into the dips on our backsides and scrambling up vertical cliffs.... The final approach to Nipple was almost vertical rock ... but we made it, only slowed down by the constant stream of wounded making their way back from the RAP to the valley below. Many were in a bad way and had great difficulty in negotiating the cliff-holds.

I ... sped to Subadar Dost Mohamad of the machine-gun platoon. The enemy fire was intense as the number of dead and wounded on that small hilltop showed. More were arriving every minute from the hill beyond. Frank, the doctor, was not far away behind a rocky outcrop; his hands were red with blood as he splinted a knee-bone shattered by a dumdum bullet. "The Dost" put me in the picture which was a black story of disaster. No Battalion Headquarters left as they had all gone forward with the six leading platoons, the battered remains of which were now in full flight down the hillside. "All the Sahibs killed," said he.'

The end on Pt 4080 was watched through field-glasses by the FOO with another battalion. Tribesmen started collecting the arms of the dead and wounded. Five of the Guides struggled up again to fight and killed one of them. A signaller, propped up against a rock, started flashing a lamp, a signal which no one read. Meynell was seen standing on a rock defending himself with a clubbed rifle. Soon all were shot or stabbed.

But to Hamilton it was not apparent that it was all over.

'I decided I must get forward at once and try to do something to help. The Khattaks tore after me as we left Nipple, and streamed down the forward slope towards the lower reaches of Pt 4080.

I had gone about a hundred yards when I was hit in the stomach by what felt like the kick of a horse, which spun me round in my tracks. I paused and, I suppose, stood gazing with fatuous amazement at Pt 4080 whence the bullet must have come, for I heard my orderly, Aspirla Khan shout, "Don't stand there! We must go forward." I now saw what he had seen, the rocky outcrop named Pimple ahead of us, where the two platoons of C Company had halted earlier to cover the advance of A Company. I found I could still move on all fours, and covered the 200 yards or so to Pimple like a chimpanzee. Six men of the platoon had also been wounded. Naik Said Mohamad, hit near the edge of the ridge, had rolled with a shattered thigh down a thousand feet to the bottom.

I took stock of our position. The Khattaks who were left were now in firing positions among the rocks around me. Looking back I could see the Dogras were valiantly following. . . . I saw Havildar Mohan Singh hit in the chest and roll down the lower foothills of the ridge. . . .

Having sorted out the Dogras in some sort of position I looked at my shirt, which was soaked in blood, in the shelter of a friendly slab of rock. I appeared to have been hit by a bullet in the stomach where there was a neat hole, with another jagged wound behind my right hip. I tried to wriggle my toes. They wriggled. I urinated against the rock, much to Aspirla Khan's embarrassment. It was gin clear. I decided I could carry on. . . .

It seemed . . . that there were no Guides left alive on Pt 4080 and that the hill was occupied by tribesmen in force. . . .

I was certain there would be a counter-attack to recover our wounded, and decided to stay put on Pimple despite our casualties. . . . For the next hour we . . . fired at anything that moved on the hill and spurs, but the tribesmen were some hundred feet above us and well concealed. We saw little.'

They did not see the withdrawal of a few Guides still alive on the lower slopes of Pt 4080, organized by Good (who was wounded) down a ravine and into the Wucha Jawar valley. The arrival of a platoon of the 2/15 Punjabis and an artillery FOO made their position healthier, but there was no sign of a counter-attack. Then, as there seemed to be no chance of any Guides surviving on Pt 4080, the guns started shelling it to stop the tribesmen getting away with the rifles. Through the shell-bursts men could be seen running about collecting the spoils of victory. With that, Hamilton realized there would be no counter-attack, and the battle was over. 'I suddenly felt very tired and let Aspirla Khan lead me back through Frank's RAP and down the hill.'

Next day the Mohmands sued for peace and the little war was ended. Against all precedent, they returned unharmed the eight wounded Guides they had captured. Naik Said Mohamad, who with a shattered thigh had rolled a thousand feet down the hill, was found by one of the enemy, an ex-Havildar of the Guides, honourably discharged and 'eating pension'. He got hold of a donkey, put his former comrade onto it and sent him too into camp. Out of 140 Guides who reached Pt 4080, only 31 came off it unscathed.

Meynell was awarded a posthumous VC, the first on the Frontier since 1920; Doherty and Hamilton got DSOs, an unusual gong for a battalion MO and a 23-year old subaltern. As for the Mohmands, they reckoned they had done all right.

The next trouble was in Waziristan where a generation had grown up nurtured on tales of their fathers' deeds in 1919–20 and longing to emulate them.

It started early in 1936 with what should have been a mere police court case. A Moslem student in Bannu abducted – or eloped with – a Hindu girl, more or less willing, who turned Moslem, more or less willing, and married her seducer, more or less willing, taking the name of Islam Bibi. Her parents took the matter to court, and this small dispute promptly took on an ugly communal character. A holy man known as the Fakir of Ipi, one of the kind who have always been the plague of the Frontier, raised the cry that Islam was in danger and called Moslems to the Holy War. The Bannu Magistrate directed that the girl, until she came of age, should reside in the custody of a respectable Moslem gentleman in Bannu. The temperature dropped and Political Agents heaved a collective sigh of relief. But the Judicial Commissioner, reviewing the case, awarded the girl's custody to her Hindu parents, and the fat was in the fire, blazing up nicely, particularly in the country of the Tori Khel Wazirs, the Fakir's tribe.

Some time previously the Tori Khel had agreed that a road should be made from the Tochi valley southwards into the Khaisora valley, through the heart of their country. It seemed a good time to hold the tribe to their undertaking; but although the elders again agreed, the young men shouted them down.

The Tori Khel must be brought to heel. A plan was drawn up for two brigades to march through their country on 25 November 1936. The Razmak Brigade (Razcol) would move eastward down the Khaisora valley, and the Bannu Brigade (Tocol) southward from Mirali. They would meet at Biche Kashkai, tell the Tori Khel not to be so silly, and return home. It would be an exemplary demonstration of the Government's might, enlivened, perhaps, with a little long-range sniping.

It did not work out like that. Razcol reached Biche Kashkai, but not until after dark and after some quite hard fighting. Tocol fared worse, largely because its brigade staff underestimated the Tori Khel and did not have proper control; and one of the battalions, the 3/7th Rajputs, was a new arrival.

They set off from Mirali in the early morning of the 25th, their flanks guarded by the Tochi Scouts, not part of the army but for this operation under the brigadier's command. By 8.30 they had reached the Katira river where they were joined by some Tori Khel maliks who warned of trouble ahead. When they crossed the Katira river, they came under quite heavy fire from tribesmen in sangars among the hills south of it. The advanced guard, the 1/17th Dogras, was held up; and the 3/7th Rajputs were ordered to drive the tribesmen from the hills to the right front. To Lieutenant V. L. M. Wainright of the Tochi Scouts who watched their performance from the right flank, they seemed 'very brave but hadn't a clue, and got shot down in clumps'. Their attack was halted by fire from well concealed sangars, all the officers of their leading companies being killed or wounded. It was now about 14.30 hrs.

According to the *Official History*, 'Orders were given to the squadron Probyn's Horse to carry out a mounted attack on the enemy holding up the Rajputs. . . . The cavalry galloped the hills in about four or five minutes, with only two casualties. . . . and the Rajputs were enabled to continue their advance.' Actually, it wasn't quite like that. Captain J. A. Steward of Probyn's Horse tells what really happened:

'A Squadron and the machine-gun troop were part of Tocol. . . . I commanded the MG Troop. The 3/7th Rajputs went through us and took casualties including two company commanders whom I saw being carried back.

The squadron was ordered to gallop the high ground east of the Katira. One troop was to lead up the track, followed by the MG troop to give covering fire to the squadron's attack. I was riding a charger, Leraka ("the quarrelsome one"), which I had in training for point-to-points that winter. The troop in front was fired on and went off in top gear, veering left.

The MG packs [packhorses] were very restive and, at a hand-gallop, the noise of the ammunition-boxes banging up and down was too much for Leraka, and we reached the high ground at great speed. I managed to stop him in a slight hollow at the top which gave some cover, and set up my four machine-guns. . . . We fired off a lot of ammunition at the backs of the sangars before the rest of A Squadron came up and made us feel a bit less exposed. . . .

It is not for me to dispute the Official History. We galloped the high ground out of control. The opposition melted away, partly because we were behind them. It must by definition have been a "mounted attack", but it was odd for the machine-guns to arrive before the sabre squadron they were supposed to be supporting, and for that I can only blame Leraka.'

It was high time Tocol stopped and made its perimeter camp for the night, an operation best not undertaken in darkness. But the Brigadier felt he must press on six miles further to Biche Kashkai. At 19.30 the advance was resumed, by moonlight, with four platoons of Tochi Scouts as advanced guard. First the left of the column was shot up, then the rear; each time there was a stampede of animals, including the Brigadier's horse, and touch was lost with the advanced guard. At 20.30 a Tori Khel malik arrived with a message from Razcol, saying they had reached Biche Kashkai, and the Brigadier decided to bash on. Almost immediately there was heavy fire, at short range, on the advanced guard, yet another stampede of horses, camels and mules, and yet another long delay while officers tried to sort out the chaos in the dark. The Brigadier bowed to the inevitable and halted the column for the night. Behind a screen of Tochi Scouts some sort of perimeter wall was thrown up, and by one in the morning the Brigade Major at least was tucked up in bed (a situation rectified by Wainright, who came in to report).

Light is thrown on the staff work of this operation by the fact that when Razcol wished to inform Tocol that it had reached Biche Kashkai, word was sent by a Tori Khel malik; and when Tocol wished to inform Razcol that it was still far short of Biche Kashkai, word was sent by a Mahsud Khassadar. The two columns had suffered 131 casualties. It was not, perhaps, the Tori Khel who had been taught a lesson.

This was the beginning of a war which was to continue in Waziristan, sometimes crescendo, sometimes diminuendo, for nine years, keeping busy, at peak, six regular brigades and the equivalent of two brigades of Scouts.

The most notable operation was on 11/12 May, 1937. The Fakir of Ipi was the key to the whole situation. If he could be captured, killed or even discredited, the war would be over. Reports located his headquarters in a complex of caves and fortified towers at Arsal Kot, in the Shaktu valley. He must be chivvied out, even if he could not be caught. From the Khaisora into the Shaktu valley the only practical route was over the high Sham Plain, which would normally be reached from Dosalli Scouts Post southwards up the steep Sre Mela valley and gorge, piqueting the heights on either hand as the column crept slowly along the valley. But Major General A. F. Hartley, commanding a division made up of the Bannu and Abbottabad Brigades, looked at the problem from another point of view. Why not surprise the enemy by advancing at night along an unexpected route?

Almost parallel with the Sre Mela valley and a mile or two to the east of it runs the steep, narrow, rugged Iblanke ridge. It has been compared to a lean crouching lion. From the tail, in the Khaisora, the path follows the spine, a mile and three quarters long, up to the shoulder blades; then down the neck and between the ears; over the skull, the Iblanke Narai (col); and down between the outstretched forelegs to the Sham plain. Was it passable by a brigade with machine-guns and mountain artillery? Maps and air photos being useless, and reconnaissance impossible lest the game be given away, Hartley could rely only on the recollections of sundry Tochi Scouts who had been over it in the past. These included no British Officers. The consensus was that it was just passable at night by infantry and mules. On the word of these Pathans Hartley staked the Bannu Brigade and his own reputation: if they proved wrong, dawn would have found the brigade jam-packed on a narrow ridge, fired at from three sides and unable to deploy its own supporting arms. The disaster to the Guides at Pt 4080 was fresh in the memory of Major W. A. Gimson, commanding the Tochi Scouts detachment, himself a Guide. Afterwards he wrote: 'The responsibility of getting the brigade there and of having said that the mules could get over

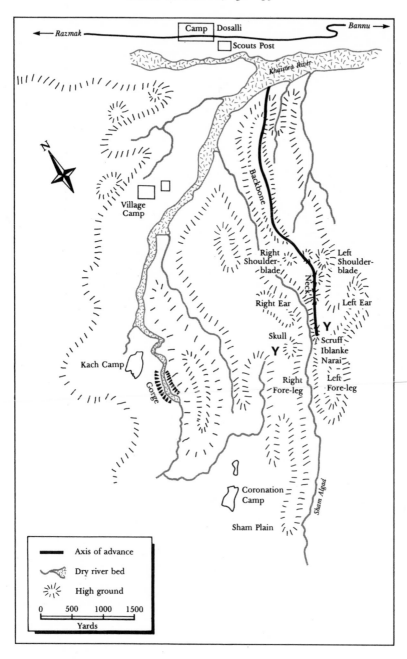

Razmak ← Camp Dosalli → Bannu
Scouts Post
Khaisora River
Backbone
Village Camp
N
Right Shoulder-blade
Left Shoulder-blade
Neck
Right Ear
Left Ear
Skull
Scruff
Iblanke Narai
Y
Y
Kach Camp
Gorge
Right Fore-leg
Left Fore-leg
Coronation Camp
Sham Algad
Sham Plain

Axis of advance
Dry river bed
High ground

0   500   1000   1500
Yards

Waziristan: Iblanke, 11–12 May 1937

the very difficult ground was on my shoulders, and if the expedition had failed, I would have been for the high jump.'

The essence of the plan was surprise, and Dosalli was crawling with Wazir Maliks, contractors and Khassadars, for whose benefit an elaborate deception plan was put into operation.

The mules accompanying the column were reduced to a minimum, but the brigade must have machine-guns and 3.7 howitzers to make sure of getting through. They would also need ammunition, entrenching tools, signalling and medical stores, one blanket to be shared between two, tea and sugar for two days. All these required 725 mules. No riding animals were to be taken, and no mule addicted to braying. Because of the difficult going, there would be one leader per mule. Every man carried hard rations for two days.

The brigade would be led by eight platoons of Scouts under Gimson, moving at their own pace, which would be faster than the infantry behind. They would seize the 'shoulder blade' heights and hold them until the advanced guard, the 2/11th Sikhs, arrived and took over. Behind the Sikhs the 2/4th Gurkhas would place piquets of five men every hundred yards, on alternate sides, not more than ten yards from the path, to prevent anyone going astray. Each piquet commander, on his predecessor being posted, would seize the hand of the Commanding Officer and hold it until he was posted. (The Adjutant had some difficulty in impressing on young Lance Naiks that they really must take this liberty with the Colonel Sahib.) Behind the Gurkhas followed the rest of the column.

There is no operation of war more apt to go wrong than a night march over difficult, unreconnoitred country, and none more likely to produce greater dividends in surprise if it is successful. The Tochi Scouts were practised in night work; they carried no more than their rifles and were unimpeded by mules. Wearing sandals made of grass-rope which clung to rock and made no noise, swift and silent as wraiths, they set off at 2100 hours, in pitch darkness, and half an hour after midnight they were on the 'shoulder-blade' heights exchanging with Wazir outposts the taunts and insults customary between the Pathan Scouts and the Pathan opposition. The Wazirs were quite confident that they could hold the pass against the rifle-armed 'militia', and had no suspicion that the brigade with all its fire-power was following.

Gimson expected the 2/11th Sikhs to arrive by 0130, and by 0430 hours there was still no sign of them. 'My heart was in my boots, and I thought they must have got stuck.'

They were having a terrible time. In addition to all the normal hazards of a night march – the loss of touch between the head of the column which is always creeping along and the tail which is always hurrying to catch up, the fear of losing one's way, the terrible, atavistic dread of being left alone in the hostile darkness – there were the appalling difficulties of coaxing and dragging mules along a knife-edged ridge, up unseen rock steps two foot and more high, across scree slopes of unknown steepness. Now and then a mule laden with radio sets or picks and shovels would lose its footing and roll with a rattle and a crash down two hundred feet of mountain, its leader and helpers following blasphemously to re-load and bring it up again to the top. To those in the middle of it, the din of the column's progress seemed to reverberate through the mountains; but to Gimson and his Scouts, and to the Wazirs further away, nothing was audible.

At 0500 hours a runner from Brigadier Maynard reached Gimson, with information that the advanced guard was still some way behind, and orders to push on and secure the hills on either side of the Iblanke Narai. It was getting light, and as they moved forward they came under heavy fire from the front and both sides.

A Scouts officer, John Prendergast, looked back

'and saw a close-packed column of the 11th Sikhs below me in the gathering light – close-packed as they were edging along the narrow spine. At the firing the column bent like a cornfield and for that sort of vital second all training was forgotten and panic reigned. I heard a high, calm voice. It was their commander, Colonel Keyes, as he called them to order. They knew him and steadied at once. . . . A Scout near me was firing calmly and deliberately. His wadded skull-cap round which his turban was wound showed a puff of cotton-wool. A bullet had pierced it and missed his skull by an inch.'

With daylight, the machine-guns and 3.7 howitzers came into action. Shells burst along the enemy sangars, machine-gun bullets crackled overhead, sending stones and rock-chips flying. The enemy, taken by surprise, melted away. The Sikhs arrived and took over from the Scouts, who pressed on down the hill to the Sham plain and the site of a camp known as Coronation Camp because on that day King George VI and Queen Elizabeth were crowned.

During the First World War the Indian Army hardly ever attacked at night. Nor did anyone else: it was thought to be far too difficult. During the Second World War the Indian Army made a speciality of night attacks. Perhaps the experience of the Iblanke Ridge suggested to some people that a night attack by an unexpected route was not so difficult after all, if properly prepared.

From Coronation Camp the column pushed down to Arsal Kot and had the satisfaction of blowing up the Fakir's headquarters, three linked caves swarming with fleas. He withdrew to the Afghan frontier, where he was safer but not so well placed for making trouble. His influence seemed to be on the wane, road-making continued apace, and by December 1937 two of the three extra brigades could be withdrawn, leaving only one to support the normal garrison.

With the Hitler-Stalin pact and the outbreak of war with Germany, jirga after jirga of Mahsuds and Wazirs pledged undying attachment to the British cause. If the atheist Germans and Russians invaded Waziristan, they swore, the Mahsuds and Wazirs would send them packing. At the same time they behaved very much as they had for the previous three years. Sustained by ample funds from the German and Italian legations in Kabul, the Fakir was able, for the first time in frontier history, to give his warriors regular pay and rations. In North Waziristan, where his influence was greatest, the guerrilla war continued. The Mahsuds were more or less neutral; but when they did fight, their action was well planned, well commanded and bloody.

Such was the action on 6 December 1940.

It was decided that the Razmak brigade, Razcol, would sort out one of the Mahsud hard men, Mohamad Hayat, whose gang hung out in near-inaccessible mountain country south of Razmak. The first day's march would be to Tauda China.

The column's difficulties began when the advanced guard had almost reached camp at Tauda China and the rearguard, the 1/19th Hyderabad Regiment (Lieutenant Colonel J. B. Macdonald), had only four miles to go. They were abreast of Pakalita Sar, a huge, forbidding feature with three peaks, A, B and C, piqueted by a company of the 5/8th Punjabis (Lieutenant Colonel C. F. Faulkner). Macdonald, as rearguard commander, was responsible for withdrawing the piquets by signalling with a large red flag. When the time came to withdraw the piquets at A, the yellow piquet screen could be seen, but no sign of a soldier. The signaller did not answer, but eventually some men under a Sikh officer began a slow, difficult descent and disappeared into a gorge. Next day their mutilated bodies were found there.

With the rearguard commander was C. H. T. MacFetridge, a subaltern in temporary command of 15th (Jhelum) Mountain Battery. He had one section already in action about nine hundred yards down the road, and another coming into action further back. A mounted signaller rode up at a collected canter with an excellent panorama of Pakalita Sar as seen from the section in action. This was a speciality of mountain gunners. MacFetridge was astonished to see that the angle of sight was 18° elevation. As soon as his second section was in action, he ordered the first back to join it.

Another signaller rode up at an urgent gallop with a message from the Gun Position Officer that he had seen enemy moving about on Pakalita Sar. Faulkner and Macdonald were incredulous, for the piquet screen was still correctly placed. But MacFetridge, scenting trouble, had a telephone line laid to him from the battery position.

There being no further communication with the piquets on B and C, Macdonald sent a company of 1/19th Hyderabad to reinforce them. Faulkner said he would go up too, and it was arranged that he would take command of everyone on Pakalita Sar and would stay there all night. This was an important decision, not lightly made. MacFetridge sent with them a Forward Observation Party of a VCO and signallers, but decided that his place was with the rearguard commander during the three miles withdrawal in fading light to the perimeter camp.

'We arrived at our camp at Tauda China in complete darkness. . . . During the night a few Sikhs of 5/8th Punjab arrived in camp. They were almost incoherent with fright and strain, but it became evident that they had been overrun in the darkness. Many had been ambushed when running the gauntlet to the camp. The battery FOO reported that first the company commander and then the Commanding Officer had been killed. The troops had fled in confusion.'

Major A. J. Dring, Political Officer with the column, adds that the fugitives declared that the Colonel had shouted, 'Every man for himself.' Dring thought this unlikely. It would have been a crazy order to give, and when Faulkner's body was brought in it was found that he had been killed instantaneously, by a bullet in the head, probably not in hand-to-hand fighting.

MacFetridge's narrative continues:

'No men of the 1/19th Hyderabad appeared, and a solitary lamp flickered at intervals from Pakalita Sar. Both batteries engaged A throughout the night (at a near extreme range of 6,000 yards without ranging and with self-devised meteor) in a desperate attempt to encourage the survivors. . . .

A relief column left the camp at first light. . . . It was unopposed, but we found a number of Sikh bodies, some mutilated and all stripped of arms and ammunition. They had clearly been caught while fleeing to the camp. . . . On approaching Pakalita Sar I was horrified to see that the company 1/19th Hyderabad occupied A which we had shelled frequently during the night, while B and C were not occupied. The company came down in good order . . . always in sight. The commander, Jemadar Umrao Singh, reported with cool confidence and self-possession that the CO 5/8th Punjab had appreciated on arrival that A was the salient feature and must be held. He had been ordered to capture it in the fading light. This he had done and then ordered his inexperienced troops to sit tight at all costs, not to fire but to use their bayonets. . . . I asked him about the artillery fire and was apprehensive as to his reply. He replied, "Very good SOS. It fell close and all around us. . . ." I smiled and held my tongue.'

Umrao Singh received an immediate MC and a King's Commission.

Of the 5/8th Punjabis, 66 were killed and as many wounded, quite a lot for the 'phony war'. It was an Indianized battalion, only the CO and second-in-command being British, which caused some to say, 'I told you so'. Unfairly, as events during the next six years were to prove.

Through the early 1940s the Frontier was never at peace. The Fakir, sustained by Axis money and arms and by the belief that Britain would lose the war, tied up in the barren hills three regular brigades and the greatly expanded Tochi and South Waziristan Scouts. Many good men were killed in little battles with Mahsuds and Wazirs. But it is time to leave the Frontier, for more important matters are pending.

CHAPTER 11

Getting Ready

Busy mainly on the Frontier, the Indian Army between the wars acted also as a sort of Asia Fire Brigade, quenching blazes in South India (Moplah Rebellion) in 1921, Shanghai in 1926, and Burma in 1931. The possibility that it might have to fight a more serious war first became apparent in 1934 when bellicose speeches by Mussolini and nervous twitterings in the League of Nations indicated that the new Caesar was about to launch his legions against Abyssinia. The British Minister in Addis Ababa sought military aid to defend British interests in the event of an Abyssinian defeat sparking off anti-foreign riots and attacks in the capital. It arrived in the shape of the Sikh Company of the 5/14th Punjabis, the old 40th Pathans.

When in April 1936 the Emperor's army was routed, looting in the city was universal, fires blazed everywhere. But lorry patrols of the 5/14th kept touch between foreign legations; issued rifles to Americans, Japanese, Italians and Germans; escorted 1,770 refugees of thirty nationalities to the British Legation and defended them there; fought a pitched battle with the Imperial Guard who were attacking the Belgian Legation; and evacuated the American diplomats as their Legation went up in flames. After five days of mayhem, the Italian army arrived and restored order with a heavy hand.

Watched by *carabinieri* and blackshirt militia, the 5/14th company paraded to celebrate the King's birthday and were formally thanked for their services by the new Italian Viceroy, the Duke of Aosta.

Some – not enough – attempt was made to modernize the British Army in the early 1930s: none to modernize the Indian Army. For this one must blame, first, the parsimony of the Indian Government. Moreover, Congress politicians grudged every anna spent on the army, and it was a top political priority to persuade them to form elected provincial governments. Internal security required a lot of men on foot with rifles, not a few men in tanks. To every suggestion for modernization the conservative-minded could reply, 'Oh, but the Frontier. . . .' Thus transport could not be mechanized because there were still parts of the frontier accessible only by mules; and more support weapons for the infantry battalion meant fewer men with rifles for piqueting. General Skeen, Chief of General Staff in the late 1920s, viewed with disfavour any training in which the enemy was supposed to have artillery and machine-guns: this, he said, was unrealistic: Mahsuds did not have them.

The litmus test of modernization was the rate of conversion of horsed cavalry into armour. In India this proceeded at snail's pace. Cavalry officers pointed to Allenby's campaign as proof that there was a place for horsed regiments in modern war. It seems strange that men who loved horses should have wished to expose them to artillery and machine-guns, but so they did, not really believing that another war was possible.

All their arguments were rationalizations of their wish to remain horsed because it was such fun. Where but in Indian cavalry could a comparatively poor man have as many horses as he wanted for polo, pig-sticking, hunting, point-to-points at a cost of only ten shillings a month insurance premium?

Indian cavalry regiments included ocean yachtsmen, mountaineers, watercolour artists, authors, Persian scholars, Staff College instructors, future parsons; but Larry Esmonde-White, joining the Poona Horse in 1937, found that:

'the first requisite was to be able to sit on a horse, regardless of how much the horse objected. . . .

The sight of cavalry en masse is awesome and exhilarating, but there are other times when horses in large numbers are sheer delight. One such is at the end of a hot, dusty march when a regiment halts by a river. When saddles have been removed and four hundred horses are all rolling in the sand with their legs in the air one can feel the delight this back-scratching gives to each animal as he prepares to roll just once more before dashing into the river to drink, wade and swim. And who can forget the whinnying from a squadron of hungry horses when their nosebags are being replenished?'

No wonder horsey young men viewed without enthusiasm the prospect – with no war apparently in sight – of exchanging these glorious creatures for greasy, smelly tanks.

Three commanders-in-chief between the wars were cavalrymen. They were not Blimps. Birdwood had commanded Australian infantry with conspicuous success. Chetwode speeded up Indianization and the foundation of the Indian Military Academy. Cassells saw perfectly well the need for armour, but was inarticulate in putting the case to Treasury officials and politicians. But all three could sympathize with the gut-reactions of cavalry officers. The Scinde Horse and the 13th Lancers were mechanized in 1937, and then no more until 1940.

There was, however, one significant innovation during the doldrums of the 1930s. In January 1935, the 1st Field Brigade of Indian Artillery was formed, with batteries composed of Madrassis, Punjabi Mussulmans, Rajputs and Ranghars. Moreover it was Indianized: after its formation, all new officers posted to it would be Indians. Also, the Lewis-gun was replaced by the Vickers-Berthier, a much lighter and more reliable weapon, which was soon replaced by the very similar Bren-gun. Nevertheless, in 1938 the Indian Army was behind even the Iraq Army in its equipment and readiness for modern war.

In that year Auchinleck became Deputy Chief of General Staff. He was sure that war with Germany and Italy was inevitable, sooner rather than later. He formed a committee to consider its implications, and found that the Indian Army must be prepared for five tasks in a major war, viz:

1. Frontier defence
2. Coastal and anti-aircraft defence
3. External defence, e.g. Persia, Iraq, Malaya
4. Internal security
5. To provide a general-purpose reserve

For these roles, troops with varying scales of equipment would be needed. The whole army need not be mechanized, but the reserve should be highly mobile and include armour and brigades with motor transport. The British Government was persuaded to contribute £34 million to the modernization of the Indian Army on the grounds that it would be necessary for imperial purposes. Not least of the services of 'the Auk' to the Indian Army was the fact that in September 1939, the groundwork of modernization had at least been thought out, agreed in principle, and money made available to pay for it.

At about the same time the Viceroy, Lord Linlithgow, noted the lack of preparation for an attack by the Japanese through Malaya and Burma. He was told not to worry: with the American Pacific Fleet at Pearl Harbor, the Japanese would never risk it.

CHAPTER 12

The Second World War: Opening Bids, 1939–40

Britain declared war against Germany on 3 September 1939. Automatically India was at war, too. That was the constitutional position, but it was politically vulnerable as 'bringing India into war without consulting a single Indian'. Gandhi immediately indicated to Linlithgow that he would support the war effort in his 'individual capacity', and that he viewed it 'with an English heart'. Nehru was fervently anti-Nazi. Nevertheless, after lengthy debate, Congress refused any co-operation with the war effort except on conditions which would outrage the Moslem League and politicians who put no price on their help. So Congress Provincial Governments resigned, and later Congress promoted a rebellion and the sabotage of rail communications with the Burma front at the most critical stage of the war with Japan.

The attitude of Congress made no difference to recruiting: potential recruits were not Congresswallahs. But it affected the supply of officers: many patriotic, educated young Hindus and Sikhs, perfectly good officer-material, must have been put off applying for commissions by the attitude of the organization which they regarded as representing India and likely before long to govern the country.

There was no conflict of conscience such as that of Moslems in the war against Turkey. But a faint question-mark hung over Sikhs, the most politically-minded of the martial races, who had been 'got at' by persons warning them of a nefarious British plot to have them exterminated so that the Punjab would be ruled by Moslems. The Sikh squadron of a cavalry regiment refused to embark for overseas, and there were other incidents. But they were magnificent fighters, with the panache and recklessness of the 36th and 45th Sikhs in the Hai Salient.

Whatever the prewar plans, modern equipment was not available for India. So cavalry were mechanized only in that their horses were taken from them. For the first year of the war infantry had no carriers, mortars or anti-tank weapons, and no one below brigade had wireless. The Indian Government was eager to help, but the received wisdom in Whitehall was that the war would be won by the naval blockade and the trusty French: there was little need for the British Army to exert itself, none for the Indian Army to do so. Word of this discouraging response filtered – leaked – down to every officers' mess in India, a damper on martial ardour. There seemed to be nothing for the Indian Army but the Frontier, to which a new hazard was added by the Hitler-Stalin Pact. It seemed quite possible that Cossacks and Waffen SS might together pour across the Oxus and through the passes, and there was a hurried construction of air-raid shelters and anti-tank defences. In May 1940, the Indian Government offered five infantry and one armoured division for this emergency, available for use elsewhere if it did not occur. His Majesty's Government accepted the infantry, but to the offer of the armoured division replied, 'Sorry, no tanks.' So the cavalry 'trained' in ancient lorries to which coloured flags were attached to represent tanks. When Pat Keenan, a squadron commander in Hodson's Horse, was asked by an eminent brass-hat how he communicated with his troop-leaders, he replied sourly, 'Thought-reading'.

The only Indian Army contributions to the German war were a few Frontier experts sent to Norway to persuade Guards and Territorial battalions that the only way to prevail in mountain warfare was to walk to the tops of the mountains; and four Animal Transport Companies of the Royal Indian Army Service Corps, with pack-mules that could work when lorries were bogged down or snowed up. They acquitted themselves well and during the chaos of the German breakthrough and the retreat to Dunkirk, maintained the discipline, turn-out and self-respect which many around them lost, greatly enhancing the reputation of the Indian Army.

The only Indian soldiers who were adequately equipped, sure they would fight and busy training for it in an environment which was not wholly strange, were the 11th and 5th Indian Infantry Brigade Groups which arrived in Egypt in August and September 1939 to form the nucleus of the 4th Indian Division. (A year later they were joined by the 7th Indian Infantry Brigade.)

In Cairo and in the Delta they set an example which was to be followed by hundreds of thousands of Indian troops in the Middle East, of being the best behaved and best disciplined of all the Allied contingents. They set another precedent: their rations – variations on the theme of meat and vegetable curries, dhal and chupattis – were excellent and appetizing, they knew it and often spoke of it; British rations – variations on the theme of bully-beef, stew, hardtack biscuits and the infamous soya-link sausages – were the reverse, and they knew it and often spoke of it. British Officers in Indian units fed as much as possible from their company cook-houses. I once asked a British Signals corporal what his terrier was doing. 'He's just eaten a soya-link, Sir,' the corporal replied, 'and he's licking his arse to take away the taste.'

Another precedent set was in the excellent relations between British and Indian soldiers within the division. (Both could be critical of other divisions.) In India they had been not unfriendly but not close: their cantonments were usually far apart, and they played different games – the British, football; the Indians, hockey. But in the desert they lived and fought side by side and in identical conditions. There was much coming and going between them, and it would have been unthinkable for an Indian visiting a British unit with a message not to be offered a mug of tea, and vice versa. They would then sit round gossiping in a mixture of Urdu and English, bewildering to an outsider but perfectly intelligible to themselves. (But not, as yet, Gurkhali. Gurkha-fans – and who isn't one? –

sometimes forget that the 4th and 5th Indian Divisions, who went into action first and remained in action longest of all the Indian divisions, initially made their great names without a single Gurkha battalion.)

It was assumed that against a European enemy the Indians needed one regular British battalion in each brigade to set an example of steadiness. (Later in the war this was not considered necessary.) The Indian battalions set an example of cross-country mobility and of frugality: not for them the clutter of welfare services and amenities assumed to be necessary for Thomas Atkins.

The 5th and 11th Brigades had the priceless advantages of training in active service conditions for the war they would have to fight; and of cutting their teeth on an enemy who often fought bravely, but not as skilfully as Germans, and without such good equipment. Before going into action they learned the tricks of the desert: how to navigate with sun-compass over a featureless land; how to move widely dispersed yet keeping contact; how to cross rocky ridges, sand-dunes and steep-sided wadis, and to extricate a lorry buried to its axles in mud; how to collect into harbour after dark and scatter before dawn; how to brew-up over sand soaked with petrol in a stove made of half a water-can, to keep reasonably dry and warm in a winter night without a tent and to keep clean the camp site lest one be driven mad by flies; how to do with very little water; and how to prevent the barrel of a Bren-gun clogging up with sand (pull a french letter over the muzzle).

In a war that was the tactician's paradise and the quartermaster's hell, transport was of supreme importance. First-line transport, used by fighting units in battle – to tow or carry weapons, ammunition, reconnaissance parties, radio sets, commanders – was an integral part of each unit, maintained by the unit's own drivers who in 1939–40 were very inexperienced. Second-line transport, 3-ton lorries carrying rations, water, petrol, ammunition up to battalions and batteries, was the responsibility of the Royal Indian Army Service Corps (RIASC). Each brigade, and divisional troops, included one transport company, RIASC. For large-scale troop-carrying it was necessary to call on higher formations. RIASC drivers had rather more driving experience than battalion drivers, but most of them, a couple of years earlier, had been driving mules.

On 8 June 1940, Italy declared war. Soon after, the defection of the French multiplied the odds against Britain holding the Middle East, the vital land bridge between Asia and Africa. There would now be no friendly French fleet, no reinforcements from Syria, nothing to keep half the Italian forces in Libya facing towards Tunisia. But although Mussolini had in Libya fourteen divisions, against only 7th Armoured and 4th Indian Divisions, their advance into Egypt was cautious and circumspect. By September they had halted south of Sidi Barani in five camps protected by mines, barbed wire, sangars and perimeter walls. These General Wavell, C-in-C Middle East Land Forces, determined to attack – as a mere raid if the first attack proved too expensive, but as the start of something bigger if the opportunity arose.

He had, recently arrived from England, a secret weapon: the 7th Royal Tank Regiment with fifty 'infantry' ('I') tanks far more thickly armoured than any the Italians had.

7th Armoured, by day and night patrolling right up to the walls of the camps, established such a moral ascendancy that the Italians rarely ventured into the desert. They established that, at the key Nibeiwa camp, traffic always entered and left by the north-west corner, which could therefore be presumed free of mines. So the basic plan was for the 7th RTR, followed by the 11th Infantry Brigade, to attack Nibeiwa from that direction. Depending on their fortunes there, the division would either pull out and proclaim a successful raid, or it would press on to deal similarly with camps at Tummar West, Tummar East and Point 90. The 16th British Brigade, from Palestine and under command of 4th Indian, would then attack Sidi Barani. Meanwhile 7th Armoured would hold the ring, west of Sidi Barani, preventing the escape of the camp garrisons or the arrival of reinforcements.

It was the sort of operation which is easy on a map – round the enemy's flank, then attack him from the rear – but presents problems on the ground. It was afterwards said, by Lieutenant Colonel A. Anderson – commanding the Cameron Highlanders – in a lecture to staff officers, 'Aye, and if ye'd done such a thing in your Promotion Exam ye'd never have passed it.' But the country had been driven over, manoeuvred over, had 'going' maps made of it, by 4th Indian Division for months and by 7th Armoured for years. And the Italians were quite accustomed to the noise of their vehicles at night.

Nevertheless, there were difficult problems. Thirty thousand men in 5,000 vehicles would have to move forward a hundred miles across a waterless desert, relying on forward dumps of petrol and water, without the Italians realizing what they were up to, although the RAF did not have command of the air. The balance of strength was, on paper, unfavourable. On the British side were 31,000 men, 120 guns and 225 tanks; on the Italian side, 80,000 men, 250 guns and 120 tanks. But the I tanks of 7th RTR were better than any the Italians had, and many of the latter's 80,000 were mere cannon-fodder.

To lull Italian suspicions, several training exercises were held east of Sidi Barani. Neither the Italians nor the troops taking part realized that some of these were rehearsals for the real operation, the imaginary 'enemy' being positioned like the real enemy. Camouflaged forward supply dumps were placed beside tracks regularly used by 7th Armoured Division.

On 27 November, General O'Connor, commanding Western Desert Force, disclosed the plan to divisional and brigade commanders, and the rendezvous area was sealed off, visitors who came into it not being allowed out. In the early morning of 6 December 4th Indian Division moved out from its positions east of Mersa Matruh and headed into the desert, for a 'training exercise'. In the evening of the 7th they were told this was not training: it was the real thing.

Few battles go exactly as the attacker plans. This did.

During the next day they crawled forward sixty miles, arriving in mid-afternoon at their concentration area fifteen miles south-east of Nibeiwa camp. The RAF sent up anything that could fly, but it seemed amazing that they had not been spotted. Actually, they had: one Italian pilot reported them, and was told to 'take more water with his wine'.

At dusk guides from 7th Armoured arrived to lead 11th Infantry Brigade, 7th RTR and four artillery regiments to their battle positions – 4/7th Rajputs for a feint attack on the east side of the camp, the remainder of the brigade and the tanks for the real attack. The artillery were dropped off at their gun-positions; the others halted, two hours before dawn, four miles from the north-west corner. They were still undetected. The divisional commander, General Beresford Peirse, and the 11th Brigade commander, Brigadier Savory, sat on a small hillock to watch battle commence.

At 0700 hrs the artillery began to register on the doomed camp, and the lines of heavy tanks roared and barged forward in billowing dust-clouds. They smashed into scrap some Italian tanks warming up their engines outside the perimeter, hesitated a moment, and heaved over ditch and wall into the camp which seethed like a disturbed ant-heap. Through the tents, dugouts and slit trenches they ground their remorseless way, machine-gunning everything in sight while bullets spattered against or ricocheted off their thick hides. Some Italian gunners fought bravely, but they might as well have saved their lives like the majority who surrendered. Not until the tanks had been inside the perimeter for fifteen minutes did the 2nd Cameron Highlanders jump from the lorries and go in with the bayonet while their gravely pacing pipers played them forward. Passing through them, the 1/6th Rajputana Rifles mopped up the last pockets of hopeless resistance. In less than an hour, at a trifling cost, 7th RTR and 11th Infantry Brigade had captured over 4,000 prisoners, 23 tanks, scores of guns and lorries.

The act was repeated at Tummar West. Isolated, Tummar East was harmless, and could be contained until the garrison surrendered.

Next morning the 16th British Brigade broke into the southern perimeter of the Sidi Barani defences and got astride the coast road, a reception committee for thousands of Italians who arrived with suitcases packed for travel. To 7th Armoured Division, cordoning off the battlefield to the west, Italians and Libyans surrendered 'by the acre'.

Although it proved to be only the start of a see-saw campaign which was to last for two years, it was a famous victory with far-reaching effects. In the United States it abashed those who were arguing that sending help to the British was a waste of dollars as they were losing the war. General Franco got the message and pigeon-holed any plans he might have had for Gibraltar. The Turks were firmer in their pro-British neutrality. Italian morale got a knock from which it never recovered; and Indian morale a boost which it could have done with in 1914–15.

CHAPTER 13

East Africa,
1939–41

In Eritrea and Abyssinia were a quarter of a million Italian and colonial troops, many of excellent quality, two hundred military aircraft, sixty tanks, a hundred armoured cars, ten groups (equivalent to British regiments) of field artillery which in the Italian Army was always good, and fifty-eight batteries of pack-artillery. Their central position seemed to facilitate a move north or west into the Sudan, held by three British battalions and the Sudan Defence Force some 9,000 strong; south into Kenya, held by two East African, two West African and one untrained South African brigade; or east into British Somaliland, in which the cause of freedom was defended only by the Camel Corps, an irregular gendarmerie maintained for internal security and grazing control.

But from the Italian viewpoint the situation was far from rosy. There were still remote parts of Abyssinia not fully subdued. Militarily, the continuing resistance was hardly formidable; the Eritreans and most of the minority Abyssinian tribes were well disposed to the Italians as liberators from Amhara tyranny. But scattered over the East African empire were thousands of Italian settlers, hostages to fortune who must be protected. Every man, gun, plane, tank, lorry and gallon of petrol expended was irreplaceable: there was no hope of reinforcement or replenishment. The Duke of Aosta, like Von Lettow Vorbeck, must have decided that he could best serve his country by a protracted rearguard action, drawing into this military backwater as many enemy troops as possible. So while the British saw the Italians as poised to pounce, the Italians saw themselves as a beleaguered garrison.

General Wavell sensed the weakness in the Italian position, that it was vulnerable to smaller but better equipped forces who could concentrate, while the Italians must be dispersed. There were two compelling reasons for liquidating Italian East Africa: the first, that it tied up British formations which were needed elsewhere; the second, that Italian submarines and destroyers based on Massawa threatened communications with Egypt and made the Red Sea a 'combat area' closed by US law to US ships carrying Lend-Lease supplies.

The seasonal rains from June to September 1940 turned most of eastern Sudan into a quagmire. In July the Italians captured – against token opposition – Kassala and Gallabat, just inside the Sudan, and then bogged down. At the end of September they lined up twenty-six battalions, fifty-seven aircraft, artillery, light tanks and armoured cars for a promenade to Berbera in British Somaliland. Wavell decided that it would be unbecoming to scuttle out without firing a shot, so the invasion was opposed by a mixed British-Indian-East African-Somali brigade which fought a good rearguard action and was tidily evacuated to Aden.

General Platt, the Kaid (C-in-C) of the Sudan, had a 1200-mile frontier with Abyssinia to watch with his meagre forces. But the arrival at Port Sudan in September of the 5th Indian Division, commanded by Major General L. M. Heath, transformed his position. With the addition of the three British battalions already in the Sudan, the division's two brigades were made up to three, the 9th, 10th and 29th, each of one British and two Indian battalions. It also provided most of 'Gazelle Force', one of those piratical semi-private armies which seem to suit the British military genius: under Brigadier Frank Messervy, this consisted of the motor-machine-gun batteries of the Sudan Defence Force, Skinner's Horse (5th Indian Divisional cavalry regiment) mounted in 15cwt trucks, a field regiment, RA, and one or two companies of infantry whenever they could be spared. Its role was to keep the Italians at Kassala in a state of jitters by giving them the impression that they were faced by overwhelming force.

From the west there were two entry ports into Italian East Africa, the southern via Gallabat into central Abyssinia; and the northern, via Keren and Asmara, to the port of Massawa. The latter was the more difficult, but would pay higher dividends.

At the end of December the leading brigade of the 4th Indian Division, the 11th Brigade, arrived straight from its victory at Sidi Barani. They went to the Kassala front, and were joined by the remainder of the division over the next six weeks. The Kaid now had the strength for an advance to take Massawa. During January the Italians made an orderly withdrawal from their advanced positions at Kassala, Agordat, Tessenei and Barentu to their main defensive position south-west of Keren. There they would stand and fight.

From Gallabat also they withdrew, unhurriedly, into the mountains, followed by a mobile column of all arms to see them off the premises. The pursuit was impeded mainly by an enormous number of mines, the first time the division had encountered them in any quantity. Sitting beside the driver of the leading carrier, his eyes keenly watching the road, was Second-Lieutenant Premindrah Singh Bhagat, 21st Field Company, Royal Bombay Sappers and Miners.

There were no electronic mine-detectors: the only way to find a mine was by watching the surface of the road and prodding any suspicious patch with a bayonet. During 1 February Bhagat's section, led by himself, cleared five minefields, and he was blown up once. On the 2nd he cleared five more without being blown up, but on the 3rd his carrier was blown up, with him in it, and the driver killed. He cleared that field and resumed the advance in another carrier. On the 4th he ran into an ambush and fought his way out of it with the anti-tank rifle on the carrier. Exhausted by continual strain, and with an eardrum blown out, he refused to be relieved, on the grounds that he now had the measure of the job and anyone else would have to learn it from scratch. Speed was of the essence, in a task which requires time, and he worked at top speed, and highest pressure, from dawn to dusk for five days. He was the key man in the pursuit, and was followed unhesitatingly through the minefields by the leading infantry in the column, the 2nd West Yorkshires. Bhagat was the first King's Commissioned Indian Officer to be awarded the VC.

Attempts to cut off the Italians retreating from Kassala failed, mainly owing to difficult terrain. In this fluid fighting there were strange adventures. A resourceful Moslem havildar of the 3/14th Punjab, finding himself at night in the midst of a company of Eritreans moving through the hills, moved with them, 'making Eritrean noises', until he could slip away. Gazelle Force were astounded to be charged by a squadron of Eritrean cavalry, erupting from the bush, kicking their shaggy horses into a furious gallop. They had to be shot down in clumps lest they get in among the guns. (Their leader, a former instructor of the cavalry school, survived to become Italian Ambassador in New Delhi, where he instructed the President's Bodyguard in show-jumping. He retired to County Meath for the fox-hunting, and used to attend Indian Army reunions in Dublin.)

On 2 February Gazelle Force came to a sudden halt against the Italian defences in the escarpment south-west of Keren. Like a mighty, craggy wall it towers up some 2,500 feet above the plain. The long-prepared defences were held by four fresh colonial brigades which had not yet been committed; six more which had been somewhat knocked about in the withdrawal to the Keren position; and a brigade of Italian infantry, Bersaglieri and Savoy Grenadiers, the best in their army, supported by field and mountain artillery. The escarpment is pierced only by the narrow and steep Dongolaas Gorge, up which wound the road to Keren. Italian engineers had blocked it by blowing down two hundred yards of cliff and boulders.

Reconnaisances by the divisional cavalry regiments, Skinner's Horse and the Central India Horse, discovered no way round. The Keren position must be stormed, and experts in mountain warfare lifted up their eyes unto the hills.

West of the gorge was a steep-sided, rocky feature later known as Cameron Ridge. About twelve hundred yards beyond, roughly parallel with and overlooking Cameron Ridge, was another ridge with Brig's Peak at the left end and the towering Mount Sanchil at the right end, rising steeply from the Dongolaas Gorge. Following the contours along the foot of Cameron Ridge and Sanchil ran the railway down to Keren. Across the gorge from Sanchil, and rather lower, was Mount Dologorodoc with a rudimentary fort on top.

The hills were as steep as anything in Waziristan, covered with immense boulders and wait-a-bit thorn. No army was more capable than the Indian Army of tackling them; but in haste to mechanize, they had discarded the best pack-transport and mountain artillery in the world. The first-line transport had to be the labouring backs of the infantry, one company

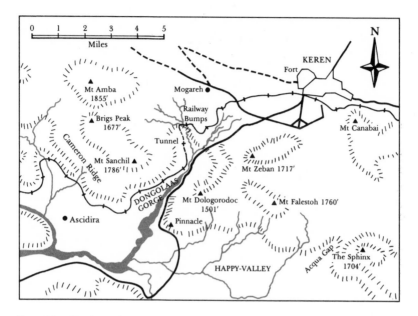

East Africa: Keren, February–March 1941

acting as porters for a battalion, or one platoon for a company. The Italians, in contrast, had plenty of pack-mules, and over the months had prepared mule-tracks to all the strongpoints in what was, in effect, a continuous line of wired and fortified positions. They also had ample pack-artillery, and heavy mortars with a longer range than the British 3-inch mortar.

The battle of Keren had two phases. The first, from 4 to 12 February, consisted of repeated attempts by 4th Indian Division to break through the mountain positions, first on the left, then on the right of the gorge; then again on the left. After prodigious exertions, toiling up almost perpendicular slopes burdened like Himalayan porters, grabbing and hauling with lacerated hands at the wait-a-bit thorns, the Camerons stormed Cameron Ridge. As they faced the last and steepest slope they were showered from above by hundreds of small, red, percussion grenades, exploding on impact, which were less lethal than Mills grenades but could be thrown much further and with their fine fragmentation inflicted flesh wounds which were painful and unpleasant. The Camerons took the ridge: it was never lost, and was a necessary starting-point for attacks on Brig's Peak and Sanchil.

Up and over the ridge, passing through the Camerons, toiled the 3/14th Punjab, down and across a ravine and up the even steeper slope to Brig's

Peak. From there at daybreak they looked down into Keren – and up, apprehensively, to Sanchil. Well might they be apprehensive. From behind the great mountain and along the narrow ridge linking it with Brig's Peak stormed two battalions of Savoy Grenadiers, fresh and rested. The tired Punjabis were thrust back to Cameron Ridge, which was barely held. Thereafter Cameron Ridge was manned by two battalions to whom every cartridge, biscuit and gallon of water had to be carried up two thousand feet on men's backs.

Brigadier Savory offered a handsome prize to the first battalion which – to the horror of the gunners – would take to pieces, with no proper tools, a 2-pounder anti-tank gun, carry it up to the top of a mountain and use it to blast enemy sangars. The prize was won by the 2/5th Mahrattas, their first plunging shot having a most spectacular effect.

Two days later 5th Indian Brigade tried to break through six miles to the east of the gorge, where there seemed to be a possible back way into Keren over Acqua Col. This time it was the 4/6th Rajputana Rifles' turn to face the exhausting climb through boulders and thorn-bushes, the shower of grenades and the counter-attacks as, breathless, they neared the top. The leading company commander was killed and Subadar Richpal Ram, a Jat, led the scramble over the crest. With only thirty men he stopped five counter-attacks and then, without a round of ammunition left, withdrew the survivors to the battalion's position below.

The battles of 10 and 11 February were carbon copies of those on the 5th and 7th. The Italians made skilful use of the steep reverse slopes behind each of their mountain-top positions. There they were safe from everything except high-angle fire of mountain howitzers and long-range mortars, of which the British had none. There they could assemble and await the moment for a counter-attack when their toiling, gasping opponents could hardly climb another step. The 3/1st Punjab, attacking from Cameron Ridge, actually reached the lower slopes of Sanchil before being driven back to their start-line having lost two commanding officers, three company commanders and 280 others. The 4/6th Rajputana Rifles fared no better than before on Acqua Col, and lost the valiant Subadar Richpal Ram, who was awarded a posthumous VC.

4th Indian Division had shot their bolt and needed a rest; 5th Indian Division was sent back for intensive training on the stiffest mountains they could find. The pause lasted from 12 February to 15 March while the sappers and miners performed prodigies of ingenuity and improvisation. They cleared blocked wells and sunk bore-holes, hacked mule-tracks out of the mountainsides, built defilading walls to protect the infantry. They even got the narrow-gauge railway working. It zigzagged from Biscia in the valley below, by the easiest gradients, to Keren, passing behind and below Cameron Ridge, potentially a most useful supply-line if only it could be made operational. The sappers rebuilt culverts, replaced rails buckled by explosives, converted a tunnel below Cameron Ridge into a shell-proof supply dump, cut the tops off wagons to lighten them and towed trains of them with a 15-cwt truck. Their masterpiece was a truck on a railway carriage, the truck engine driving the carriage wheels by means of a chain salvaged from a derelict lorry. Some useful reinforcements arrived: 40 captured mules, a Cypriot mule company, and a Palestine Commando, half-Jew, half-Arab. (How incredible that now sounds! Scarcely less incredible at that time was their CO's assessment of them: 'The Arabs aren't up to much, but the Jewboys are bloody marvellous.') From Port Sudan, 7th Brigade of the 4th Indian Division, with two Free French battalions, reached to within fifteen miles of Keren and made the Italians nervous about their right rear.

Gazelle Force was broken up, its harrassing task done, and Messervy took over command of 9th Brigade. He had commanded the first Indian cavalry regiment to be converted into armour, and combined the qualities of a high handicap polo-player and a staff college instructor. He was better at leading from the front than at driving from behind. Later, in the desert, the polo-player rather took over from the staff college instructor, and he learned the hard way that one could not take with Germans the liberties he had taken with Italians. But he made a wonderful recovery from what might have been a blighted career, and was the first divisional commander to beat the Japanese at their own game.

On the night of 14/15 March 5th Indian Division came up, and the two divisional commanders, Beresford-Peirse and Heath, set up adjacent headquarters for an attack by both divisions. Their plan was based on two assumptions: that it would take the sappers ten days to clear a way for the tanks through Dongolaas Gorge; and that they could not start work while the enemy had mortars, machine-guns and artillery observation posts on Sanchil on one side and Dologorodoc on the other. So 4th Indian Division must have another go at Brig's Peak and Sanchil. When Sanchil was taken, Messervy's 9th Indian Brigade, of 5th Indian Division, would take the fort on top of Dologorodoc. The gorge would then be strongly piqueted on both sides, and the sappers could get to work.

Again the attack on Sanchil failed, but Heath nevertheless went ahead with his attack on Dologorodoc. At 1030 hours on the 15th the 2nd Highland Light Infantry, temporarily under command of 9th Brigade, attacked the first hill, Pinnacle, on the lower slopes of the brigade's objective. Under very heavy fire from Sanchil their attack faltered, and they were pinned down for the whole of a hellish day, under a roasting sun, every move drawing fire. In the evening they were withdrawn.

From the easternmost spur of Cameron Ridge, Heath and Messervy looked down on the battlefield and made a new plan. They would try at night, when the fire from Sanchil would not be so devastating, initially with Lieutenant Colonel D. W. Reid's 3/5th Mahrattas and two companies of the 3/12th Frontier Force under command. The Mahrattas started up after last light, scrambling up the boulder-strewn slope while the percussion grenades exploded among them. Across the valley Heath and Messervy could hear through the din of battle – unusually loud, for the hills seemed to bottle it in – the Mahratta warcry, 'Shivaji Maharaj ki Jai!', and Reid muttering, 'Good little chaps! Stout little chaps!' At the fourth attempt they gained the summit of Pinnacle, and stayed there.

Reid joined them, and said to the 3/12th CO, 'My chaps seem to have shot their bolt. It's up to you now.' So the two Frontier Force companies passed through the Mahrattas and made for the next hillock, Pimple. The Mahrattas saw the flash of grenades and small-arms fire, heard the shots and shouts and screams – and then the Dogras and Pathans had Pimple.

For the 2nd West Yorkshires, the third battalion in the 9th Brigade, was reserved Dologorodoc itself. Their CO bade the company and platoon commanders note the inspiring effect their warcry had had on the Mahrattas: 'Shouldn't we have one too?' There was a pregnant pause, broken at last by a sergeant's constructive suggestion, 'What about "Fook! Fook!", Sir?'

So this warcry resounded through the night as the Yorkshiremen scaled Dologorodoc, and by dawn they had it. The 'fort' was a single concrete-lined trench, with neither traverses nor dugouts, girdling the rocky summit. It was a nasty place, under constant fire from Sanchil, Mount Zeban to the north-east and Mount Falestoh to the east. 29th Brigade tried, and failed, to take the last two. But to Dologorodoc the 9th Brigade clung like limpets, for it had a priceless, hitherto unsuspected asset: from it one could look down on, and at night reconnoitre, the roadblock in the Dongolaas gorge.

On the next two nights this was examined by sapper officers, who reported that it could be cleared in three days. Moreover, a patrol of the 6/13th Frontier Force Rifles, protecting the sapper recce, moved out along the railway line towards Railway Bumps, which seemed to be untenanted. It also seemed that these, not Sanchil, were the key to the gorge, which was actually in dead ground to Sanchil. And if once they could pass through the gorge the heavy I tanks to which the enemy had no answer, the battle was won. Said Heath, not given to dramatic utterances: 'Keren is ours!'

While 9 Brigade advanced down the reverse slopes of Dologorodoc to clear the southern defences of the roadblock, to 10 Brigade was given the vital task of capturing Railway Bumps. 10 Brigade was commanded by the little Welshman, T. W. ('Pete') Rees, who twenty-three years earlier had leaped onto a captured horse to pursue an escaping Turkish field-gun.

The Highland Light Infantry and the 4/10th Baluch spent a comfortable night in the tunnel below Cameron Ridge, smoking, drinking tea and rum, occasionally bursting into song. At 0330 hrs on 25 March they emerged cautiously from the tunnel mouth, half-expecting a blast of machine-gun fire; but nothing of the sort happened, so they deployed and advanced along the line of the railway, Baluchis to the right, HLI to the left. A few grenades were thrown from the lower slopes of Sanchil at the left-hand company of the Jocks, but the leading companies walked steadily on, neither shooting nor being shot at. By 0530 hrs they had taken the Railway Bumps, five hundred prisoners and a Bersaglieri Colonel, furious at this rude awakening.

At 0630 hrs the Sappers and Miners started work on the roadblock with pick and shovel and gelignite, working in relays, five-hour shifts. It took them two days and one night to clear it. The Italians, who for six weeks had fought so well, now seemed apathetic, and from their mountain eyries 4th Indian Division reported signs of them pulling out. At dawn on the 27th white flags were seen fluttering on the top of Sanchil, and soon the tanks and carriers were clanking and roaring over the rough new surface through the gorge.

Keren fell almost without fighting, and 5th Indian Division were welcomed by the Italians of Asmara, who dreaded a breakdown of law and order. The proprietor of the best hotel, a former Savoy Hotel waiter, served a grand celebration dinner in honour of the happy occasion.

Negotiations for the surrender of Massawa were conducted by Rees over the civil telephone line. The admiral commanding the port spun them out while as many ships as possible were scuttled, but surrendered on 8 April.

4th Indian Division returned in haste to Egypt, where it was needed. Heath departed to command a corps in Malaya, and was succeeded in command of 5th Indian Division by Brigadier A. G. O. M. Mayne from 9th Indian Brigade. In five weeks he ran to ground in Amba Alagi mountain – 11,000 feet high and honeycombed with caves and rock defences – the last 6,000 Italians who still had fight in them, under the Duke of Aosta himself.

Here, 235 miles from Asmara, it was an administrative rather than a military problem, solved by the exertions of the Sappers and Miners, the RIASC lorry drivers, and seven hundred local donkeys pressed into service as mule-substitutes. The enemy were shouldered off their forward positions, back to the massif itself. On 16 May, just when plans were being made for the assault, envoys with white flags arrived at an outpost of Skinner's Horse. By singular good fortune a shell had landed in a fuel store, and hundreds of gallons of petrol and oil had run into their main reservoir of drinking water. That finished them. On 19 May the Italian Army, with the traditional honours of war on which they set such store, marched past a guard of honour, deposited their arms and patiently awaited lorries to take them away. The Duke of Aosta entertained Mayne and his staff to luncheon. Over the port the Duke, a lover of England, remarked wistfully: 'I wonder if the days will ever return when one lunched at the Cavalry Club and drove down to Hurlingham for the polo.'

CHAPTER 14

The Arrival of Afrika Korps,
1941

After the departure of 4th Indian Division to Keren, no Indian formation took part in General O'Connor's amazing pursuit and destruction of the Italian Tenth Army. Even before it was over, the British Government was faced with a momentous choice: whether to press on to Tripoli, driving the Italians from North Africa and safeguarding Malta and its convoys from airfields in Libya; or whether to go to the aid of the Greeks who had heroically flung back an Italian invasion and were now faced by a German invasion. For reasons which perhaps owed more to admiration for a small and gallant ally than to the possibilities of a campaign against Germans on the mainland of Europe less than a year after being ignominiously ejected from Dunkirk, it was decided to send one Australian and one New Zealand division, and an armoured brigade, to Greece, giving this expedition the highest priority and all the best tanks; and relegating Cyrenaica to a care-and-maintenance basis, held only by 9th Australian Division, not fully trained or equipped, and the newly arrived 2nd Armoured Division (less one brigade in Greece), who were inexperienced, strangers to the desert and mounted largely in captured Italian M13 tanks, inferior machines and mechanically unreliable. In March 1941 there arrived Brigadier E. W. D. Vaughan's 3rd Indian Motor Brigade, consisting of the 2nd Royal Lancers, the 11th Prince Albert Victors Own Cavalry (PAVO) and the 18th Cavalry. They were mounted in unarmoured trucks without wireless, and armed with rifles, Bren-guns and a few Boyes anti-tank rifles ineffective against armour much thicker than a biscuit-tin. Their job was training and internal security, which meant guarding airfields and protecting Italian settlers against rapacious Arabs. A divisional cavalry regiment in unarmoured trucks could be very useful – mobile and employed mainly on reconnaissance, but with the division's infantry and artillery packing a punch behind. But three such regiments, with no infantry and guns behind them, did not make military sense. No one, however, imagined they would have to fight for months, least of all against German armour.

It was known in Cairo that some Germans had arrived in Tripoli in February, but it was not thought that they could mount a serious attack before May, by which time the British would have more and better tanks. But there was a new factor in the desert: General Erwin Rommel. By 24 March the Germans were fighting 2nd Armoured Division at El Agheila, and a week later they were chasing it helter-skelter back to Egypt, reduced to twenty-two medium and twenty-five light tanks and losing one every ten miles to mechanical failure.

The coastline of Cyrenaica may be likened to a bent bow, with the string represented by a 260-mile-long desert track stretching from Tobruk to the Gulf of Sirte west of Antelat. An army in pursuit, whether from the east or the west, may by following this desert track cut off the retreat of an army strung out along the coast between Benghazi and Derna. 7th Armoured Division had done that. It was to prevent Rommel doing likewise, in the opposite direction, that 3rd Indian Motor Brigade was ordered post-haste to El Mechili, a hundred miles west of Tobruk, to hold it as a base on which 2nd Armoured Division could withdraw and to delay the enemy until the Australians from Benghazi got back to Tobruk. The significance of El Mechili was that it was a big petrol- and supply-dump, and its wells were the only water on that desert route: without it no large force could drive from coast to coast.

The brigade arrived on the afternoon of 4 April only two regiments strong, the 18th Cavalry having been detached to Tobruk. They occupied a perimeter, about a mile in diameter, round an old Italian fort, the 2nd Lancers on the west and the PAVO on the east. They were joined by the 2nd Australian Anti-Tank Regiment, armed with Bofors AA guns which they had never fired, to be used in an anti-tank role but ineffective against medium tanks except at very close range.

The 5th was spent reconnoitring and digging. Enemy were located to the south and north-west, but there was no great apprehension because Brigadier Vaughan had been told that 2nd Armoured Division would soon be arriving. And arrive it did, on the 6th and 7th; Divisional Headquarters with 180 miscellaneous lorries, trucks, water-trailers, signals- and command-vehicles, hordes of clerks, signallers, storemen, mess servants, workshop personnel, mobile launderers – and one tank. The divisional commander put Vaughan in charge of this travelling circus and departed. In the evening of the 6th there arrived a German officer with a white flag, who recommended them to surrender as they were surrounded by overwhelming force.

A Blenheim bomber dropped a message which confirmed the surrounding, but Captain Jack Barlow's squadron of the 18th Cavalry found their way in from the north, having evaded some German armoured cars. The enemy positioned a dozen guns on a ridge 4,000 yards to the east, and there was nothing that could be done about them: a sortie by the Australians resulted only in the loss of one Bofors and several men. Another demand for surrender was rejected; and in a skirmish against Italian lorried infantry, thirty prisoners were taken.

On the 7th a third demand for surrender was brought in, signed by Rommel himself who was impatient to swat this fly and get his tanks to Tobruk. While it was being presented a light German plane flew slowly and insolently round, just out of range, examining every detail of the defences. When the German officer departed with the usual answer, a brisk bombardment started and went on for an hour and a half. Two more probing attacks were repulsed that night.

In denying El Mechili to the enemy for four days while the Tobruk defences were completed, the brigade had done its job. Vaughan ordered a break-out, heading east to El Adem, at first light on the 8th. The great amorphous mass of soft-skinned headquarters vehicles would move inside a protective box, the PAVO leading and guarding the flanks, the 2nd Lancers doing rearguard. But they must pass at short range five enemy guns positioned just outside the perimeter, so first these would be taken out by Barlow's squadron of the 18th and the armoured division's tank. The night was spent in preparations for the move, in reflection on what was awaiting them in the morning, and in 'wistful regret that the powers that be could not have arranged things a little better'.

Having waited in vain for the tank and lost the advantage of the half-light, Barlow's squadron took off at 0630 hrs. They swung round to the left of the guns, and then drove all out at them, dismounted and went in with the bayonet. After killing many of the crews and putting four guns out of action, they remounted and drove on, having lost only fifteen killed and missing in a very dashing exploit. The tank arrived late and was brewed up.

Tiny Gait was a sixteen-stone Calcutta business man, a supernumerary officer in the PAVO Sikh squadron: that is to say, he should have been in Cairo waiting to replace the first officer casualty. He was therefore expendable, and was accordingly detailed to lead the first troop out, but not to lose touch with the squadron commander, Brian Prosser, who would be following behind.

'As we started to move off, the enemy guns opened up a terrific barrage at us, and the dust and smoke from exploding shells, together with the bright sunlight in our eyes, made it difficult to see. I realized we were losing touch, so halted the troop in the middle of the barrage, whilst other trucks and lorries continued to move past us. I was very scared and smoking furiously to try to cover this up. My driver was swaying back and forth in his seat, chanting prayers, and I thought my last moment had come when a shell landed within a few feet but failed to explode. I was relieved to see Brian coming up out of the dust and smoke and we got going again'

All the detailed orders for advanced guards and flank guards, and for speed and distance between vehicles and columns went by the board. In the dust and smoke and all-pervading confusion trucks jinked and dodged like snipe between enemy tanks and guns, with many a collision avoided by a few feet. The PAVO got out with the loss of about two troops. Brigade headquarters followed them, and a number of the leading vehicles broke through. 'The ancillary troops and the tail of the main body, however, turned back and huddled in a mass near the fort.' As for 2nd Armoured Division, 'they never made any noticeable effort to move'. The PAVO, quite rightly, pressed on rather than be put in the bag with the two headquarters. Brigadier Vaughan, who could have got away, decided he should stay with divisional headquarters. There also remained the 2nd Lancers, who would have been rearguard in the dash for freedom.

To Major Rajendrasinhji, commanding B Squadron, the situation was far from clear. He had a wireless set, but it was of little use as the only other set in the regiment, at RHQ, was off the air. So he sent his second-in-command, Desmond Reynolds, to find out what was happening. Reynolds returned with the news that the PAVO had gone; so Rajendra went to RHQ where Lieutenant Colonel de Salis told him that orders for the break-out were cancelled: he should return to his position on the perimeter. As he was re-positioning his squadron, he saw Reynolds with two troops surrounded by enemy tanks, and mentally wrote them off.

He drove to A Squadron to ask if they were in touch with RHQ. Major Dorman replied, 'No, and not likely to be.' Looking where he pointed, Rajendra was appalled to see enemy tanks standing round his regiment's headquarters. (The Colonel was captured and the Adjutant dead.) He was contemplating a rescue or counter-attack when he received a message from the Brigadier that another break-out, to the west, was to be attempted, and he would again be rearguard.

Having disposed his troops accordingly he watched the armoured divisional headquarters move out. They did not move far: coming under artillery and machine-gun fire, they stopped and turned back. He then happened to meet Major Eden, commanding the Australian Bofors battery, who told him that divisional headquarters had surrendered. Rajendra suggested 'beating it', and Eden heartily agreed.

They drove off westward, in two columns, at about 0815 hours

'The trucks were well spread out. We moved fast and by zigzagging through enemy fire-belts across our path we were able to get through without any casualties. We could see the strike of the machine-gun bullets on the sandy ground and it was fairly easy to avoid them. Some enemy guns were in our path and we just drove at and through them, the gunners throwing up their hands as the trucks roared past. We were soon clear of the opposition and continued going until about 1230 hours, when it was decided to turn north and get into a hide in some broken ground. This we reckoned to be about 35 to 40 miles from Mechili.'

They posted sentries, redistributed loads and petrol, made tea, cooked a meal and slept, for almost the first time in three days. In late afternoon an enemy column of tanks and other vehicles halted about two thousand yards from them and two scout cars came closer, but they lay doggo and were not spotted. At dusk the enemy withdrew to the south, and at 2030 hours they set off again, in three columns, line ahead, with thirty-yard intervals between columns.

'Just before dawn we had 15 minutes' halt, had some tea and decided to wheel homeward to the east. The columns now opened out to about 100 yards intervals and the pace was increased. There was a slight early morning ground mist. We had hardly gone a mile when suddenly a harbour loomed up out of the mist, straight in our path and only about 300 yards away. We could not swerve so made straight for them. The two flank columns swung round outwards and opened fire with their two-

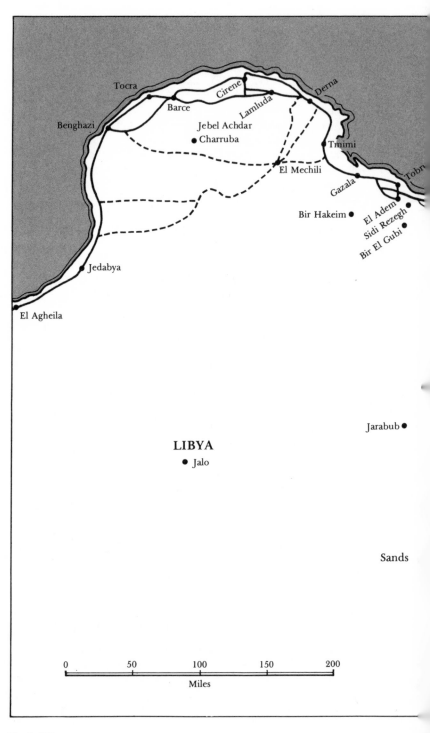

Tocra

Cirene

Derna

Barce

Lamluda

Benghazi

Jebel Achdar

Charruba

Tmimi

El Mechili

Tobr

Gazala

Bir Hakeim

El Adem

Sidi Rezegh

Bir El Gubi

Jedabya

El Agheila

Jarabub

LIBYA

Jalo

Sands

0   50   100   150   200

Miles

North Africa

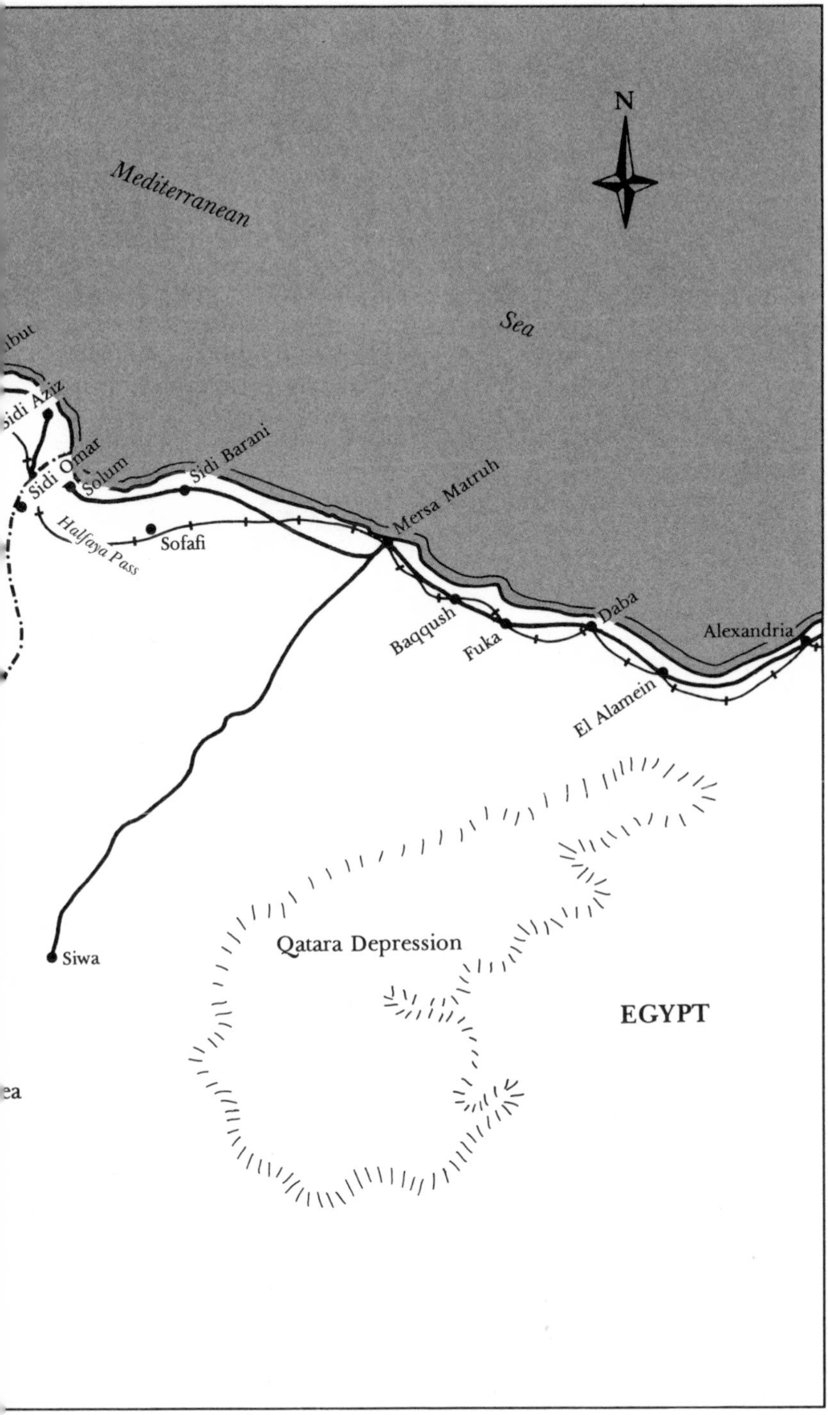

Mediterranean

Sea

N

Sidi Aziz

Sidi Omar

Solum

Sidi Barani

Mersa Matruh

Halfaya Pass

Sofafi

Baqqush

Fuka

Daba

Alexandria

El Alamein

Qatara Depression

EGYPT

Siwa

pounders while our trucks dashed straight at the harbour. The noise of trucks, guns and men shouting and letting off a few rounds was too much for the enemy, and we found them all with their hands up. . . . It was a wonderful sight; here were in our hands some 300 of the enemy who could have shot us to ribbons had they observed even the most elementary precautions. The morale of our troops went up sky-high. The enemy were made to sit down, searched, and their trucks made unserviceable with hammers. We also relieved them of water and petrol (and most probably valuables as well).'

They kept the best prisoners, let the rest go and drove on. Their luck held, and at two o'clock next morning they arrived at El Adem and slumped down beside the road like corpses. At daybreak they found Reynolds and thirty-seven men of B Squadron, which was thus almost complete; Dorman had brought out twenty from A; so only C Squadron was missing.

The 18th Cavalry, less Barlow's squadron, were the only Indians in Tobruk, with the Australian garrison. Until relieved in July they held a sector of the perimeter, wired, dug, patrolled, raided and got on extremely well with the Australians. They also acquired the Admiral Sahib.

No one really knew how Admiral Sir Walter Cowan, DSO, ever got to Tobruk. It seems to have been in his capacity of Honorary Secretary to the Warwickshire Hunt, and it is doubtful if his name appeared on any Middle East Forces establishment or pay-roll. But he adopted the 18th and they adopted him, as 'Naval Liaison Officer'. He was immensely popular with officers and men, and invaluable, for his knowledge of war extended from a gunboat on the Nile during Kitchener's Omdurman campaign (where he won his first DSO) to the bridge of a battleship at Jutland. The jawans used to say that if Britain's old men were like the Admiral Sahib, what hope had Germany of winning the war? He was often heard humming 'Danny Boy' – 'a favourite of Kitchener's. I've heard him singing it as he rode across the desert.'

Tobruk was held, a strong point on Rommel's flank inhibiting any dash for the Nile valley. But when 4th Indian Division arrived back from Eritrea, looking forward to rest and recuperation in Cairo, they found that the position in the Middle East was far more serious than it had been before Sidi Barani. Greece and Crete were lost. Only half of the 60,000 men sent there had returned, badly mauled, having lost all their tanks, and in no state to fight for some time. Cyprus seemed open to an airborne invasion like Crete, facilitated by the Vichy French in Syria who were always ready to oblige the Germans. Iraq and Persia were seething with German intrigue and propaganda. Worst of all, Rommel's Afrika Korps – three German and six Italian divisions – having invested and bypassed Tobruk, were ten miles inside Egypt, holding the Halfaya Pass.

With two divisions shut up in Tobruk, 2nd Armoured Division destroyed and 7th Armoured Division back in the Delta without tanks, Wavell could muster only five infantry brigades and part of an armoured brigade to defend Egypt. Nevertheless the Prime Minister, indomitable, implacable, impossible to please and having no empathy with a dour, inarticulate military genius, constantly nagged him to embark on a fresh offensive to relieve Tobruk long before Wavell was ready. The arrival of 4th Indian Division, and of the replacement tanks for 7th Armoured Division at Alexandria on 12 May, made such an operation just possible, once the tanks had been overhauled after their long sea voyage and modified for desert conditions, and the crews had been given a few days to get to know them. Operation Battleaxe was fixed for 15 June.

Its intention was firstly to destroy the enemy armour, and secondly to relieve Tobruk, invested by about two thirds of the enemy forces. The remaining third – 13,200 infantry, 70 field guns and 100 tanks, two-fifths German – were strongly entrenched in positions north and west of the Halfaya Pass, and on the coastal plain. These must be defeated before Tobruk could be relieved. Wavell's forces were about equal to Rommel's except in the vital arm, tanks, in which they were markedly inferior in quantity and, as it transpired, in quality, maintenance and tactical training.

Operation Battleaxe was a total failure. Seventeen out of the eighteen I tanks supporting 4th Indian Division's attack from Halfaya to the sea were ablaze in the first few minutes. The Germans had unmasked the weapon which was to dominate the armoured battle for the next four years: the 88-millimetre anti-aircraft gun adapted for an anti-tank role. With its 16lbs shell, very high velocity and flat trajectory, it was the ultimate anti-tank weapon of its day, able to smash the heaviest tank at 2,000 yards. When the British rear was threatened by German armour, almost intact while the British had lost in all ninety-six tanks, there was nothing for it but to call the attack a reconnaissance and withdraw to the original positions.

Battleaxe made it distressingly clear that British tanks were no match for the Panzers in quality. The Crusader, of which there had been high hopes, was mechanically unreliable and armed only with a 2-pounder (40mm) gun, quite outclassed by the 50mm gun in the Panzer III firing a 4$\frac{1}{2}$lbs shot. The I tank, with an effective cross-country speed of only about 6 m.p.h., was too slow to operate with Crusaders in the armoured division, and it also was armed only with the 2-pounder. Numbers might compensate for British deficiencies in quality, training and doctrine, but in the summer of 1941 numbers were lacking.

CHAPTER 15

Sideshows,

1941–42

Meanwhile a military coup in Britain's most pampered ally, Iraq, had installed a government headed by the pro-German General Rashid Ali Gailani. With commendable celerity and in accordance with treaty rights with the ousted but legitimate government, the 8th Indian Division was sent to Basra, where it landed unopposed. Rashid Ali countered by investing the RAF base at Habbaniya, defended by the British-officered Iraq Levies. Advancing from Basra with a good deal more efficiency than had been displayed in 1914–16, the 8th Indian Division occupied Bagdad and, in conjunction with a mobile column from Palestine, raised the siege of Habbaniya. Rashid Ali's rebellion, potentially a most dangerous threat to the Abadan oil installations, collapsed. (It did not escape notice that the Iraq army was plentifully supplied, by Britain, with modern equipment for which India had been pleading in vain.) 10th Indian Division joined 8th, and both remained in Iraq – just in case. The oil installations were even more vital to Britain than they had been in 1914–18.

Syria, under Vichy French administrators and an anglophobe Resident General, Dentz, was a tougher proposition. The authorities deemed it their duty, as patriotic Frenchmen, to mitigate the rigours of the German occupation of Northern France by indulging every German wish, even giving facilities on Syrian airfields for Axis planes on their way to help Rashid Ali. General Catroux, the Free French Commissioner in the Middle East, believed that Axis ground and airborne forces would soon be in Syria, probably via Cyprus, and welcomed by Dentz. Wavell was obliged, with extreme reluctance, to open up another front. Dentz had under his command twenty infantry battalions, ninety good tanks, and about a hundred aircraft. Against these Wavell could field two Australian brigades, 5th Brigade of 4th Indian Division, part of 1st (horsed) Cavalry Division in Palestine, and six Free French battalions somewhat mixed in quality. The risk seemed to be justified by the erroneous belief that the Vichy French would not fight hard, especially against their Gaullist compatriots. But they did, hating the Gaullists as traitors to Marshal Pétain and the British as deserters at Dunkirk and subsequently stabbers-in-the-back. However, within three weeks Damascus was taken, and the Vichy authorities accepted defeat and departed.

On 22 June, the day the Australians and Free French went into Damascus, the Germans went into Russia. This changed the whole character of the war: it raised the stakes. Since Dunkirk, the most optimistic could not realistically hope for better than a stalemate, Britain and

Germany each unable decisively to defeat the other. Now, if only the Red Army would hold and the Americans increase their help through Lend-Lease, one could even fantasize about winning. If the Red Army did not hold – and the most informed military opinion was divided on this – it was no fantasy at all to envisage losing; for the summer of 1942 would see the Panzer divisions pouring through the Caucasus, heading for the Iraq and Persian oilfields, with little to stop them. On the pretext that the Persian government would not or could not expel Axis agents, but really to give depth to the defence of the oilfields and to open a supply route to Russia, on 25 August a joint invasion of Persia was mounted by the Russians in the north and the 8th and 10th Indian Divisions from Iraq which, against very little opposition, occupied as much of Persia as suited their purposes. The old Shah Reza was deposed and his son, supposedly more compliant, installed in his place. It was all a most unprincipled transaction, justifiable only on grounds of war-necessity.

The Chiefs of Staff considered a German advance on the oilfields to be a greater risk than a breakthrough to Alexandria and the Suez Canal. So up to six infantry divisions and one Indian armoured division were tied up in Persia, Iraq and northern Syria, even after events at Stalingrad had ruled out the possibility of such a disaster. Bored, bitterly resentful at being left out of the war, neglected and apparently forgotten, they planned and trained for a campaign which never took place, constructed 'brigade boxes' and 'defended localities' and anti-tank defences in every pass through which the enemy might come. Their Russian allies were far from helpful. The only people who can have got any satisfaction out of the job were the RIASC companies, 203 and 204, who carried supplies from Baluchistan to the Russians. In six-wheeled, 'ten-ton' lorries (which in fact weighed twenty-one tons loaded) they drove 730 miles from Baluchistan to Tabriz, and back, again and again and again, carrying ammunition, bitumen, food, petrol, supplies of all kinds, starting their journey in a temperature of 126 degrees and ending it in blizzards, snow and ice. Some of the roads were terrifying, zigzagging down from high passes with a sheer drop of hundreds of feet over the edge. The first convoy to arrive at Tabriz, with a load of artillery ammunition, was met by a guard of honour; and when it was all over, a subadar and a havildar were awarded the Order of the Red Star. At least the Russians appreciated *their* efforts.

Whatever the long-term, strategic results of our acquiring a gallant, if unwilling, ally, the immediate results were far from welcome. All sorts of British and American hardware – tanks, planes, lorries, guns and much else – which had been promised to the Middle East Command and India, were sent instead to Russia, and much of it went to the bottom of the Barents Sea while our gallant ally complained in the most objectionable terms of the cowardice and incompetence of the British sailors who went to the bottom with it.

In India the war effort was perceptible, though often frustrated. Officers and men worked extremely hard, even in the afternoons, and there was very little leave. The modernization of the army proceeded apace: that is to say, as apace as was possible with only a trickle of modern equipment. It was far more difficult than in Britain because there was no civilian motor infrastucture – no car factories, no village garages or petrol stations, very few mechanics and public buses and transport companies. However, apprehensive jawans chugged over parade grounds and ventured into the countryside in decrepit lorries; and cavalry regiments received a few obsolete tanks. They used to break down in the most awkward circumstances for reasons which defeated their drivers and officers. One ground to a halt, and remained for a long time awaiting the arrival of spare parts, outside the gate of the Viceroy's House in New Delhi. The regiment was mortified when the Delhi Hunt's Appointments Card announced that hounds would meet 'At the Old Tank'.

Some armoured cars arrived, improvised in South Africa. Faith in them was undermined by the discovery that the armour could be penetrated by an ordinary .303 bullet; but they *looked* better than a battered truck. In India a factory started producing an armoured carrier, to do the job of the Bren carrier, but on wheels, not tracks. It was a creditable improvisation, under-powered but better than nothing.

In armoured regiments much effort was devoted to training the gunners to fire when moving across country. It was the received wisdom that the ability to shoot straight while on the move, while the Germans always halted to fire, would confer an advantage to compensate for puny tank-guns. Moreover, by racing round their flanks, while they obligingly stood still, one would be able to shoot at the thinly armoured sides of their tanks. The flaw in this was that no one could shoot straight while on the move.

Squadron and company commanders made tremendous efforts to fit square pegs into square holes. The brightest jawans were generally chosen to be wireless operators, the next brightest to be mechanics. The least intellectually gifted tended to be detailed as gunners, which was all wrong because everyone's object was to put the gunner within range of the enemy. There did seem to be some correlation between horsemanship and driving: the best remount-riders often made the best drivers and mechanics; and certainly the prize marksmen with the rifle were best at hitting the target with every kind of weapon, including, eventually, 75mm guns.

Indian signallers were superbly trained in sending and receiving by Morse code with flag, Aldis lamp and helio. But these recondite arts were useless in mobile desert war. Nor was line much use, even in defensive positions: inevitably it would be cut, or the earth-pins uprooted by the passage of a tank or carrier. 'Line dis *hai*, Sahib,' the signaller would say resignedly, and trudge off into the dark to find and repair the break. In the desert only radio telephony (R/T) was of the slightest use for signalling, but in 1940 and 1941 replacement signallers, perfect in flag, lamp and helio, would arrive at 4th and 5th Indian Division having never even seen a wireless set.

Harry Clive, a subaltern of the Royal Corps of Signals in 7th Indian

Brigade, watched their struggles with admiration and sympathy.

'These gentle men had a sympathy with those satanic machines. Today when radio communication is almost indistinguishable from telephone communication, and frequently more reliable, few people can realize the uncertainty of those far-off days of valves, tuning dials, massive aerials, cumbersome batteries and the terrible two-stroke charging engines which kept everyone awake at night. Today a handset is lifted or a button pressed and conversation begins. Yesterday endless fiddling with knobs, coarse and fine tuning dials had to take place before the radio operator could turn with a look of joy in his eyes to an impatient staff officer and say the words, unforgettable to any signaller, "Through, Sahib." Later in Italy many was the time when a battle hinged on a Punjabi signaller forcing those magic invisible waves through the ether by sheer will-power.'

All training in India was planned with a view to fighting in the Western Desert and Persia. That would be the Indian Army's war, and for that they prepared in the Punjab, the Sind desert and Baluchistan. Hardly a thought was given to Burma and Malaya, except to sympathize with the poor buggers who were bogged down there, with no chance of ever seeing action.

CHAPTER 16

Eighth Army Advances, 1941

In July 1941 Wavell was replaced as C-in-C Middle East by Auchinleck. Wavell was, in the best German opinion, that very rare phenomenon: a British general with a touch of genius. But his taciturnity and his patent distrust of all politicians displeased the Prime Minister. The change was welcomed by the Indian Army. They had nothing against Wavell; indeed they greatly admired him. But Auchinleck was something special and their very own. He was their ideal of a general, with a noble presence, a reputation for winning, a thorough understanding of the Indian Army and an empathy with the jawan. On 27 September Western Desert Force was upgraded (though not otherwise strengthened) into Eighth Army.

Like Wavell, Auchinleck was under ceaseless pressure from Downing Street to attack and relieve Tobruk *now*, or at the latest next week. The enemy in the Western Desert consisted of 15 and 21 Panzer Divisions; 90 Light Division, motorized infantry very strong in armoured vehicles, self-propelled and anti-tank guns; Ariete, the not-to-be-despised Italian armoured division; and seven Italian infantry divisions, of which two were motorized. Four of these infantry divisions were investing Tobruk; one was on lines of communication in Tripolitania; and the remaining two were deployed in a number of all-round-defended localities or 'boxes' in an arc stretching into the desert from its extremities near Tobruk and Halfaya. Based on these boxes, poised to sally forth to attack or counter-attack, were the German divisions and Ariete.

Early in September 1941, 4th Indian Division, commanded by Major General Messervy, moved up to the frontier area. The infantry busied themselves with reconnoitring enemy positions from Halfaya to three 'boxes', Libyan Omar, Omar Nuova and Cove (known collectively as 'the Omars'), twenty miles south-west of Halfaya. The Central India Horse (CIH), the divisional cavalry regiment, still mounted in unarmoured trucks, roamed far into the desert, mapping minefields, supply dumps, enemy positions and gaps in the wire; shadowing and shooting up enemy convoys; rescuing baled-out RAF pilots.

The date of Auchinleck's offensive, Operation Crusader, was fixed at 18 November. The lead role was allocated to XXX Corps, consisting of 7th Armoured Division (which had two armoured brigades), 4th Armoured Brigade, 1st South African Division and 22nd Guards Brigade. These would swing wide round the Omars to destroy the enemy armour and relieve Tobruk. The Tobruk garrison would sally out at the opportune moment to join hands with XXX Corps. To XIII Corps, consisting of 4th

Indian Division, 2nd New Zealand Division and 1st Army Tank Brigade, was allocated a supporting role: to contain the enemy in the frontier area in order to protect the right flank of XXX Corps.

Even the Prime Minister realized that the vital arm in the desert was armour. In this, Eighth Army had a numerical advantage: 665 tanks against 505. But (as the Prime Minister failed to grasp) the Germans had a huge advantage in quality. Of the British tanks 210 were the I tanks in the Army Tank Brigades, heavily armoured but very slow. They had been effective against Italians, but were sitting ducks for German anti-tank guns. The 290 tanks in the two brigades of 7th Armoured Division were mainly Crusaders, known to be mechanically unreliable; and the 165 tanks in 4th Armoured Brigade were the new American General Stuart tanks (euphemistically known to the media as 'the Honey'), very fast and mechanically excellent, but lightly armoured. On the German side half the tanks were the Mk III and Mk IV, mounting 50mm and 75mm guns which fired HE shells and solid, armour-piercing shot weighing respectively $4\frac{1}{2}$ and 14lbs. No British tank had a gun bigger than the 2-pounder, and the 37mm gun in the Stuart tank was even smaller. So no British tank could kill a German tank at a range longer than about 600 yards, if that, but a German Mk III or Mk IV could kill a British tank at twice that range. In anti-tank guns the discrepancy was even greater. The Germans had the terrible 88mm, long-barrelled 7.62 guns captured from the Russians, 75mm guns and their standard, long barrelled 50mm. The British had only the 2-pounder. In fact the only British weapon which could knock out a panzer at, say, 1,000 yards was the 25-pounder gun-howitzer, firing solid shot over open sights. But this was a field gun, far from suitable for anti-tank work since its trajectory was too high. Moreover 25-pounders shooting at tanks were not doing the job for which they were designed: firing HE shells at infantry and transport. When, therefore, the Prime Minister informed the House of Commons that Eighth Army was 'at least as well armed' as the Germans, he was talking through his hat. But the two forces were about equal in the air.

The Germans were also much more skilled in armoured warfare. The inadequacy of the pop-guns in their tanks encouraged the British in the idea that to destroy the panzers they must charge in to close quarters, relying on speed to escape punishment. But the Germans were already beginning to realize that the best tank-killer was not another tank (as the British supposed) but the anti-tank gun, and their anti-tank guns were such that they could put this theory into practice. So they were more adept than Eighth Army in the integration of armour, infantry and anti-tank guns. Time and again they lured the British onto a screen of anti-tank guns cunningly concealed.

At the start of 'Crusader' 4th Indian Division had only 7th Indian Brigade available. 5th and 11th Brigades, for which there was no transport, remained respectively at Mersa Matruh and Halfaya. 7th Brigade's role was to attack, and if possible capture but at least mask, the Omars; while the New Zealanders swung further out into the desert and behind the enemy positions on the frontier.

During the night of 28/29 November XXX Corps passed through the frontier wire at Bir Sheferzen and headed north-west. XIII Corps followed, and at dawn 7th Brigade passed through the gap and right-wheeled to head north, the New Zealand division on its left. Eighth Army moving across the desert in open formation was an extraordinary sight, thousands of trucks, tanks, carriers, armoured cars and gun-towers like a great fleet at sea, all keeping station, their wireless aerials bending and swaying with the speed of their progress. For once there was little dust: it had rained heavily during the night and the atmosphere was crystal-clear.

At first all went very well. 7th Armoured Division had a successful encounter with Ariete. The armour then wheeled north to Sidi Rezegh, only eighteen miles south-east of Tobruk. On the morning of the 20th the South Africans arrived there, freeing the armour for its battle with the panzers, and the Tobruk garrison was told to break out next day.

XIII Corps, which had been held back until it was seen how XXX Corps fared, were now ordered forward. The New Zealanders swung round behind the Omars and drove north to the Trigh Capuzzo road. The CIH cut the Omars' communications, and 7th Brigade prepared to attack them on the 22nd. The 1st Royal Sussex were to go for Omar Nuova, the 4/16th Punjab for Libyan Omar two miles to the west; and 4/11th Sikhs were to mask, but not assault, Cove, four miles to the north.

The Royal Sussex had two squadrons of I tanks in support. Six of these had tracks blown off by mines, but the infantry surged forward through the trenches and weapon-pits, taking 1,500 prisoners.

4/16th Punjab, with two more tank squadrons, then passed through Omar Nuova heading for Libyan Omar. The tanks made for a gap in the minefield, but it was covered by 88s, dug in flush with the ground. In a few minutes nearly all the tanks of the leading squadron were ablaze, belching flames and black greasy smoke. The second squadron sheered away from trouble and ran slap into a minefield where a dozen tanks, immobilized by mines, were smashed by the 88s. When the Punjabis debused and formed up to attack, they had only five tanks instead of thirty. Nevertheless they went in, stalking, moving round, taking from the rear each weapon-pit and strongpoint, hurling hundreds of the red Italian grenades they had brought from Keren. By evening they had 500 prisoners and had cleared the eastern part of the box. Next day, in many little platoon and company actions, they took a thousand more prisoners and increased their hold to one third of the box. But they were then told to go no further, for elsewhere 23 November had been a day of disaster.

The sortie from Tobruk, having got within five miles of the South Africans, was forced back again. 7th Armoured Division and 4th Armoured Brigade did indeed seek out the enemy armour, as ordered, and were almost destroyed. The 5th South African Brigade was overrun by a hundred panzers. The New Zealanders, having taken Capuzzo, Solum and

Sidi Aziz, could move no further westward. XXX Corps and XIII Corps were separated by some fifty miles with the German armour between them. The situation was so serious that General Cunningham, commanding Eighth Army, recommended that the operation be called off while he still had some tanks to defend Egypt. Auchinleck sacked him, took control of the battle himself, and then gave command of the Army to General Neil Ritchie. This was over-calling the hand of a very capable Deputy Chief-of-Staff who had never commanded even a division in action. It was Auchinleck's weakness that he picked his subordinates badly. As an Indian Army officer he perhaps did not know enough senior officers in the British service.

If XXX Corps could not relieve Tobruk, XIII Corps must do so, moving along the coast. But Rommel had other ideas, and launched – or, rather, led – his armour on a great raid, a sort of Jeb Stuart ride, deep into Eighth Army's soft, headquarters-cluttered rear. Messervy was astonished to see hundreds of lorries stampeding past his headquarters at Bir Sheferzen, heading with extreme speed in an easterly direction. Late in the afternoon XXX Corps headquarters arrived with news that the panzers were on their heels. The utter confusion was compounded by the RAF raining bombs on just and unjust alike. All through the night the withdrawal, to use a polite term, continued. 4th Indian, however, did not join it, but closed up its harbours, recalled the 4/11th Sikhs from Cove, escorted a supply convoy to the New Zealanders, and arranged the defence of sundry supply dumps. Messervy had already summoned 5th Brigade, and now heard that 11th Brigade would soon join him. The night was bright with German flares: enemy harbours seemed to be all round them, and a panzer column drove past only a mile away. They judged it prudent to move, 'almost on tiptoe', through seven miles of enemy-infested desert to Omar Nuova.

But from the flap and chaos resulted two significant little victories, both won by the British field gunners of 4th Indian Division. The first was south-east of Cove, where a South African armoured car raced up to 4/11th Sikhs with news of enemy armour approaching. The Sikhs were accompanied by 1st Field Regiment, which promptly got down its trails, loaded with solid shot and prepared for action over open sights. Out of the dust twenty-eight Mk IIIs and Mk IVs appeared and advanced at speed, firing their machine-guns while the gunners lay very flat beside their 25-pounders. When the tanks were within 800 yards, the gunners jumped up and opened fire, loading, sighting and firing at top speed. Twice the panzers came on, twice they went back, and eventually withdrew, leaving seven blazing wrecks. A few hours later an exact replica of this battle was fought on the south perimeter of Omar Nuova, with even a Medium Regiment depressing its guns to take advantage of a unique opportunity. There six tanks were brewed up and five more, disabled, were dealt with by the sappers during the night.

Extraordinary things happened during these two days of chaos. A field ambulance of 4th Indian Division was captured by German armoured

North Africa: Jebel Achdar, 1941

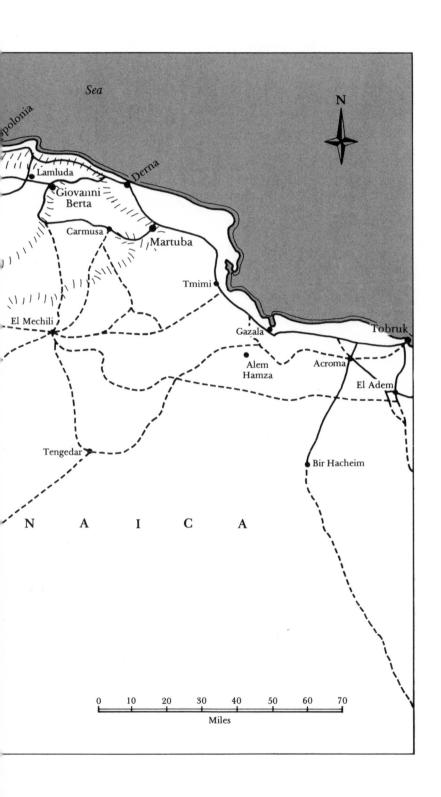

Sea

N

polonia

Lamluda

Derna

Giovanni
Berta

Carmusa

Martuba

Tmimi

El Mechili

Gazala

Tobruk

Alem
Hamza

Acroma

El Adem

Tengedar

Bir Hacheim

N A I C A

0   10   20   30   40   50   60   70
Miles

cars, and told to continue working under orders of an Italian officer who a few minutes earlier had been a prisoner-patient. During the night a British gunner officer arrived and asked where he was.

'At Boundary Post 57 on the Libyan border,' muttered Major Aird, busy operating. 'It is in enemy hands and we are prisoners of war. The guard happens to have stepped outside for the moment.'

'How very embarrassing,' said the visitor, 'I don't think I should linger.' And departed.

Next day the field ambulance was rescued by a patrol of the CIH and the prisoners became the jailers.

Elsewhere an Indian lorry full of wounded arrived by mistake in a German harbour. The Germans, having no food for prisoners, mended two punctures, re-dressed some wounds and directed them to the nearest British harbour. Such events set the pattern for a sort of rough chivalry which distinguished the desert war from other campaigns in World War II.

If Rommel hoped that his foray would frighten Auchinleck into pulling back from Tobruk, he mistook his man. The Auk maintained his objective, and it was the panzer divisions who had to pull back, disappointed in their hopes of linking up with the garrisons of the Omars or of replenishing their petrol tanks from Eighth Army dumps. The New Zealanders battered their way along the coast road and the Trigh Capuzzo, and by the 25th were within five miles of Tobruk. 4th Indian Division resumed its attack on Libyan Omar.

This was stoutly defended by a tough, capable German commander. There was no question of quickly over-running the last square mile of the box still in enemy hands. But the 3/1st Punjab from 5th Indian Brigade, and the 4/16th Punjab from 7th Brigade, bombed and shot and bayoneted their way into one weapon-pit and strongpoint after another, until the night of 29/30 November when the last hundred defenders slipped quietly away.

There followed several days of confused fighting, during which 11th Brigade arrived, commanded by Brigadier Anderson who had led the Camerons at Sidi Barani. By 7 December the division, now part of XXX Corps, was reorganized into three brigade groups, each with infantry, tanks and guns, for the pursuit.

That day news was received of the Japanese attack on Pearl Harbor. To men in the desert this seemed of less interest than making contact two days later with the defenders of Tobruk.

There followed an exhilarating chase through the scrubby, boulder-strewn Jebel Achdar hills, a fearful obstacle-course for drivers accustomed only to the open desert. The CIH acted as cavalry should, galloping their old trucks through the rugged country parallel with the coastal road, scrambling down the escarpment to shoot up group after group of lorries streaming away to the west. One squadron was swept along helplessly with the tide of retreat, and extricated itself with difficulty in the darkness with 150 of the 'best' prisoners, mostly German.

Two companies and the carriers of the 4/11th Sikhs, crashing and skidding and slithering down the escarpment, reached Derna airfield just as twelve laden Junkers transport planes arrived overhead, circled and settled in. The Sikhs held their fire until the last plane landed, and then opened up with every weapon they had. Only two Junkers got away, and the jubilant Sikhs found themselves possessed of tremendous booty – petrol, food, wine, weapons of all kinds and 185 aircraft in various states of air-worthiness.

But it was no rout. Rommel withdrew with expert celerity, but used his dwindling supply of tanks to turn on his pursuers. At El Gubi on 5 December they overran two companies of Mahrattas; and at Alem Hamza on the 16th destroyed a whole battalion, the 1st Buffs. At the end of the month, near Antelat, they knocked out 65 tanks of 22nd Armoured Brigade. He was a master of the aggressive rearguard action, and while 4th Indian Division were enjoying the limited amenities of Benghazi, entered by the CIH on Christmas Eve, the Afrika Korps was ensconsed behind the marshes of El Agheila, not (as the media suggested) 'licking its wounds', but awaiting the arrival of new tanks and reinforcements. They had not lost many Germans; only tanks, which were replaceable, and Italians which were expendable.

Nevertheless Eighth Army had won a famous victory. They had relieved Tobruk, driven the enemy out of Cyrenaica and reduced him from eight divisions to the equivalent of two. In this victory 4th Indian Division had played not the lead, but a very strong supporting part, proving that the Indian Army of 1941 could fight the best troops that the best army in the world could put in the field. The Germans took the point. A captured note by a German staff officer read, 'So long as 7th Armoured Division and the Indian division are in the desert, we must watch out. They will be the spearhead of any attack.'

CHAPTER 17

Eighth Army Retreats,

1942

In the Far East the little cloud out of the sea like a man's hand had swelled and darkened until it filled the sky to bring a hurricane which swept over Hong Kong, the Philippines, the Dutch East Indies, Malaya and Burma. Just as a year earlier Wavell's Western Desert Force had been stripped of its best men and machines for Greece, so now 7th Armoured Brigade was shipped to Burma, and two of the three Australian divisions were called home. Modern fighters and tanks earmarked for the Middle East were diverted to India; and a British division, actually at sea on its way to Suez, was taken to Singapore, where it arrived too late.

Nevertheless planning proceeded for an advance to carry Eighth Army through to Tripoli. But Rommel struck first. The flotilla of light cruisers and destroyers, based on Malta, which had decimated Axis convoys, suffered crippling losses in a minefield. So unmolested convoys brought to Tripoli in January enough men, tanks, lorries and guns to replace all he had lost.

7th Armoured Division had been withdrawn to the Delta for rest and re-equipment, and facing the Afrika Korps was 1st (British) Armoured Division, as new to the desert and to fighting Germans as 2nd had been a year earlier. Frank Messervy had been put in command of it, a desert veteran in charge of desert tyros. On the morning of 21 January British patrols along the road from El Agheila to Agedabia were pushed back, and by evening the panzers were forty miles on, at Antelat.

Intelligence reports suggested that this was merely a reconnaissance in force, but the new commander of 4th Indian Division did not believe a word of them. He was Major General F. I. S. ('Gertie') Tuker, a Goorkha of Goorkhas (1/2nd, God's Own) who combined an addiction to polo with an intellectual approach to war and a keen delight in questioning accepted military practices. Not least of his services to 4th Indian Division was to redesign its badge so that it looked more like a Red Eagle and less like a red shite-hawk. He was given as his task the control of the corridor between the escarpment and the sea, and the defence of Benghazi. For this he had 11th Brigade back in Tobruk, 5th Brigade in the Barce area, and 7th Brigade around Benghazi.

On hearing the news from the south, he sent 7th Brigade to a covering position fourteen miles from Benghazi, and light forces to watch the Sidi Brahim and Sceledeima passes through the escarpment, between coastal corridor and desert; and he asked for 11th Brigade to be sent up from Tobruk. He had plans prepared for demolitions and the evacuation of

Benghazi if the worst came to the worst; and proposed to XIII Corps that he attack the enemy rear at Agedabia while the panzers were engaged with 1st Armoured Division further north. Too late. On that very day Rommel attacked 1st Armoured Division and got very much the better of it. On 25 January Tuker was ordered by XIII Corps to evacuate Benghazi and withdraw to Derna while the remaining British tanks were in full retreat from Msus. The 'Benghazi Handicap' was being run for the second time.

On the 26th the Army Commander, General Ritchie, intervened. Mindful, perhaps, of the circumstances in which he had replaced General Cunningham, he countermanded the order to withdraw. His robust view was that the enemy opposite 4th Indian were only Italians. Tuker must now attack them, as he had suggested three days earlier. Tuker, never afraid and seldom respectful of senior officers whom he believed to be in error, demurred. The opportunity to attack had been lost. 1st Armoured, he knew from intercepted signals, had lost so many tanks that it could not protect his desert flank; moreover, there was a ninety-mile gap between 4th Indian and 1st Armoured, widening every hour, with the panzers between them. Tuker was overruled, had to do as he was told, and was placed directly under Eighth Army command.

The rapid flow of events absolved him from obeying orders which he knew were unsound. On the 28th the CIH, withdrawing northwards up the coastal corridor, reported two columns, each of about forty tanks with self-propelled guns and lorries, one moving along the coastal road and the other along the escarpment. Much of this information came from Lance Daffadar Attar Singh, who with two trucks came upon German armour near Antelat. Having no wireless, he sent back one truck to report, and himself followed the enemy. Irritated by this surveillance, they detached armoured cars to chase him off. His truck being faster than they, he scuttled away, doubled back round a hill and continued his watch. They sniped him with field guns, without success; and from time to time he encountered stray British trucks and gave them reports to be passed on. At dusk he returned to his squadron after an interesting and profitable day.

Light forces holding the passes through the escarpment south-east of Benghazi were driven back; and further north 1/6th Rajputana Rifles had a miraculous escape. They were almost surrounded by enemy armour, and had no troop-carrying transport. But the battalion transport officer, Lieutenant Mehbub Singh, cut the superstructure off all battalion vehicles, filled them up at one end of a petrol dump* while the Germans were filling up at the other, jettisoned everything but arms and ammunition and packed all the men onto the lorries, jammed tight as sardines. With the springs flat and the bodies bumping on the back axles, this extraordinary cavalcade drove slowly back to safety.

---

*A petrol dump, widely dispersed as a precaution against bombing, could cover a hundred acres.

With 90 Light and 21st Panzer both positively identified in the coastal corridor, it was now obvious that the main enemy effort was directed against Benghazi. It was out of the question for 4th Indian Division to do anything but defend the port, and that would be possible only if 1st Armoured turned back to help. Tuker telephoned Eighth Army, reported the situation, and asked what 1st Armoured was doing. To his dismay he learned that it was still moving east towards El Mechili. He urged that Benghazi must be evacuated before 7th Brigade was cut off, and reluctantly Ritchie consented.

Leaving 7th Brigade to delay the enemy as long as possible south of the town, and ordering 5th Brigade to hold fall-back positions fifty miles to the rear, divisional headquarters got out of Benghazi just in time, while the rumble of demolitions and columns of smoke told them that the sappers were destroying the port installations which they had recently got working. 7th Brigade followed, but too late. German armour, bumping down the escarpment, set up a roadblock behind divisional headquarters and in front of 7th Brigade, seven miles north of Benghazi. It was across a narrow causeway, with the brackish foreshore on one side and deep ditches on the other. There was no possibility of forcing a way through before the main enemy columns arrived from the south. 7th Brigade was cut off.

At 2100 hrs on the 28th, a day full of incident, Tuker, now in Barce, again telephoned the Army commander to report the situation, and was again informed that he had got it all wrong: only Italians were approaching Benghazi. Ritchie suggested that 7th Brigade remain there and defend the place, or at least leave a battalion group. At 0500 hrs on the 29th a wireless message was picked up reporting the roadblock and that the blocking force was German. At this Tuker ordered 5th Brigade to send patrols to try to contact 7th Brigade, which had gone off the air, and sent another appeal to 1st Armoured Division. They, however, could do little to help, their tanks having been reduced to twenty-two runners.

Later in the morning, with no more word from 7th Brigade, Tuker was told that losses must be cut (i.e. 7th Brigade left to its fate), the passes on the two Benghazi-Barce roads must be blown, and the two remaining brigades of 4th Indian Division must continue their retreat.

This was done. 11th Brigade was joined, fortuitously and fortunately, by a detachment of 5th Indian Division which had made a remarkable trek from the Jalo Oasis, 230 miles to the south, across a desert swarming with enemy. They had been on half-rations for a week and their vehicles were at their last gasp, but they brought a very useful reinforcement – the 1/2nd Punjab, a battery of 25-pounders and eight armoured cars.

5th and 11th Brigades withdrew across a nightmare country – far worse when retreating than when advancing – of little rocky hills and steep-sided ravines, constantly pressed by enemy armour. Their transport drivers were heroic, wrestling with lorries which crashed at night into invisible holes, got bellied on rocks, bashed sumps and differentials. 18th Field Company's tale is one of many:

'We have only 38 vehicles and we need 100. We have 13 different types, which makes spares hard to obtain. 13 of our lorries are over two years old and completely worn out. 7 are relics which formerly towed trucks up the Keren railway. Their engines are finished, their steering deplorable, their frames out of alignment. The remainder are veterans of Sudan, Syria and Libya. . . . One is a captured French lorry that no one knows anything about. Another was picked up in a minefield and repaired by our own LAD.'

But they reached at last the line on which Eighth Army made its stand, the Gazala position, a few miles west of Tobruk.

7th Brigade was left in Benghazi, its retreat to the north cut off. By all the rules and probabilities of war they should have fought until overrun, and then departed to honourable captivity. Brigadier Briggs decided on the desperate hazard of a breakout to the south, across the enemy lines of communication, and then east across two hundred miles of desert.

For this the brigade was divided into three columns, moving independently – Headquarters, Gold and Silver. They had three hundred miles to go. Documents, codes and marked maps were burnt, private kit ruthlessly jettisoned. By 2300 on the 28th they had started on the most dangerous part of the drive, seventy-five miles through the crowded coastal strip and into the desert beyond Antelat.

Gold and Silver Groups had surprisingly uneventful drives. Headquarters Group had more trouble.

It consisted of 1,200 men in 300 vehicles – four and a half companies of infantry, eight anti-tank guns, a Field Company Sappers and Miners, and HQ Squadron of the CIH. They moved through a known gap in the minefield and wound their way slowly between the flares sent up from enemy harbours. At 0230 hrs they halted to allow stragglers to catch up, and a number of unfit vehicles were destroyed. A cock crowing shortly before dawn suggested that they were about to blunder into a village: they swung away: there was another lusty crow; and another. Their navigator wondered desperately if they were going round in circles – but the cock was next day's lunch of a sepoy in the leading lorry.

Soon after daybreak they reached the Beda Fomm-Antelat track. They were now crossing the enemy supply lines, so they opened out and straggled and broke formation, hoping to be taken for a number of independent parties, each going innocently about its own business. Where the coastal plain narrowed as the escarpment swung towards the sea, they halted short of a track along which enemy traffic was passing in both directions, including a convoy escorted by armoured cars. When there was a lull in the traffic, Briggs ordered, 'Cross the road.' The story is told by an anonymous officer in the CIH.

'Nearing the trail we could see four tanks, about 800 yards away, with men working on them. A motorcyclist passed along the track 200 yards ahead of our leading truck. A staff car coming from the opposite direction halted for a few minutes beside the tanks and then went on. Just as we crossed the road, two big lorries which had been moving towards us apparently became suspicious, and halted near the tanks. A big gun on tow, a straggler from one of the enemy convoys, was only fifty yards away. Its driver . . . pulled up to allow one of our three-tonners to pass in front. In one of our vehicles were five German prisoners. The sowars stood over them, with the butts of their rifles ready to bash their heads if they attempted to give the alarm. One started to pull himself to his feet, but was quickly hauled down by his comrades.'

With every mile into the desert they felt safer, bowling briskly over hard sand and gravel, occasionally stopping to replenish petrol tanks. All through the day and night they drove, heading now towards the east. At dawn on the 30th they stopped for breakfast. They badly needed petrol. Briggs reckoned they were now about eighty miles south of El Mechili, but he did not know who was there. At 0700 hrs he risked breaking wireless silence and, having destroyed his codebooks in Benghazi, asked in clear if there were friends in El Mechili. Back came the answer, 'Many friends.' He was asked for his position, but dared not give it in clear. However, there were in his party several New Zealand signallers who had served in XIII Corps headquarters where each operator had a code number. For the figures of the map reference they signalled the corresponding names. At 1500 hrs they met the Free French and Polish outposts.

There were many individual escapes, Dogras and Mahrattas and Punjabi Mussulmans were provided with Senussi Bedouin clothes and passed from one Senussi camp to another. (The devotion of this tribe to the democratic cause was stimulated by rewards.) Two Mahsud truck drivers walked all the way to El Alamein. With typical Mahsud guile, one painted a hideous sore on his leg and hobbled along leaning on his 'brother', who ceaselessly complained of being encumbered with a cripple. They noted on their Arab clothes the location of all enemy installations and minefields which they passed on their way.

Among those who did not get away were the Sappers and Miners who stayed in Benghazi to the last, destroying the harbour and all its works. One is believed to have smuggled explosives aboard a ship and blown it up, and later to have been killed doing likewise to an ammunition train. Certainly a ship and an ammunition train did mysteriously blow up, and the RAF never claimed credit for them.

In extricating itself from a very difficult situation, 4th Indian Division lost only about 600 men out of 12,000. It was a remarkable achievement, due largely to the sagacity and foresight of 'Gertie' Tuker.

CHAPTER 18

Eighth Army Defeated,
1942

From March to May 1942 there was stalemate in the desert, both sides hurriedly building up their forces for an offensive. The British were receiving a trickle of heavier tanks, the American General Grant which carried a 75mm gun. But even this was no match for the Panzer Mk III and Mk IV, for its 75 was mounted low in the hull, not in the turret, so that it had only a few degrees' traverse and could not be fired from a 'hull down' position.

The British position consisted of a number of self-contained, all-round-defended boxes, behind a minefield, each held by a brigade with supporting arms. They were intended as pivots of manoeuvre for armour, but Tuker forcefully pointed out the folly of immobilizing one's troops in boxes, like the Italians at Sidi Barani, unless one had superiority in armour. And although Eighth Army had many more tanks, the enemy still had better ones.*

4th Indian Division was not involved. 7th Brigade went to Cyprus, 11th Brigade to the Canal zone and 5th Brigade to Palestine to prepare for a German attack through Turkey and/or Persia and Iraq. The 4/11th Sikhs and the 1/6th Rajputana Rifles were sent to PAIFORCE (Persia and Iraq Force) to show them how things should be done, and in their place, at Tuker's special request, came the 1/2nd Goorkhas and the 2/7th Gurkhas, the first of the little men to sew the Red Eagle on their sleeves.

Tuker even went to Cairo to press his views on the C-in-C himself, and was appointed to command a number of miscellaneous forces on the left (desert) flank of the Gazala position, viz. a Free French brigade, 29th Infantry Brigade of 5th Indian Division, 7th Motor Brigade of 7th Armoured Division and the 3rd Indian Motor Brigade, still mounted in Chevrolet trucks as it had been at El Mechili in April 1941. (It was characteristic of Eighth Army at that time, and the subject of unfavourable comment by Tuker and others, that it never seemed to fight in divisions, always in brigade groups and even battalion groups.) He set off from Cairo in a fever of impatience to unpack his heterogeneous command from its boxes and get it out on wheels, mobile, in the friendly desert where it could not be pinned to the ground and battered by the panzers. But he arrived too late. In the race between Eighth Army and Afrika Korps to attack, Rommel again struck first.

*Including 1st Armoured Brigade in Egypt but under orders to join it, Eighth Army had 242 Grants, 257 Crusaders, 219 Stuarts and 276 I Tanks: a total of 894. The enemy had 292 German Mk IIIs and IVs and 228 Italian mediums, a total of 520.

He swung his armour round the open desert flank, and his blow again fell on the 3rd Indian Motor Brigade in a box on the extreme left of the Gazala position. This time each of the three cavalry regiments had eight 2-pounder anti-tank guns; and Brigadier Filose had under his command 2nd Indian Field Regiment (the first of the Indian artillery to be in action), consisting of 3rd Battery (Madrassis), 4th battery (Mahrattas) and 7th battery (Sikhs), each armed with six 25-pounders; and one anti-tank battery of six 2-pounders.

The box was roughly square, with the 2nd Royal Lancers facing south, the 18th Cavalry facing west and the PAVO facing north. The east face was held by the Sappers and Miners and the anti-tank battery of the 2nd Field Regiment. The 25-pounders were inside the square. They had no time to lay mines. They were stronger than they had been at El Mechili, for they had the field regiment in support, and at close range the 2-pounder could kill tanks. But the enemy were in immeasurably greater strength. Rommel attacked on the morning of 27 May, and at 0615 hours it seemed to Brigadier Filose as though the whole of the Afrika Korps was drawn up facing him as on a ceremonial parade, about five miles to the west. Immediately opposite his brigade, on the left of the enemy line, was Ariete division, and next to it, 21st Panzer.

The field regiment opened fire at 0630 hours on the enemy soft-skinned lorries and troop-carriers. The first attack was from the west, by about a hundred tanks, mainly Ariete with some Mk IIIs and IVs of 21st Panzer, aimed at the 18th Cavalry and the 7th (Sikh) Battery of 25-pounders. The second, a little later, by about the same number of tanks, all Mk IIIs and IVs, was from the south, against the 2nd Lancers and the 3rd (Madrassi) Battery.

The Brigade Major, Miles Smeeton of Hodson's Horse, took a message at Brigade headquarters that a squadron of infantry tanks was on its way to support them, and hurried with it to Filose at Battle Headquarters.

'My Sikh driver was waiting with my Chev pick-up, a fast little truck with balloon tyres and no windscreen. I jumped in, took the wheel and we set off together. The enemy artillery was retaliating now. . . . The desert in front began to look like brown soup just coming to the boil with bursting bubbles of sand and rolls of black smoke. I looked at the face of my young companion, so bearded and intent, and shouted "*Sath Sri Akal!*" (the Sikh warcry) to him. He shook his head sentimentally and wagged his beard and shouted back, "Sahib, when you say that, a great love strikes me." . . . So we shouted "*Sath Sri Akal*" together and drove on. . . .

We got to Battle HQ just as the Brigadier finished his orders. There was not much to say except that we were going to hang on. . . .

I gave the Brigadier the message about the tanks. "Good," he said, "they'll have to be quick. You never saw such an array as we've got in front of us." But the tanks never arrived. . . .

The shelling continued, and our own guns from inside the position . . .

26 North-West Frontier, machine-gun section, 1937.

27 *(right)* Volunteers: 14 Punjab Regiment recruits. Left to right: Khattack Pathans, Dogras, Yusafzai Pathans. More than a million and a half such recruits volunteered for war service.

28 *(below)* 12 Mountain Battery firing 3.7-inch mountain howitzers, Shawangi, North-West Frontier, 1938.

29 *(above left)* Indian troops offloading water casks from naval landing-craft for Eighth Army during the advance to Benghazi, 1941.

30–33 *(below left)* Sepoys, 1941. Left to right: Rajput of 6th Rajputana Rifles; Sikh of 11th Sikh Regiment; Dogra of 12th Frontier Force Regiment; Mahratta of 5th Mahratta Light Infantry.

34 The author in Persia, 1941. The vehicle is an Indian-built armoured carrier.

35 *(above)* Gurkhas in Tunisia, 1943: the mountain warfare experts of Eighth Army.

36 Indian troops first to enter Derna, Western Desert, 27 December 1941.

37 Holding a captured German flag, Sidi Omar 1941: the first Indian Army success against Germans.

barked angrily back, sending their shells rattling away towards the enemy lorried infantry. . . . The main attack was forming on the front of the 18th Cavalry, and it seemed that the PAVO on the right flank would be least involved.

"Go and take two anti-tank guns from the PAVO up to the 18th. That's where they are going to be most needed," said the Brigadier. . . .

The PAVO Colonel might have put up a strong resistance, but this was a special day, and he surrendered them and their crews with only a hurt look.

I led them towards the forward position of the 18th. The shelling was continuous, and except for a few scattered vehicles, there was very little of our own troops to be seen. Only our coughing guns, with smoke-shrouded kneeling figures and a glimpse of an upraised arm behind the thin shields. . . . I saw an Indian squatting with an ineffective rifle in the little hole he had scratched. He grinned up at me, and I saw he was a soldier of the 18th.

"Where are your headquarters?" I asked him.

"Over there," he said, pointing, "by the Admiral Sahib." He said it with a possessive pride, as a girl might show her engagement ring. I looked and saw a small figure, hands linked behind his back, pacing up and down, ten steps one way and ten steps the other, as if he had been on the lee side of his bridge. Up and down he went, rejoicing in the smell of cordite and hoping that perhaps he might die on this day, before he got too old, and in action as sailors and soldiers should.

"Good morning, Miles," he said as I came up to him. "A wonderful morning, a wonderful morning." The Colonel was sitting in a shallow scrape in the ground with earphones on his head and puffing at a cigarette.

"Good man," he said to me when I told him I had a couple of guns for him. "We'll need them. It looks as if they're coming in any minute now." Not having the same inclinations as the Admiral, I jumped into my truck and hurried back.

By the time I got back to Battle HQ the anti-tank guns were beginning to fire, and we could hear their sharper cracks between the thumping of the field guns. Bob Prentice, the DQ with the merry crumpled face . . . looked at me with a wry grimace. "Take a look behind you," he said.

On the ridge behind our position, . . . coming up from the south having turned our flank, was a long frieze of German tanks, anti-tank guns, half-tracks and lorried infantry. We could see the gunners on the towed 88s slamming a shell into the breech as they stopped for a moment to fire. We could see the tank commanders with their heads out of the turrets of their tanks. We could see the infantry in the half-tracks and the drivers in the cabs of the lorries. . . .

Enemy tanks were soon swarming onto our position and down our right flank too, where I had so recently deprived the PAVO of two of their guns. Italian tanks on our right and German tanks on our front, and between our position and Bir Hachim I could see more tanks of the Ariete Division hurrying past. . . . The air was alive with the crackle of automatic fire as if we had been caught in an electrical storm, and the surface of our position was cut and crossed with lines of spurting sand which we regarded with an impersonal detachment as long as they weren't coming our way. . . . Besides the automatic fire there was a continuous thump and twang, thump and crack, from the heavier tank guns. We could watch the tanks as they came on, sometimes with a great spurt of sand about them as the armour-piercing shells of the field-guns struck low, sometimes stopping so that we thought they had been hit in the vitals, only to see them fire and roll on again; and sometimes they stopped to fall apart in red flame and billowing black smoke.

There seemed to be an inexhaustible supply of them. They rolled over the gun positions and the brave fire of the guns was silenced. We had no idea of time. It was as if only a moment before a few toy tanks like models on an indoor battle range had appeared, and gradually, in a nightmare of the day, they had grown and swelled and multiplied until they filled the whole stage and the deep throbbing of their engines beat on all sides of us.

"We've got to get out what we can," said the Brigadier, "to a rear rendezvous." . . . Telephone lines had been broken by the mangling tracks and we could only raise one regiment on the radio, but what we could do towards getting a message out, we did. . . .

"If we don't do something pretty soon, we've had it," Bob said. As he said it, three tanks which had driven past and had been standing behind us, caught sight of us and drove towards the small, disconsolate group. We made a dash for the cars . . . driving forward because that was the way they were facing, and there were some tanks close on our heels. . . . As we picked our way between the German tanks in front they were uncertain as to who we were or what we were doing, and I could see the commanders look down in surprise from the turrets as we passed. We were too quick for them, and we swung left-handed to the south.

Behind us the enemy lorried infantry were flooding up, dismounted between the tanks, and our men were surrendering in little uncertain groups. Others, particularly those amongst the guns, stayed still and were neither perplexed nor disappointed any more.'

In the 18th Cavalry sector the Admiral and Colonel Fowler were called upon to surrender. 'Dog!' replied the Admiral, 'I will NOT surrender.' He emptied his revolver at the tanks and was unarmed when seized with Fowler and carried into captivity. (The strain of holding this spirited captive was too much for the Italians, who released him, as being too old to fight, a year later. He ended the war fighting with the Partisans in Yugoslavia.)

When the 25-pounders had fired off all their ammunition, Major Kumara Mangalam managed to extricate five of the six troops of 2nd Field Regiment, for which he was awarded the DSO.

Captain Desmond Reynolds was commanding B Squadron of the 2nd Lancers. His strongest recollection of the action is of the 'appalling communications at that stage of the war. We would have done better with trumpeters and gallopers.' His squadron held the south-west corner of the box, with two troops of anti-tank guns and a 3-inch mortar detachment.

'My squadron position was attacked by Italian M13 tanks of Ariete Division. The attack was in two waves, the first frontal by tanks alone, the second from the south supported by lorry-borne infantry. The anti-tank gunners needed little encouragement or orders as targets were so numerous. From my slit trench I took over one Bren to direct the fire of the other Brens onto the lorried infantry. . . . Both attacks were beaten off and the position was not penetrated. The enemy left ten tanks, seven on fire, the nearest being about 75 yards off. . . . The mortar detachment did much damage to the packed lorries.

The enemy broke off the engagement and wheeled away to the north-east . . . leaving the squadron isolated. There was now a lull, and I walked back to find out what was happening elsewhere and to arrange for more ammunition. Regimental headquarters was not in its old location. Except for one troop of 2nd Field Regiment, there was nothing but the burning hulks of some Mk III panzers. . . . The Battery captain informed me that the remnants of the brigade had withdrawn on a bearing of 119° and that he was going as soon as he had limbered up.

On return to my squadron I met Major Macnamara (A Squadron). He said we too should withdraw to the east. . . . Then as quickly as possible we got on the few available trucks and moved off. . . . After a day and a night's drive and many close brushes, we managed to reach Tobruk.'

The brigade had destroyed at least fifty-two enemy tanks. With the enemy actually overrunning the position, even the 2-pounders had scored. Lance Daffadar Ali Mahboob Khan was found dead beside his gun, with six knocked-out tanks in front of him, two within fifty yards. The enemy had been delayed for several vital hours. About six hundred officers and men of the cavalry regiments got away, together with eleven 25-pounders, through the maelstrom of Axis columns. About 250 were killed and a thousand captured. But of the latter, six hundred were rescued by a roving armoured car troop. So within ten days the Brigadier was able to report that he was ready for action again, and the brigade acted as rearguard during the long retreat to El Alamein.

June was a month of sheer chaos, with brigades attacking and being attacked, retiring into boxes and emerging from them; with 4th, 5th and 10th Indian Divisions (the last two newly arrived), swopping brigades and brigades swopping battalions. In one month 5th Indian Division had twenty-two changes in brigades. There were mobile columns, generally named after their commanders – 'Gleecol' commanded by Gleeson, 'Leathercol' commanded by Leatherdale – swanning about all over the desert. It was a pernicious system, or lack of system, to some degree enforced by the lack of proper anti-tank guns. No force could survive an encounter with tanks unless it had a few 25-pounders, so a column might be composed basically of a section or a battery of 25-pounders, with just enough infantry to escort them and armoured cars to reconnoitre for them. Everything seemed to be improvised, at the last moment, nothing planned. In short, Rommel had the initiative.

There were isolated successes, such as that of Leathercol from 29th Brigade of 5th Indian Division, which came upon twenty-five Mk III and IV panzers, helpless, having run out of petrol. Their crews departed, and Leatherdale longed to bring in his prizes and use them; but Brigadier Reid ordered, 'Bust them.' So they were busted.

The only coherent feature of the chaos in the area known as the Cauldron was that the German armour, always concentrated, knocked hell out of the British armour, generally dispersed. About 800 British tanks were lost – most to 88s and long-barrelled 50mm anti-tank guns onto which they were lured by superior tactics. With only 50 cruiser and 20 I tanks left, the infantry were helpless in that open desert. A whole brigade of 50th Northumbrian Division was overrun by panzers and destroyed, as were the 10th Brigade and half of the 9th Brigade and 5th Indian Division. Saddest was the fate of 11th Indian Brigade, which had stormed the Italian camps at Sidi Barani and Cameron Ridge at Keren, chased the enemy from the Jebel Achdar and covered the retreat from Benghazi. Sent to Tobruk to help defend a fortress which no one decided to defend until it was too late, 11th Brigade was put under command of 2nd South African Division. When the divisional commander surrendered, 11th Brigade had to surrender too, though the Camerons and the 2/7th Gurkhas went on fighting for thirty-six hours after the general capitulation.

Then it was back – back – back, through Halfaya and Sidi Barani and Mersa Matruh to the place Auchinleck had chosen and had prepared for Eighth Army's last stand, El Alamein. Only the terrific efforts of the RAF and its own rearguards saved the army. The retreat was far from orderly. Miles Smeeton and an American war correspondent were watching a shoal of trucks and lorries moving rapidly eastward like fish pursued by a shark when suddenly a water-truck stopped with a jerk. The driver jumped out, ran round behind, turned on all the taps and drove on, with increasing speed as his precious load drained way.

'You may think,' said the American consolingly, 'that your army is a shambles. But, gee, wait till you see ours!'

Everyone's fear was of his vehicle breaking down and being left behind. A subaltern of the Guides, divisional cavalry of 10th Indian Divisions, stopped his armoured car, a true Samaritan, beside a lorry halted in the dark and asked solicitously, 'Will I send the breakdown lorry for you?'

'We are the breakdown lorry,' was the gloomy reply.

At first it was intended to make a stand at Mersa Matruh, but when the remnants of the armour had passed through, Auchinleck decided that men and guns were more valuable than ground, and ordered it to be evacuated.

Captain P. H. MacDwyer's company of the 2/11th Sikhs in 10th Indian Division was the last of the rearguard.

'Shortly after midnight the battalion began thinning out to the troop-carrying transports . . . of a RASC company. A lot of the drivers were the worse for wear, having taken advantage of the burning NAAFI to ensure that all the beer and spirits did not fall into enemy hands, and I had to risk court-martial by using my fists. . . .'

It was a nightmare drive. They blundered into an enemy laager and fled from it like a lot of hysterical hens. Then – 'a miracle took place: a desert fog suddenly came down and blanketed us'.

MacDwyer took stock in daylight and found he had company headquarters, one and a half platoons, one 25-pounder, two 2-pounders from a Mahratta Anti-Tank Regiment, a lorry full of sappers, a lorry full of signallers and an ambulance.

'I was not sure where I was. . . . I felt alone and frightened. I was the only British Officer, but I had my Subadar and one Jemadar and 237 men, enough water for three days and food for a week. . . . Shortly after dawn we formed up and pressed on.

At mid-day, to my front on a sand dune, there suddenly appeared three German armoured cars. . . . It was hopeless against their guns: ours were still limbered up, and rifle fire was useless. . . . I surrendered.

My column was escorted to the west, and after three hours of very fast going came upon a small party of vehicles, tanks and armoured cars heading north-east at speed. We all halted. I was ordered from my truck and marched to an open staff car. To my astonishment I recognized the man who sat there: it was Field Marshal Rommel.

I was presented to him. . . . He asked if I spoke German, and I replied in the affirmative. He was a fine-looking man, greying slightly, with sharp but friendly eyes. . . . He was wearing goggles pushed up over the peak of his cap and was very dusty.

He shook hands and bade me stand at ease. We talked for about fifteen minutes of everything except the war. . . . He offered me cigarettes and a drink. The cigarettes were a well known British brand at which I smiled, and he remarked with a laugh . . . "*Rauch mal, Herr Hauptman, sind besser als unsere.*" Turning to an aide, he ordered me and my men to be taken away, but before we were dismissed he smiled and shook hands again, saying, "I gave special orders for the last man out of Mersa Matruh to be taken prisoner and brought to me. I wanted to tell him that all your rearguards had fought well. It was easy to find you. Have care and good-bye, I don't expect to see you again. Go." He then gave me a wide wink and indicated the open desert. It was an invitation to escape, I thought. Anyway, only one armoured car and three elderly guards escorted us to the north-east until we camped for the night in the open desert.

I entertained the three Germans to the remains of my whiskey and some rum the Subadar had. . . . I helped them into a false sense of security by telling them several jokes in their own language, which they thought very funny. Subadar Jagat Singh and I then quietly removed their rifles, and I told them we were all going back to Cairo. . . . They smiled sheepishly and did not seem surprised.'

MacDwyer and his little column got back to El Alamein. They were lucky. Brigadier Reid wasn't. To cover the withdrawal of XIII Corps, he was ordered to hold a rearguard position at Fuka, fifty miles back from Mersa Matruh: 'the position will be held until it is impossible to hold it without being cut off.' His force consisted of the equivalent of three and a half companies from three battalions, some sappers, and five 25-pounders. Late in the evening sixty panzers roared along the escarpment, smothering and blinding with dust the two companies of 3/2nd Punjab who were in position at the top of the Fuka Pass. While most of the panzers continued east, heading for Alexandria, about twenty lurched down the escarpment and drove in line ahead straight at Reid's modest headquarters. Three or four were stopped by 25-pounders, but the remainder charged into the little group of tents and slit trenches, and roamed round shooting up everything they saw. Having smashed the wireless sets, Reid and some others hid, hoping to make a getaway in the dark. But they were caught: the only escapers were two platoons of HLI.

Nevertheless, most of the Mersa Matruh garrison, most of the miscellaneous columns and hundreds of individuals reached the El Alamein position. Flanked on the right by the sea, on the left by the impassable Qatara Depression, it was, in Sir Arthur Bryant's words, the 'British Army's spiritual home, the last ditch'. There, under the personal command of the Auk who seemed to be wherever there was a crisis, Eighth Army held firm, saving the Middle East and the war.

The men who fought in the desert under Wavell and the Auk tended to regard themselves as the real Eighth Army, foundation members, and those who came later, when things were easier, as parvenus. They were outraged when the Eighth Army Clasp was awarded only to those who fought in it under Montgomery, as though Eighth Army never existed until he commanded it – which, one can only suppose, was precisely the impression Montgomery wished to give.

CHAPTER 19

Rising Sun,
1941–42

There was never a hope of holding Hong Kong against the Japanese. The garrison consisted of two British, two Canadian and two Indian battalions (5/7th Rajput and 2/14th Punjab) with attached troops. With no prospect of reinforcement or evacuation, they held out for eighteen days against two first-class Japanese divisions before surrender.

The campaign in Malaya and Singapore was a different story. Work on the Singapore base had started in 1922. Expert opinion was that:

1. An attack from the mainland was impossible because of difficulties of terrain. Any attack must therefore come by sea.
2. The Japanese would never risk it with the US Pacific Fleet poised at Pearl Harbor.
3. If they did take a chance on it, the Mediterranean could be left to the French, and the British Mediterranean Fleet move to Singapore.
4. Malaya and Singapore could best be defended by bombers. To this end, a number of airfields were constructed up and down the peninsular, mainly in the north.

Events in the summer of 1940 invalidated several of these assumptions. With the French out of the war and bent on appeasing the victorious Axis powers, the British fleet could not leave the Mediterranean, and the Japanese could use (Vichy) French Indo-China as a springboard for an invasion of Malaya. For the defence of Malaya there were only 158 obsolete planes available, as against an estimated minimum requirement of 582 modern aircraft; so the airfields became a tactical and strategic liability, useless, but distorting any defence plans because they must be denied to the Japanese. Moreover, the peninsular was *not* impassable to a modern army.

Without the warships and the aircraft on which were based the plans, or at least the hopes, for the defence of Malaya, the main burden would fall on the army. In December 1941, this consisted of two Australian, one British and five Indian brigades, with attached troops. But Malaya was at the bottom of the list for modern equipment of all kinds, so they had no tanks, no mobile AA guns, and very few 2-pounder anti-tank guns. But they *did* have motor-, instead of pack-, transport, which confined them to the roads. Their only armour was the 3rd Cavalry in armoured cars with armour that would not stop an ordinary .303 bullet.

The general belief was that they were out of the war. Plainly neither the civil government nor the population took the war seriously. There were hundreds of thousands of hard-working Chinese labourers in the country, but no attempt was made to enlist them in labour battalions to prepare defences. Until the weekend before Pearl Harbor troops were forbidden to inconvenience people by clearing fields of fire, or laying minefields. This attitude was not conducive to tough, purposeful military training.

Nor was the belief that, if they ever did come, the Japanese would not prove very formidable. They were seen as little, buck-toothed yellow men, deficient in initiative, quite unable to move through the jungle, and so short-sighted that their pilots could not operate at night or make low-level attacks. They couldn't invent anything, could they? Only copy Western inventions.

However, in case they were so crazy as to try an invasion, something had better be done, or considered, to prevent them getting awkwardly close to Singapore – and to deny to them half a dozen airfields, unfortunately situated in the north, 340 miles from Singapore. Had it not been for this embarrassing commitment, the defence might have been based on a much better line half way up the peninsular.

The north was the responsibility of III Corps, commanded by Lieutenant General Heath, who had commanded 5th Indian Division in Eritrea. He had 9th Indian Division on the east side, covering an airfield and miles of beaches at Kota Bahru, and another airfield 150 miles south of this at Kuantan; and 11th Indian Division on the left side covering the Alor Star group of airfields. This division was teed-up to advance fifty miles into Siam and grab the port and railhead of Singora before the Japanese got there. There were some rather farcical reconnaissances by British officers posing as tourists, their footsteps dogged and their passport photographs taken by Japanese agents, one of whom jocularly signed their hotel register, 'The Rev. Suzuki-Major'. After a good deal of high-level havering, and moves up to the frontier and back, much to the detriment of the defence of Alor Star, at the last moment this operation was called off.

The first and strongest defence of Malaya was the US Pacific Fleet in Pearl Harbor. When this was sent to the bottom, Malaya was suddenly and dramatically opened wide to invasion.

It came within hours, launched from French Indo-China. During the night of 7/8 December 1941 three Japanese regiments (which we would call brigades) landed on the east coast at Singora and Patani in Siam, and a fourth at Kota Bahru in northern Malaya. Unimpeded – indeed assisted – by the Siamese authorities, the former marched on Alor Star.

At Kota Bahru the 3/17th Dogras were spread thinly to cover ten miles of beaches. They fought hard, but could not stop the enemy getting ashore. Bombers flown in from Singapore sank one and damaged two Japanese ships, and were then all destroyed by Japanese fighters while re-fuelling on the Kota Bahru airfield. On a rumour that the enemy were approaching the perimeter, the ground staff departed, without setting a match to the petrol dump. The 1/13th Frontier Force Rifles ('Cookies') counter-attacked to retake the airfield but got stuck among impassable streams. The *Prince of Wales* and the *Repulse* steamed up from Singapore, without fighter cover, to smash up the Japanese invasion fleet; and on the 10th were sunk by Japanese aircraft, one of the worst disasters of the war, which lost the Allies command of the Indian Ocean. The Japanese could then pour reinforcements onto the beaches, and there was nothing for 8th Brigade but an orderly withdrawal, having killed and wounded some 3,000 of the enemy in what the Japanese described as the hardest fight of the campaign.

On the western side of the peninsular 28th Brigade's front was broken by forty Japanese tanks driving straight down the road, against which they had nothing but Bren-guns and one or two of the useless Boyes anti-tank rifles. Back they had to go next day, leaving to the enemy the Alor Star, as well as the Kota Bahru, airfields.

We will not follow step by step the misfortunes of the army withdrawing down the Malayan peninsular. The British, Indian and Australian brigades were outfought and defeated by an enemy which was no more numerous, but of top quality, perfectly trained and equipped for this particular war, enjoying unchallenged air superiority. The British forces, with only motor transport, were completely road-bound; the enemy moved fast and freely through the jungle to outflank and cut in behind the retreating battalions; they used their 200 tanks boldly along the roads, against negligible anti-tank fire; they could bypass the British positions by landing anywhere along the coasts.

Tony Chenevix Trench, a battery captain in 4th Hazara Mountain Battery, wrote:

'My chief memory is of a total absence of reliable communications. None of us knew what was happening anywhere. Wireless was unpredictable, for some reason it always went "on the blink" in rubber plantations, and the telephone was worse. . . . I remember ringing up for ammunition and getting a Japanese officer on the phone.'

There was another fundamental breakdown in communication – between officer and man. Units in Malaya had been 'milked' again and again for experienced officers, NCOs and men to form new divisions for the Middle East: what was left contained far too high a proportion of very young soldiers, eighteen and nineteen years old, and Emergency Commissioned Officers who had very little Urdu.

They were buoyed up as they retreated by the confidence that when they neared Singapore they would find proper defences, dug, wired and mined, in which they could make a stand. All they found was total unpreparedness, no defences dug, no labour corps raised to dig them, and in Singapore parties going on until the small hours as though there were not a Japanese within a thousand miles. An officer of the 3rd Cavalry, arriving at six in the evening at the Ordnance Depot to collect some urgently needed armoured car spares, was advised to call again next morning, when it might be open.

There were individual successes and heroic deeds; ambushes which bloodily checked the pursuers; counter-attacks which proved that Japanese were as vulnerable as anyone else to bullet, bayonet and kukri; last-man, last-round stands; companies and platoons, surrounded by the enemy, breaking out to rejoin their battalions. The 5/11th Sikhs could boast: 'The battalion when given an objective to take, took it; when given a position to hold, held it; in no instance did the battalion withdraw from any position till ordered to.' Many others could make the same boast; but this was not the general picture.

The excuse for failure is that there was not enough of everything to go round, and that if the little there was had been spread evenly between the United Kingdom, the Middle East and Malaya, the Suez Canal and the Persian oilfields would have been lost. This is a valid excuse for material deficiencies. It does not excuse psychological unpreparedness: the total lack of prepared defences; the general atmosphere of 'It can't happen here'; the failure to prepare troops for the war they would have to fight if it did happen, to train them to fight and move in the jungle, to free them from dependence on roads by bringing out some of the excellent mule transport companies sitting idle in India.

The result of these failures was that on 14 February 1942, the general officer commanding the Singapore defences surrendered with 85,000 British, Indian and Australian troops.

The most disgraceful surrender in British history was compounded by a disgraceful episode in the history of the Indian Army. Of 60,000 Indian prisoners-of-war, about 25,000 joined the Japanese-sponsored, traitor Indian National Army (INA).*

The motives for their treachery varied. Perhaps 500, including their founder, Captain Mohan Singh, regarded themselves as Indian patriots, the Japanese as their allies against British oppression. Some were afraid, not without reason, of torture and death if they refused. Some hoped for a chance to desert back to the British, and some actually did so in Burma. The vast majority joined in a state of bewilderment, persuaded by Japanese and Congress propagandists that Britain had lost the war, and that the Japanese and Congress would be the next rulers of India. If, therefore, they wished to continue in their honourable profession as soldiers, they could do so only by serving the Japanese, as Rajputs in the past had served without shame their Moghul conquerors. The alternative was to be employed until the end of the war, and long after, in the most degrading, caste-destroying work. Separated from their British Officers immediately after their surrender, some heard no powerful voices arguing, urging, ordering them the other way.

Some did, for the Japanese did not at first separate Indian Commissioned Officers and VCOs from their men. Many – most – of these resisted every pressure, including torture, to make them break faith. (Some of the worst torturers of Indians were Indians.) Captain Durrani was tortured for days to make him collaborate. (He was awarded the George Cross for his heroism.) Captains Hari Badhwar and Dhargalkar of the 3rd Cavalry were, in Dhargalkar's words:

*Details from Philip Mason, who was involved in the postwar trials of INA officers and has closely studied the subject.

'taken to the Japanese Gestapo Headquarters where we were locked in underground cages, which were about five feet long by five feet wide and seven feet high, and sometimes held as many as five or six prisoners of war. We were kept inside these cages for eighty-eight days during which time we saw nothing of the outside world. We had to answer all nature's calls in the cage.'

VCOs of the same regiment were confined in latrines for eleven days as a punishment for refusal to collaborate. Said Risaldar Major Ismail Khan, 'You could hardly sit in them when used for their proper purpose, so you can imagine what it was like being confined in them.'

Another who set a wonderful example was Captain Parshotam Das. He was a Brahmin who hailed, improbably, from a Brahmin village on the Frontier in Abbottabad District. He served from 1914 to 1918 as a clerk in a mountain battery; was discharged in 1919, and re-enlisted as a gunner. Through efficiency, smartness and intelligence, he rose to be Subadar Major, Lieutenant and Captain. He was a devout Hindu but, while a prisoner, had only one book which he read many times, the Gospel according to St John. He visualized all religions as being on the circumference of a circle, equidistant from God at the centre.

Most of the men in units with such officers remained faithful. A disproportionate number of those who did not were Sikhs; few, if any, were Gurkhas. There was a snowball movement to treachery: the more men who defected, the more brutally were treated the brave and faithful. Some had second thoughts and tried to redeem their honour by getting out of the INA: but not many, after Captain Burhan-ud-Din had ordered and personally supervised the punishment of two who were hung up by the arms and flogged, every man in their battalion giving them one lash each. When they were cut down, one was dead.

All the more honour to those who remained true to their salt. The Indian soldiers in Burma regarded the INA with disfavour: later in the war, when the INA were surrendering and deserting in droves, bringing much useful information, special orders had to be issued to prevent them being shot out of hand. As for the Indian National Congress, which started the whole thing, they exploited the INA for all it was worth in the run-up to Independence, but were very careful after Independence not to take any back into the Army. Hari Badhwar, Dhargalkar and others of the faithful rose to high rank.

Meanwhile, the British Officers were kept separate from their men. The tale of their treatment, and of the infamous Siam Railway, has been told many times.

In the afternoon of the day of the surrender the 40th Pathans (5/14th Punjab) were ordered to cease fire and await the Japanese who would come to collect them in the morning. It was no surprise: they were utterly exhausted, and had suffered heavy losses when overrun by tanks at the Slim River. The officers said what could be said to their men, who took it amazingly well, and foregathered at the officers' mess in the evening, as though each sought consolation from others as despondent as himself.

Among them was Bob Cavill, an Australian, a member of the Malay States Volunteers with an emergency commission in the battalion. He spoke Malay and knew something about boats.

'I reckon,' he said, 'I could find a motorboat down at the docks. Would anyone like to come with me and try to make Sumatra?'

Two subalterns volunteered, A. T. Johnston and Cecil Hopkins-Husson. The Colonel wished them luck. 'If you do get out, tell all our next-of-kin that we were alive when you last saw us.'

After dark they drove towards the docks. Encountering a Japanese patrol, they talked their way through: they were, they said, liaison officers going round to make sure that all units knew about the surrender. The Japanese let them through. They abandoned their truck and headed for the beach, as being safer than the docks. From the darkness to their right they heard a fusilade of shots and a scream, but no enemy came their way. They found not a motor-boat, but a sampan with oars and sails, and embarked.

For three weeks they sailed from island to island, ignored by Japanese patrol-boats as too insignificant to merit suspicion. A boatload of Dutch sailors made them the princely gift of an outboard motor and five gallons of petrol, which took them to the east coast of Sumatra and up a wide river leading into the interior. There, from Malays from whom they bought food, they learned that the enemy had occupied the two ends of the 700-mile long island, but the Dutch were still in control of the middle. So across the middle they went – first by river-steamer, having sold their sampan for food; then on foot; finally by a narrow-gauge railway to the west-coast port of Padang, where they found an Australian destroyer, and all their troubles were over.

In April 1937, the Government of Burma Act severed Burma constitutionally from India. Geography and common sense demanded that the defence of Burma continue to be the responsibility of the Commander-in-Chief, India. But Burmese pride – that is to say, the pride of the British officials governing Burma – demanded a separate Burma military establishment, with its own Burma Army and its own Army Headquarters. Four times in the next five years was this arrangement altered, the defence of Burma being tossed in turn to the Far East Command at Singapore, back to India, to the South-West Pacific Command in Java, and back to India. This was not conducive to continuity or clarity in defence planning. Army Headquarters was an administrative body, not an operational headquarters geared to defence planning: it did not set up its own Intelligence Department, but relied for intelligence about potential enemies on the experts in Singapore, who had a poor track-record in crystal-gazing. It relied on the Royal Navy to defend its 1,200-mile coastline, and on mountains, jungles and the Siamese to discourage overland invasion from the east. The peacetime garrison of Burma consisted of two British battalions; four battalions of Burma Rifles, newly raised and with no

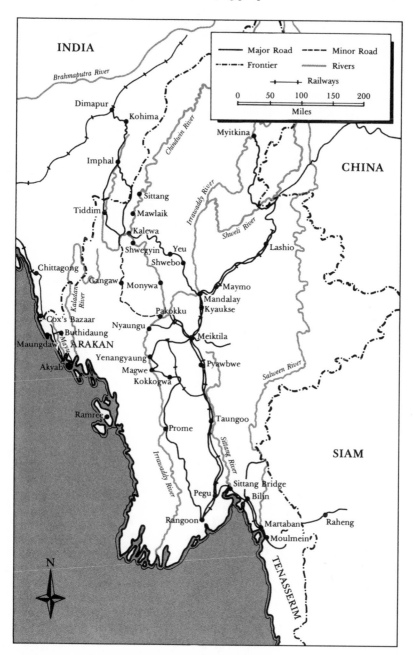

Burma

military traditions; and the Burma Frontier Force, a gendarmerie recruited largely from the Punjab.

Between February 1941 and the Japanese attack on Pearl Harbor, this force was increased by two Indian brigades. In January 1942 there arrived the headquarters and one brigade of 17th Indian Division, which had been training for the Caucasus. (The other two brigades of the division had been sent to Singapore, arriving just in time for the surrender.) The brigades in Burma were then organized:

1st Burma Division (Major General J. Bruce Scott)	13th Indian Brigade 1st Burma Brigade
17th Indian Division (Major General J. G. Smyth, VC)	46th Indian Brigade 16th Indian Brigade 48th Indian Brigade (arrived 31 January) 2nd Burma Brigade

In 1941 there were three RAF fighter squadrons in part-worn Hurricanes, veterans of the Battle of Britain, and three squadrons of Blenheim bombers. There was also a fighter squadron of the American Volunteer Force, regular US Army pilots who were fighting for Chiang Kai-shek's China against the Japanese. They were experienced, skilled, and flying P40 fighters, slightly better than anything the Japanese had. The Generalissimo had made them available for the defence of Burma, because through Burma passed the only road to China. These air forces totalled about half what had been estimated as the essential minimum for the defence of Burma, and much less than half the modern aircraft the Japanese had within range of Rangoon.

Three great north-south rivers run through Burma. The most easterly, the Salween, flowing into the sea at Moulmein, is roughly parallel to and for eighty miles forms the Siam border. Approximately fifty miles to the west of this is the Sittang; and one hundred miles west of the Sittang is the great Irrawaddy, navigable by steamships for a thousand miles, which empties itself into the sea through a multi-channelled delta on the eastern edge of which is Rangoon. From Moulmein south to Victoria Point is Tenasserim, a strip of Burmese territory four hundred miles long by thirty to sixty miles wide, between the Bay of Bengal to the west and Siam to the east. It contained three airfields on the reinforcement route to Singapore.

Presiding over the defence of Malaya and Burma was Wavell, first as C-in-C India, then as C-in-C South-West Asia Command, then, after the fall of Singapore, again as C-in-C India. He appointed to the command of the forces in Burma his Chief of Staff, Lieutenant General Sir Thomas Hutton, who was not, however, provided with an operational corps headquarters, but had to make do with Army Headquarters, Burma. He was a competent staff officer.

Hutton's first responsibility was to keep open Rangoon, through which alone reinforcements and supplies could reach Burma: there was no road from India. Second, the protection of the Tenasserim airfields. Third, defence against overland attacks from Siam which could be directed against Moulmein and Rangoon, or further north against Toungoo, or further north still against Meiktila. For reasons which always seemed more convincing to the Americans than to the British, he also had to protect the so-called Burma Road, reaching north-east from Mandalay through Lashio, along which Lend-Lease supplies flowed into that bottomless pit of ineptitude and corruption, Chiang Kai-shek's China.

The Intelligence Department of Far East Command in Singapore informed Hutton that the only immediate danger was of air-raids on the Tenasserim airfields. Later there might be an attack directed on Meiktila. A Japanese move through Raheng towards Moulmein was not considered likely: the mountains and jungle along the Siam border were almost impenetrable. By early January he had 1st Burma Division in the Mandalay area; and 17th Indian Division in Tenasserim with 16th Brigade across the route from Raheng, 2nd Burma Brigade at Moulmein and 46th Brigade in reserve at Bilin. The Burma Rifles were an unknown quantity. In the event, they fought quite well until almost every man decided that his first duty in these troubled times was to go home and look after his family. The Burmese population of the river valleys was at best neutral, more frequently (especially the Buddhist priests) murderously anti-British and anti-Indian. The Japanese lost no time in raising and arming the Burma National Army, which had considerable nuisance value. But the hill tribes of the frontier areas were pro-British, and gave invaluable help throughout the war.

The Japanese had no difficulty, with Siamese help, in making their way through the mountains and jungles into Tenasserim. On 10 December they captured the airfield at Victoria Point, in the extreme south, and on 10 January the airfield at Tavoy, half-way up Tenasserim. By the 20th they were pushing hard down the road from Raheng towards Moulmein, and 16th Brigade, under orders not to get heavily involved on the frontier, withdrew to Martaban, three miles across the bay from Moulmein.

In their first battle, the Burma Rifles fought quite well at Moulmein, and were then withdrawn by river steamer to Martaban. Staying to the last moment to complete demolitions was a section of 60 Field Company, Madras Sappers and Miners, under Captain A. R. Jardine. At last they embarked on a launch, but as they were about to leave, a party of stragglers arrived on the jetty and the Brigade Major ordered the sappers off the boat to defend the jetty while the stragglers got away. So Jardine, Jemadar Malligarjunan and their men built parapets out of bedding-rolls and held off the Japanese. Jardine was wounded, and the Jemadar assumed command. The party was joined by Lieutenant Colonel Taylor, OC 8th Burma Rifles. When it became obvious that no ferry was returning for them (the crew would not risk it), the whole party took refuge under a jetty while the Japanese arrived and set up mortars above them. After dark Taylor 'heard odd sounds coming from an adjacent yard and found that the sappers had disappeared. Peeping round a wall I was staggered to see them industriously building a petrol-barrel raft with their Jemadar giving instructions in whispers. Having completed the raft, they launched it; but the Jemadar, apparently not satisfied, had the raft pulled ashore and taken to pieces to replace a leaking barrel. It was then re-launched, but still the Jemadar was not happy about it, and had it re-built a second time. Then he smiled his satisfaction, came up to me and, saluting, said, "Raft ready, Sahib." We climbed aboard, but as we dared not use paddles, the Jemadar and his men stripped and gently slid the raft into the water and guided it to safety.'

Having complete command of the Bay of Bengal, the Japanese then landed west of Martaban, which in turn was evacuated.

Much depended on holding Rangoon as long as possible. 48th Infantry Brigade from India disembarked during the night 30/31 January; another brigade and a field regiment from India, and an armoured brigade from the Middle East were at sea heading for Rangoon. The natural defence line against an attack from the east was the Sittang River, fast flowing and up to a thousand yards wide. It was bridged in two places, three miles from its mouth by the Sittang Bridge and, 110 miles upstream, at Toungoo. Obviously the Sittang Bridge was vital to holding Rangoon. The river there was only about 500 yards wide, but widened to 800 yards above and below it.

To hold the line of the Sittang and deny the bridge to the enemy was the responsibility of 17th Indian Division, commanded by Major General J. G. Smyth. 'Jackie' Smyth was a well-known and somewhat flamboyant Indian Army character. He had won in France a very 'good' – and much publicized – VC; and was the author of a book about winning VCs. He would have liked to concentrate his three brigades – to which a fourth, the 48th, now in Rangoon, was about to be added – and fight a divisional battle for the bridge. But he was overruled and ordered to give ground as slowly as possible, as being the best way to keep Rangoon open. In accordance with these orders, he held the line of the Bilin river, west of the Salween, as a rearguard position. Withdrawing to it, the 7/10th Baluchis, a young, wartime battalion in 46th Brigade, for the whole of the night of 11/12 February, fought a Thermopylae-style battle against a Japanese regiment (brigade). An immediate DSO was won by Captain Siri Kanth Korla, commanding the Dogra company, who led many counter-attacks in person, was captured by the Japanese and escaped. But when the battalion was almost annihilated, the colonel and six British Officers dead, the Japanese were across the Salween.

The Japanese plan was to cross the Sittang Bridge with two divisions. The 33rd, having crossed, would head south-west for Rangoon, eighty miles away, and the 55th would go north to Toungoo. The Bilin position, some forty-six miles from the bridge, held them up for only four days; but

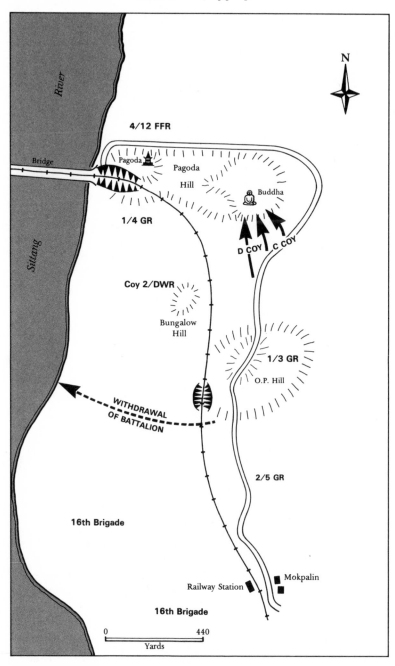

Burma: Sittang Bridge, 21–22 February 1942

every day was precious with 7th Armoured Brigade approaching Rangoon. Then the Japanese outflanked the rearguard and raced for the Sittang Bridge.

To hold the bridge, Smyth had one fresh brigade, the newly arrived 48th (Brigadier N. Hugh-Jones); the 16th and 46th Brigades (Brigadiers J. K. Jones and R. G. Ekin), somewhat battered; and the remains of 2nd Burma Brigade, almost disintegrated. The withdrawal from the Bilin position to the bridge was led by 48th, followed by 16th, with 46th as rearguard.

48th Brigade consisted of three Gurkha battalions, the 1/3rd, 1/4th and 2/5th (Royal). Very tired, they reached Kyaikto, sixteen miles short of the Sittang bridge, at midnight of 20/21 February, dossed down and slept like logs. Shortly before dawn they were awakened by the screaming, jackal-howling, gibbering and manic noises which the Japanese made to scare young soldiers. Round the perimeter rapid fire was directed at nothing, but order was soon restored and Lieutenant Colonel W. D. A. Lentaigne, commanding the 1/4th, decided that a hot meal would do them no harm. So at 0930 when Brigadier Hugh-Jones ordered an immediate move to the bridge, his battalion was leading, a very fortunate chance for them.

Owing to someone's blunder, the brigade as it marched was subjected to the most vicious attacks by RAF and American Volunteer Force planes which circled over the Japanese, the pilots cheerily waving at them, and then zoomed down bombing and machine-gunning the Gurkhas, which shook even those stolid little men. Worse, it stampeded most of their mules, which were almost untrained since they had been taken over only at Rangoon, and which disappeared into the jungle with their wireless sets and 3-inch mortars. In the evening of the 21st the Gurkhas arrived at Mokpalin Quarries, some nine miles short of the bridge; and spent the night with the 2/5th in the quarries, the 1/4th north of the quarries, nearest to the bridge, and the 1/3rd about two miles to the east.

At midnight Lentaigne was ordered by the divisional commander to march his battalion with all speed to the bridge and across it, for a parachute drop was expected on the west bank that morning. This he did, after shoving his way through a fearful traffic-jam in Mokpalin village. There was no parachute drop, but the 1/4th were a welcome addition to the bridgehead force, which up to then consisted only of the 4/12th Frontier Force Regiment and a very shaky battalion of Burma Rifles holding a perimeter round the east end of the bridge, and a company of the 2nd Duke of Wellington's Regiment in reserve on the west bank.

At 0830 on the 22nd the enemy attacked the bridgehead from the north and the Burma Rifles disintegrated. But the 4/12th Frontier Force in a fine counter-attack restored the situation. During this action the Sikh Section (two guns) of 12th (Poonch) Mountain Battery arrived on the river bank and the section commander made the sensible decision to get his guns across and into action on the west bank. The bridge was blocked with lorries, so he got his guns off the mules and onto a small steamer. Enemy fire set this alight but he managed to take his guns ashore, manhandled them up the far bank and into action from the jungle-edge. He was just in time, for soon after this the CRE ordered all steamers, ferries and three hundred sampans to be made unserviceable. Later, the section's mules crossed by the bridge.

Brigadier Hugh-Jones, arriving at 1030, took command of the bridgehead and sent across the river the 1/4th Gurkhas to hold the perimeter to the right of the 4/12th Frontier Force, and the company of the Duke of Wellington's Regiment to hold Bungalow Hill.

At 0400 hrs in Mokpalin Quarries the 2/5th received verbal orders to march straight for the bridge, sending their motor transport on ahead. The lorries got across safely, and it seemed as though the battalion would also, subject to air attack. The CO, Lieutenant Colonel Cameron, rode on with a small party on liberated bicycles to reconnoitre the crossing, but were held up by lorries jammed nose-to-tail in Mokpalin village, under fire from the village temples. He sent his battalion in to clear the village, which they did, incinerating most of the enemy in the wooden houses.

It seemed that the enemy were holding a jungle-covered hill, crowned by a huge stone Buddha, about a mile north of Mokpalin and commanding the approach to the bridge. Four or five hundred yards to the west of Buddha Hill, and on the same ridge, was Pagoda Hill, also assumed to be held by the Japanese although in fact a company of the 4/12th Frontier Force were on it. Cameron was also unaware of the company of the Duke's on Bungalow Hill. The 1/3rd Gurkhas then came up, and the two COs made a plan for the 1/3rd to attack Buddha and Pagoda Hills, supported by two and a half mountain batteries (ten guns).

Half of the twenty-minute artillery concentration fell with deadly accuracy on the Frontier Force company holding Pagoda Hill. They withdrew (but returned later). At 1130 the 1/3rd Gurkhas went in, B Company on the left going for Pagoda Hill, C and D on the right going for Buddha Hill.

Battalion headquarters was on OP Hill, about half a mile to the south. For the next three hours Colonel Ballinger waited for news of his forward companies. All he heard was the sound of heavy firing, mortars and automatics. He said to his Adjutant, Captain B. G. Kinloch, 'Bruce, I want you to go and find out what's happening to the forward companies.'

Kinloch, without even an orderly (for his had been killed by the RAF bombing), set off into the jungle, feeling remarkably lonely and apprehensive. Then Ballinger called him back, 'I think I'll go myself, with the recce group. You stay here with Major Bradford.' Ballinger and the recce group disappeared into the jungle, whence a few minutes later was heard the sound of automatic fire. Only the Subadar Major returned, to describe how the Colonel was killed as he went towards some Japanese who raised their hands in surrender. Half an hour later there arrived Lieutenant Fay, wounded, with news that C and D Companies were on Buddha Hill but could go no further because the enemy were dug in on the reverse slopes. There was no news of B.

Bradford, with two companies pinned down and a third disappeared into the blue, went back to Mokpalin to get help. There he found Brigadier J. K. Jones, commanding 16th Brigade, who had no one to send and ordered Bradford to withdraw his forward companies, concentrate on OP Hill and hold it at all costs. But by that time C and D company were surrounded: there was no way of recalling them, or B Company. So the battalion, with only A Company and two platoons of the 2/5th Gurkhas under command, took up a strong position on OP Hill based on a sunken road. They held the north face of a box, with the 2/5th between them and Mokpalin railway station, facing east; and 16th Brigade facing south and west. Apart from hearing nothing of B, C and D Companies except intermittent firing from their direction, their position seemed fairly stable.

So it was at the bridgehead. The perimeter was still intact, held by the 4/12th Frontier Force on the left, Lentaigne's 1/4th Gurkhas in the centre, and the company of the Duke's on Bungalow Hill, with what was left of the Burma Rifles on the right. On Pagoda Hill, not part of the bridgehead force and probably not even in contact with it, were C and D Companies of the 1/3rd Gurkhas.

But this comparatively tidy picture was not what Brigadier Hugh-Jones, the bridgehead commander, saw. His only news of 46th Brigade, still back at Kyaikto, came from stragglers with wild stories of the brigade destroyed and 16th Brigade reduced to six hundred men. The truth was that the Japanese had set up a roadblock between 46th and 16th Brigades, and both had suffered casualties; but they were far from broken: the Mokpalin box held, and some units of 46th Brigade managed to reach it. But Hugh-Jones had no contact, by wireless or any other means, with Mokpalin less than a mile away.

It had been impressed on him that the decision on when to blow the bridge was his alone, but in no circumstances must it fall intact into enemy hands. At 1930 hours the previous evening the Malerkotla State Field Company of Sappers and Miners had been ordered to prepare the bridge for demolition by dusk on the following day (the 22nd). A steel-girder bridge cannot be demolished by a few big charges; many small charges of plastic explosives must be attached to key girders and detonated simultaneously. The 17th Division had no Field Park Company and was short of engineer stores: it had only enough cable to blow one span electrically (by far the most reliable method), another span by instantaneous fuse (FID), and a third span with safety fuses setting off one charge and the remainder, it was hoped, going off sympathetically.*

---

*FID must be set off by a detonator joining it to a length of safety fuse which is lit by a match. The FID at that time was notoriously unreliable. Both the electric cable and the FID could explode simultaneously several charges; but the slow-burning safety-fuse couldn't: if it was laid to a number of charges, the first to explode would probably cut the fuse to the others. Hence the hope that the charges under the third span would explode sympathetically, as the first went up. They didn't.

Moreover, there did not seem to be enough cable or FID for the charges to be detonated from the safety of the west bank: the demolition party, calculated the CO of the Malerkotlas, Major R. C. Orgill, would have to be actually on the bridge, close to the spans to be demolished. It was not easy to fix the charges and prepare the demolition of the narrow bridge while lorries were passing ceaselessly over it. For twenty-four hours the Malerkotlas worked on the job, and guarded their work against Japanese swimmers or boatmen.

At 0200 hours on the 23rd the Brigadier asked Orgill if he could guarantee to blow the bridge in daylight. Orgill couldn't. Already the Japanese had infiltrated to the railway cutting and were firing a light machine-gun straight down the bridge, the bullets sending up showers of sparks from the girders; and in daylight it would be under much heavier fire from upstream.

Brigadier Hugh-Jones then called a conference of battalion commanders and explained the position as he saw it. It was vital that the enemy should not capture the bridge intact. He did not think the bridgehead force could hold out against a strong attack in the morning. They could not count on the bridge being blown in daylight.

It is extraordinary that at this conference Major Orgill was not present. He was asleep in bed some distance away. He was an outstandingly enterprising and adventurous officer, and it is inconceivable that he could have deliberately absented himself from a very important action and left the demolition to a subaltern, Lieutenant Bashir Ahmed Khan. Either he was utterly exhausted after working non-stop for thirty hours; or – and this seems much more likely – he did not expect the bridge to be blown that night. Another mystery is that Bashir Ahmed Khan did, apparently, find enough cable to blow one span electrically from a foxhole beside the west bank abutment of the bridge. This is what he actually did, and he could presumably have done it safely in daylight. Did Orgill know this? What *exactly* had Orgill said to Hugh-Jones? One can only speculate: the facts are not known.

Hugh-Jones and the battalion commanders agreed in that desperate hour before dawn that the bridge must be blown, and quickly too, while it was still dark. But with most of 17th Division on the wrong side, the dreadful decision could be made only by the divisional commander, who was awakened and asked for his orders. The man who had won the VC twenty-eight years ago took five minutes to make up his mind. He gave the order, 'Blow it.'

There was just time to bring back the 1/4th Gurkhas and the 1/12th Frontier Force, but the Duke's could not be contacted, and the Burma Rifles had gone. On the bridge was only the firing party of Malerkotla sappers under Bashir Ahmed Khan, who lit the safety fuse and then touched off the instantaneous fuse and electrical circuit while the battle raged practically on the bridge itself.

On OP Hill Bruce Kinloch, lying on the lip of the sunken road with his

Tommy gun, felt comparatively safe, though it was a very noisy night with shelling and mortaring, and streams of red tracer and Very lights providing a dazzling fireworks display.

'Then, at 0530 hours, as the first light of dawn appeared in the eastern sky, from the direction of the river came the reverberating roar of three enormous explosions, and on the instant we realized that the bridge had been blown and our lifeline cut. As the echoes died away, there was complete silence. All firing ceased, and every living thing seemed to be holding its breath. Then the Japanese, like a troop of excited monkeys, broke into shrill chattering. Believing that everyone else had crossed over and abandoned us to our fate, we were filled with anger.

When dawn broke I got into a carrier with two volunteers and drove down to reconnoitre the Mokpalin station area. To my surprise and delight I discovered that the other troops were still there. So I loaded the carrier with water and ammunition and returned to OP Hill. There was a long lull until about 0730 when there appeared to our astonished eyes some thirty Japs, marching in close formation along the railway line below us, singing and laughing, only about 150 yards away. Our Brens opened with good effect, and the survivors dived over the railway line. Soon after a Jap reconnaissance plane flew slowly over us, so low that I could distinctly see the pilot's goggled face peering down. Everyone opened up on it, and I emptied a full drum of my Tommy gun. We could see the bullet strikes on the fabric, and over the station the plane suddenly banked and dived to the ground, exploding in a ball of flame. A great cheer went up, like a football crowd applauding the winning goal.'

Later in the morning Brigadier Jones, now in command of all the troops on the east bank, arrived at OP Hill and issued orders that the 1/3rd Gurkhas, with the company of Duke's under command, and the 2/5th Gurkhas hold their positions until the following morning, the 24th, to cover the withdrawal of 16th Brigade during the night to the river bank, and their rafting across. A few survivors of C and D Companies trickled in, the remainder having been killed or captured when their ammunition ran out. The Gurkhas neither saw nor heard a single Japanese, but there was firing from the direction of Mokpalin, so Kinloch went to investigate. The firing, he discovered, was ammunition exploding in a line of burning lorries. No one was there.

What had happened was that in the early afternoon the Japanese had attacked the south-eastern face of the perimeter and pushed the defenders back. Brigadier Jones had decided that they must cross at once, not wait until dark, and had accordingly sent a message to the 1/3rd Gurkhas which never arrived. Already the wounded were being carried to the bank and rafted across by Captain Sundaram, Medical Officer of the 2/5th. Two or three burning lorries gave Colonel Cameron an idea: he had the remainder set alight, and under cover of the smoke and explosions, moved down to the river, half a mile away, behind 16th Brigade, every man laden with as many bamboos and empty tins as he could carry. From these, with rifle-slings and pull-throughs, they constructed rough rafts on which were sent across first the wounded, then the bolder of the non-swimmers, finally the swimmers. Some drowned, some had their throats cut by ghoulish saffron-robed priests as they struggled exhausted ashore; but about two hundred of the 2/5th reached the west bank safely.

Bradford and Kinloch on OP Hill deduced that all the other troops had withdrawn to the river, but that the order for their battalion to withdraw had gone astray. So at 1530 hours they set off, reaching the river an hour later, unimpeded by Japanese, about eight hundred yards below the bridge. On the east bank there were only some wounded, too bad to try to swim or raft. Looking upstream, Kinloch

'stared resentfully at the broken bridge. Then my interest quickened. I noticed that only two spans had been blown, and that the ends of these were resting in the water where the gap between them looked tantalizingly small. If the bridgehead could be secured, it might still be possible to get the battalion across in the dark.'

After a perimeter had been formed and the men put to work building rafts, Kinloch stalked cautiously through the jungle towards the bridge. He left his Tommy gun with Bradford, but carried three grenades, the pins flattened for quick use, in his binoculars case. An experienced shikari, he moved without a sound through the jungle, watching warily for any movement. He reached the end of the bridge: no one was there. Slowly, carefully, he moved up a path leading to the Pagoda. About a hundred yards from the bridge, he came upon a huge tree, forked ten feet above the ground. In the shadow of the fork he made out a head wearing a British-pattern steel helmet. He challenged, and the head disappeared.

'With one bound I reached the tree and peered cautiously round it – to find myself looking straight into the face of a Jap officer so close that I could have touched him – black knee-boots, soft khaki peaked cap, samurai sword. I whipped out a grenade, let the lever go and rolled it gently round the other side of the tree. I heard a gasp, a shuffle of feet and an explosion. Then the air came alive with the whip-like crack of bullets. My guardian angel was working overtime, for I reached the bridge without a scratch.'

He ran back to the battalion and, since the Gurkhas were flaked out, collected two platoons of the Duke's, who had had an easier time. But he was too late: the Japanese reached the bridge before them, and held in force the railway line.

After dark Kinloch and Captain Darley, the Quarter Master, constructed a raft of water-tanks and bamboos, piled their clothes and arms on top and pushed it across, taking an hour over the crossing. They searched the west bank for good boats, but all had the planks stoved in, except one with which they returned to the east bank. During the rest of the night the wounded and about a hundred men made the crossing.

In the morning Kinloch and Darley again swam across, to try to organize a better ferry service for the following night. But they heard firing and watched helplessly as the Japanese rushed the men who remained. Some swam across, bullets pocking the water beside their bobbing heads, and told him that Bradford had surrendered, to save the lives of the rest of his men. But surrender was not in the military code of the Subadar Major, who pulled a pistol, shot a Japanese officer and then shot himself. Bradford was then killed, and a Gurkha shot the man who killed him. But there was no more shooting: the Subadar Major had behaved exactly as the Japanese would have behaved in his place. The rest of the Gurkhas were marched away, prisoners.

So, barefoot and almost naked, Kinloch, Darley and the survivors of the 1/3rd set off across to the west. Apart from being bitten by a snake, and having the poison sucked out by Darley, Kinloch had no more adventures until he was challenged by a Cameronians' sentry.

It took the Japanese a fortnight to make a road from Kyaikto, bring up bridging material and make a crossing in force. During that time 17th Division re-formed at Pegu. Most of the sappers and gunners, with most of their guns, were there. (The 3rd Indian Light AA Battery, in almost its first action, here shot down with its Bofors guns six planes in a day.) The 1/4th Gurkhas and 4/12th Frontier Force were almost complete. Other battalions varied in strength from 1/9th Royal Jats, 550, to 5/17th Dogras, 30. Eighty officers, 68 VCOs and 3,325 Other Ranks reached Pegu.

Forty-five years later opinion among those who were there is still divided about the decision to blow the bridge while most of the division was on the wrong side. Even hindsight gives no clear answer: the troops on the east bank held out for twenty-four hours after the explosion, but the Japanese did not press them. Someone had to carry the can, and that, of course, was Jackie Smyth, VC, as he knew he would when he gave the order. But perhaps the real fault lay with those who insisted that he fight too far forward, instead of staging a divisional battle to hold the line of the Sittang. Wavell always under-estimated the Japanese, and Hutton was an extremely good staff officer but not an experienced field commander.

Right or wrong, the decision taken set the pattern for the Burma campaign of 1942. It ruled out any possibility of holding Rangoon for any length of time by defending the line of the Sittang river. On the other hand, blowing the bridge enabled Rangoon to be held for two vital weeks during which reinforcements, especially 7th Armoured Brigade, were disembarked, without which the two divisions in Burma could never have been withdrawn to India.

7th Armoured Brigade consisted of the 7th Hussars and the 2nd Royal Tank Regiment, with a battery of Royal Horse Artillery, veterans of the desert battles. To it was attached sometimes one, sometimes both of the unbrigaded British battalions from India, the 1st Cameronians and the 1st West Yorkshire Regiment. The armoured regiments had Stuart tanks: inadequate in the desert, these were enough for Burma; for the Japanese, unsurpassed as infantry in this kind of war, were not nearly as formidable as

Germans with tanks and anti-tank guns.

On 5 March General Sir Harold Alexander relieved Hutton, who became his Chief of Staff. Alexander's greatest asset was that he was always calm, always 'unflappable', even during the retreat to and from Dunkirk. No quality could be more valuable in Burma in 1942. His command included the British troops, and the Chinese IV and V Armies (each of the strength of about two very weak divisions) put at his disposal by Generalissimo Chiang Kai-shek. He formed the British troops into a corps, Burcorps, to command which General W. J. Slim was flown in.

Slim, who had been wounded commanding 10th Indian Brigade at Gallabat, was the best British, perhaps the best Allied, commander in World War II. Certainly he was the one who, to adapt a military aphorism, 'made the mostest out of the leastest'. He was a man of great mental and physical resilience, no showman but a strong personality with wit and style. When he gave a pep-talk to a newly arrived British battalion in his brigade, an enthusiastic corporal exclaimed: 'Don't you worry, sir, we'll follow you anywhere.' 'Not bloody likely,' retorted Bill Slim, 'I'll follow you.'

He found 17th Division and the armoured brigade about thirty miles south of Prome, and 1st Burma Division at Toungoo, waiting for the Chinese to arrive. He and Alexander were handicapped by lack of instructions about the overall plan. Were they supposed to try to hold any part of Burma, or to fight a rearguard action back to India? Like the Duke of Aosta in Abyssinia, they had no hope of reinforcements. Nothing they expended could be replaced. They were hampered by many thousands of Indian settlers, who must be fed and protected. Most of the Burmese, but not the hill tribes, were hostile. But they had one enormous advantage denied to the Duke of Aosta, and to the defenders of Hong Kong and Malaya: it was just possible that they would get back to India. And the Japanese treatment of prisoners – throats cut, beheaded, used for bayonet practice, flogged, starved, worked to death – was not such as to encourage surrender.

Slim decided to concentrate the British troops in the Prome area for a counter-attack against an enemy who he believed might be overstretched, and to leave the Sittang valley to the Chinese.

The Chinese, as allies, had virtues and defects. They fought well and cleverly when they could be persuaded to fight at all. They were as likely to retreat as to advance, and to do either at four o'clock or twelve o'clock when they had promised to do it at eight. Their chain-of-command was tortuous, not such as to facilitate quick decision, and not understood even by their field commander, the limey-hating American General 'Vinegar Joe' Stilwell, who was also supposed to be Chiang Kai-shek's Chief of Staff. They had been made available to Alexander only on condition that they were rationed by the British, who were finding it none too easy to ration themselves. They were compulsive pillagers: anything not nailed down they would remove, including their allies' transport, weapons and supplies.

While 1st Burma Division were at Toungoo waiting to hand over to the

Chinese, there occurred an incident trivial in itself, but in its way historic: the last charge of British/Indian horsed cavalry. It was led by Arthur Sandeman of the Central India Horse, a Don Quixote, brave as a lion, affecting the style and costume of a bygone age (in his case, Edwardian), and so short-sighted that he could not see a polo ball and had therefore taken to pig-sticking, as a boar was large enough to be visible. Never for one moment did he contemplate going to war other than on the back of a horse; so 22 March 1942 found him at Toungoo commanding a mounted squadron, Sikhs, of the Burma Frontier Force. With a clink of curb-chains and a rattle of hooves on gravel they rode out of history to reconnoitre the country to the south-east and perhaps link up with some Chinese who were supposed to be there. Four or five miles out, Sandeman saw what he myopically took to be the Chinese, and rode towards them making allied noises. When machine-gun bullets started kicking up dust, he realized they were Japanese. He drew his sword, ordered his trumpeter to sound the charge and galloped straight at them, followed by his Sikhs yelling their warcry. None reached the enemy: most were killed, and survivors did what they should have done at first, galloped back to Toungoo with information.

Back in Toungoo 1st Burma Division had begun its move to a concentration area thirty miles north of Prome. Among those remaining was 23rd Mountain Battery, near whom shells began to fall. Pat Carmichael, a wartime subaltern, spotted the muzzle flashes of a Japanese battery, and was told 'Well, if you can see them, go and set up an OP on the road and sort them out. Zero line 270 degrees.' He dismounted and, with a signaller unreeling a line, walked to the road.

'Meanwhile our guns had been run up to the forward edge of the copse and Zero Lines recorded. The element of surprise was in our favour, but it was essential that ranging should be quick so that we could go to fire for effect as fast as possible. . . . I ranged on the right hand gun, their Number 4, which was the most visible, using our Number 1 gun. I needed four rounds to get a respectable bracket, and had just ordered One Round Gunfire with a slight lift in range for the Left Section when a shell burst in the trees above us with a shattering explosion. . . . I watched for the fall of shot with my glasses and saw the bursts suddenly flower out and mask the enemy guns. As I was ordering a correction for the next round of Gun Fire, a second shell exploded in our trees. . . . No time for more than a fleeting thought as our next rounds were on their way. They were good, bursting on the fringe of the wood. While I waited for the dust to clear, small arms fire started down the road on my left. . . . A mass of infantry was advancing towards the road, at a walk, in the open paddy. . . .

Were they enemy or Chinese? [Their uniforms were very similar.] I had to be sure and check with the Chinese on my right, but before moving I ordered two rounds Gun Fire for good measure. I ran the fifty yards to the Chinese and grabbed what I assumed to be the senior man, pointing at the advancing troops.

"Japani?" I asked. He grinned and gave me the metronome nod, which could mean both Yes and No.

"Chinoise?" The beaming and nodding continued. I jabbed my left arm towards the Japs, bared my teeth, screwed up my eyes and drew a hand across my throat.

"Japani? Nipponi?" The nodding was more vigorous. I ran back.

"GF Target" I shouted at the signaller before I reached him. I ordered switch and range with Number 1 gun ranging, and saw the round burst well behind them. I dropped the range. The burst was just short. I corrected left and went for One Round Gun Fire. The four bursts spattered out across the dry paddy and totally obscured the lines of men, who immediately started to emerge from the dust of the explosions, still walking steadily towards the road. But now there were some gaps in the lines. I dropped 25 yards for two more rounds. . . .

"Left One Degree. Drop Fifty. Two Rounds Gun Fire."

The enemy infantry had been cut down to small groups. . . . The next two lines of bursts finally scattered them.'

Next day the battery was on its way by rail to the Irrawaddy valley.

In the Prome area Slim had his corps concentrated. It was of the greatest value that Major General Bruce Scott, commanding 1st Burma Division, and Major General D. T. ('Punch') Cowan, commanding 17th Division, were from Slim's own battalion, the 1/6th Gurkhas. They had been friends for years and each knew how the others would react to any circumstances.

No sooner did 1st Burma Division leave Toungoo than the Chinese did likewise. With his left flank wide open, Slim had to give up all idea of a counter-attack and withdraw from Prome. Another grievous setback was the destruction on the ground, by Japanese fighters, of nearly all the RAF and American Volunteer Force planes in Burma. Thereafter Burcorps never saw a friendly plane. Unfriendly planes day after day straffed troops and transport which was helplessly road-bound.

As in Malaya, the greatest weakness of the British forces in Burma was that their motor transport tied them to the roads. This the Japanese exploited skilfully. A British rearguard would take up a position across a road. The Japanese would circle round it and set up a roadblock some miles behind. If the rearguard stayed put, it would starve: so it withdrew to try to break through the roadblock. It might succeed, with considerable losses: if it failed, it would have to go round, abandoning its transport on the road. In either case it had given up ground. This happened time and again. There was a way to defeat the Japanese tactics, but it depended on supplying the isolated rearguard by air-drop, and in 1942 there were no planes.

Least roadbound were the Mountain Artillery, who performed extraordinarily well. Others might occasionally be carried back in lorries, but the brave, enduring, patient mules and their devoted drivers marched every yard of the long retreat. On two occasions the 12th (Poonch) Mountain Battery marched 47 miles in a day and night, and 23rd Mountain Battery did 53 miles in 17 hours. To cover these great distances they never marched in step: each man marched with strides as long as he could manage: and they had no regular halts, like the infantry's ten minutes in the hour, but stopped only when it was absolutely necessary; because at a halt the mules got no rest, they had to stand with their loads on, so it was better for them to finish the day's march as soon as possible. The first job when the march was over was to water the mules. A mule is very fussy about what he drinks: if water is in the least tainted or brackish, he will sniff at it and stare into the distance with studied disdain. If the water is drinkable, he likes to take his time over it, savouring the flavour; so watering the 120 mules of a battery with buckets from a single village well was a long process. After watering, grooming: not to make the mules look smart, but to keep them going at all. A big mule needs 12lbs of oats a day to keep him in condition. Failing oats, maize will do. But during the Burma retreat there was neither oats nor maize, only paddy, which does not have the necessary vitamins. So they lost condition, their back muscles shrunk so that the saddle rested on spine and withers giving sore backs. During the grooming hour sores were dressed, methods devised of relieving the sores next day, and the men thumped and rubbed the mules' backs to get the circulation going. After grooming, the nosebags were put on, containing whatever had been found for the mules to eat. Then only could the men attend to their own needs, the first of which was hot, sweet tea, consumed with much sucking and smacking of the lips while each man squatted in front of his mule talking quietly to him while he snuffled contentedly in the nosebag. And *after* the men, the officers. Only the most dedicated care kept the mules going at all: it was agony to the men to load their beloved animals with the heavy parts of the gun, knowing it would hurt them. Towards the end of the long retreat, about half a dozen mules a day could no longer keep up, and had to be shot, rather than be left to die or to the Japanese and Burmans. Of all Carmichael's jobs, this was the worst: shooting a calm, trusting mule while the mule's driver pleaded in tears for his life.

Not infrequently the mountain guns were far too close to the enemy, often firing over open sights in gun-against-gun duels. Near Prome the FOO of 12th Battery was startled to see Japanese emerging from the bush not ten yards away. He backed quickly into cover, firing his Tommy gun: his signaller was slower off the mark and, as he turned, felt a hand grab his web-equipment. He had the presence of mind to slip it off his shoulders and run. The batteries' riflemen and Lewis-gunners were often in action, though where possible they had infantry escorts.

Burcorps held Yenangyaung long enough for the oil-installations there to be reduced to smoking black wreckage. Then, with the Chinese running hard for China and the enemy reaching round behind them, they could linger no longer. On 28 April Slim, to his great relief, received orders to do what everyone realized had to be done – give up Burma and withdraw to India. Burcorps, and the best of the Chinese divisions, the 38th, were to cross the Irrawaddy and move up the valley of its tributary, the Chindwin, as far as Kalewa. Thence by a new road, if it were completed in time, through the jungle-covered mountains to Imphal in Assam. It was a race. Could the roadmakers, labour and supervisors provided by the Assam tea planters, complete their task in time to meet Burcorps before the monsoon made operations impossible? Could Burcorps get there in time, and before the Japanese?

They could never have done it but for 7th Armoured Brigade. The tanks broke roadblocks, fought rearguard actions, ferried infantry, carried off wounded who would otherwise have been left to the enemy, and sometimes provided the only reliable radio communication between corps, division and brigades.

Gurkhas showed up outstandingly well in this retreat, on two occasions demonstrating that Japanese were not supermen. The first was on 11/12 April at Kokkogwa, during the fighting for the oilfields. A tremendous thunderstorm was raging, the night ablaze with sheet-lightning. The 2/5th Royal Gurkhas had repulsed one attack, and there were signs of another. According to the Regimental History:

'The enemy could be heard moving about and the clinking of metal indicated the mounting of mortars. A moment later a blinding flash proved the correctness of the deduction. A Bren gun opened fire on the flash and a combination of good marksmanship and good luck was decisive, for in the morning the complete mortar crew was found dead beside their mortar. Shortly after this the Japanese very helpfully announced their intention to attack by the fixing of bayonets. The attack when it came was met by such intensity of fire that it withered and broke.'

The second occasion was when 48th Brigade was holding a covering position at Kyaukse while the rest of the division, the armoured brigade and the Chinese crossed the Irrawaddy by the Ava bridge near Mandalay. The Japanese attacked at 2200 hours in bright moonlight. The 1/7th Gurkhas held their fire until the enemy were 150 yards away, and then opened up the 'mad minute', Brens, Tommy guns and all. Twice more during the night the Japanese attacked, and twice were decimated. In the morning Gurkhas and tanks sallied out and went through a village in front, bayonet, bomb and kukri. Over a hundred Japanese were killed for the loss of one Gurkha killed and three wounded. The Japanese were not supermen, and were not invincible.

1st Burma Division crossed the Irrawaddy near its junction with the Chindwin by a ferry improvised by the sappers, and marched thirty miles north-west to Monywa on the Chindwin. Divisional headquarters arrived after dark, and the Japanese arrived too, having come upriver by powered barges. Confused fighting in the dark resulted in a partitioning of the village. In the morning Major Hartley, commanding the 2nd (Derajat) Mountain Battery, established his OP within a few yards of divisional HQ, an unusual situation even in this unusual campaign. Suddenly some barges appeared, crammed with Japanese, moving rapidly upstream about four hundred yards away. The divisional commander shouted, 'Gunner, those barges!'; Hartley shouted to his signaller, 'GF target'; and the barges heeled over and began to sink. Warm were the congratulations on the Mountain Gunners' amazing speed and accuracy: but Hartley, a modest man, gave credit where it was due, to the Bofors guns of 3rd Indian Light Anti-Aircraft Battery, commanded by C. H. T. MacFetridge, who were almost within stone's throw of the target.

Nevertheless, Burma Div HQ had to decamp with unbecoming celerity, General Bruce Scott, his staff and office clerks clutching rifle or Tommy gun in one hand, cypher-books and secret papers in the other.

The last and most crucial battle was at Shwegyin, on the left bank of the Chindwin, the end of the road. The next stage would be a six-mile run on river-steamers up to Kalewa, whence the retreating army would strike off across the mountains towards Imphal in Assam. There was at Shwegyin a landing-stage, and adjoining it, 'the Basin', an egg-shaped depression about eight hundred by four hundred yards, surrounded, like the rim of a basin, by jungle-covered cliffs. Into this, for embarkation, poured all Burma Army, so that it was jam-packed with troops, guns, lorries, tanks. There were six steamers, each capable of carrying about six hundred men, plus one or two lorries, guns and jeeps. But it was rare for all six to be operating, for their civilian crews could only with great difficulty be persuaded to venture down to Shwegyin, and were alert for any opportunity to disappear.

Slim laid down that priorities for embarkation should be men, guns and four-wheel-drive vehicles. All other lorries would have to be burnt, and the tank crews, having fired off all their ammunition, must run their engines without oil until they seized up. The defence of the Basin was entrusted to 1/9th Royal Jats (Lieutenant Colonel Godley) and the last four Bofors guns of the 3rd Indian Light AA Battery. The Basin could never have been held without these Bofors, commanded by Lieutenant F. D. Webber. One was deployed primarily in an AA role, and three for action against ground targets in support of the Jats on the southern face of the Basin. The position was a perfect target for air-raids, and the Bofors shot down two planes, bringing their total bag since Moulmein to twenty-two planes and three troop-carrying barges.

At dawn on the 10th the enemy attacked, established themselves on the southern lip of the Basin and even got into it. Counter-attacks by the Jats and a battalion made up of 1/7th and 3/7th Gurkhas, supported by the closest and heaviest covering fire from the AA troop, which could now be prodigal of ammunition, thrust them back to the lip of the Basin but could not dislodge them from it. The enemy brought up a 70mm infantry gun which could fire down into the crowded Basin with devastating effect. In a dramatic duel over open sights it was knocked over and the gunners killed by a Bofors.

Loading men, guns and vehicles onto the steamers continued spasmodically until early afternoon, when the steamer-crews downed tools: nothing would induce them to make another trip down to such a deathtrap as the Basin. Then there was nothing for it but a night-march for men and mules, and what they could carry, over the roughest of hill paths towards Kalewa. In the evening the 2/5th Royal Gurkhas took up fall-back positions: the 1/9th Royal Jats and 7th Gurkhas then withdrew at speed, as though from a frontier piquet, under a terrific 20-minute rapid-fire barrage by the Bofors, tracer-shells streaming across the Basin in the gloaming. It silenced the enemy, who made not a move. The last shell fired by the last Bofors exploded in the red-hot barrel, and the Number 1 reported simply, 'Finished'. Then the gunners destroyed their guns and followed the infantry on the night march to Kalewa.

One Punjabi Mussulman gunner was too badly wounded to make the march, and a selfless comrade stayed to look after him. MacFetridge could do nothing but shake their hands and wish them luck.

Perhaps 100,000 Indian refugees trekked through Burma hoping to reach Assam. They were accompanied – often preceded – by many hundreds of terrified low-grade Indian troops and base personnel, soldiers only in that they wore uniform, without officers, without discipline, without shame, who robbed and murdered the villagers, in some degree justifying the hatred felt by Burmans for all Indians, from which the fighting troops suffered. Perhaps half the refugees died in the last stages of the retreat, of starvation, malaria, cholera and sheer loss of hope. The jungle on either side of the track was littered with their putrifying corpses, the stench overpowering and the disease-risk considerable. That cholera never did break out in epidemic was a great tribute to the Indian Medical Service.

On 12 May, under black, lowering clouds, they set off into the hills towards Imphal. They had a few four-wheel-drive vehicles, one Stuart tank, and fifteen guns, ten of these being 3.7 howitzers. As the rearguard left Kalewa, the monsoon burst in its full fury. It made the march a misery, struggling up steep hills along a track deep in slippery or glutinous mud. But it stopped the Japanese; and twenty-five miles out of Kalewa they reached the end of the road from Imphal, and the lorries of a RIASC transport company came slithering down to meet them.

On the last day of the 900-mile retreat, Slim recalled, he

'stood on a bank beside the road and watched the rearguard march into India. All of them, British, Indian and Gurkha, were gaunt and ragged as scarecrows. Yet as they trudged behind their surviving officers in groups pitifully small, they still carried their arms and kept their ranks, they were still recognizable as fighting units. They might look like scarecrows, but they looked like soldiers too.'

Pearl Harbor made it India's war, but with Congress on the wrong side, prepared to welcome the enemy with open arms, quite confident that he would hand the country over to Congress and then depart. If he declined to depart, he would be ejected by 'soul-force'. Apart from Congress, India was now in the front line with equipment arriving in quite satisfactory quantities, given that the Allies' first strategic priority was the defeat of Germany. Armoured regiments actually began to receive armour, Stuarts and Grants; the infantry got carriers, mortars, anti-tank guns – everything they had hitherto done without. Even wireless sets.

In no arm of the service was expansion so rapid, and so difficult, as in anti-aircraft artillery, when once India became a possible target for air-raids. In 1939 there was one British Heavy AA regiment in India, no Light AA. In 1940 one Indian Heavy AA regiment was raised; in 1941, before Pearl Harbor, three Heavy and two Light AA regiments, Indian, were raised; and in the first six months of 1942 five Heavy and seven Light, seven being converted infantry battalions. The training problems were awesome. The technique of anti-aircraft fire is difficult to master: there were few instructors, and the only previous experience on which to build was that of the Mountain Artillery and the 1st Indian Field Regiment.

Yet one Heavy regiment took part in the defence of Singapore, manning not only its own sixteen 3-inch guns, but also sixty-three Bofors which were found spare in the docks. They shot down a significant number of the 124 Japanese aircraft destroyed during the campaign. In Burma the first Heavy Battery in action defended the oilfields with converted 18-pounder field guns on improvised high-angle mountings. Their early-warning system was provided mainly by railway stationmasters and the civil telephones. The 3rd Light AA Battery was in the retreat, sometimes too close to enemy infantry for their comfort. Nearly all the AA regiments saw service somewhere – in Burma, Assam, defending Calcutta and other sea-ports.

Fighter, bomber and transport squadrons, British and American, were arriving all through 1942 and 1943, with the result that eventually they enjoyed complete command of the air.

Before Pearl Harbor all military thinking was directed westward: after Pearl Harbor it was directed eastward. The front was in Assam and the Arakan; half-trained formations were stationed to repel a landing on the east coast. A huge programme of road-, rail-, pipeline and airfield construction was started. Intensive training was given in jungle war by instructors not too well versed in it themselves.

By the autumn of 1942 morale, still low but recovering, needed the tonic of a victory. Wavell ordered an operation aimed at recapturing the port of Akyab on an island off the Arakan coast. It would be a limited affair, because the Arakan is separated from the rest of Burma by wide rivers and supposedly impassable jungle-clad mountains. The plan was for 14th Indian Division to advance ninety miles from Cox's Bazaar, down the narrow Mayu peninsular to capture Foul Point at its southern end. 6th British Brigade would then take Akyab from the sea.

At first all went well. The little port of Maungdaw, fifty miles south of Cox's Bazaar, and the only lateral road across the peninsular, passing by a tunnel under the Mayu range to Buthidaung, were captured in mid-December without difficulty. The division pressed on, one brigade on each side of the peninsular but keeping clear of the rocky spine which was 'impassable', to within seven miles of Foul Point.

There they met for the first time the Japanese 'bunker'. This was a strongpoint, held by perhaps a platoon, dug into the ground and roofed by heavy treetrunks with four or five feet of earth on top. It was camouflaged so as to be invisible at fifty yards. The occupants, well supplied with machine-guns, fired through narrow slits just above ground level. It was proof against a direct hit from a 25-pounder, and the garrison always fought to the last man. Bunkers were sited so as to be mutually supporting. Attacking infantry could be standing on top of one, with no means of breaking in; then mortar and artillery fire would come down on them, and machine-gun fire from neighbouring bunkers, and they would have to retreat, baffled and decimated.

Then the Japanese struck out of 'impassable' jungle, over the 'impassable' Mayu ridge, and set up roadblocks behind 14th Division. In near-panic it retreated to the Maungdaw-Buthidaung line. On the assumption that the Japanese would again encircle, a trap was laid for them, into which they obligingly walked. But the jaws of the trap failed to snap shut. Soon the 14th Division was back at Cox's Bazaar, whence it had set off four months earlier.

It was evident that divisions on the Burma front were still no match for the Japanese in jungles. Slim, soon to be promoted to the command of what became Fourteenth Army, determined to make them masters of the jungle, and of the Japanese.

A somewhat more successful amphibious operation was launched from India at that time by, improbably, two Auxiliary Force units, the Calcutta Light Horse and the Calcutta Scottish. All their young and fit had gone to the war, and there remained on the muster-rolls only those whom the Manpower Committee retained as too old, unfit or indispensable at their desks to the war effort. They were overjoyed at being asked to supply volunteers for a dangerous secret mission against Germans. From many applicants, fourteen of the Calcutta Light Horse and four of the Calcutta Scottish were chosen, and given special instruction in revolver and Sten-gun shooting.

Although they did not yet know it, they were to board and capture or sink a German ship, the *Ehrenfels*, safe with three other Axis ships in the harbour of neutral Portuguese Goa. Captain Röfer, skipper of the *Ehrenfels*, was a member of an intelligence team organized by a German spy named Trompeta, who was established as a businessman in Goa. Trompeta collated reports on shipping movements from enemy agents in Indian ports, and Röfer transmitted these through a special, secret set in his ship to German and Japanese submarines, whose successes were damaging.

To attack these ships in the harbour of a neutral state (albeit Britain's ally) was an act of piracy.* If captured, the best the pirates could expect

*Surviving 'Goans' do not wish their true names to be revealed, in case even now the owners of the *Ehrenfels* or the relatives of the crew sue them for damages. Also, there is the problem of holiday homes in Portugal.

would be a long term in a Goan prison, no fun-palace. If successful, they would receive no medals. The diplomatic consequences of disclosure could be horrendous, just when the Western Allies were hoping that the Portuguese might offer them base facilities in the Azores. If the job were done by regular forces, it would be impossible for His Majesty's Government to disclaim responsibility. But the escapade of a party of Calcutta boxwallahs might be dismissed as a drunken frolic. Administratively it might have been easier to launch the operation from Bombay, where the boxwallahs were no less eager and able. But with Bombay so close to Goa, security might be jeopardized.

The operation was organized by the Commanding Officer of the Light Horse, 'Chips' Grice, who had fought in the Zeebrugge raid and had been in business in Calcutta between the wars, and an SOE operative named Pugh. As the first step, Pugh kidnapped Trompeta and his wife at gunpoint from Goa and removed them to internment in India.

A sea-going vessel had to be acquired, capable of the voyage from Calcutta to Goa – but not too sea-going, lest its acquisition occasion unhelpful gossip. The choice settled on *Phoebe*, a Hooghly river hopper-barge, used for taking out to sea mud tipped into her by dredgers. She was simply an iron tank, 206 feet long, with a coal-burning engine, unsatisfactory at sea but not quite unseaworthy. Her temporary skipper was a retired naval officer, also in business in Calcutta. Her crew were lascars, ignorant of the treat in store.

To Trooper Cartwright, whose dicky heart precluded an active role in the operation, was allotted the delicate duty of persuading, and paying, Goa's brothel-keepers to offer, as a gesture of international amity, free entertainment to all foreign seamen in Goa during 'D' Night.

Because eighteen Light Horsemen and Calcutta Scots with middle-aged spreads might be too much for *Phoebe* – and the long voyage too much for them – they travelled by train, innocent tourists and commercial gents, to Cochin, still in ignorance of what lay ahead. There, from their hotel verandah, Chips Grice indicated a funny little boat with a long funnel.

'Gentlemen, you are looking at the boat which is going to take us to our assignment.'

'What, that little tiddler?'

'Are you serious?'

'Yes indeed. I will give out orders when we are at sea.'

They had imagined a dashing landing craft, not a wallowing little tub reeking of oil and coal and Hooghly river mud.

Out at sea, men were detailed to deal with the German crew, seize the bridge and captain's cabin, destroy the ship's and the secret radio, cut the anchor-chain with plastic explosive, fight fires, start the engines and navigate the ship. If captured, their cover-story was of a boozy cruise to Bombay, an illegal entry into Goa for a lark, an accidental collision with the *Ehrenfels* and an unprovoked attack by the *Ehrenfels* crew. It sounded pretty thin. They practised shooting, were instructed in plastic explosives, made bamboo ladders for the boarding party. They were issued with Goan currency in case they were cast ashore, and with German ammunition for their Sten guns. (In an enquiry by the Goan authorities after the operation, British empty cases would be damning; but German empty cases might be attributed to mutiny or quarrels aboard.) The Medical Officer, a Calcutta GP, placed on the deck a tin bath, filled with a solution of potassium permanganate, for the treatment of the wounded. Some of them felt rather sick.

Someone on the *Ehrenfels* had a premonition of trouble. Preparations were made to repel boarders with knives, iron bars and the like; and charges were laid to scuttle her if necessary. But on 'D' Night, thanks to Trooper Cartwright's wiles, only a few men were aboard.

It was pitch dark as the *Phoebe* crept into Goa harbour. Waiting on deck, faces blackened, were the boarding party.

'Who are you?' hailed a voice from the deck.

'Harbour barge,' replied Grice in German.

Then the two ships bumped. 'Now!' he shouted.

Bamboo ladders scraped against *Ehrenfels*'s side, grapnels were flung, hooked on and held. Up the ladders and over the gunwhale went the middle-aged boarders. A searchlight blinded them, but Trooper MacFarlane shot it out with his Sten. Then they were on deck, fighting with the crew. Captain Röfer was shot as he reached for a pistol, and the First Officer as he sounded the alarm siren. Pugh and Trooper Breene made for the secret radio cabin, shot open the door and smashed the set; but the radio operator managed to destroy the cypher-books with a white-hot incendiary bomb. Someone blew the anchor-chain, but the German crew flooded the deck with kerosene and set it alight with flares. Then the whole ship rocked with a deep explosion, and all the lights went out, as the scuttling charges exploded.

As the *Ehrenfels* went down, blazing and belching smoke, the other Axis ships were scuttled too. The boarding party returned to the *Phoebe* and set a course for the bar of the Taj Mahal Hotel in Bombay.

But they never got even the 1939–45 Star for it.

One more unusual amphibious operation deserves mention. The 45th Cavalry were a wartime unit, training near the little port of Karwar, on the Bay of Bengal. Suddenly there came panting up to 'Oscar' Jenkins an excited sowar from the Dogra Squadron. 'Sahib, an enormous fish!'

'It was a whale, stranded on the shore. Someone had been there before us and in the manner of India had made propitiation and passed on, leaving a hibiscus flower and a little formal pattern of pink and scarlet petals on its smooth dark hide. . . . At intervals it opened a brown eye, large, dark and tranquil, or expelled from its single nostril a blast of hot and foul-smelling air. A gasping inhalation followed and the nostril screwed itself shut like a rubber tobacco-pouch. . . .

The beach was flat and the sea now some three hundred yards away. If we could keep it cool, we might get it back into the ocean at high water.

We detailed men with canvas buckets to pour water over the whale and dug trenches to assist in the operation. I was struck by the complete impotence of the creature. . . .

High water came and it was soon plain that even with our digging it was not deep enough. The whale remained limp and powerless. Lifting was impossible. We decided at the risk of damage to its flippers to roll it down the beach. Its flat belly was white and furrowed fore and aft like a ploughed field.

Risaldar Nawaz Khan and his Pathans joined the Dogras, patting and exhorting the creature to cheer up; giving, receiving and disobeying orders all in the same breath. Pandemonium of the most exhilarating kind! Nawaz had obviously been salvaging whales all his life. Numbers made all the difference. Over and over went the whale until suddenly the deepening water gave it life. An abrupt heave tipped a young Pathan off its back into the water. Slowly it began to swim and then, gathering speed and spouting water, set course for the horizon.'

CHAPTER 20

Eighth Army Triumphs,
1942–43

Only gradually did it become apparent that the El Alamein position would be held, largely because the Afrika Korps had shot its bolt and run out of supplies. Eighth Army's defence was vigorously – if sometimes confusedly – offensive. A key to the position was the Ruweisat Ridge, running east and west through the middle of it. It rose only some sixty or seventy metres above sea level, but it commanded the battlefield to the north and to the south.

On 14 July 1942 5th Indian Brigade – of, but hardly in, 5th Indian Division – attacked in a westerly direction along the ridge, with a New Zealand brigade on its left. A night attack by the 3/10th Baluchis and the 4/6th Rajputana Rifles, continued all through the day, collected about a thousand Italian prisoners but left the Indians and New Zealanders holding a salient like a long finger stuck into the enemy's midriff. Uncomfortable. Thanks to the carelessness of Germans speaking over the air in clear, or in clumsy *doubles entendres*, they expected to be attacked by panzers in the evening, and were. But the Germans got an unpleasant surprise: during the day there had been brought to the Indian position, and dug in flush with the ground, a number of newly arrived 6-pounder anti-tank guns, which could actually knock out tanks at further than point-blank range. It was these wonderful little guns that were to end the tyranny of the German armour. The Germans attacked in the evening, as they preferred, with the setting sun in the defenders' eyes, and the fighting went on through the night. Daylight disclosed on the 5th Brigade front twenty-four dead tanks, eight armoured cars, six 88s and many lesser guns. It was a wonderful experience, the shape of things to come. More than any other weapon, the 6-pounder won the war in the desert. Next, perhaps, in importance was the four-wheel-drive jeep, available in quantity for the first time at El Alamein.

There ensued a further stalemate, each side striving to build up its strength for a knock-out in the autumn. For 5th Indian Brigade on Ruweisat Ridge it was extraordinarily unpleasant, largely because it was so *crowded* – more latrines, more 'desert roses' (urinals), more scraps of food lying around, more corpses in burnt-out tanks, and above all more flies. A. G. Barron, who had just joined the 4/6th Rajputana Rifles, will never forget them:

'During daylight hours everyone had a black mass of flies about the size of a football hovering over his head. If two men met for a talk, the two masses would amalgamate into one, but then split up again when the men went their respective ways. . . . If one had the good fortune to get a bottle of beer, one had to be adept at whipping off the crown stopper and getting the mouth of the bottle into one's mouth with the absolute minimum of delay or the beer would be black with flies that had gone down the neck of the bottle. . . . It was usual to delay eating till after sunset when the flies would have settled down for the night.'

But the last ditch held compensations. It was only sixty miles from Alexandria. For those lucky enough to get a couple of days' leave or a quick dash back on some convenient duty, there were the delights of a proper bedroom and bath at the Hotel Mediterranée, *crevettes chasseurs* and Chablis at the Union Bar, the latest movie; even – who knows? – a bit of crumpet. For in Alex were ATS, FANNYS, Wrens, WAAFs, nurses and VADs. To say nothing of other girls whose charms were loudly advertised at every street corner. 'Hey! Meester Captain! You like my seester? She white girl, ver' nice, ver' cheap, ver' clean.' Then the irresistible sales-point, the very hallmark of perfection, 'I fuck her myself.'

The replacement of Auchinleck by Alexander as Commander-in-Chief, Middle East, and by Montgomery as commander of the Eighth Army, was much regretted by the Indian Army. It seemed very unjust to the Auk, a poor sort of reward for stopping Rommel at El Alamein. But on the whole most Eighth Army men would agree that it was time for a new general to meet the new situation of men and weapons pouring into Egypt in lavish profusion: bomber and fighter squadrons, including Spitfires, which were to win complete command of the air; two new British infantry and one new armoured division; 300 Sherman tanks mounting a 75mm gun in the turret, a match for nearly all the German tanks then in the desert; armoured, self-propelled 25-pounders and 105mm guns; and, above all, hundreds of 6-pounders, the tank-killers. Montgomery had more and better of everything than Rommel, far more and better than Auchinleck ever had. And he knew how to take advantage of overwhelming strength. To begin with, he scrapped all the Gleecols and Leathercols: in future Eighth Army would fight in divisions, with the 25-pounders doing the field gun's proper job. He tidied up the battlefield, replacing confusion and improvisation by order and balance. He infused everyone with the conviction not just that Rommel would get no further, but that he would be knocked right out of Africa.

He gave the impression of being one of those British service officers who did not want to know about the Indian Army. He made a tremendous impact on British troops, but not on Indians: he was not their style, though they might recognize his competence. So in Montgomery's plan for his great battle, to 4th Indian Division (of two brigades only), which had relieved 5th Indian Division on Ruweisat Ridge, was allotted a minor role. Only in SUPERCHARGE, his second plan when the first had been foiled by enemy minefields, was it given a worthy task. Brigadier Russell's 5th Indian Brigade (transferred back from 5th Indian Divsion), under temporary command of 51st Highland, would cut a lane south-west from

Kidney Ridge through which 7th Armoured and the New Zealand Divisions, the *corps de chasse*, would pass to complete the destruction of the Axis forces.

The plan required of Russell's brigade an approach march of seventeen miles, largely by unknown tracks in the dark. But the attack itself, behind a tremendous barrage moving forward at a pace of exactly thirty-five yards a minute, was almost a walkover. The guns obliterated all opposition, and when they stopped firing the brigade had only to round up a few hundred shaking Italians who were waiting to surrender. Then the Sherman tanks poured through: the battle was won.

(At the same time Anglo-American forces moved into French North Africa, the French authorities there with some hesitation declared for the Allies, and the Germans occupied Tunisia in force.)

General Tuker assumed that his division would be launched in pursuit. 'We knew we were the only fresh, desert-worthy troops now left in the Eighth Army. We were stripped ready. Our target was about two hundred and fifty miles away at Halfaya.' They could have reached it, and cut off the Afrika Korps, before the torrential rain which, according to Montgomery, prevented the *corps de chasse* getting there. Instead, 4th Indian had to hand over the troop-carrying lorries to a Greek brigade whose sole contribution to the desert war was a mutiny in Cairo some months later. Tuker's men were put to clearing up the battlefield and salvaging anything worth salvaging.

Well-founded rumours began to circulate that Montgomery did not want Indians in Eighth Army; they were to be relegated to garrison duties. Tuker was not the man to put up with this, and addressed a strong protest to XXX Corps Commander, Lieutenant General Horrocks:

'We feel most strongly that this division does not deserve such a fate. . . . I do not think anyone would deny that this is the most experienced division in the Empire, having been the only formation which fought at Sidi Barani, . . . the desert and mountain campaign of Eritrea, in the Syrian campaign, in the summer attacks last year in the Western Desert, throughout the Tobruk operations a year ago to Agedabia and through the withdrawal from there . . . and now having been engaged in this recent battle. Further, it looks as though mountain fighting may yet develop. I think we have more experience than most in this sort of warfare. . . . I should find it hard to explain to my officers and men that they are no longer needed.'

Horrocks forwarded this protest to Montgomery with the comment:

'I concur with the remarks in the attached letter. There is no doubt that this is an experienced division, more experienced probably than any other division in the Middle East. . . . Generally speaking the standard of training among the forces available here is not very high, but in the 4th Indian Division this is not the case.'

The division was moved westward, but only as far as Benghazi for garrison duties and stevedores' work. At the entry into Tripoli only two platoons, Army Headquarters guards, represented the army's most battle-worthy division. But in March 1943 Tuker's own former battalion, the 1/2nd Goorkhas, was brought forward as mountain specialists to probe and reconnoitre the enemy defences in the Matmata mountains along the Libyan-Tunisian border, which formed part of the Mareth Line originally built by the French. Naturally Tuker went up too. Although the 1/2nd Goorkhas had 'covered more ground in a night than anyone else in a week', it was broken to Tuker that there was no role for his division: its two brigades would go to X and XXX Corps respectively, and his divisional headquarters would come directly under Eighth Army, where it would have absolutely nothing to do. He said he could not accept this and asked to be relieved of his command. Then Montgomery changed his mind. He would, after all, need a division which understood mountain war and could climb mountains.

Fate was kind to them. During the night of 16/17th March the 1/2nd Goorkhas took out a German strongpoint and killed at least nine with the kukri. There was an American war correspondent there who told the world the story – 'with advantages'. Gurkhas became news. Montgomery never missed a trick in his handling of the media: it would now be quite impossible to relegate 4th Indian Division to the collection of scrap.

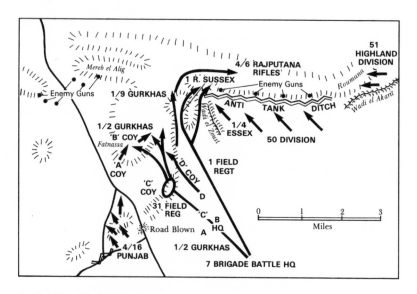

North Africa: Wadi Akarit, April 1943

His first attempt on the Mareth Line, a frontal attack by 50th Division, failed. His next ploy was a left hook, round the foot of the Matmata Mountains, by 1st Armoured and 2nd New Zealand Divisions. But there was a rough track, right through the middle of the mountains. If this could be forced, it would shorten the New Zealanders' supply line and with luck enable the Mareth Line to be taken from the rear. It was a job for 4th Indian.

They did it perfectly. There was not much enemy opposition, but a great deal of trouble from sophisticated minefields with anti-lifting devices, from the mountains themselves and from demolitions to the zig-zag mountain track, all overcome by infantry and Sappers and Miners. As they emerged into the Gabes plain, the enemy pulled out of the Mareth Line and retired thirty miles to the Wadi Akarit position.

Horrocks was generous in his praise. 'I congratulate all ranks on an outstanding performance – which could only have been carried out by troops highly trained in mountain warfare.'

The Wadi Akarit position covered a fifteen-mile gap between the sea and impassable salt marshes. On the five-mile-wide coastal plain, the defences were based on the deep, steep-sided Wadi itself; then on the 500-foot hill, Roumana; and on the right, on the much higher mountain massif, Fatnassa, a fantastic pile, like a fairy-tale mountain, split by chimneys and fissures, layered by escarpments and crowned by rock pinnacles. Between Roumana and Fatnassa the country is open and rolling, good tank country, so it was covered by a two-mile-long anti-tank ditch. The position could not be outflanked. It was held by the best of the German desert divisions, 90 Light and 164 Light Divisions, with Italians sandwiched between them.

Montgomery's original plan was for a breakthrough along the coast by 51st Highland, with 4th Indian taking Roumana to guard their flank. Tuker objected. It was no use in mountain war holding the second highest point: on Roumana his division would be overlooked by artillery OPs on Fatnassa and shelled to pieces. Fatnassa was the key to the Wadi Akarit position and must be taken. His 4th Indian was the division to take it. The whole enemy position would then be untenable. Montgomery accepted this view. In his revised plan 51st Highland would attack from the sea to Roumana; 50th Division would go for the open country between Roumana and Fatnassa; and 4th Indian for Fatnassa.

In front of the Fatnassa massif are two parallel escarpments with a deep re-entrant between them running into the middle of the massif. Tuker, who in Waziristan had been an articulate and often lonely advocate of silent, surprise night advances, saw this re-entrant as the key to the mountain, and planned for it to be made good at night by 7th Indian Brigade. 5th Indian Brigade would then pass through and go over the top of Fatnassa, opening the gate for the armour in the morning.

7th Brigade commander was O. de T. ('Os') Lovett, also a 2nd Goorkha. He naturally gave his own regiment the task of taking the highest ridges and peaks of Fatnassa, 'horses for courses'; while the 1st Royal Sussex and

4/16th Punjab, just as good soldiers but not as good hillmen, went for the lower features to the right and left, respectively. The attack by 50th and 51st Divisions would not start until 0430 hours; by which time, Tuker hoped, the battle would be virtually over. From a sand-table model company and platoon commanders made careful study of the ground they must cover in the dark.

During the night of 5/6 April the 1/2nd Goorkhas advanced silently, C Company on the left and D on the right leading. With them were a platoon of the machine-gun battalion of the 6th Rajputana Rifles. Crossing the outer escarpment, C came upon an Italian sentry asleep. He never woke up, but the alarm was given: along the escarpment the machine-guns opened up and the red grenades exploded among the Gurkhas, who ran up the slope with bayonet and kukri. Through the night could be heard not cheers or warcries, but an excited whimpering, like that of foxhounds in covert on a doubtful line – the bloodthirsty little men guiding one another to the kill. C made good the first escarpment, and A and B passed through them, their way illuminated by flares dropped from an enemy plane. On the left A came up against an unscaleable cliff, worked round it to the left and found easier slopes leading up to Pt 275, the highest peak of Fatnassa, occupied only by an artillery OP. B had some trouble with an anti-tank gun covering the narrow path they were using, but the crew were cut down and the company clambered to the top of the massif.

D Company had struck off to the right, to make good a couloir up which a narrow, winding path gave access to the top of the inner escarpment. It was vital to seize and hold this escarpment, piqueting the side of the re-entrant up which 5th Brigade would advance. This couloir was the scene of one of those individual feats of arms which, very rarely, tip the scales of battle. The regimental history of the 2nd Goorkhas tells the story.

'As D Company closed up on the entrance to the corridor, Subadar Lalbahadur Thapa with two sections of 16 Platoon led the way. Enemy sentries in an outpost sangar suddenly discerned figures leaping through the darkness. The Italians died to a man under the kukris. As the Gurkhas raced up the widening passage the arena before them was swept by machine-gun fire; grenades arched down from posts on both escarpments and shook the night with their blasts. A number of men fell, but the dauntless Subadar headed the rush which overwhelmed the next machine-gun nest. He killed two enemies with his kukri and shot down two others. Gaining the twisty track leading to the crest of the escarpment and followed only by Rifleman Harakbahadur Gurung and Rifleman Inrabahadur Gurung, he managed to close on the machine-gun nest which guarded the top of the path. Again he struck two men dead with his kukri, while two others fell before the weapons of the riflemen.

The corridor had been won and the way was open. Subadar Lalbahadur Thapa and the two riflemen stood guard at the top of the path while D Company passed through. Fanning out along the top of the escarpment the Gurkhas quickly put an end to resistance.'

The leading battalions of 5th Brigade, the 1/9th Gurkhas and 4/6th Rajputana Rifles, were awaiting the signal to go through. As soon as they got it, they were off – the Gurkhas aiming for the centre of the massif to the right of B Company of the 1/2nd, the Rajputana Rifles passing through them and swinging right to head towards Roumana. Two hours before the Eighth Army main attack was due to start, 4th Indian Division had ensured that it could not fail.

Captain A. G. Barron, commanding the Rajput Company of the 4/6th, was established by daybreak on the extreme right-hand ridge of Fatnassa, enjoying a bird's-eye view of the Highlanders attacking Roumana, of 50th Division advancing on the anti-tank ditch, and of all the enemy rear areas. He could see a battery of 88s in an orchard firing at tanks in hull-down positions across the anti-tank ditch, and hear the 'horrible screeching sound of a solid shot hitting a tank'.

'Unfortunately our own artillery had been left behind by our quick advance, were on the move and could not be brought to bear on the battery of 88s. I passed all the information I had back to battalion HQ and for the rest of the day sent back situation reports.'

It had all the makings of a complete victory and the destruction of the Afrika Korps. At 0845 hours Tuker

'pointed out to the commander, X Corps [which included 1st and 7th Armoured Divisions] that he had broken the enemy; that the way was clear for X Corps to go through; that immediate offensive action would finish the campaign in North Africa. Now was the time to get the whips out and spare neither men nor machines.'

But the armour did not go through all day. Excessive caution in face of the 88s – muddled orders – a lack of zeal for pursuit in the Army Commander: the delay has never been satisfactorily explained, least of all in Montgomery's account. It is a familiar story in British military history. When, next morning, the armour did debouch onto the Sfax plain, the Germans had gone to fight another day. All that were left were disconsolate groups of Italians.

Considering the magnitude of their victory, 4th Indian Division's casualties were light, as is often the case in well executed night attacks. Fanning out across the plain they made contact with the Americans, accompanied as usual by serried ranks of war correspondents. Of all the tributes paid to the division, from Mr Churchill downwards, the most perceptive was that of an American:

'You have only to see these tall, proud fighting men to realize what an asset the Allied forces possess. These are not civilians fumbling towards a knowledge of war. . . . To me the most astonishing thing was not what they achieved on the summits of these mountains, but their calm and relaxed behaviour while waiting for their turn.'

With the Wadi Akarit the desert ended. To the Eighth Army it was a strange experience, driving through fields and orchards, with white farmhouses and villages. One could even walk into a village shop and *buy* things, bread, sugar, dried fruit.

One hundred and fifty miles north of the Wadi Akarit was the coastal town of Emfidaville, dominated by the mountain block which guards the southern approaches to Tunis. General Alexander, as Deputy to the American General Eisenhower, was in overall command of all the Allied land forces in Tunisia. His plan to finish the campaign was for the Americans to take Bizerta, and the British First Army to take Tunis, from the west; while Eighth Army attacked from the south, not with much hope of breaking through the mountains, but to distract the defenders.

General Montgomery took a robust view of orders to play only a bit part. He determined to 'bounce' the enemy out of their mountain stronghold and beat First Army to Tunis. But the German position above Emfidaville was of immense natural strength. The 4/6th Rajputana Rifles were founder-members of 4th Indian Division, veterans of Sidi Barani, Keren, Syria, the Omars, the Jebel, the 'Benghazi Handicap', Alamein and the Wadi Akarit. They had won more medals than any other battalion in the army. Here they had their hardest fight yet. Barron and his Rajput company were in reserve, waiting in the dark to go through. He could hear the slow knock-knock-knock of Brens, the faster rattle of Spandaus, the thump of grenades and through it all the shouts of '*Maro, maro, Allah ho Akbar!*' and '*Maro, maro, Raja Ram Chandraji ki jai!*' * which told him that the Punjabi Mussulman and Jat companies were fighting hand-to-hand against Germans. At half-light he was ordered to relieve the pressure on them by taking a high shoulder to their left, which he did, having his first unpleasant experience of German 6-barrelled rocket launchers, Nebelwerfers, their missiles passing over with a low moaning sound and obliterating with their multiple explosions everything in the area where they landed. Through one of these terrifying Nebelwerfer bombardments he saw his company signaller walking calmly down the hill running a telephone cable through his hands:

> 'Suddenly he stopped, squatted down and started to mend a break in the cable. . . . When he got back I reprimanded him for risking his life mending a telephone cable when we had perfectly good wireless contact with battalion. He replied with dignity that it was his duty to ensure that we had full contact at all times, by all methods.'

It was in the fierce night battle that the Havildar Major of the Jat Company won the battalion's second VC in two years.

But it was to no avail: the Germans were not to be bounced out of their very strong defences. So by a quick change of plan 4th Indian and 7th Armoured were transferred to First Army to strengthen the attack on Tunis from the west.

The lean, hard-bitten Eighth Army, their officers wearing corduroy trousers, silk scarves, suede 'brothel-creepers' – almost anything but

---

* 'Kill, kill, God is great!' and 'Kill, kill, Victory to the Lord Chandra!'

conventional uniform, in battered trucks with no windscreens and mudguards tied on with wire, met to their mutual surprise the spick-and-span First Army, every officer and man dressed according to regulations; and were not invariably tactful in their patronizing of 'these bloody Inglese'.

In the last operation of the war in Africa 4th Indian Division, on Tuker's insistence and despite the misgivings of 4th British Division on their left, again attacked at night. They were supported by such artillery fire as they had never imagined, of 1917–18 dimensions, and by the morning of 6 May 1943 they were through with very little loss. There was the customary delay in sending through the armour, but for once this did not matter. Five days later Colonel General von Arnim, Commander-in-Chief of all Axis forces in Tunisia, surrendered his own headquarters and Fifth Panzer Armee to Lieutenant Colonel L. C. J. Showers, commanding the 1/2nd King Edward VII's Own Goorkha Rifles.

A few weeks later General Montgomery, in a lecture to officers, made handsome amends for the past: 'I sent First Army my best, 7th Armoured and 4th Indian.'

CHAPTER 21

Italy: the Gustav Line,
1943–44

British and American troops landed in Sicily on 10 July 1943 and in five weeks overran the island. During this short campaign Mussolini was overthrown and the Italian Government sued for peace which was signed, after regrettable delays, on 3 September. On that day Eighth Army crossed the Straits of Messina and landed on the 'toe' of Italy. Six days later Fifth Army (British and American) landed at Salerno. But the delay between finishing the Sicilian operation and landing on the mainland enabled the Germans to pour troops into Italy, so that Fifth Army at Salerno was nearly flung back into the sea. They made good their foothold, however, and Eighth Army linked up with them; but it was evident that although Italy had capitulated, and the Italian people longed only for peace, the advance to the Alps, under General Alexander's overall command, would be opposed by many German divisions of the highest quality, in mountainous country which favoured the defence, with innumerable rivers which the attackers must cross. The justification for the campaign was that it would draw Germans into Italy and the Balkans, making possible the landings in Normandy in 1944. This, in fact, is what happened.

Because conditions on the beaches were likely to be so tough that only good fighting troops could stand them, two Indian battalions, 3/10th Baluchis and 3/12th Frontier Force, were employed as beachhead labour in Sicily, humping supplies from the boats to lorries and by no means overjoyed to be used as coolies; and the very fine States Force battalion, the Jodhpur Sardar Light Infantry, was similarly used at Salerno, where Major Ram Singh was awarded the DSO, the Indian Army's first decoration in Europe in World War II. On 19 September the 8th Indian Division (Major General Dudley Russell) landed unopposed at Taranto. 'Russell Pasha', a 'Piffer', was an extremely able commander, with an eye for country and a keen tactical sense, who could certainly have gone further had he wished. But all he wanted was to command 8th Indian Division until the end of the war; and that was what his division wanted too. They moved up the Adriatic coast to join Eighth Army's advance up the east of the peninsular while Fifth Army advanced up the west.

Neither advanced very far. With great speed the Germans had improved on nature to construct the Gustav Line from the Garigliano on the west coast to the Sangro river on the east, with the mountain and monastery of Cassino as its mightiest bastion, dominating Highway Six from Naples to Rome. The exhilarating dash up Italy came to a sudden halt. 8th Indian Division joined V Corps at Termoli. Its other division was 78th British.

8th Indian consisted of the 17th, 19th and 21st Brigades, with attached troops. Its divisional cavalry regiment was the 6th Lancers which had a strange and ever-changing establishment. On landing at Taranto, each of the three squadrons had three carrier troops, each of four Bren carriers; one mortar troop, with three 3-inch mortars; and one rifle troop, twentieth-century Mounted Infantry. After four years training it was aggressive, adventurous and less cunning than with experience it later became. On 13 November B Squadron (Sikhs) picked up two escaped British prisoners of war (the country swarmed with them) who reported unwary Germans in Rosello village, four miles behind the enemy lines. A patrol from the rifle troop arrived near Rosello, stalked it on foot and watched Germans going about their normal business without a care in the world. Two ventured close to the lurking Sikhs, who grabbed one and shot the other. It was like poking a stick into a wasps' nest: Rosello buzzed with indignation and some very unfriendly motorcyclists came charging out with machine-guns blazing from sidecars. But the Sikhs got away, and their prisoner turned out to be from 1st Parachute Division, a very significant discovery: the Germans were sending their best to Italy. A week later the regiment received enough Humber Armoured Cars, mounting 37mm guns, to convert one carrier troop in each squadron. They were in action with these within twenty-four hours of receiving them.

Any illusions about Sunny Italy were dispelled. Icy rain, rivers in spate and glutinous mud dominated the military situation. The first river, the Biferno, was crossed without great difficulty. Fifteen miles on was the Trigno, and the division closed up to its south bank.

It was a torrent a hundred yards wide between high escarpments. All the bridges had been blown, and all approaches mined with anti-tank mines, *schuh* mines which merely blew off your foot, S-mines which jumped three feet into the air and exploded with shrapnel. Many of the mines were made of plastic or wood, and could not be located by a mine-detector. The Italian campaign was very much a sappers' war: it was the sappers and miners who cleared the minefields, bulldozed the approaches, pushed the wonderful, Meccano-like Bailey bridges across the rivers. At 0345 hrs on 2 November the 6/13th Frontier Force Rifles opened the division's first attack by wading chest-deep through the rushing, icy waters: the bridges went across behind them, and in three days they were through the German positions covering the Trigno and moving on to the next river, the Sangro.

The Germans overlooked the Sangro and its southern approaches from a high escarpment crowned by five hummocked villages, the sort you see in hundreds of Renaissance landscapes. Each was constructed of close-packed, solidly built stone houses, miniature fortresses with all-round defence. It required little work to 'hedgehog' the villages with wire, mines, and machine-guns in houses and weapon-pits with interlocking lines of fire. The two 'hedgehogs' with which 8th Indian Division were concerned were Mozzagrogna and, on the same ridge, San Maria. Around them the *schuh*-mines were broadcast in thousands.

The corps plan was for 78th Division to establish a bridgehead across the Sangro through which 8th Division would advance to the two hedgehogs on the escarpment. Rain and mud made a foothold across the river a major achievement. Then a torrential downpour in the mountains brought the Sangro up to flood the whole valley, washing away the half-built bridge abutments, leaving a brigade of 78th Division isolated on the far side. Three days' ceaseless labour by the sappers got a bridge across, and some tanks were able to pass over it. Then the floods rose again. On 25 November the river subsided and 8th Division was at last able to cross. But the river continued to go up and down like a yo-yo, making the division's supply extremely precarious.

Across the river eight miles upstream was another 'hedgehogged' village, Calvario, which was given as its objective to 19th Brigade to screen the deployment of the 2nd New Zealand Division, coming up on the left of 8th Indian. The 3/8th Punjab waded across the chest-deep flood, and with the 1/5th Essex took Calvario, but were then cut off by floods. Very thin on the ground, they were ordered back from the bridgehead they had won with such blood and labour. But next morning Captain Gardhari Singh of the 3/8th, feeling a proprietary interest in Calvario, submitted to Brigadier Dobree that the Germans were in as bad a state as themselves and had probably pulled out: could he go and see? His hunch was correct: he occupied Calvario with thirty-five men without firing a shot. The bridgehead for the New Zealanders was made good, and 19th Brigade went back to join the rest of the division.

At midnight on the 27/28th the 2/5th Gurkhas advanced through the rain on Mozzagrogna, with the 1st Royal Fusiliers in support. The ground off any tracks – and indeed on them – was littered with mines, most scarifying. The Gurkhas got well into the village, but the Germans emerged from cellars and re-occupied houses and weapon-pits behind them. Gurkhas, British and Germans were soon chaotically intermingled. The main feature of the village was the square dominated by the church tower in which Major Morland Hughes, commanding the Gurkhas, established battalion headquarters. By daybreak they were hoping for the arrival of some tanks, but these had been held up by mud and mines.

Then two German flame-thrower tanks arrived, burst through the forward companies and lumbered into the square, sousing the church walls with burning oil. The first tank-commander, putting his head out of the turret, was shot by a Fusilier. The second turned his flame-thrower to avenge his comrade and fell to a brilliant snap-shot by Morland Hughes. Both tanks then turned their guns onto the tower and set the bells ringing in a wild carillon while the Major came rapidly to earth in a shower of bricks and debris.

As the Shermans could not get up in support, Morland Hughes was ordered by brigade to withdraw so that the artillery could properly stonk the village. He protested that all he needed was ammunition, but the order was repeated. (For once, the wireless was working.) The Fusiliers insisted

38 An OP of the 4/13th Frontier Force Rifles, Mount Vigese, Italy.

39 *(above)* 8th Indian 4.2-inch mortar crew in action in Italy, 1944.

40 *(below)* Fighting in Italy, winter 1944–45.

41 *(above)* Recce patrol of 6th Duke of Connaught's Own Lancers (Indian Armoured Corps) at San Felice, overlooking the Trigno River valley, 1944. The men are all from the Punjab.

42 *(below)* Cassino, March 1944.

43 *(above)* Mountain Artillery at Shwegyin on the Chindwin, May 1942.

44 *(below)* Arakan, 1945: 19th Lancers in Sherman tanks moving forward to support infantry.

45 *(above)* In a heavily camouflaged foxhole at an outpost of the Burma front, a Gurkha keeps guard with his Bren-gun.

46 *(above)* Sikh troops in Burma, 1945.

47 *(below)* Snipers being cleared from a pagoda on Mandalay Hill, 1945.

48 (*above*) The young and debonair Lieutenant Bahadur Singh, MC, of Probyn's Horse, shortly before he became Maharajah of Bundi, during the advance on Meiktila, March 1945.

49 (*below*) The road to Mandalay, 1945: Gurkhas with a Punjabi Mussulman military policeman.

50 King George VI decorating Sepoy Kamal Ram with the VC in Italy: the youngest Indian ever to win the award.

that the Gurkhas, who were in the more forward positions, should go first, and as they sprinted in groups across the square, shouted 'Run, Johnny!' and kept up a rapid fire at every door and window to cover their retreat. The Gurkhas and Fusiliers got back to their start-line, angry at having to give up all they had won.

In the early hours of the 30th the 1/12th Frontier Force attacked, this time with tanks in support. The tanks' technique was very effective: make a hole in a house with armour-piercing shot, and then fire HE through it; or fire HE with a delayed action fuse so that it burst inside. This time Mozzagrogna was taken and held. The Sangro line was broken. When it was all over Morland Hughes gave orders for nine dead Germans, found in the cellar of the house he had chosen for his headquarters, to be buried. While they were being carried out, one came to life. A Gurkha casually drew a kukri to finish him off and a nearby British soldier protested, 'Hey, Johnny, you can't just kill him like that.' The Gurkha, shocked by this inhumanity, replied, 'We were told to bury nine. Surely you don't want me to bury him *alive!*'

From Mozzagrogna the 6th Lancers probed towards the road junction of Lanciano. Dismounted night patrols came upon German engineers preparing two bridges for demolition and interrupted the good work, reporting to squadron headquarters that the enemy seemed to be on their way out. So in the morning C Squadron, its armoured car troop leading, approached the village and lost a brand-new Humber to the much heavier metal of a Mk IV tank. But this was a parting shot, and the occupation of the village was delayed only by mines and shelling.

The next river to cross was the Moro. The corps plan was for the 1st Canadian Division (which had relieved 78th) to cross on the right, by the sea, and the New Zealanders on the left; while in the centre 8th Indian made offensive noises to draw German reserves. But neither of the flanking attacks succeeded, so Russell was ordered to cross and take Caldari, a mile beyond the river.

There was a problem. If Caldari were to be taken and held, it would be necessary to bridge the Moro so that tanks could cross. A Bailey bridge required a stretch of straight road at right angles to the river, on which the bridge could be assembled while being pushed over. But the Lanciano-Caldari road crossed the river in a ravine, making a sharp bend as it approached the bank from the south. The collective wisdom of the corps engineers ruled that a bridge there was impossible. But 8th Division CRE, Colonel MacLachlan, came up with a novel idea: the bridge must be assembled on a straight stretch of road on the enemy bank, and pushed *back*. So it was done. Behind a screen of 3/15th Punjab and a company of 5th Mahrattas machine-gun battalion, all the bridge parts were ferried over in rafts, assault craft and rubber dinghies, assembled by 7th, 67th and 69th Field Companies, Bengal Sappers and Miners, and pushed back to the south bank. Next morning tanks were crawling across the 'Impossible Bridge'.

The next 'hedgehog' on 8th Division's front was Villa Grande. It was 19th Brigade's turn. Early on 22 December, in arctic conditions, the 1/5th Essex followed the artillery barrage and through the murk of smoke and fires entered the village. There followed the usual murderous hide-and-seek in houses and cellars – a corporal's battle: not even platoon commanders could know what their men were doing. The Essex men had to pull out. Twenty-four hours later they tried again from the south while the 3/8th Punjab attacked from the west. Interlocking machine-gun fire sent the Punjabis to ground, but Gardhari Singh, now a major, was inspired to set two sodden haystacks alight with captured spandaus loaded with tracer. Behind the dense smoke-screen the Punjabis got into the village. Two days later the ground had dried and the tanks could come forward. The German parachutists, faced by hopeless odds, made an orderly withdrawal.

In many ways the Eighth Army was very like Wellington's Peninsular Army, far from home, wearing the most varied and outrageous clothing which Montgomery minded no more than Wellington, and enjoying, on appropriate occasions, wine, women and dancing. Such an occasion for 17th brigade was Christmas Day, when they were in reserve in the bank building in Lanciano, expecting the arrival of their new brigadier, Charles Boucher, who had been taken prisoner in the desert and recently escaped. Women were no problem; the villages were full of them, and they full of the party spirit. The problem was wine, the Germans having drunk any which was drinkable. But the Canadians had perfected a method of distilling spirits with the condenser which recycled steam from over-heated radiators of desert jeeps. The result was a colourless, tasteless spirit, pure alcohol. Tasteless: that was the trouble. After midnight, when the Brigade Major, Bill Moberly, was virtuously drafting orders for the day, his orderly arrived at the double to announce that the new Brigadier Sahib was at the door. The Brigadier Sahib had to pick his way over bodies, male and female, recumbent but far beyond amorous thoughts or actions. He never mentioned the matter.

At the end of the year General Montgomery left Eighth Army to command the invasion forces for the Second Front. In his farewell talk to the press he stressed in his usual staccato speech, 'My Eighth Army's tails are up, right up!' He was interrupted by the rich Dublin brogue of Dennis Johnson, BBC commentator: 'Excuse me, General, up what?'

As 8th Indian Division settled down to survive a snowbound winter, 4th Indian Division arrived from a six months' rest in Palestine. It now consisted of three brigades, 5th, 7th and a re-formed 11th, to replace that which had been lost in Tobruk. But its divisional commander, 'Gertie' Tuker, was a sick man, never out of pain with racking headaches, albeit as clear as ever in his mind.

The Italian campaign would not be won on the Adriatic side, where the coastal plain was too narrow, served by too few roads and crossed by too many rivers. One did not have to be a Churchill to see that it could best be won by amphibious landings behind the German lines. 'Why crawl up the leg like a harvest-bug?' enquired that noble voice from Downing Street. 'Let us rather strike at the knee!' But although the Americans formally subscribed to the strategy of General Sir Alan Brooke, Chief of the Imperial General Staff, of drawing Germans into the Mediterranean area to make possible the Normandy landings, at heart they suspected a sinister plot to further British imperialist designs in the Balkans, and purposely kept the armies in Italy short of landing craft. So there was no alternative but a slog up the west side of Italy – Naples, Rome, Florence – with perhaps one landing to help it along.

A third of the way from Naples to Rome Highway 6, of which the general direction is south to north, swings left to approach Cassino from the east, crosses the Rapido river, skirts Cassino town and passes under Monte Cassino crowned by its famous medieval monastery. Monte Cassino is the southernmost feature of a great mountain block, to the east of which is a three-mile wide valley down which runs, north to south, the Rapido. With Monte Cassino in enemy hands, no army advancing from Naples to Rome could go a step further: from the monastery walls, the Germans could almost toss a stone down onto Highway 6.

In January 1944 the Americans, characteristically resorting to a frontal attack backed by tremendous firepower rather than to manoeuvre, assaulted Cassino from the south. At the same time, to take the enemy in the rear, a corps was landed at Anzio. There, complained Churchill, instead of tearing like a tiger-cat at the enemy's vitals, it emulated a huge, helpless, stranded whale. Their frontal attack having been bloodily repulsed, the Americans tried again, with more promising tactics. They crossed the Rapido north-east of Cassino, moved westward into the mountains, and then turned south along Snake's Head Ridge to attack Monte Cassino from the rear. But it had no rear. It had complete and most formidable all-round defence. The Americans reached Pt 593, a quarter of a mile north-west of the towering monastery walls, and could get no further.

Early in February 4th Indian and 2nd New Zealand Divisions were brought across from the Adriatic coast for another attack on Cassino, directed by the New Zealand commander, Lieutenant General Sir Bernard Freyburg, VC, whose gallantry and wide battle experience perhaps exceeded his tactical sagacity. (Some of his own men said he was a butcher.) He was not provided with a proper corps headquarters but had to improvise one, which did not make his task easier.

Although ill, Tuker applied his mind to the monastery, which everyone assumed (wrongly) to form the hard core of the defence. No one seemed to know anything about it, but he learned from a secondhand book picked up in Naples that it was a fortress which could not be reduced with the division's weapons. The walls were of solid masonry at least ten feet thick. It could be destroyed only by air bombardment with blockbuster bombs: 'the 1,000 bomb would be next to useless'. Whether or not the monastery was actually occupied by the enemy (they said it wasn't), it must be demolished

Italy: Monte Cassino, 1944

to prevent them occupying it. 'When a formation is called upon to reduce such a place, it should be apparent that the place is reducible by means at the disposal of that division . . . without having to go to the bookstalls of Naples to find out what should have been fully considered many weeks ago.' If demolishing the monastery was for political, aesthetic or religious reasons unacceptable, the only alternative was to isolate it by a wide turning movement through the mountains, cutting Highway 6 west of Cassino.

But Tuker when he wrote this assessment was no longer in command of 4th Indian Division, having been taken to hospital. His temporary successor did not carry his weight, and the wide detour was modified into what was essentially a repetition of the American attack down Snake's Head Ridge, combined with a repetition of the American first attack, frontal, against Cassino from the south. The first would be carried out by 4th Indian, the second by the New Zealand Division.

On 14 February the Americans on Snake's Head Ridge were relieved by Lovett's 7th Brigade. These had been led to believe that the Americans still held Pt 593, but this was not so: it had to be re-captured.

A bombardment of the monastery by American Flying Fortresses had been laid on for the morning of the 15th. 'It appears that the monks had been told, the enemy had been told, indeed the world at large knew about it. The only people who did not know were the forward [7th] Brigade who might have profited from it.' * The bombardment – such of it as did not fall

*Major General J. G. Elliott, *A Roll of Honour.*

on the New Zealand headquarters – blew the roof off the monastery and wrecked the medieval interior, but hardly shook the massive walls. Brigadier Lovett submitted that Pt 593 must be taken as a preliminary to the main assault on the monastery, and 1st Royal Sussex attacked it but were repulsed with dreadful losses.

Next night, 18/19 February, the 4/6th Rajputana Rifles tried. Some actually gained the summit of Pt 593: months afterwards the graves of a company commander and some men were found in the very heart of the enemy defences. But they too were driven back, with the loss of 196 officers and men. The 1/2nd Goorkhas worked towards a low wrinkle of ground beyond which the hillside sloped down to the very foot of the monastery wall. Air-photos showed just a patch of scrub, but it was a deathtrap, thickly sown with *schuh-* and S-mines, laced with tripwires connected to booby traps. The leading platoons dashed into the scrub and were blown up almost to a man. Colonel Showers was shot through the stomach. Two-thirds of the leading company were killed or wounded, but the survivors pushed through, some with three or four tripwires round their legs. When they were withdrawn, seven British and four Gurkha officers, and 138 riflemen were dead or wounded. By daybreak, despite terrible losses, not a yard of ground had been gained. Nor had the New Zealanders, in their desperate attacks on Cassino town, been any more successful. 'Unfortunately,' wrote General Alexander, 'we are fighting the best soldiers in the world – what men!' They were the 1st Parachute Division.

An assault on the monastery from Snake's Head Ridge would require at least two brigades, but only one could be maintained there, with immense difficulty. All supplies had to be carried up from the Rapido by 800 mules and five companies of porters, under observation and fire every yard of the way.

Before their next attempt the New Zealanders withdrew from what they held of Cassino town in order that it might be flattened by a thousand tons of bombs. Flattened it was, but valiant machine-gunners survived in the ruins, and tanks could not get at them over the huge piles of rubble and flooded bomb craters. The New Zealanders, with fearful losses, took Castle Hill, overlooking the town, but itself overlooked by Monastery Hill with its huge boulders and concrete strongpoints. They were relieved by 5th Indian Brigade. A company of the 1/9th Gurkhas fought their way still further, to Hangman's Hill, only a little way from the grim monastery walls. Their every move was seen and drew spandau, mortar and artillery fire from above. It was on Hangman's Hill that both sides concentrated their efforts, the British to supply and reinforce it, the Germans to surround and cut it off. A group of 4/6th Rajputana Rifles, acting as porters when the real porters, of a labour battalion, refused to go any further, actually reached it with food and ammunition, and more was air-dropped but rolled down the steep slope below.

The German parachutists made a full-scale attack on Castle Hill, the defenders of which (Essex and 1/6th Rajputana Rifles) manned the medieval walls and fired rifles and Bren guns through arrow-slits. Their mortars were fired until the barrels became red-hot, and bent. A heroic German officer placed an explosive charge, nineteenth-century fashion, under one of the bastions; but parachutists storming the breach were all shot down. In the castle were some prisoners who volunteered as stretcher-bearers. Their sergeant major strolled round with a proprietorial air, as though supervising the defence, and congratulated Major Beckett on a soldierly performance. Indians and Germans had no difficulty in conversing – in Italian.

By 23 March there was a stalemate. 5th Brigade could not be turned off Hangman's Hill and Castle Hill, but equally could go no further. There was no wireless communication with Hangman's Hill because the batteries were flat and new batteries dropped on the hill had rolled down the slope. Two officers, each with a carrier-pigeon to report his arrival, made their way there with orders for a withdrawal. The Gurkhas pulled out just before midnight, perforce leaving their wounded. These were returned next day with a polite note to say that no more would be sent back.

4th Indian Division lost 4,000 men on Cassino and gained nothing. Tuker, on his way back to hospital in India, must have thought, 'I told you so'. This was just the sort of operation he abhorred. There was a general feeling that if 4th Indian and the New Zealanders could not take Cassino, who could? But someone had to, so Eighth Army took on the job, secretly bringing over from the Adriatic side the Polish Corps, 8th Indian Division and the 2nd Canadian Armoured Brigade.

This time there would be no frontal attack on an impregnable position. The Polish Corps would strike westward out of the Rapido valley, across the mountains and into the valley beyond, down which the Liri river flows in a south-easterly direction to join the Gari* six miles south of Cassino. The British 78th Division and 6th Armoured Division would move up the Liri valley to meet the Poles, thus isolating Cassino. To let them through, XIII Corps, consisting of 4th (British) and 8th Indian Divisions, and the Canadian Armoured Brigade, would bridge the Gari, hold a bridgehead over it and breach the Gustav Line. The operation would not be possible until the flattish, sodden land of the Liri Appendix, the tongue of land in the apex of the Liri and Gari rivers, had dried out enough for tanks. The Gustav Line behind the Gari river was very strong, a feature of it being Panther tank turrets, armed with extra long-barrelled 75mm guns, anchored to concrete platforms and supported by ordinary anti-tank guns, Nebelwurfers, spandaus with interlocking fields of fire and extensive minefields. But the garrison was not of the quality of 1st Parachute Division.

Americans who had failed at Cassino were offering ten to one against the Indians doing any better, which the Canadians tank crews, who had worked with 8th Indian on the Sangro, eagerly took up.

*The Rapido river becomes the Gari south of Cassino.

They had trained at river crossings in the Canal Zone, a year earlier, and they did more training on the Volturno river, twenty miles south of Cassino. There were two great differences from their previous experience: the Mark III Assault boat, a heavy, collapsible affair made of wood and canvas, which the assault companies had to assemble and carry some 400 yards to the river bank; and the strength of the current in Italian rivers. According to the manual of instructions the boat, having been paddled across on its initial crossing, should then be towed back and forth by ropes attached to bow and stern. But if it was thus held side-on to a strong current, the collapsible boat collapsed, so they tied both ropes to the bow and let the stern swing free. There were other novelties. Captain A. F. Chown, Adjutant of the 1/12th Frontier Force, watched on the Volturno 'two crowded boatloads of 1/5th Gurkhas moving swiftly downstream, out of control and swirling round and round, to the obvious enjoyment of their beaming occupants going goodness knows where'.

On 1 May 8th Indian and the Canadians were filtered up with great secrecy to their positions on the left bank of the Gari, to the left of 4th (British) Division. 8th Division's line-up from right to left was 17th Brigade with 1st Royal Fusiliers and 1/12th Frontier Force up and 1/5th Gurkhas in reserve; then 19th Brigade with 3/8th Punjab and 1st Argyll and Sutherland Highlanders up and 6/13th Frontier Force Rifles in reserve. 21st Brigade formed the division's reserve.

With the division's right little more than two miles from Cassino, the utmost care had to be taken to preserve secrecy for twelve days before the attack. There was wireless silence; no movement by day outside camouflage netting; no looking up when aircraft passed over; and for the whole twelve days Monte Cassino was blanketed with smoke-shell. By day everyone tried to sleep. By night they worked hard for there was much to do. Routes forward, over irrigation ditches six foot deep and wide, to the crossing places over the Gari had to be delicately reconnoitred and marked; patrols on the near bank of the river had to learn what they could about enemy dispositions; there were dumps to be made and camouflaged for bridging material, engineer stores, boats, duckboards, ammunition; minefields left by the Americans on the near side of the river had to be found, marked and perhaps lifted; hard roads had to be built across the soggy fields to the crossing places. T. J. Thornton, a subaltern of 7th Field Company, Bengal Sappers and Miners, felt shudders down his spine every time the night silence was broken by the thunderous unloading of crushed rock from tip-trucks. But the enemy seemed unaware of anything going on. 1/12th patrols listened to a gramophone playing in a German dugout while a powerful voice sang, 'When will this ruddy war end?' It was an area much favoured by nightingales, whose songs seemed eerily out of place among shell-holes, minefields and the smell of death.

As the moon rose at 2300 hours on the night of 11/12 May, 800 guns started pounding the enemy positions. The sappers and forward infantry companies carried the heavy assault boats to the river bank, as they had

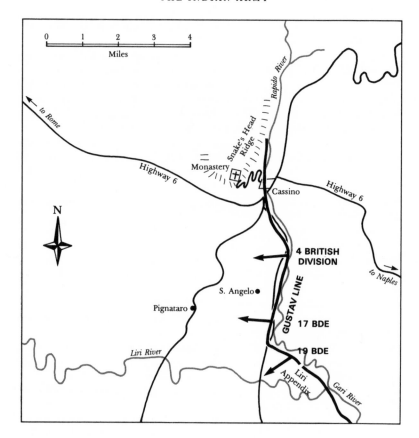

Italy: Monte Cassino area

done so often in practice. At 2345 the guns changed targets and started firing a close barrage starting from the far bank of the Gari and moving forward a hundred yards every six minutes. The boats were slid down the bank and launched, and the first wave paddled across the forty feet of fast-flowing water.

The dust and cordite fumes from the shellbursts, a truck full of smoke canisters set alight by a shell and the heavy river-valley mist produced a peasoup fog which, while it blinded enemy gunners, made control almost impossible. On the 1/12th front the Beachmaster himself lost his river and had to be directed to it. This was compounded, as soon as the twelve-days' wireless-silence was lifted, by a complete breakdown of wireless discipline; a babble of English, French, Polish, Gaelic, Urdu, Pushtu and Gurkhali set up an impenetrable blanket of sound. Chown remembers most the confusion.

'White tapes disappeared into the mud and coloured AA shells fired overhead as guidelines were invisible. Lost and wounded men straggled by as we, in our tight little boat-groups, pressed forward seeking the river-bank. Calls from the billowing, noisy blackness, "*Colonel Sahib ke kishti hai*" and "*Adjeetant Sahib ke kishti hai*" [Colonel's boat, Adjutant's boat] kept us vaguely in touch as we all cursed and stumbled forward, hanging onto one another's hands, back-packs or bayonet-scabbards. We located the river and the ferrymen, who had been over with the first wave and had returned, called and guided us down the slippery bank and with their hands guided our feet into the invisible boats.

The boat-trip over the swirling water and the scramble up the far bank was followed by a quick re-organization and sorting-out. The jawans were taking it all amazingly well, with the old stalwarts encouraging the youngsters and all of us glad to be across, trying to pretend we felt happier than we did. There was a good deal of spandau and mortar fire.'

Lieutenant Colonel H. E. Cubitt-Smith, commanding the 1/12th Frontier Force, found the fog of war thicker than ever on the far bank, visibility down to a yard. The enemy had laid tripwires which ignited smoke-canisters and started spandaus firing on fixed lines. Strong words were spoken in four languages as men stumbled into shell-holes and ditches. The forward companies groped their way on compass-bearings, sometimes encountering enemy parties equally lost. To give the Colonel their direction, they shouted their warcries, which served also to confuse the enemy. They reached their first objective, a lateral road along the top of a bank; and following the battalion plan, A Company (Major Amar Singh) attacked it from the south, thus avoiding in the fog the enemy's frontal fire. Dugouts and quarries favoured the defence, but the fog favoured the attack; and just as Amar Singh was killed, part of 'The Bank' was overrun. The confused night continued, sometimes strangely quiet, except for the singing of the nightingales, generally noisy and nasty.

Behind the 1/12th and the Fusiliers 7th Field Company cleared mines from the tracks and rafted anti-tank guns across. Work was started on the Bailey bridges. Of these there were to be three: CARDIFF, by 7th Field Company, to support the Fusiliers; OXFORD, by 65th Field Company, to support the 1/12th; and PLYMOUTH, by 69th Field Company, to support 19th Brigade.

CARDIFF was expected to be the easiest. The main difficulty was in finding a launching-site, because the river ran between high embankments; but a place had been found where a ramp ran up to the top of the near embankment. But when Captain Howarth found this site, he

'discovered it was already occupied, and the centre of considerable attention. The Royal Fusiliers had chosen this precise point for their crossing and their Beachmaster had established his command-post slap in the middle of my only possible launching-site. . . . The enemy were bringing considerable fire to bear on it. The arrival of a sapper bridging party which was likely to attract even more unwelcome attention was not good news and there was no way he could or would re-locate. I crawled up the bank to assess the bridging problem but there was nothing to see. The water was invisible somewhere below me. I could hear it but not see it, altogether a peculiar sensation.'

Howarth set off upstream to look for an alternative site, but there was none. On his return he found another problem: men ramping up earth to the ends of the steel bridging ramps were digging up *schuh*-mines. Soon four men had feet or legs blown off, and they spent the rest of the night working with the knowledge that every step was a hazard. Daybreak came, and with it heavy machine-gun fire from the village of S. Angelo. They had to give up their attempts until the following night. In the end the bridge was only completed after S. Angelo had been captured.

Elsewhere, however, it had been easier. The first bridge to be completed, at 0840 hours, was OXFORD, and soon the 1/12th heard the welcome sound of Sherman tanks crossing. PLYMOUTH was a most ingenious effort. A turretless tank carrying a span of Bailey bridge descended into the river and surged across until it could go no further and the crew baled out. The links steadying the span were cut by plastic explosive, and a second tank shoved the span across until its end overlapped the far bank; the carrying tank settled lower into the river bottom, the span dropped into position and soon tanks were crossing.

A hurly-burly in the dark was hardly the cavalry's scene, but the 6th Lancers were usefully employed making bridge-building noises – hammering at rails and angle-irons – in a place where no bridge was being built, thus drawing a good deal of shell and mortar fire which the Germans might more profitably have directed elsewhere.

It is curious how the human spirit rises above noisy and unpleasant circumstances. Thornton at the height of the barrage was

'returning from the river-bank to the off-loading zone to chivvy up the sappers when I came across a group of them collecting fireflies (there were thousands of winking lights) and throwing them up in the air like a fireworks display. Children could not have been happier.'

Later in the morning Chown was accosted by a tough, dusty, Pathan havildar major with hand outstretched, admiring with real enjoyment, a scarlet anemone.

By mid-day, when the fog had cleared, the 1/12th were established, not too securely, on 'The Bank', and on their right the Fusiliers had reached about as far. But S. Angelo had not been taken, and both battalions were held up by fire from it. This was the objective of the 1/5th Gurkhas, passing through either the Fusiliers or the 1/12th, whichever had made more progress. At 0200 hours they reached the river bank to find that only four out of sixteen boats were still afloat. This delayed matters, but eventually they got across. Then Major Winstanley, commanding the company which was to attack S. Angelo, reported that he had lost contact with two of his platoons. Chown was surprised to see 'Derek Organ, the 1/5th Adjutant, looking very cheerful, come belting through our area with two platoons to reinforce the attack on St Angelo'. But he missed his way; Winstanley had to attack S. Angelo with only twenty-five men, and was held up three hundred yards short of it. His missing platoons had become mixed up with the 1/12th whom they helped all day against parties of Germans who had been bypassed in the dark but now came to vigorous life.

Another attempt on S. Angelo was made with tank support, but the Shermans bogged down, and by evening it was still in enemy hands, and holding up the advance of the whole division. A full-scale attack by two companies with two squadrons in support was laid on for noon on the 13th. Fifteen minutes after the start the leading platoons entered the village, and there was desperate house-to-house fighting like the shambles of Mozzagrogna. By 1330 the whole village was in Gurkha hands, but for hours after Germans continued to appear from holes and corners looking for a kind face to whom to surrender. Gurkhas in such circumstances are not kind.

On 19th Brigade front the 3/8th Punjab had trouble with their boats, losing several washed down by the powerful current and others from enemy fire. However, with a single boat pulled back and forth by ropes and some rafts, they made the crossing, but then had to attack without benefit of darkness or barrage. D Company (Sikhs), impetuously charging, was brought to a sudden halt by a belt of barbed wire and spandaus firing at point-blank range: the company commander, Major Sujan Singh, and a whole Sikh platoon were wiped out as they tried to cross the wire. B and C Companies, under Major Gardhari Singh, were also held up by machine-guns; but the day was saved by Kamal Ram, a nineteen-year-old Jat sepoy, in action for the first time.

An officer called for a volunteer to deal with a particularly troublesome gun on the right. Kamal Ram crawled through the wire, shot the gunner, bayoneted the feeder and swung round to shoot an officer who came at him from behind. He pressed on, sniped the gunner of the next spandau nest, and killed the crew with a grenade. With a havildar, he dealt similarly with a third machine-gun post; and, later, with a fourth. He was awarded the VC.

Except on the extreme left, the leading battalions were well into the Gustav line defences. With S. Angelo taken, the Fusiliers and 1/12th could push on; and soon Chown was 'well into the bridgehead, sitting beside my slit trench in the sun, eating Bosche chocolate and using rather a good line in Berlin hair-tonic'. On the 14th, 21st Brigade, led by a squadron of 6th Lancers, came through to take Pignataro, the division's final objective. Twenty-four hours later the Polish attack from the Rapido valley went in, and 78th Division went through to link up with them.

17th Brigade had about thirty per cent casualties, 19th Brigade rather less, and 21st Brigade fewer still. It was a small price to pay for a great victory, which opened the way for the reduction of Cassino and a great gap torn in the Gustav Line through which the armour poured.

On the coast Fifth Army linked up with the corps which had landed at Anzio, the American commander of which did not see fit to obey orders and cut off the retreating German army, the whole purpose of the landing, but preferred instead the fame of being first into Rome, on 4 June. It was a great triumph for the Fifth and Eighth Armies, but on the next day the Anglo-American armies landed in Normandy, and the Italian campaign became a sideshow.

Sideshow or not, the pursuit of the German army was an exhilarating experience, and 8th Indian Division was in it. Generally a squadron of the 6th Lancers was in the lead, bowling along the excellent roads through Tivoli, Terni and Foligno. Except for the ever-present fear of mines – particularly the horrid little *schuh*-mine which might be in any dusty road-verge, scattered among demolitions, placed so as to get you as you pushed a derelict truck off the road – it was for most people pleasantly exciting to drive over bridges prepared for demolition before they could be blown, to pass abandoned tanks, guns, vehicles of all kinds, horses and mules, a complete workshop, a staff car with maps still on the seat. In villages the people handed one flowers and wine in gratitude for their liberation. 'I suppose,' I said to a German officer prisoner, 'it was just the same for you?' 'In this very village,' he replied, 'last week.' But someone had to be in the leading armoured car, and for them it was exciting but not so pleasant. You could not creep along looking for enemy everywhere but had to keep moving, knowing that at any moment there might be a great jolt to the car, a smell of hot metal, and you baled out if you were lucky.

A curious task was given to P. H. MacDwyer, now Staff Captain to 25th Brigade in 10th Indian Division: to take a patrol into Rome and ensure that the great opera singer, Benjamino Gigli, was not removed by the Germans.

'He lived in a villa not far from the Castello Sant' Angelo. I drove up at dusk with John Denning, my subaltern, and two jeep-loads of Indian troops. The door was opened by a terrified old woman who, after taking one look at us, screamed over her shoulder. "*Mama mia, Mama mia, niente Tedeschi, esta Inglese, benissima, benissima. Gracia, avante, avante!*"'

Gigli then came out and greeted them, talking volubly in Italian and English. His house was well stocked with food: he had been a privileged person under both Fascists and Nazis, but hastened to explain that he was not a fascist by choice; so after wine and food, he said he would play and sing to them.

'He sat at one of the two grand pianos and gave us an impromptu concert for about half an hour. He sang first *Die Lorelei*, obviously one of his favourites, then branched off into Tosca, Traviata, Il Trovatore and many others. He was enjoying himself enormously, and so were we. . . .

He was vibrant, vivacious, noisy at times and deeply passionate.'

A unique experience came to an end with the arrival of an American officer to take charge of the maestro.

People were going to Rome on leave within a few days of its capture. It was strange to see Hindu, Sikh and Moslem soldiers being conducted round the Vatican by a Punjabi-speaking Italian priest.

Just short of Perugia 8th Indian Division was relieved by 10th Indian Division, fresh from the Middle East, and retired to a rest area after eight and a half months' almost continuous fighting and advancing 240 miles in five weeks. The pursuit was slowing down as the campaign moved into its next stage, with the Germans back on their Gothic Line.

CHAPTER 22

Burma: the Turning Tide, 1943–44

After, and indeed before, the Arakan fiasco, Slim realized that a lot must be done before divisions in Burma were a match for the Japanese. When he took command of the Fourteenth Army in August 1943, he was in a position to do it with the unfailing and vigorous support of the new Commander-in-Chief, Auchinleck. There were three main problems, each aggravating the others: supply, health and morale.

At the heart of the supply problem was communications. The 700-mile Burma front passed through country as badly served by roads as any in Asia. One ramshackle railway, three quarters of it narrow gauge, served the central front in the sense that it reached within 110 miles of the base of Imphal. In 1941 its daily capacity was 600 tons; by August 1943, it was 2,800 tons; and by October 1944, 4,400 tons. It was washed away by floods, broken by bombing, swept down by landslides, closed by train wrecks and finally shattered by an earthquake; but it was Fourteenth Army's main artery. The Arakan was served by a combination of railways, river steamers and country boats. A huge programme of all-weather road construction proceeded from 1942 to the end of the war.

This eased the supply problem except for rations. Nothing could solve that. Fighting men need fresh meat and vegetables. Indian troops can to some extent substitute fresh milk and ghee for meat. Without refrigerator cars, meat, vegetables and milk were all stinking by the time they reached the front; and there were no local supplies. Tinned food was infinitely worse and less varied than in the desert. Bully-beef, liquefied in the heat, was not an adequate fresh-meat substitute for British troops, while Indians and Gurkhas could not eat it at all. But there was always tea.

Much more could be done about health. In 1942, for every man evacuated with wounds, 120 were evacuated sick. The common ailments were dysentery, jaundice, jungle sores and, far worse than all the rest, malaria. Stern measures to improve hygiene reduced the intestinal diseases. Malaria responded to discipline: make men roll down their sleeves in the evening, use mosquito nets where possible and take every day a nauseating prophylactic pill, Mepacrine. Instead of being sent back to India and not returning to their units for months, malaria patients were treated at special centres just behind the line, and were back with their units in three weeks. Slim believed that the biggest life-saver and morale-booster was the evacuation of wounded and seriously ill men by air. In 1942 the daily rate of admission to hospital was twelve per thousand, one third of the army every month. By 1945 it had fallen to one per thousand. This gave

Fourteenth Army an enormous advantage over the Japanese, who suffered dreadfully from malaria.

After the disasters of 1942 morale could hardly have been lower. A beaten army makes out the enemy to be bigger and better than he really is, and rumour portrayed the Japanese as invincible. Slim pondered this, and concluded that morale depended on: (1) an object worth fighting for: the destruction of that evil thing, the Japanese army; (2) a belief in every man, from general down to the pioneer labouring on the roads, that he is contributing something vital towards that object; (3) a conviction that the object is attainable.

The first two of these factors could be promoted by personal contact, talks by himself and others who could do it well, not only with the fighting units but with men in the rear areas, doing dull and non-dangerous jobs, who far outnumber the fighting troops and are more prone to boredom and despondency.

The conviction that the Japanese could be beaten was to some extent developed by Wingate's first Chindit operations. Militarily they achieved very little at a very high cost, though they did point the way to bigger operations of the same kind supplied by air. But as propaganda, well handled by the Allied media, they were beyond price. The impression was given that the Chindits had run rings round the Japanese, and what they could do, others could also. A more genuine morale-builder was the defeat, total and undeniable, of the Japanese in New Guinea by the Australians in September 1942.

By far the best way to convince Fourteenth Army that it could beat the enemy was to provide opportunities to do so. Every battalion started sending into the jungle, for several days, small patrols whose sole object was to kill Japanese. This was far easier than collecting information, or identifying enemy units, or taking prisoners, and less liable to end in disaster, because the 'Tiger-patrols' needed to go only for soft targets. Thus, Tiger-patrols sent out by the 14/13th Frontier Force Rifles, who fancied themselves at the job, consisted of a rifle section less the Bren numbers, each man carrying four grenades and rations for five or six days. Their method was to lie up, perhaps for days, beside a jungle track used by the enemy, let his scouts pass through, open up with Tommy guns and grenades on the main body, and then get the hell out of it. Of course they could make no body-count, but knew they killed many Japanese; and an enemy map was found which showed an estimated 3,000 Indian troops in the area in which only a few Tiger-patrols had been operating. Quickly the idea got round that the Japanese, so far from being of superhuman cunning, were rather thick, hidebound in their tactics, and easy to surprise: when taken by surprise, they reacted much like other people, running away or doing something stupid.

The next step in morale-building was to lay on small attacks which could hardly fail – a whole brigade attacking a Japanese company, a battalion attacking a platoon.

A big area of jungle round Ranchi was turned into a training area, and two divisions were converted into jungle-training divisions, through which all drafts for combatant units had to pass, so that they arrived at the front knowing something, and did not have to learn it all the hard way. The jungle training was tough, varied and on occasion dangerous. Major L. F. Steele, 3/14th Punjab, was leading through dense jungle a patrol of Pathans who had, of course, never experienced anything like this. They were almost deafened by a menacing roar, and Steele said, 'What the hell was that?' 'Camel, Sahib,' replied the company know-all. It was, of course, a tiger.

The main lesson impressed on all was that if the Japanese got behind them they must sit tight, *not* try to clear their communications by withdrawing and attacking the enemy roadblock as had always been done during the Burma retreat. They would be supplied by air, the enemy would not, so it was the Japanese who would in effect be surrounded.

Slim's re-forged weapon was ready to be tested in November 1943. There would be another attempt to clear the Arakan using XV Corps (General Christison) which consisted of 5th Indian Division, back from the Middle East, under General Briggs, and the untried 7th Indian Division commanded by General Messervy. Frank Messervy had been rather in eclipse since the 7th Armoured Division, under his command, lost nearly all its tanks in the Cauldron. But on his return to India he was given an infantry division, with which he was about to make a splendid comeback. Among the corps troops was the 25th Dragoons, a British regiment in Lee Grant tanks, very similar to the Grant.

The first object of XV Corps was to capture the lateral road and tunnel Maungdaw-Buthidaung, whence they would press on to Foul Point. 5th Indian Division advanced on the right, 7th Indian Division on the left, the Mayu ridge between them. Wide to the east the 81st West African Division moved down the Kaladan valley to protect that flank.

The operation did not go according to plan. It went much better.

As a preliminary, a lateral jeep-track to link 5th and 7th Divisions was made across the Ngakyedauk Pass, four miles north of the tunnel. Pushing back enemy rearguards, 5th Division occupied Maungdaw on 10 January. Through this small port 5th Division could then be supplied largely by sea.

On 14 January they attacked Razabil, the most easterly of the strong-points in the main Japanese position, and its outlying bastions, a complex of deep, mutually supporting bunkers and wire. They had not yet got the measure of the Japanese bunkers. Again and again battalions of 161 and 123 Brigades stormed the enemy positions, got on top of the bunkers – and were then shot off them by machine-guns and mortars in neighbouring bunkers, while the garrison remained safe under ground.

General Christison decided to switch the main effort to the other side of the Mayu peninsular, and Messervy's 7th Indian Division prepared to attack Buthidaung on 8 February. The initial assault would be by 33rd Brigade. To support it, 89th Brigade was sidestepped to the left, and

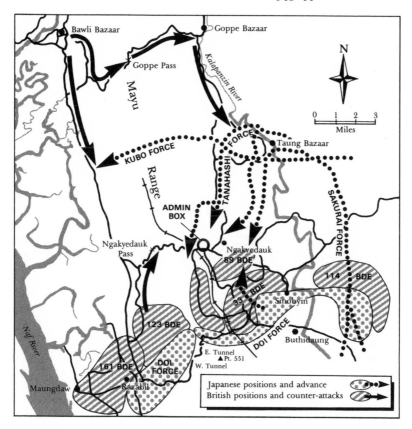

Burma: Ngakyedauk, February 1944

replaced in the area of the Ngakyedauk Pass by 9th Brigade of 5th Division. 114th Brigade, to the east of the Kalapanzin river, protected 33's left flank. Two squadrons of the 25th Dragoons and 6th Medium Regiment, RA, crossed the pass to strenghten 7th Division. At Sinzweya, a mile north of the eastern end of the pass, was established the 'Administrative Box' of 7th Division, to hold reserves of rations, ammunition and stores of all kinds, and that part of the divisional staff and headquarters personnel which was not immediately required for operations. This was known as the 'Admin Box'.

During the night of 3/4 February, men of 114th Brigade heard the sound of men and mules moving up a valley which passed north and south through their positions. They thought it must be the brigade's mule company, and let it pass unchallenged. They were wrong. The Japanese had taken the extraordinary risk of sending through the brigade position a solid phalanx of mules and men, sixteen files wide, which by daybreak had disappeared to the north.

During the morning, however, their supply column was spotted. Its escort was destroyed, its locally conscripted porters disappeared into the jungle and all the supplies were captured. The enemy were running this operation with a very narrow margin of administrative safety, trusting to acquire all 7th Division's supplies. They even brought spare drivers for captured lorries and gunners for captured guns. So the loss of their own supplies was in the long run a serious blow.

The next development, later in the morning of 4 February, was a report from a mounted patrol of Gwalior Lancers of 900 Japs at Taung Bazaar, seven miles behind 114th Brigade. In fact they were about 7,000, hell-bent for the Ngakyedauk Pass to surround 7th Division. At the same time a Japanese battalion crossed the Mayu range, hauling machine-guns and mortars by ropes up precipices, to raid and burn lorries in 5th Division's administrative area. But 5th Division was not completely cut off; the Japanese force was not enough to establish a proper roadblock, and they received much of their supplies by sea.

Messervy, on hearing of Japs near Taung Bazaar, ordered his reserve, 89th Brigade, to face north and deal with them. In two days' fighting the brigade was able to slow the Japs down, but not push them back.

On the evening of 6 February Messervy, now surrounded, had to decide whether his headquarters should move from its exposed position near Laungg Yaung. The headquarters defence company of 1/11th Sikhs having been sent to help 89th Brigade, the only defence now left was provided by divisional signals, an engineer company, and headquarters clerks and storemen, about 120 in all. Nevertheless, he made the characteristic decision to stay put. Having ordered everyone else when surrounded to stand firm, it would be unbecoming for his headquarters to scuttle. Brigadier Hobson, the divisional signals officer, organized a makeshift perimeter, and they were left alone that night. In the morning of 5 February, however, out of the dawn mists, charged some 500 Japanese, screaming their jackal noises and catcalls. The thin clerks' line threw them back, but the whole headquarters area remained under heavy mortar and machine-gun fire and all communications were cut. Messervy, realizing they could not stand another attack, ordered cyphers and secret papers to be destroyed, and everyone to break out in small parties and make their way to the Admin Box at Sinzweya, two miles to the south-west. He and the CRA, Brigadier Hely, escaped down a chaung and hid while Japanese hurried past them not ten yards away.

Commanding 9th Brigade of 5th Indian Division was Brigadier Geoffrey Evans, a fire-eater with a great reputation from the desert. His divisional commander, Major General Briggs, hearing that 7th Division Headquarters was under attack and that there was no wireless contact, assumed the worst and ordered Evans to move into 7th Division's Admin Box with all of his own brigade who could be spared from guarding the Ngakyedauk Pass, and hold it to the last. Ordering 2nd West Yorkshires and 24th Mountain Artillery Regiment to follow, Evans set off in a jeep through heavy rain, slithering about jungle paths, and eventually arrived in the Admin Box on foot, having abandoned his jeep. There he found Lieutenant Colonel R. B. Cole organizing his 24th Light AA-Anti-Tank Artillery Regiment (with Bofors guns) into perimeter infantry, supported by the two squadrons of the 25th Dragoons. Later in the afternoon the 2nd West Yorks and the 24th Mountain Artillery Regiment arrived; and later still the somewhat bedraggled General Messervy and his CRA. Messervy, having re-established wireless contact with his brigades, left Evans in charge of the defence of the box while he commanded the division.

The Box was a bad place to defend. It had been selected for administrative convenience, not for defence. It resembled a saucer, fairly flat and open but surrounded by jungle-covered hills. It was about 1,200 yards across, so every yard of it was overlooked and within mortar and machine-gun range of the surrounding hills. In the centre was a scrub-covered hillock, about 150 feet high, known as Ammunition Hill because it was the site of ammunition and engineer stores dumps, a considerable hazard to anyone in the vicinity when under shellfire. That evening the 4/8th Gurkhas came into the perimeter, less two companies who were lost, with a mortar battery and a medium battery. They now had plenty of supporting arms, but few infantry: too few, even with every clerk and mess waiter, to man a proper perimeter. The enemy would probably get in, and must then be driven out. The first attack came in that night. It hit a sector held by the Animal Transport company, pack-mules led mainly by trans-Frontier Pathans. These had little musketry training but plenty of practical experience. They held their fire until the Japanese were so close that they could not miss – and did not miss.

By next morning, 8 February, 7th Division was established in a number of self-contained, all-round defended boxes: 33rd Brigade opposite Buthidaung; 114th Brigade across the Kalapanzin river, guarding that flank; and 89th Brigade north of the Admin Box. The weak point was the Admin Box itself, the nerve-centre of the division but short of infantry, tactically not well placed; with a plenitude of headquarters personnel who would normally be regarded as non-combatant; and an embarrassing superfluity of mules who contributed nothing to the defence, but a great deal, dead or alive, to the all-pervading stench and flies which plagued the garrison, and had to be watered, fed and cherished under constant fire.

At Corps Headquarters, north of Bawli Bazaar, the fog of war was clearing. Reinforcements were now on their way from the north. 5th Division was ordered to clear the Ngakyedauk Pass, across which the Japanese were by now well established, and link up with the Admin Box. Plans, long prepared for exactly this eventuality, were now put in motion to supply 7th Division by air. The Japanese were still completely confident. The seductive voice of Tokyo Rose crooned over the radio that it was all over in Burma, 7th Division annihilated and the March on Delhi begun. But in fact 7th Division had recovered its balance.

The air-drop started on the 10th, under cover of Spitfire and Hurricane fighters which, if they did not yet enjoy complete command of the air, were denying it to the Japanese. Every day there came armadas of American Dakotas, carrying not merely the basics of food, mule-fodder, rum, ammunition and petrol, but such extras as spectacles to the correct prescription, boots of unusual size, false teeth, razors, soap, private mail and newspapers. The moral effect was enormous: however frightened, exhausted and stinking one might be – the stench of unburied corpses, human and animal faeces, and unwashed bodies was soon overpowering – everyone knew that he would in time be relieved.

There were bad times still to come. The worst was when the Japanese got through at night the thinly held perimeter and attacked the Main Dressing Station. They lined up all the doctors and shot them, except one who feigned dead, and bayoneted the sick and wounded on their stretchers. This stiffened the resolve of any who might have been contemplating surrender.

Without the tanks of the 25th Dragoons the box could not have been held. The Grant might have its shortcomings in the desert, but in the Admin Box it was worth its considerable weight in gold. Its thick armour was proof against any Japanese guns which could be brought close enough to the Box to fire over open sights, and its 75mm gun, firing HE or solid shot, was accurate at close range to an inch. The Dragoons and the West Yorks developed a system of infantry-tank co-operation which became standard in Burma. First the tank fired HE with instantaneous fuse to clear the jungle and expose the enemy position; then HE with a delayed action fuse to smash through the bunker and explode inside; finally, to cover the infantry for the last few yards to the bunkers, solid shot which kept the Japanese down but did not endanger the West Yorks.

During the night of the 9/10th the Japanese got their 71mm infantry guns onto a ridge from which in daylight they could direct plunging fire over open sights at any target in the Box. The ammunition dump was hit and the consequent fires and explosions endangered anyone near it. Then the enemy guns were engaged by the tanks and a medium battery, and blown to smithereens.

9th Brigade's B Echelon, administrative personnel too old for front-line service, under Captain E. D. Chaytor and Regimental Sergeant Major Malony, scored a spectacular success. At two in the morning some fifty Japanese, marching in column of fours and conversing loudly, approached their sector of the perimeter, having perhaps lost their way. Malony held his fire until they were a few yards away, and then killed the lot with grenades and Tommy guns. A search of their bodies produced some satisfactory trophies: a marked map, some rations taken from the Main Dressing Station, and Messervy's red-banded General's cap.

The map, with details of the Japanese plans and the dates of their expected victories, showed that the operation was well behind schedule, and that they must soon be short of food. The enemy commander, General Hanaya, would at this stage have been wise to cut his losses, withdraw, and concentrate on holding his main position. But no Japanese commander would contemplate retreat and loss of face while there remained the smallest chance of victory. So attacks on the Admin Box continued.

Twice they got through the perimeter and onto Ammunition Hill, where they were blasted by a terrific concentration of close-range fire. INA patrols called out invitations in Punjabi to desert, but there were no takers. But taut nerves could be shaken by such cries in the night as, 'We're coming to kill you, Johnny.' Every morning, however, morale was revived by the armada of Dakotas raining down parachutes.

The Box was strengthened by 89th Brigade moving into it on the night of the 14/15th; and two companies of the 4/8th Gurkhas, which for days had been playing hide-and-seek with Japanese in the jungle, found their way in. After this the Box was pretty secure.

The first attempt by 5th Division to force the Ngakyedauk Pass almost succeeded: indeed a telephone line was laid by which Messervy and Briggs conversed briefly before the Japanese discovered and cut it. Then a key point above the pass was retaken by the enemy and the Admin Box was isolated again. But from the north 26th Indian and 36th British Divisions were making their presence felt: just as the Admin Box was besieged, so were its besiegers, and they were sustained by no air-drop. By the 19th they were beginning to pull out. There was a last suicide-attack on the Box, which reached within two hundred yards of Messervy's Command Post before being blasted away by overwhelming fire-power.

That was the end. On 24 February 1944, early in the morning, a Grant tank emerged from the eastern end of the Ngakyedauk Pass and lurched into the Admin Box. From the turret emerged the grinning face of 'Briggo', who shook hands with Frank Messervy as though it were the Relief of Ladysmith, and handed him a bottle of whisky.

The victory was not so much the body-count of over 5,000 Japanese dead in the jungles and paddy-fields as the fact that the enemy encirclement tactics had been, for the first time, defeated. It was not a great victory in terms of the number of men engaged, but it made history.

5th Division then renewed its attacks on the Razabil strongpoint, this time from the rear, and using the new methods of tank-infantry co-operation, took it at last. They found that the enemy had hollowed out in the top of the hill an immense cavern, with dressing stations and gun positions from which field guns could be fired from perfect cover. 5th and 7th Divisions were then called by more important events to Assam.

Slim's sources of intelligence were limited: no Enigma decypherings, no Burmese resistance movement. He had to rely entirely on air and ground reconnaissance. But during the cold weather of 1943-4 many signs – a build-up of Japanese divisions in Burma, the pattern of road construction, logs being stock-piled along the Chindwin, herds of cattle being driven westwards, marked maps and documents captured in raids on small Japanese headquarters – all indicated a major Japanese offensive aimed at capturing Imphal and Kohima, cutting the railway supplying the whole central front, and a breakthrough into Bengal. A Japanese move into the Imphal plain, where he would have comparatively good – and the enemy very bad – lines of communication would give Slim the chance to destroy the attacking divisions, thus making possible an invasion of Burma in 1945. Since the Japanese would probably take great administrative risks, their destruction would be complete if, by the time the monsoon burst, they had not overrun the Imphal plain and replenished their supplies from Fourteenth Army supply dumps and lorry parks.

IV Corps was itself advancing towards the Chindwin; 17th Division southwards through Tiddim, 20th Division south-eastwards through Tamu. These must be concentrated in good time, with the reserve 23rd Division, in the Imphal area. The Imphal plain, crammed with base installations and supply dumps, and with all-weather airfields at Imphal and Palel, must be put in a state of defence – non-essentials evacuated, essentials gathered into defended boxes, administrative personnel organized to fight. Warning orders for withdrawal were issued to 17th and 20th Divisions, and to 5th Indian Division for a move from the Arakan by air.

There remained the delicate matter of timing. A premature withdrawal of the forward divisions, for no apparent reason, would be demoralizing. Slim reckoned that the enemy would not advance before mid-March, so a few days before that would be time enough.

He was wrong. On 6 March the Japanese 33rd Division attacked their old enemy the 17th Division and, moving wide through jungly hills, suddenly appeared near a road-construction camp at Milestone 109, sixty miles behind the front. It held no fighting troops except some Sappers and Miners. Part of a Jat machine-gun battalion was hurriedly sent there to protect an exposed camp and five thousand unarmed road-coolies.

17th Division had to withdraw. Some preliminary measures had aleady been taken. Jemadar Dharam Singh, Dogra, a well-known character in 70th Field Company, Bengal Sappers and Miners, was preparing to demolish the road at a point where it crossed a vertical rock-face. It took three days and nights of shift work to complete the job, and the road was blown as soon as the rearguard has passed through, making a block impossible to repair: the Japanese had to cut another road round it, which took them days.

At Milestone 109 the Japanese shelled the congested camp, but did not entirely surround it, and during the night of the 16/17th the non-combatants were led out by jungle paths to the north. The Jat machine-gunners held on for two more days and then broke out, while the exultant enemy swarmed through the stores and abandoned lorries. They occupied two positions, not inter-visible, on a steep ridge athwart the road and prepared to contest 17th Division's withdrawal. Was it to be 1942 again?

It wasn't. The 2/5th Gurkhas got between the enemy positions; and 70th Field Company cut at top speed a zigzag track for mortar and ammunition mules to reach them. After a devastating mortar bombardment, the Gurkhas charged into the first position and killed every Japanese within it. The second position was then untenable, and the enemy cleared out. Meanwhile, two brigades had come from Imphal to help 17th Division out of trouble: when they linked up, the way was clear through to Imphal.

20th Division disengaged and withdrew from the Chindwin valley without great difficulty, followed by the Japanese 15th Division with a regiment of tanks. By 2 April two brigades were covering Palel and a third in reserve at Imphal. Slim's concentration was achieved, though not as neatly as he had planned.

Further north the situation was more serious. The Intelligence appreciation was that the Japanese could not maintain more than one regiment in the Kohima area. In fact the whole 31st Division was heading for it. At Ukhrul the Indian Parachute Brigade, which happened to be training in the area, held them for two days, but the enemy broke through and set up a roadblock on the Kohima-Imphal road. Imphal was thus cut off from India except by air and a jeep track to the railway at Silchar; and Kohima was in great peril.

It was defended only by two battalions of the Assam Regiment which, although newly raised, fought splendidly; a company of the Nepalese army, not up to much; the hastily organized inmates of convalescent and transit camps, who did far better than could be reasonably expected of 'odds and sods' – all commanded by Colonel H. V. Richards. Thirty miles behind Kohima was Dimapur, a big supply base on the railway, the loss of which would be a disaster. But on 29 March the 161st Brigade of 5th Indian Division flew into Dimapur from the Arakan.

The brigade went straight up to Kohima, to the manifest relief of the garrison. Then, by an unfortunate misunderstanding, it was withdrawn to Dimapur, departing shamefacedly under the reproachful gaze of those who stayed behind. But on 5 April it was sent back to Kohima, 4th Royal West Kents leading. They arrived just in time. The Japanese were already in Kohima village, to the east of the main position, and the odds-and-sods were visibly despondent. Not so the Deputy Commissioner, Mr Charles Pawsey, who in grey flannels and Panama hat strolled about as though hosting a garden party. Of 161 Brigade only the Royal West Kents and 20th Mountain Battery actually entered Kohima. With the other two battalions (1/1st Punjab and 4/7th Rajputs) Brigadier Warren formed a box across the Dimapur road about two miles to the west. His reason for doing so was that the Kohima box was so small and congested, and overlooked by the enemy, that guns could not come into action there; while from gun positions in the box outside Kohima, with FOOs inside it, 2nd (Derajat), 11th (Dehra Dun) and 12th (Poonch) Mountain Batteries could give very good support, especially as they had raided Dimapur for 5,000 rounds of extra 3.7 ammunition and brought it up in purloined lorries. In fact 20th Mountain Battery, in Kohima, was obliged to dismantle its guns, and the gunners to fight as infantry. But its Battery officers acted as FOOs for the other batteries.

Lieutenant Colonel R. H. M. Hill, commanding 24th Mountain Artillery Regiment, the parent unit of these batteries, found in the box a perfect gun position.

'From that position and from one close by we fired many thousands of rounds by day and night for more than eight weeks at a mean range of 3,500 yards. The Jap never found our guns. . . . It was a 3.7 position, no use for 25-pounders. . . . 161 Brigade would have been in a proper pickle with [only] 25-pounders. . . .

2 (Derajat) Mountain Battery was soon in action, and 11 (Dehra Dun) Mountain Battery later the same day, dug in, camouflaged and registering Defensive Fire tasks. . . . We had only eight guns for that critical first fortnight. It was enough for close Defensive Fire and for smashing Jap attacks forming up.'

Beside the Royal West Kents and Assam Rifles in Kohima was 2nd Battery Commander, Major Dick Yeo, and his two officers

'with resources fully stretched calling for and directing fire from our guns. It was a matter of honour for us never to deny them a round or hint that we were running out of ammunition. Nor were we, though I watched it like a hawk. Starting with 5,440 rounds of HE on the 6th April, we still had 886 on the 14th. Thereafter air-drops kept us ticking over.'

On the 7th a company of 4/7th Rajputs made their way into Kohima with another gunner FOO, Lieutenant J. S. Punnia. The Japanese then closed the ring. The FOOs were often within grenade-throwing distance of the Japanese. Not once did their wireless communication with the gun position break down, though it was not easy to keep batteries charged so close to the enemy. Indeed, when Colonel Richards's set was 'on the blink', he had to use Yeo's to communicate with Brigadier Warren.

Artillery support was greatly helped when, after the first week, there fell like manna from heaven a supply of excellent 1/25,000 maps. But there was no meteor or survey data, so the shooting was somewhat bow-and-arrow. But effective.

Two weeks earlier Kohima had been a pleasant little hill station with rest camp, hospital, DC's bungalow, gardens, tennis courts and friendly Naga peasants. In a few days of siege it was reduced to unspeakable squalor: every building in ruins, littered with corpses, faeces, corrugated iron, tin cans and rubbish. No sanitary digging was possible, overlooked at close range by the enemy. The stench was appalling, the flies worse. Inexorably the Japanese ring closed: the perimeter shrank from 1,000 by 1,000 yards to 800 by 300. Royal West Kents and Japanese were dug in on opposite sides of the DC's tennis court.

The garrison's water supply was captured. Thereafter they were dependent on one small spring and air-drops of water in inner tubes: the daily ration was half a mug. Every square yard of the position was under enemy fire. There was no proper shelter for the wounded, many of whom were wounded a second and third time while lying in the 'hospital', heroically tended by Lieutenant Colonel J. Young's 75th Indian Field Ambulance. The garrison could not have survived without the magnificent support afforded by 24th Mountain Artillery Regiment.

The Japanese commander was singularly unenterprising. He could have left a force to mask Kohima and gone straight for Dimapur. But that danger was reduced by the arrival there of the 2nd (British) Division in the first week of April. The 5th Brigade of that division moved up the road towards Kohima, and on 15 April were within 25-pounder range. 24 Mountain Artillery Signals Officer was 'fishing for their gunner frequencies', but contact was first made by lamp, and fire-orders passed from Yeo to the gun position by wireless were passed on by old-fashioned visual signalling.

With the arrival at his box of 5th Brigade on the 16th, Warren could send his two battalions into Kohima; and on the 18th the garrison, at the last inch of their endurance, was relieved. 7th Indian Division was also now being flown in to Dimapur, so the crisis was over.

The Royal West Kent regimental history records that:

'The fire of these gunners was so careful and accurate that they were able to bring down fire at call on the other side of the tennis court with no danger whatsoever to our troops. They were frequently called on to bring down Defensive Fire within twenty-five yards of our forward positions, a feat which they could do at any time without danger to us. The 3.7-inch howitzer was a wonderful little gun.'

When the regiment came up to Kohima, the mules had been left behind and they had moved by lorry. But with the prospect of mobile operations being resumed, the mules were sent for. The regiment had only one tent, of which the sole occupant was Memsahib, its prize and most beautiful mule. When General Mansergh asked why she was given such favoured treatment, he was told, 'Sahib, there will be a Horse Show.'

There was hard fighting to clear the Japanese off the hills east and south of Kohima, so as to open the road to Imphal. Within a couple of days of joining 24th Mountain Artillery Regiment, P. A. Densham was FOO with an Indian battalion of very high reputation, but tired and long overdue for relief, watching the battering of Church Knoll by RAF fighter-bombers, 25-pounders, and medium guns.

'I could not believe that anyone could possibly remain there. Then I saw a discouraging sight. The mediums got a direct hit on the centre bunker. It was only a small slit in the hillside, with doubtless a small dugout behind it. . . . The direct hit was magnificent, and when the smoke cleared I saw that the earth had been dented in and the slit closed. But even as I watched through my glasses I saw the earth move, a stone went slithering down the hill, and then a hand and an arm appeared. It carefully cleared the earth away. . . . I rang up the CO and reported that the Knoll was definitely occupied. "Oh, blast!" he said.'

Two days later the battalion's attack was due to go in at 1300 hours. Densham went to the battalion headquarters for lunch.

'Most of the officers were drinking rum and I had a goodish peg too. There was a lot of laughter and joking, quite genuine, not of the film variety.... At last someone said, "We had better be getting along", and we filed out to put on tin hats and equipment. The start line for the attack was a nullah near my OP, well out of sight of the enemy, and here the two companies were formed up, waiting listlessly for zero hour.... British Other Ranks generally talk on these occasions, but Indians don't; they squatted on their haunches, looking straight ahead.'

Two companies got onto their objective, a big Japanese bunker, and were then shelled off it, with heavy loss. Then another company tried.

'I found the company commander lying in a shallow depression at the bottom of the hill. He said, "I can't get my men to go in. Can you get your guns on to the top and try to keep the Japs' heads down?" I got orders through and heard shells going over. Suddenly there was a dull clang in my head and everything went black and far away. When I came to, I found my signaller dead, sitting beside me about two feet away. The Company Commander said, "Sorry about that, Gunner; he's mortaring us, I'm afraid."'

The next mortar bomb mortally wounded the Company Commander and Densham's other signaller and smashed the wireless set. All the men had gone. He tried to pull the Company Commander back but could not until he got help.

'I went back to the nullah and found everyone very upset. The attack had been a complete failure and we had nearly 100 casualties.... The rest of the day was grim.... The men couldn't be got to attack again; they just sat on the ground, not looking or thinking about anything. This sounds very terrible, but I am told it is what happens when a unit has been kept in too long.'

Eventually 2nd British Division cleared the hills round Kohima and pushed down the road towards Imphal, rather slowly for it was their first experience of action. 7th Indian Division, with pack transport, moved through the hills on their left.

Imphal is like the hub of a wheel with six roads or tracks radiating like spokes from it. All were scenes of fierce fighting as the Japanese 33rd and 15th Divisions tried to close in on Imphal.

The most dangerous thrust was from the north-east, down the Ukhrul road. The enemy took Nunshigum hill, and had to be turned off it because it overlooked Imphal airfield. 123rd Brigade of 5th Indian Division had been flown in to Imphal, and from it the 1/17th Dogras with two squadrons of Carbineers (Grant tanks) counter-attacked Nunshigum on 13 April, an early example of infantry-tank co-operation on a hill so steep that most people regarded it as 'untankable'. Indeed, at one point tanks had to be winched up; one reared over backwards and rolled over and over down the hill. Drivers could see nothing, so tank commanders had to lean head and shoulders out of the turrets to guide them, with the Japanese so close that they were using revolvers and grenades. All the officers in the Dogras' attacking companies were killed or wounded, as were all the tank commanders except one – Squadron Sergeant Major Craddock who, with Subadars Tiru and Ranbir Singh, none of them linguists, made a plan for the final assault and carried the enemy position where 270 Japanese lay dead in bunkers smashed by 75mm solid and delayed action HE shells.

Along the Palel road, south-east of Imphal, the Gandhi Brigade of the Indian National Army saw action, but not for long after it was ambushed and scattered. Thereafter it confined its military activities to shouting nationalist slogans at night. Many of its soldiers tried to surrender, and were given short shrift by their former comrades, who disapproved of traitors. As, however, they brought useful information, orders were issued to give them a kinder welcome.

There was a battle for the Shenam Pass, between Tamu and Palel, where the 3/1st Gurhas held a forward position. The Regimental History records:

'Warning of an assault came from the explosion of mines. Then showers of grenades were followed by a line of attacking infantry led by officers with drawn swords. The line melted as it met the fire of A Company, but its place was taken by wave after wave of yelling Japs hurling themselves forward to be mown down. At about 0530 a new plot seemed to be hatching, to the accompaniment of much jabbering and waving of swords. Number 7 Platoon reported that a party of about twenty enemy were trying to place Bangalore torpedoes under the wire. Havildar Minhahadur Rana seized two sandbags full of grenades and [made his way] over the parapet to the threatened wire. There, standing up alone and fully exposed, he flung grenade after grenade on the bunch of crouching enemy trying to place the explosives under the wire. His last bomb thrown, he was about to return when he was killed.

By then the Madrassi signallers had at last managed to get through by wireless to summon help from the battalion. These men earned everyone's praise, unmoved by the inferno and imperturbable even when two percussion fuses, with shells attached, penetrated the trench and hung perilously over their heads.'

Next day the Gurkhas went in with the kukri.

'With blood-curdling yells the men rushed the bunkers and soon not a Jap remained alive inside the position. Outside the bunkers about twenty Japs still lay in groups, covering the flanks, but at the sight of Number 16 Platoon charging over the top with bloody kukris, they fled in panic.'

There was a curious, and in the war against Japan perhaps unique, sequel to this little battle: a cease-fire so that both sides could carry away their wounded.

Bishenpur, at the junction of the road leading south from Imphal to Tiddim and that leading west to Silchar on the railway, was an important place, the scene of very heavy fighting, including a night attack on the 4/8th Gurkhas. They were supported by tanks which had climbed two thousand feet up a zigzag path hacked out of the bamboo jungle by Sappers and

Miners. They used their headlights to illuminate the screaming suicide attacks, mowing down the Japanese with their machine-guns.

In an Order to the 33rd Division Major General Tanaka told them that he expected them to be almost annihilated in capturing Imphal; and that if any soldier flinched, 'a commander may have to use his sword as a weapon of punishment'. Slim knew of no army to equal the Japanese in courage.

But Tanaka's division, like the 15th and the 31st, was beaten. By June the monsoon had broken – the nemesis which had overhung the commanders who attacked without adequate logistic support. Now all they could hope was to get back to the Chindwin valley without dying of starvation, malaria, typhus, or sheer exhaustion. Some rearguards still fought, but every road and track was littered with the debris of defeat – abandoned arms and equipment, heaps of rotting rice and corpses. The pursuers even found Japanese stragglers, deserters and unwounded men waiting to be taken, hitherto unheard of in this war. Having lost their military honour, their spirits were so broken that they talked quite freely. The headquarters of the 31st Division, with all its maps and secret documents, was taken.

Since Imphal was no longer in danger and was getting all it wanted by air, Slim was in no hurry to 'relieve' it: he was far keener to complete the destruction of the Japanese divisions so as to facilitate his advance into Burma during the cold weather. But, for the record, on 22 June the last roadblock on the Kohima road was cleared and the lorry convoys rolled down to Imphal.

On 5 March two brigades of Wingate's second Chindit expedition were flown into Burma. (A third brigade marched in, and two more were flown in later.) They were mainly British, with some Gurkhas and West Africans, since Wingate was prejudiced against Indians. They were to disrupt communications to the northern front where Stilwell's Chinese-American force was advancing on Myitkina; and to prevent the enemy reinforcing the 'March on Delhi' via Imphal. With air supplies and medical arrangements much improved, they were far more effective than the first Chindit expedition in 1942, particularly in indirect help to Stilwell which he never acknowledged. Their heaviest fighting was the defence of their 'Blackpool' box, attacked by overwhelming numbers of infantry and bombarded by everything up to 155mm guns and 6-inch mortars. When the monsoon rains made their airstrip almost unusable, and their food and ammunition was running out, the acting brigade commander, Major Jack Masters, decided they must go. They shot their own mortally wounded, rather than leave them to the Japanese, and fought a bitter rearguard action for four days to Mokso, held by another Chindit column, beside a lake which could be used by flying boats even in the rains.

A few days later the 3/9th Gurkhas had to attack a hill, Pt 2171, held in force by the Japanese. Their CO was, improbably, an officer of the Royal Deccan Horse, Alec Harper, who had volunteered for Chindits.

'We attacked "two-up", B Company (Major Thorpe) straight up the hill, and C Company (Major Blaker) a left hook, down a ravine and up the mountain. B Company got to close quarters too soon and had about thirty casualties. They stopped and exchanged fire with the Japs at about thirty yards, both sides being held. I went up and joined them, and talked with Thorpe who had a Jap bullet through the skin of the back of his neck but was in good heart. On my way I met Jemadar Yem Bahadur, leader of the left platoon, who was being carried down with a thigh broken by a burst of machine-gun. He gave me a clear account of the situation, said the way into the Japs' right flank was open and practically ordered me to continue the attack. This Gurkha officer had the aquiline face of an Elizabethan buccaneer and the same mentality, a dangerous man. During training he had pistolled two of his men who were insubordinate and seemed to be going for their kukris.

As I expected C Company on the Japs' right flank, I told Thorpe to wait for them. When C Company hit the Jap flank they were met at very close range by a machine-gun raking the jungle and mortars, and lay down. But Jim Blaker got up and rushed the gun personally, firing his carbine, and getting them all moving again. The Japs ran, and C Company had only about ten casualties. Blaker was the only one killed, by a burst of machine-gun fire through the stomach. He was awarded a posthumous VC.'

For all their battles and privations, the Chindits' effect on the main, Assam, front was minimal. The Japs diverted no troops from the March on Delhi to deal with them. Slim believed that transport planes and troops of the highest quality could have been better used in the main battle. When Wingate was killed in a plane crash, the whole Chindit concept was downgraded. Harper, although immensely inspired by this magnificent adventure, concluded in retrospect that their greatest contribution was to prove the efficacy, and limitations, of regular British troops using all the resources of modern medicine but with nothing but air-supply, in tropical jungle. They learned, too, lessons from the Japanese: how to construct bunkers, and never to surrender.

Another unorthodox formation, the light-hearted Lushai Brigade, two Indian battalions and the Lushai Levies, with no artillery, no engineers and, it was said, only one map, did great work harrying the Japanese advance and subsequent withdrawal south of Tiddim. And the even more irregular Kachin Levies, in the furthest north-east corner of Burma, were extraordinarily cost-effective, killing many Japanese and providing much useful information.

CHAPTER 23

Italy: *Guerra è finita,*

1945

Any chance of bouncing the Germans out of their Gothic Line and ending the war in Italy in 1944 was lost by the removal of seven divisions from General Alexander's command for a landing in the south of France in August which, for all the opposition it encountered, could have been done by a single brigade.

Prepared for months, the Gothic Line stretched for 130 miles from Pesaro on the Adriatic to La Spezia on the Gulf of Genoa. Its strength was the mountains on which it was based. It was not continuous: it did not have to be; but wherever there was a practicable way through, there it was fortified. There was only one way round, a thirteen-mile gap between the mountains and the Adriatic.

10th Indian Division, having relieved 8th Indian Division, pushed into the mountains east of Florence. It was commanded by Major General Denys Reid, who had escaped from an Italian prison camp with Brigadier Charles Boucher. He was a mountain war expert, with a wonderful eye for ground vital to attack or defence. Such a feature was one of many Italian mountains called Monte Grande which 25th Brigade attacked on 5 August. After a week battering at the formidable defences, it was decided to try a silent night attack by the Gurkhas, using kukris, impeded only by one rifle per section.

It had been a hard week for MacDwyer, but 'curry and whisky were a great help in keeping up flagging spirits. I should think I drank a bottle a day with no ill effects whatsoever.' As DQ it was his duty to be close behind the Gurkhas to deal with various administrative problems which would arise when Monte Grande was taken.

'The Gurkhas attacked silently just before dawn and swarmed through the minefields and over the German positions, taking the enemy by surprise. It was all over in a short time, Monte Grande was ours and the battalion in waiting moved in to relieve the Gurkhas and consolidate. Few Germans escaped and we took a large number of very bewildered prisoners, literally shocked and stunned by the suddenness and swiftness of the attack. I was not really very surprised at the slaughter I saw. There were many dead Germans, mainly decapitated or with limbs chopped off with those deadly kukris. It was a scene of carnage. We made the prisoners bury their own dead and help the less badly wounded down the mountain. I spoke to several prisoners who were terrified of "those little black devils" and thought the slaughter might start again.'

North of Monte Grande, Brigade headquarters was shelled accurately and often, although there seemed to be no place where the Germans could possibly have an OP from which they could be seen. Finally a search of a nearby monastery disclosed, in monks' robes, four very brave Italians (one a woman) who were directing the enemy's fire. In the confusion attending their capture, they were somehow shot – a more merciful end than the court-martial and firing squad which would otherwise have awaited them.

In the middle of August 8th Indian Division reached Florence. By an unwritten, civilized agreement, the city was spared the fighting which would have damaged its antiquities and art treasures: within hours of its capture, Bill Moberly was being taken on a conducted tour of the Pitti Palace. Other bridges across the Arno were blown by the Germans, but not the Ponte Vecchio, and the British treated it as a no-go area for military purposes. UNRRA, however, asked for it to be opened so that food could be taken to civilians on the north bank, so Howarth's 7th Field Company cleared it of mines and demolition charges. He then drove the leading jeep across the ancient bridge, turned right along the colonnaded side-walk and bumped down the steps to the Uffizi.

By early September the 6th Lancers, after slow progress along mined and demolished roads, reached the Gothic Line in wild mountain country. Halt!

The main effort of Eighth Army, in which 4th and 10th Indian Divisions took part, was now on the right, between the high Apennines and the coast. A new arrival was 43rd Gurkha Lorried Brigade, under Brigadier 'Tochi' Barker, seething with impatience after rusticating for three years in PAIFORCE. On 12 September they made a brilliant debut under command of 1st Armoured Division, storming the Pesaro ridge in hill-farm country not unlike the Normandy *bocage*, cut up by high banks and deep ditches. During the night they took all their objectives in hand-to-hand fighting; but would they be able to hold them against the inevitable panzer counter-attacks in the morning? The sappers were doing all they could to throw Ark-bridges* across the Fosse de Valle stream in time, but one went astray in the dark and the other was wrecked by a direct hit as soon as it was completed. There was a fearful traffic-jam of vehicles waiting to cross, but the Queen's Bays and some 17-pounder anti-tank guns extricated themselves from the queue, went looking for a crossing place, found one and arrived just in time to break up the panzers when they came in later in the morning.

Eighth Army had turned the Gothic Line and entered the flat, semi-flooded Emilian plain, heading for Bologna.

(In October, 4th Indian Division was diverted to Greece, not so much to chase out the remaining Germans as to keep the peace between rival Greek parties, royalist and communist, and see that the latter did not prevail. This

---

*An Ark-bridge was a Bailey bridge span laid on top of a tank driven into the river, a technique first tried at the Gari crossing.

they did with discipline, self-restraint and very little fighting. There were thirty-nine recognized political parties in the country. Greeks postured and orated; newspapers invented lurid tales of oriental atrocities, while the Indians tactfully discouraged them from killing one another, repaired roads and bridges, brought in food convoys, created a more or less well-behaved anti-communist National Guard, and listened to their interminable speeches.)

By Christmas, when torrential rain in the plain and snow in the mountains had reduced military operations to patrolling and skirmishing, Eighth Army had reached the Senio river, forty miles short of Bologna.

8th Indian Division spent most of the winter in the high mountains, patrolling in snow and learning, without conspicuous success, to ski. The 6th Lancers operated as infantry. 'Russell Pasha paid us the back-handed compliment of calling us the best foot-soldiers in his division.'

Just before Christmas, 8th Indian Division made a dramatic dash across Italy to plug a gap left in the line by the precipitate departure of the 92nd American (all-Negro) Division. They were preceded by the Commanding Officer of the 6th Lancers, immaculate as usual in prewar Sam Browne belt and glistening field boots. Seeking some headquarters with whom to make his number, he pushed open a door to be confronted, through clouds of cigar-smoke, with half a dozen shining black faces and the soles of a dozen combat-boots resting on the table. 'Good morning,' he said. 'I am Lieutenant Colonel Robinson, commanding the 6th Lancers. I gather that you may need some help from my regiment.'

The largest cigar was waved in his direction. 'Ain't that dandy? Ma name is Robinson too, and Ah'm a colonel too, only Ah'm a bird-Colonel. Sure, some of the boys have been psyched.'

It transpired that the 92nd had over-assessed the emergency which so stirred them. 19th and 21st Brigades restored the *status quo ante* without difficulty.

They had a short but agreeable sojourn in the Lucca area, their main problem being the traffic discipline of the US forces. On one occasion a huge lorry stopped just outside divisional headquarters and the driver got out to relieve himself. A Sikh military policeman swaggered up to him. 'Hi! Midnight, you know bloody well you're not allowed to stop there, even if your bladder is bursting.'

'Who you calling Midnight? You ain't far short of a quarter to twelve yourself.'

In April it was time to think of ending the war. The task of 8th Indian Division was to cross the Senio and form a bridgehead over the Santerno, seven miles on, through which would pass 10th Indian, the New Zealanders, the Gurkha lorry brigade, 6th Armoured and 78th British divisions, to administer the *coup de grâce* to the German Tenth Army.

The two rivers were formidable obstacles. The approaches were flat and open. The rivers ran between high flood-banks which the Germans had honeycombed with dugouts so that attackers who had managed to get across the first flood-bank were, as they forded or swam the river, caught in enfilade by scores of spandaus firing through loopholes in the inner side of the flood-banks.

The attack started on 9 April. 19th and 21st Brigades were to cross the Senio; 17th Brigade would go through them to cross the Santerno. It was a very bloody battle, particularly the actual crossing of the water. Two VCs were won that day, by Ali Haidar, a Pathan of the 6/13th Frontier Force Rifles, and Namdeo Jadhao, of the 1/5th Mahrattas, in much the same manner: attacking single-handed, with grenades and Tommy gun, spandau teams enfilading the river.

6th Lancers had to provide a dismounted squadron to cross with the Argylls and protect the right flank of 19th Brigade. The Colonel, 'Bingall' Ingall, summoned the squadron commanders and asked, 'Any offers?' There was, recalls R. A. A. Dawes, commanding C Squadron, dead silence.

'"Alright, you miserable buggers," said Bingall, "we'll draw for it." Of course poor old C Squadron drew the short straw. As it turned out I was rather glad, because when we had the bridgehead, the US Air Force mixed up the rivers and delivered a load of bombs on the rest of the regiment in their vehicles waiting to cross.'

It was the job of 7, 66 and 69 Field Companies to bridge the Senio and the Santerno. At the latter:

'At 0445 hours a bulldozer broke its track and partially blocked the near approach to our bridge site. Then the demolition charges in the flood-bank failed to explode. A report reached us that a Tiger tank was waiting for us on the far side of the Salterno, two hundred yards away. Our near approach was widened round the disabled bulldozer and a Sherman tank . . . was positioned to take on the Tiger the instant the gap in the far bank was blown. No mistake was made this time: up went the bank. . . . The only enemy in sight . . . were two bomb-happy Germans who staggered out of a deep dugout not twenty yards from the crater.'

Through the gap punched by 8th Indian Division poured the divisions of the pursuit. Well to the fore was the 43rd Gurkha Lorried Brigade, in their armoured carriers or riding on the tanks of the 14/20th Hussars. On the 16th, in the darkness just before dawn, they reached the village of Medecina.

It was imprudent for tanks to enter the narrow lanes of a village in the dark, but this was no time for prudence. The leading tank brewed up a SP (self-propelled) gun and sprayed with machine-gun bullets the crews of two 88s at fifty yards range, but was then itself knocked out. The SP gun blew up, bringing down several houses behind the leading troop and trapping it. But by that time the 2/6th Gurkhas were in, led by Major Greenwood, bareheaded, armed with a walking-stick and wearing a red scarf for identification. Through cellars and attics, over roofs and under culverts, they hunted the paratroopers, and by daylight the village was cleared.

10th Indian Division took up the running with a crossing of the Lidice, the last river before the Po. The flood-banks were thirty feet high, held by

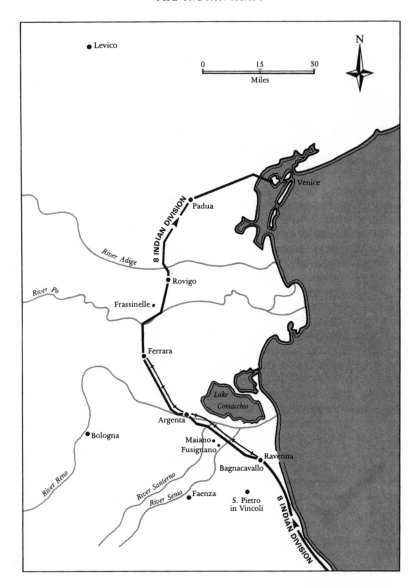

Italy: February–May 1945

troops as brave and skilful as any in the Wehrmacht. Of the leading battalion, the 1/2nd Punjab, only two Dogra platoons reached the far bank and were trapped against wire by spandau fire. The supporting tanks, bogged while crossing an irrigation ditch, could not help them, and they were assailed on all sides. Every Dogra was killed; but by morning the Germans had gone.

The next river was the Po. It was swift, two hundred yards wide, and all the bridges were blown. Too wide to be bridged in a hurry, it had to be crossed by assault craft, cable-ways, amphibious Shermans and rafts. 7th Field Company were presented with rafts they had never seen before, each propelled by four outboard engines, their management requiring skills which could be acquired only by practice. Dawes's squadron of the 6th Lancers was ordered, to his horror, to make a crossing on them.

'In my usual Bolshy way I protested to Bingall that I had joined the Indian cavalry, not the bloody Indian Navy, but was told, "Stop belly-aching, for Christ's sake, and get on with it." In the middle of a dark night I sent the Rifle Troop over on the first raft, to establish some sort of bridgehead. I was never one for "Come on, lads, follow me!": "Get on, you buggers, what's keeping you?" being more my style. But it was obvious that control could be exercised only from the far bank; so once the Rifle Troop reported themselves in position, I went over on the second raft, with the first armoured car and my Tac HQ. The Suffering Miners were not all that good at controlling the rafts. The first one, being lightly loaded, went straight across; but my raft, heavily loaded, proceeded to spin like a top and eventually ended up where it started. After a lot of strong language and heavy breathing we set out again, only to collide with the first raft on its return journey. Luckily there were no hostiles on the far bank. Eventually we sorted ourselves out and made landfall in the so-called bridgehead. The Suffering Miners improved their technique with every journey, and by first light all the vehicles had reached the far bank, and I sent the leading troop to look for some enemy. All they encountered was a British infantry patrol, wondering what all the noise was about.

Feeling a bit red-faced, we let in the spurs, fanned out on three parallel roads and set out for Rovigo. There were a lot of disenchanted Bosches lying around, who had to be rounded up and sent to the rear, and it was late evening when the Canale Bianco was reached, a piddling little stream, no more than twenty yards wide, but blocking any wheeled advance. It looked as if that was that for the day, so I went back to the village where Spencer, my too good-looking second-in-command had established squadron headquarters in a small, dirty house occupied by a voluble female with three buxom and over-friendly daughters, in preference to more suitable houses nearby. His reasons were obvious, his excuses pitiful. I was expressing my displeasure when Jemadar Fazal Dad, commanding my right hand troop, came up on the blower to say that he had captured a wooden bridge across the canal, that the enemy had tried to burn it, but he had driven them off and put out the fire. I told him to hang onto the bridge at all costs until the arrival of the Rifle Troop and myself. I told young Spencer to sit on the R/T till I came back, and leave the women alone, and the Rifle Troop to follow me to the captured bridge at all speed. I arrived there just before dark to find Fazal Dad had his cars covering the bridge and was engaging enemy on the far side. The Rifle Troop arrived and were able to cross unscathed and establish a firm little bridgehead. The fire damage to the bridge was not serious and during the night they were able to effect repairs to get armoured cars across. I returned to my headquarters and put young Spencer on R/T watch until further notice before retiring to bed, alone. "Fazal Dad's Bridge", as it was officially called, carried most of the division across next day.'

From there on it was roses, roses all the way: flowers and wine in the villages; kisses for any good-looking fellow the girls could get hold of; parties of theatrical-looking Italians, over-armed with weapons that had been carefully hidden until the Tedeschi departed, rounding up as 'fascists' anyone they disliked; columns of dispirited prisoners, and all the debris of a beaten army.

The last adventure of the 6th Lancers, while peace negotiations were proceeding, was to escort a special intelligence mission into the Southern Alps. There they found 1st Parachute Division, grimly holding a position and refusing to believe that their cause was lost. Lieutenant Connisbee assured them that it was so, and persuaded them to lay down their arms. It was from this matchless division that the 6th Lancers had taken their first prisoners eighteen months earlier.

CHAPTER 24

Triumph of the Forgotten Army,
1945

The Arakan and Imphal-Kohima campaigns in the first half of 1944 removed the threat to India, showed how to deal with Japanese encircling tactics and proved that whole formations could be supplied by air. Some 70,000 Japanese had been killed or died of disease. The greatest gain was to give Fourteenth Army the confidence it had lacked. 'Everything they can do, we can do better' was the spirit that prevailed. They had command of the air. They had three hundred Sherman and Grant tanks. Slim was confident of destroying the Japanese Fifteenth Army: twelve divisions, of which three were shattered.

In the master plan of the Supreme Commander, Mountbatten, the emphasis, in deference to American views, was on aid to China. Fourteenth Army was to cross the Chindwin; occupy the area between the Chindwin and the Irrawaddy; take Mandalay, and halt on the line Mandalay-Pakokku. The Chinese-American divisions in the north would advance to Lashio and link up with Chiang Kai-shek's armies in China. The Arakan would be cleared to provide airfields to help operations in central and southern Burma. Rangoon would be taken by air and sea-borne landings.

The last item Slim took with a pinch of salt. He did not believe that enough landing craft would be available. He had in mind that Rangoon would probably have to be taken by Fourteenth Army from the north, an operation which as yet had little more than a code-name, SOB – Sea or Bust. He did not think much would be achieved by lavishing aid on Chiang Kai-shek, especially after the Generalissimo sacked Stilwell in October. The destruction of the Japanese army was his object, not territorial acquisitions.

The fighting would no longer be in mountains and jungles, but in the comparatively open 'dry belt' of central Burma where armour and motor transport would be at a premium. For this his divisions must be retrained. The Japanese, who used tanks only in penny-packets, would be faced by a concentration of armour such as they had never envisaged, against which their bunker defences would be of no avail.

His appreciation was that the new commander of the Japanese Fifteenth Army, General Kimura, rather than lose face by retreating, would fight for the country between the Irrawaddy and the Chindwin and could there be brought to battle. To IV Corps, now commanded by Frank Messervy, 'not too calculating of the odds', he allotted 7th and 19th Indian Divisions, and 255 Indian Tank Brigade (150 Shermans). To XXXIII Corps, commanded by Stopford, he allotted 2nd British and 20th Indian Divisions and 254 Indian Tank Brigade (Grants and Stuarts). Using bridgeheads already taken, IV Corps would cross the Chindwin at Sittang, XXXIII Corps at Mawlaik and Kalewa. Both would then converge on the Yeu-Shwebo area where the enemy had airfields and bases for which he would fight.

XXXIII Corps crossed on 3 December, and 19th Division, of IV Corps, next day. It was 19th Division's first fight. Composed largely of regular battalions, it had been training for two years and was fuming to get into action under its 'pocket Napoleon' commander, Pete Rees. It advanced with élan and speed, if only to keep up with Rees, who was generally in the leading jeep. But, pondered Slim, eighty-five miles in twelve days – was this possible if the enemy really intended to fight for Yeu and Shwebo? He realized that he had misread Kimura's mind. All that 19th and 20th Divisions were facing were rearguards. The Japanese would fight behind, not in front of the Irrawaddy; and if he persisted in his plan his two corps would be jammed between the rivers having struck a terrific blow at – nothing.

He re-cast his plan, put it to Messervy and Stopford on a camp-table at Tamu, and flung it to his staff to fix the details.

Under the revised plan, 19th Division (transferred to XXXIII Corps) would cross the Irrawaddy eighty miles north of Mandalay and move on the city down the east bank; 20th and 2nd Divisions would cross west of Mandalay and move on it from the south. With the Japanese attention and reserves drawn off to defend Mandalay, the vital blow would be struck by IV Corps, in which 17th Division would replace 19th Division, moving across behind XXXIII Corps, up the Myittha valley past Gangaw, descending to cross the Irrawaddy in the Nyaungu area, and seizing Meiktila, the base and communications centre a hundred miles south of the Japanese divisions fighting for Mandalay.

A great problem would be transport, especially after the removal from Fourteenth Army, without any warning, of seventy-five American Dakotas to help Chiang Kai-shek. Fourteenth Army would have to rely largely on river transport. There was only one problem: they had no boats. Most of the shipping on the Chindwin and the Irrawaddy had been sunk by either the retreating British in 1942, or the retreating Japanese in 1944. Slim summoned his chief engineer, Major General W. F. Hasted and, pointing to teak forests within half a mile of the Chindwin, said, 'Billy, there's the river and there are the trees. Within two months I want five hundred tons of supplies a day down the river.'

Soon Hasted's engineers, with Burmese labour and inland water transport companies flown up from India, were turning out boats by the dozen, made of teak logs hauled from jungle to river bank by elephants. Three, lashed together and decked, would carry a Sherman. They were powered by outboard engines, reinforced by Japanese vessels of various types salvaged from the river bottom, and protected by two home-made gunboats flying the White Ensign.

The first division to cross the Irrawaddy – because the further north Japanese reserves were drawn the better – was 19th Division. On the far side they were in contact with the 36th British Division which had been operating with the Chinese-American forces in the far north, and was now moving south to come under Fourteenth Army. This all-British division contained one Indian unit, 30th Field Company, Bombay Sappers and Miners, which included one Indian officer, Lieutenant R. M. Rau.

> 'The OC, Bob Swaine, was a fine old gentleman. (He was about 30 but looked old to us.) With a fine sense of "Divide and Rule", he gave me the Punjabi Mussulman platoon, knowing I was a Hindu. To this day I remember with pride the loyalty these men gave me.'

Rau's first misfortune occurred when he was supervising the loading onto an improvised raft of a huge REME recovery vehicle.

> 'The front wheels of the vehicle were on the raft and the rear wheels on the jetty when the mooring rope on one side snapped with a sound like a pistol-shot. The raft swung away from the shore and the vehicle slid slowly into the river.'

So did Lieutenant Rau, who returned to the Mess with a heavy heart to report the mishap to his CO: 'I was a bit dramatic about it and said it was all my fault and would he please sack me? Bob Swaine roared with laughter and suggested a couple of drinks.' The court of enquiry found that Rau was not to blame as the Ordnance had provided a rotten rope.

Moving south towards Mandalay, 36th Division had to cross the Shweli river. The first crossing failed, leaving a company of the Buffs on the far bank with all its officers dead. A newly arrived Indian sapper subaltern, M. R. Rajwade, won the MC for organizing the company's defence and evacuating wounded. The divisional commander ordered another attempt upstream, and Rau, 'a lowly subaltern, was sent to choose the spot'. The crossing proceeded under unpleasant shellfire directed by a Japanese OP up a tree. As it got dark, Rau found himself on the far bank with the Royal Sussex. All his boats were damaged, he was no swimmer, so he could not get back.

> 'So there was I, a lone Indian officer in a British battalion perimeter, with no work to do and no business to be there. I jumped into a trench with a couple of Tommies. I was not exactly welcome, but we soon became friends. The Japs were all around shouting orders, and put in a couple of banzai attacks. I fired my revolver half a dozen times at nothing in particular. There was nothing but bully-beef to eat, and after surviving on water for two days, my will-power ran out. All my inhibitions disappeared as I gobbled up the stuff, and the Tommies solemnly shook my hand.'

On Rau's fourth day in the slit trench, the crossing was made good.

A hundred and fifty miles to the east, IV Corps was having problems in the Myittha valley. Secrecy was essential. Continuous fighter cover kept off any inquisitive enemy pilot who might see tanks where only the irregular Lushai Brigade was supposed to be. The genuine IV Corps headquarters observed wireless silence, but a bogus headquarters at Tamu conversed with 19th Division with indiscreet garrulity. The problems of the staff organizing the move faded into insignificance beside those of the sappers and pioneer battalions making up a winding jeep-track into a road fit to take tank-transporters which each, with a Sherman tank, weighed over fifty tons. (The tanks had to be carried, so as to conserve their track- and engine-life.) Soon the road was deep in red dust, and in places the tanks had to be off-loaded to tow the transporters. Almost as hard pressed as the engineers were the IEME workshops. All day and night they worked to keep vehicles running through suffocating dust which clogged air-filters and carburettors, blanketed radiators and penetrated every bearing.

To time the crossings of XXXIII Corps moving on Mandalay and IV Corps moving on Meiktila was Slim's problem. Before IV Corps crossed and the secret of the tanks was revealed, enemy reserves must be drawn up north to defend Mandalay. 19th and 36th Divisions were already doing that. 2nd and 20th Divisions were poised to cross below Mandalay. When? And when should IV Corps cross? The longer they waited, the more chance there was of a bold Japanese pilot or a spy spotting the tanks. He decided that XXXIII Corps should cross on 12 February, and IV Corps as soon after that as possible.

XXXIII Corps's main crossing was by 20th Division at Myinmu, forty miles below Mandalay. The actual crossing went well, but there was difficulty in extending the bridgehead on the far side. 422 Field Company had to lay Sommerfeld track across a wide belt of sand, and then make tracks through ten-foot elephant grass to the forward positions. Snipers lurked in the grass, and direction could be maintained only by compass bearings. Bulldozers would raise dust and bring down enemy artillery fire, so grass had to be cut by hand and laid on the surface. After 481 Field Company had ferried across some Stuart tanks of the 7th Light Cavalry, the expansion of the bridgehead speeded up. Further down there was a subsidiary crossing on a raft improvised by 92nd Field Company from two Japanese pontoons with old rails as road-bearers and decking of planks.

The most vital crossing was that of IV Corps, at Nyaungu, by 7th Indian Division on the night of 14/15 February. There were enormous difficulties in bringing the engineer stores to the river bank across half a mile of soft sand. At the site chosen for the initial crossing there was a water-gap of 3,700 yards and a sandbank in midstream. The sapper companies had a prodigious task coaxing the lorries across $1\frac{1}{2}$ miles of track leading to the river: it took five hours of unremitting toil. Then the assault boats had to be manhandled across a quarter of a mile of the softest sand in Asia. The first company, of the South Lancashire Regiment, was ferried across unobserved in the dark, and took up its covering position. So far, so good. After that, with dawn breaking, it was all bad. Outboard motors refused to start. There was a muddle in midstream when the leading boats, which should have been in the rear, circled round to get in their proper place and were followed in their circle by everyone else. Enemy fire was fairly heavy and several boats were sunk. The crossing seemed to have failed, and one company of the South Lancashires was stranded on the far shore.

Then, unexpectedly, things started going well. A small boat was seen approaching from the distant shore, flying a white flag. It contained two Jiffs* who said that the Japanese had all marched away, leaving the Nehru Brigade of the INA whose only wish was to surrender. Quickly a platoon of Sikhs was ferried across and the Jiffs laid down their arms with smiles, unreciprocated. It was, wrote Slim, the chief contribution made by the INA to either side in Burma. After that, the crossings proceeded apace and by the end of the second night the bridgehead was secure. The tanks followed, on rafts built by 36th Field Squadron.

All was now set for the armoured drive on Meiktila. The British element in 255 Tank Brigade, the 116th Regiment, RAC (the Gordon Highlanders) had been diverted to 7th Indian Division; so the Brigade consisted of Probyn's Horse, the Royal Deccan Horse and the 4/4th Bombay Grenadiers. The last provided one company to each armoured regiment, making two or three infantrymen to each tank. In thick country and in close contact with the enemy, when the tank's turret was generally closed down, the tank was deaf and blind, the 'Grinders' were its ears and eyes, communicating with the tank commander through a telephone on the back of the tank. They accompanied it into action, watched treetops for snipers, guarded it against suicide-attacks. They protected it in night harbours, and the tank with its machine-guns on fixed lines protected them. It was, as scientists say, a 'symbiotic relationship', each looking after the other. Each tank's Grinders became virtually part of its crew, even helping in the tank's maintenance.

Since there were four companies to a battalion and only three regiments to a Tank Brigade, one Bombay Grenadier company, Captain Sobha Chand's D in this case, operated as a motorized company, not as tank-escorts. In the break-out from the bridgehead on 21 February D Company formed part of the advanced guard with a squadron of the PAVO (armoured cars) and other troops. It was Jemadar Mamur of this company, a champion quarter-miler, who captured the brigade's first prisoner, after a dramatic quarter-mile chase. D Company also captured the brigade's first – and only – Japanese 'comfort-girl', and her comfortee, a warrant officer. Unfortunately, or perhaps fortunately, she escaped.

On the 22nd Probyn's Horse, commanded by Miles Smeeton, was detached to clear up opposition reported by the PAVO at Oyin, to the right of the axis of advance. Co-operating with the regiment, but not of course as tank-escorts, was a 6/7th Rajputs from 17th Division, not practised in this work.

As they approached the village, sniping started from treetops. The infantry, who had been perched on the tanks like roosting hens, dropped off and spread out as the Brownings began searching the trees. Sometimes the

*Jiffs: Japanese-inspired Fifth Columnists, a term generally used for the INA.

fire resulted in a heavy shaking of the upper branches and out would topple a sprawling figure to fall with a thump to the ground. To Smeeton 'there was someting so unlikely about shooting one's fellow men out of the tops of trees like rooks that it was hard to think of them with any more compassion than might be spared for a young rook.'

The infantry, coming under heavier fire, halted and took cover.

'For the first time we were up against the difficulty of speaking to the infantry when bullets were actually flying, so very different from the cool co-ordination that we managed to achieve on training. We had a telephone on the back of our tanks, but no infantryman likes to stand up and talk down a telephone when he is being shot at; and no tank commander likes to face the moment of helpless exposure as he climbs out of the turret to speak to an infantryman on the ground, with snipers perhaps only fifty yards away.'

They could see the infantry were under fire, but not where the fire was coming from. They knew the infantry wanted them to go on and clear up the mess; but the infantry

'didn't always understand, in this very close fighting among smoke and trees and burning huts, how blind and vulnerable tanks could feel. . . . With the infantry held up, the leading tanks moved slowly on through the burning village, and as they were approaching the far end a Japanese soldier came suddenly rushing up, threw himself under the squadron commander's tank, and detonated a box of explosive he was carrying, killing himself and the driver and disabling the tank.

We were able to discover that the fire which was punishing and perplexing the infantry was coming from hedgerows on the other side of the road. . . . A troop from the second squadron was called up. . . . As the three tanks came line ahead down the lane, another Japanese soldier sprang out of a foxhole in the middle of the hedge and scrambled up onto the second tank, giving the surprised tank commander just time to duck his head in and pull the hatch shut [shouting the code-signal, "*Badmash!*" On this] the leading tank then traversed his turret and shot the Japanese while he was struggling with the hatch. During this excitement, another Japanese bounced suddenly from the hedge, and with his face twisted in frantic determination, hurled himself under the same tank. Before he could detonate his charge, the tank backed off quickly, like a horse shying, and one could imagine the crew felt the soles of their feet tingling. It left the soldier lying on the ground, curled round his box of explosives, where he was killed. . . . A moment later yet another Japanese came leaping through the hedge, swerved through a file of infantry with his box in his arms as if he were a football player, and climbed onto the front of the third tank. As he did so his charge detonated, blowing his body over the turret, without damaging the tank. If in harvest time I had seen a rabbit, shaken out of a corn stook, turn suddenly on its pursuers. . . . I couldn't have been more surprised than I was at the sudden appearance of these Japanese soldiers, with their anguished look of determination and despair, pitting their puny strength against such tremendous force. Their desperate courage was something that we . . . saw with amazement, admiration, and pity too.'

Nevertheless, wrote A. W. Lane, a troop leader in A Squadron:

'the bunkers were identified and softened up with a round of armour-piercing shot, followed by the finisher-off round of high explosive. . . . The infantry, however, were pinned down . . . the company commander was killed and his men somewhat demoralized. A Squadron commander, Bernard Loraine-Smith, dismounted several times to drive the infantry forward like a farmer with a flock of sheep. Daffadar Durga Singh got his tank stuck in a sunken roadway and was killed when he opened up to get a better view of his predicament. I was in the thick of the trees dealing with snipers and bunkers. My gunner, Bullan Singh, with eyes like a hawk, spotted snipers up the trees and let them have one murderous blast after another from his Browning. We saw the unfortunate devils disintegrate and drip out of the branches. . . . We learned a valuable lesson in mutual support. Thereafter each tank was allotted its very own section of 4/4th Bombay Grenadiers for its sole protection, bless 'em.'

That evening in harbour Miles Smeeton

'had nothing but admiration for the Rajputs, who fought at such close range without the protection of two or three inches of armour, and they were grateful to us who saved them so many casualties. We plotted how we could do still better together.'

In the gloaming he walked back through the shambles of the village.

'Only the tank-hunters had been killed outside their foxholes. All the others were full. There they still sat. Some were pocked and smashed with bullets, some with their clothes still smouldering from the tracer: some, after the brutal propaganda cartoons, surprisingly good-looking, sturdy and young. If a British regiment had fought against such odds as they had fought, the story would live forever in their history.'

Then it was on to Meiktila, Fred Joyner's squadron of the PAVO leading, and treating the Japanese just as they themselves had been treated by the Afrika Korps.

'Just before reaching Meiktila a fair proportion of the Armoured Brigade caught up with us and we joined together for what must have been one of the last cavalry charges on record. Objective, Meiktila Airfield. . . . It was a sight I shall never forget with everyone joining in, . . . just get there as quick as you can . . . tanks, armoured cars, jeeps, trucks, straight across country against fairly heavy opposition.'

The defences of Meiktila on the western side were reported to be strong. 63rd Brigade put in a holding attack, not pressed, from that direction; the main attack was by 48th Brigade with the two tank regiments from the east and north-east. It took two days' hard fighting, 1 and 2 March, to clear Meiktila; every bunker was defended to the last man against Shermans methodically destroying it with HE and solid shell until, under cover of this fire, the infantry could run in and finish off the occupants with grenades pushed through the firing slots.

One bunker, under a huge pile of rubble and bricks, absorbed many 75mm shells without its machine-guns being silenced. Finally Major Kennard, Deccan Horse, summoned Sergeant Smith who commanded the regiment's LAD which had a turretless tank fitted with a bulldozer blade. Slowly Sergeant Smith advanced on the bunker, lowering his bulldozer blade while bullets pattered against it like hail. With the bulldozer scraping the ground, he backed and shoved, backed and shoved, until he had bulldozed bunker and occupants into eternity.

There followed several days of fighting to extend the captured area, keep the enemy out of artillery range of the airfield, clear neighbouring villages, and beat up enemy columns converging, without much co-ordination, from all directions. D Company of the 4/4th Bombay Grenadiers was ordered to raid a village holding about forty Japanese and an anti-tank gun. They ran into more opposition than was expected and were ordered to pull out. But Captain Sobha Chand, who had done a mortar course, persuaded the CO, Lieutenant Colonel S. C. H. Tighe, to lay on a shoot by the battalion mortars which he, Sobha Chand, would direct by wireless. For once the wireless was working, and the mortars plastered the village. Sobha Chand, however, felt he had made a mess of his first independent command, losing one of his platoons in the dark and doing precious little damage to the enemy. Tighe advised him to take a drink, wait and see. Daylight disclosed twenty-seven dead Japanese, a captured anti-tank gun and crew, and his lost platoon, safe and sound.

The 16th Cavalry and the PAVO in their armoured cars showed exemplary cavalry spirit in raiding far afield. In one Jeb Stuart ride the PAVO destroyed a Japanese light tank and captured a 105mm gun, the crew of which was asleep. Their main difficulty was in crossing chaungs: an officer usually had to get out and reconnoitre a crossing on foot, an unnerving job. Often they were on listening watch the whole day, usually on an old battlefield, the smells and sights of which did not improve with time. They lost one armoured car, and Lieutenant Macartney, to a Japanese who leaped onto it clasping an explosive charge. The Deccan Horse found a new anti-tank device: a Japanese squatting in a hole with a 100lbs aircraft bomb and a brickbat to strike it on the head when a tank passed over. Some anti-tank guns were cleverly concealed, one disguised as a bullock-cart, and held their fire until the target was a few yards away. Thus a Deccan Horse tank was brewed up. The other tanks in the troop deluged with fire the houses in front, until the commander of the burning tank came back and told them he thought the shot came from behind. The gun was silenced only when tank shellfire brought down a whole house upon it. On the 5th Lane's tank was hit several times by 75mm guns which shook it but did not penetrate.

'We received further hits from anti-tank guns and the engine was set on fire. We were rocked by another shell and received a complete penetration in the left hand sponson between the driver's instrument panel and an ammunition bin. This grazed the back of my driver's neck and caused a fire in the electrical wirings, stopping the engine. The whole tank was filled with the stench of cordite and acrid smoke which could not be cleared as the engine fan had stopped. The heat was stifling and choking, so I opened the top of the cupola to get some air. We were able to put out the fires with fire extinguishers, but our thoughts raced to the possibility of the tank brewing up or blowing up if the fire reached the ammunition. The wireless set was dead. We seemed lost in the middle of the Jap position, but were still able to fire the guns with manual controls. In this way we dealt with a 105 gun at point-blank range as the Japs strove to get it to bear on us. We were much relieved to see Surat Singh and Sarup Singh galloping to our rescue. Opposition then ceased and I gave orders to evacuate the stricken tank. The driver was last out, trying to repair the dashboard damage. . . . The Sherman engine was a most complicated piece of engineering but, a natural mechanic, he understood its workings perfectly.'

On the 10th Miles Smeeton led – or, rather, followed – two squadrons in an attack on a low hill. The infantry were already in their lorries to return to Meiktila, and stood watching like a point-to-point crowd

'the tanks racing and snarling through the low scrub. . . . As we gained the position the enemy jumped from their trenches and fled, running along between the tanks in a slow and desperate waddle. . . . The tanks stopped to engage two 75mm guns, which they knocked over, and to pour fire into the men who were running so hopelessly. [Shades of Bir Hakim!] We were just about at the limit of our sweep when I saw an anti-tank gun coming into action on the edge of the village and stopped to engage it. There followed a quick exchange of shots. Its first ploughed a groove in the armour at the top of *Clear the Line's* turret, while ours fell some way beyond them. As I gave the correction, a second shot from the Japanese hit *Clear the Line* on the mantle of the gun, pinning it to the turret so that we could not elevate or depress the gun. We fired with the same elevation and fortunately hit the tree above the enemy so that the shell burst over the heads of the gun-crew. . . . We were now heading for home and rather a long way behind. . . . Suddenly *Clear the Line* rang like a cracked bell and flinched away, as a yacht will flinch from a heavy wave on the beam. She had been hit at close range by an armour-piercing shell which had passed through the extra armour of the ammunition bin knocking off three shell fuses. Just behind, Ted Halliwell was hit in the same place, and a moment later one of Malise's tanks had a track knocked off. We called up guns and asked for their help. Within a few moments the first shell had landed and we were able to direct their fire. We were only two or three hundred yards from the village. I watched Malise [Nicolson] climb out of his turret and jump to the ground to fasten a towline. He was glowing with youth and excitement but I, impatient and with my gun still jammed at a useless angle, was as anxious as an old hen until I saw him and the other tank commander safely back in their turrets.'

The strategy of seizing Meiktila behind the Japanese armies was a large-scale repetition of the encircling tactics which the Japanese had so often used in 1942; and the Japanese reacted just as the British had then reacted, by somewhat ineffective attempts to clear their communications. But they must not be allowed to overwhelm IV Corps; XXXIII Corps pressed hard for Mandalay, 19 Division coming down from the north, 20 Division from the south-west, so that Kimura would not be able to divert anything to Meiktila.

By early March they were in tankable country, so Rees pushed on 98 Brigade, with tanks and motor transport, while 64 Brigade followed more slowly. By 8 March they were in the outskirts of the city.

The Japanese made a stand on Mandalay Hill, an 800-foot rock, covered with pagodas and honeycombed with cellars, caves and concrete dugouts. More orthodox methods of ejecting them having failed, and the hill being quite untankable, drums of petrol were rolled down into their hideouts and ignited by tracer. Their last stronghold, Fort Dufferin, was an enclosure of about a square mile, surrounded by a high wall backed by an embankment seventy feet thick at the base. It had to be tackled as though it were Badajoz. Medium artillery was brought up to within five hundred yards to pound a breach in wall and bank; 'Forlorn Hope' parties charged forward with scaling ladders, but were repulsed. But on the morning of 20 March a party of Anglo-Burman prisoners appeared at the main gate waving white flags and Union Jacks. The Japanese had slipped away in the night.

In the aftermath of the battle for Mandalay Hill, Slim was attracted by the incongruous sound of singing. Investigating, he found a small figure in a dirty, sweaty uniform, a red scarf round his neck and a bush-hat worn at a jaunty angle, vigorously conducting a party of Christian soldiers of the Assam Regiment in singing missionary hymns. It was 19 Division's commander, Major General Pete Rees. The fact that he was singing in Welsh and they in Khasi did not in the least detract from their enjoyment.

The capture by 19 Division of Maymo, the Government of Burma's hot weather retreat twenty-five miles east of Mandalay, and by 20 Division of Kyaukse, a big railway depot thirty miles south of it, cut communications to the Japanese opposing the Chinese-American divisions in the far north-east, and provided a handsome dividend in rolling stock. This was about to come in extremely useful, as on 27 February Slim had been instructed to seize Rangoon before the monsoon. As, of course, he had always intended.

Meanwhile Christison's XV Corps, consisting of 25 and 26 Indian Divisions, two West African Divisions, 3 Commando Brigade and 50 Indian Tank Brigade, had cleared the Arakan.

By the end of 1944, 25 Division had the whole of the Mayu Peninsular. Akyab was to be taken by an assault landing but was, in fact, liberated by a gunner officer in a spotter plane who diagnosed, from the inhabitants' friendly waves, that the Japanese had left. There was a failure in communications, resulting in the Commandos storming ashore to be welcomed on the beach by their Corps Commander.

Subsequent operations consisted of sea-borne landings to get round successive enemy positions. The first was on the Myebon Peninsular, on 12 January, by the Commando brigade supported by A Squadron, 19th Lancers, in Shermans. A soft, muddy shore is not the best place for a landing; the LST commander refused to risk his vessel by running her ashore and let down the ramp when she was still three hundred yards out. Lieutenant Billimoria was obliged to hazard his tank, which descended the ramp, churned forward about five yards and then heeled sideways in four foot of water over unplumbed depths of soft mud and was seen no more. Other tanks (waterproofed with sticky tape) were landed on a rocky beach, after sappers had blasted a track across it.

The terrain was of paddy fields divided by steep little jungle-covered hills and ridges, on which the enemy had his bunkers. Where possible the tanks, with their Bombay Grenadier escort, stayed below in the paddy, firing in support of infantry attacking the hills and ridges. A Forward Tank Officer (FTO) with a 38-wireless set accompanied the infantry, on foot, to direct the tanks' fire onto what was often a very small target, a mere slit in a bunker quite invisible to tank gunner and commander. The FTO was often lying flat within yards of the bunker, giving corrections until the solid shot were thudding into the slit, enlarging it for a finisher-off of HE. Then, so as not to endanger them, the tanks would change back to solid while the infantry ran in. At the last moment the FTO would order 'Lift', and the guns would be firing over their heads as the infantry threw grenades into the gaping slit.

Sometimes these methods did not work. On 15 January the Commandos were held up by fire from a hilltop position which could not be hit by tanks in the valley below. The troop leader, Lieutenant Ben Pryde, suggested that he drive up to the top. The squadron commander, Bill Sample, had his doubts:

'Looking at the gradient and the thickness of the jungle, this seemed impossible. However, things were so unpleasant that any new idea was a good one. Ben led the climb and managed, by knocking enormous trees down, to get to the top. The Commandos took on a new lease of life and crept in behind the tank. Robin [Captain Wright, the FTO], Ben and the Commando troop leader decided that the best plan was to charge the positions with the Commandos behind. Calling up his other two tanks, he moved forward. One Jap left it too late and was run down by Ben, three were killed and the remainder fled. Ben, however, leading, was unable to see a sheer drop on his left and went over the side, turning about three somersaults to the bottom.'

The tank came to rest upside-down and the crew, considerably shaken, were rescued by their faithful attendant Grinders.

Two days later the Commandos were relieved by 3/2nd Goorkhas who attacked a pagoda-crowned hill. The tank commanders could see nothing but smoke from smoke-grenades pillaring up through the trees to mark the Gurkha advance. Eventually they emerged onto the open top of the hill. Twice the Gurkhas were repulsed by fire from an invisible bunker. Finally the FTO, Robin Wright, managed to locate it, and slowly, giving meticulous corrections, got a tank three hundred yards away firing shot after shot into the bunker-slit. Then he stopped the firing, and there was a strange silence, broken by the Gurkhas as they ran in with grenades.

That day ended, as did most days, with all-night labour by the recovery team, often under fire, to bring in tanks which were disabled and tanks which were bogged or had shed their tracks. At night they went into close harbour, protected by the Grinders. At 0530 hours on 31 January

'we were rudely awakened by very fast and accurate shellfire. A babble of voices in the nearby bushes followed by the noise of machine-guns and grenades indicated that we were being attacked. . . . Grenades were whizzing through the air from both sides. . . . Bing Wilson [Bombay Grenadiers company commander] shot the leader of the suicide squad in the face with his Sten, but after overrunning our forward position, they planted some explosive on the truck. There was a terrific green flash and a tremendous bang which drove most people back to their trenches. After things cooled down we discovered that honourable friend had succeeded in lodging himself in a small feature overlooking us. However Bing, who was to be seen jumping from tree to tree, led a section of Grinders up and pushed them off.'

It was quite a success for honourable friend, who brewed up a truck, a tank and its crew. But it was an isolated success. In late January and February, 25 Division with tank support captured Ramree and Cheduba islands, potential airfields from which Fourteenth Army's chase to Rangoon could be supported. With that, XV Corps had all of the Arakan that mattered. In what was left, the surviving Japanese could be left to perish of malaria or starvation, or to make their way to the disintegrating Japanese forces further east.

For the second time Slim had to race through Burma to beat the monsoon. Failure to do so would have dire consequences to Fourteenth Army at the end of very long and by no means all-weather lines of communication. It might even allow the enemy to stage a recovery. His transport was on its last legs, his tanks very near the end of their track- and engine-life. On these would depend the striking power and speed of the pursuit. 'I told them that when I gave the word, every tank must be a starter, and every starter must pass the post in Rangoon.' Prodigious exertions by regimental LADs and IEME workshops ensured at least the first of his requirements. Although there could be no major seaborne invasion at Rangoon, Slim asked for a modest landing to foil Japanese demolition parties; but naturally he hoped Fourteenth Army would win the race.

Before IV and XXXIII Corps came under starter's orders, the enemy must be driven from Pyawbwe, thirty miles south of Mandalay, a strong position from which 99 Brigade could not shift them. But the flanks were open, so the tanks circled round Pyawbwe and cut the Rangoon road behind it.

Probyn's Horse were in night harbour, the officers dining, when they heard the distinctive noise of Japanese tanks coming south from Pyawbwe. They ran for the nearest Shermans as the crews scrambled into their places. In the tank taken by the Colonel, Miles Smeeton, the gunner's place was taken by Lieutenant Bahadur Singh, a young and debonair Rajput with an MC, who was soon to become Maharajah of Bundi.

'As the leading tank came round a bend in the road. . . . I leant forward and touched Bahadur Singh's shoulder. A dagger of flame shot from the barrel of his gun, the enemy tank glowed redly, and immediately with a great belch of flame blew up.'

The second tank swung off the road and came towards them. Then, suddenly seeing the line of Shermans in the dark, turned sharp right and drove along it, only a few yards away, while the gunners frantically tried to depress the muzzles of their 75s. If he had stayed close to them, he might have got away with it; but the driver lost his nerve, swung back to the road, was hit, caught fire and upset. The third tank reversed at top speed, crashed into a dry river-bed and overturned. The others withdrew, but were all destroyed next day, with fifty-three staff cars and lorries which had been trying to escape.

Pyawbwe was taken and the chase was on.

Generally in the lead were the 16th Cavalry and the PAVO. Their Daimler armoured cars were so silent that they often came upon an enemy who had no idea they were near. The PAVO were first into Prome and woke up next morning to find a film unit re-enacting its capture without its true captors. The main thrust was by IV Corps, along the road and railway via Toungoo and Pegu, 320 miles to Rangoon and, with luck, forty days before the monsoon. Toungoo was halfway. Led by Stuart tanks of the 7th Light Cavalry which knocked down a Japanese military policeman directing traffic in the outskirts, 5th Indian Division chased out the Japanese on 22 April and put 3,000 Jiffs to work on the airfield. 166 miles to Rangoon and three weeks to do it in. It looked as though they would win the race.

They just lost it. The day 17th Division reached Pegu, forty miles from the finish, the monsoon broke two weeks early and a deluge of rain made all movement impossible. That day, 1 May, the 50th Indian Parachute Brigade dropped on Elephant Point at the mouth of the Irrawaddy; and a pilot flying low over the city saw on the roof of the prison in large letters, 'Japs gone. Ex-digitate.' Next day 26th Division landed.

The campaign was not quite over. There were still scattered and demoralized groups of Japanese trying to escape to Siam. But Slim's 'Forgotten Army' had destroyed the Japanese army in Burma.

CHAPTER 25

Unfinished Business, 1945–46

VE-Day, a week after the landing in Rangoon, was no great event for those fighting the Japanese: indeed they somewhat resented being told to smarten up, celebrate and look cheerful. For their D-Day was still to come, on the coast of Malaya, and it promised to be a very bloody one. Already preparations were being made by a cloak-and-dagger organization, Force 136, contacting Chinese communist guerrillas and pro-Allied Siamese. Fortunately the atom bomb and Japanese unconditional surrender on 14 August made this unnecessary.

The landing was carried out as an exercise, the most convenient way of re-occupying Malaya and Singapore. The Japanese Army, terrible in war, after surrender could not do enough to oblige its conquerors. Captain Rau, disembarking from his landing craft on the Malayan shore, was welcomed by a Japanese army detachment 'bowing with monotonous regularity'. The Japanese troops on Singapore Island had, for the most part, not fought, and had certainly not been defeated: they might have proved truculent, but they meekly left the island, with their 'comfort corps', built themselves huts on the mainland, and turned their hands to street- and sewer-cleaning, stevedoring or anything else that was required of them. Meanwhile, they were being screened to identify war criminals.

Lieutenant Colonel Brian Montgomery, commanding the 6/7th Rajputs in Burma, was ordered to the Salween to disarm and take the surrender of the Thirty-Third Army. No one could have been more co-operative than General Honda and his Chief-of-Staff, Major General Sawamoto. Montgomery treated them with scrupulous fairness and courtesy, as fellow-professionals, and they responded in the same spirit. The surrender of the officers' swords, an emotion-charged ceremony, was carried out in silence and with perfect discipline. Montgomery was amazed at how many expert artificers they could produce to build huts, an officers' mess, vehicle inspection-pits for his battalion. They even supplied six excellent horses and saddlery for his officers' morning rides. At their repatriation, Major General Sawamoto wrote a letters of thanks for the way they had been treated.

In 1941–42 the Siamese government and army had done everything in their power to assist the Japanese, but in 1945 it was considered politic to treat them rather as sinned against than sinning. The British-Indian formation which entered Siam in September was not an army of occupation, but a general do-goodery force. Its jobs were to disarm, screen and repatriate 125,000 surrendered Japanese soldiers; to succour and repatriate about 12,000 released prisoners-of-war, and about 150,000 slave labourers – Tamils, Chinese, Malayans, Javanese – brought in by the Japanese; to reconstruct the war-damaged Siamese communications, and promote the growing and export of rice, for which neighbouring countries traditionally looked to Siam.

The screening was a laborious process. The record of every Japanese was examined, and where there was prima facie evidence that he was a war criminal, it might take months to collect from former prisoners and locals evidence that would satisfy a British court. Eventually some 1,700 were sent to Singapore for trial. The remaining Japanese were usefully employed in repairing roads and railways, building camps for British-Indian troops and refugees from Java, draining swamps, constructing amenity parks and growing food to feed themselves. The last Japanese left Siam at the end of October.

By mid-October the last of the former prisoners-of-war had been flown home. It took longer to trace and repatriate the slave-labourers: some 30,000 were never found, having presumably died of starvation, disease and ill-treatment.

Work on communications was pressed with great vigour, because of the importance of getting the huge Siamese rice-crop moving. Railways, including the Burma and Kra Peninsula railways on which thousands of prisoners-of-war had died, were repaired and maintained, largely by Japanese; rolling stock was procured, and the rice was transported from where it was grown to where it was needed.

Captain Rau's 30 Field Company was sent to Siam to build a railway branch line, having under command a Japanese Railway Regiment which worked with speed and efficiency.

'They showed me special consideration as the only Asian officer in the Indian Engineers there. They had been in charge of constructing the notorious "Death Railway". It was difficult to believe that these were the same men working with us, so disciplined and obedient.

The scene at the railway station when we departed was unbelievable. Half the female population was on the platform in tears waving farewell to their boy-friends. One resourceful lady turned up in Malaya later claiming that the Education Havildar was the father of her son. . . . Siam had been a very enjoyable sojourn for everyone.'

Not so Java. A few days before their surrender the Japanese had formed a government of their Javanese collaborators headed by Dr Soekarno. These hoodlums had proceeded to treat with extreme brutality – as bad as that of the Japanese – several thousand Dutch internees. The men and boys had been taken from the internment camps and thrown into prison, the women and girls left to the mercy of the Indonesian Youth Army and the mob who, on the Japanese surrender, acquired most of their arms.

On 25 October 49th Brigade (Brigadier A. W. Mallaby) arrived at Soerabaya, charged with succouring the Dutch internees, disarming and evacuating the Japanese, and keeping the peace. It was not at first clear whether this was internal security or war. Mallaby had little difficulty in coming to an agreement with the moderate nationalist politicians who formed the local government; but these had no control whatsoever over the Indonesian army, 12,000 strong, armed and trained by the Japanese, and still less over the mob. The city was in chaos, with road-blocks and machine-gun posts manned by every kind of thug. On 28 October a 49th Brigade convoy, peacefully going about its routine business, was attacked: eleven officers and fifty other ranks were captured and shot out of hand. Another convoy, Dutch women and children being brought down to the docks, was also attacked; most of the lorries were burnt, the Dutch and their small Mahratta escort hacked to pieces. It was war, not internal security.

Mallaby arranged a truce, but within hours the radio station and jail were attacked and their Mahratta and Rajputana Rifle guards, ammunition expended, were barbarically butchered. Mallaby, trying to negotiate another cease-fire, was murdered.

The brigade second-in-command, Colonel Pugh, concentrated the brigade in two areas which were defendable and where the Dutch internees could be protected. In three days 49th Brigade had lost eighteen officers and 374 men.

5th Indian Division (Major General Mansergh) arrived to carry out the tasks which had proved beyond 49th brigade. First to disembark was the ubiquitous PAVO, now in Stuart tanks. These were not quite the thing for street fighting, but were invaluable for escorting convoys of Dutch refugees from their camp inland to the docks for evacuation. In some of these operations the PAVO was assisted by Japanese troops who had not been disarmed. They brought out over 6,000 women and children past mobs screaming for their blood and threatening every obscenity and barbarity. Any Dutch, British or Indians who fell into Japanese hands were mutilated, raped and dismembered in public.

Eventually the city had to be cleared by a methodical advance of 123rd Brigade, supported by only the moral effect of artillery and the Shermans of the 13th Lancers: it was not considered politic to use more than small arms against an enemy plentifully supplied with every weapon, including Japanese medium tanks, and with no inhibitions about using them. Not surprisingly, the battle lasted nineteen days. The severity of the fighting may be judged from the fact that the 3/9th Gurkhas lost eighty men and was awarded a DSO, two MCs, a DCM and two MMs. Many fine soldiers died in this quarrel which had nothing to do with them, men who had fought in East Africa, the Desert, the Arakan, Assam and Burma. Among these was one of the finest soldiers in the Indian Army, Lieutenant Colonel Sarbjit Singh Kalha, DSO and Bar, 2/1st Punjab, just the sort of officer that his country now most needed. But it was an odd sort of war: an officer could be fighting all morning, and in the evening playing tennis or dancing with a Dutch girl at the Soerabaya Club.

For 5th Indian Division the war ended only when they were relieved by Netherlands Marines early in 1946.

CHAPTER 26

Finis: 1946–47

During the war the Indian Army expanded from 150,000 to 1,800,000, every man a volunteer. At the beginning of the war fewer than a thousand Indians held the King's Commission; at the end, 15,740, the senior ones commanding battalions, regiments and brigades. Fifteen Indian Infantry Divisions, three Indian Tank Brigades and many independent formations such as the Lushai Brigade fought against Germans, Italians and Japanese; five brigades were on active service in Waziristan. One infantry, one armoured and one Airborne Division, to their great grief, never fought at all because the Japanese surrendered. In Burma Indian units bore an increasing share of the burden as British regiments dwindled through lack of reinforcements and repatriation. By 1945 nobody thought it necessary to 'stiffen' Indian brigades by a British battalion. It was an astonishing effort for a country which is now popularly supposed to have been groaning under the tyranny of the 'Raj'.

By 1946 it was all over, and in Delhi the staff officers were planning the reduction of the army to its peacetime establishment. There was a problem: whereas most British soldiers wanted to get out as soon as possible, most Indian soldiers wanted to stay in as long as possible. 'You are lucky commanding mercenaries,' said an envious British service officer to Alec Harper in Soerabaya.

There was no tidy, planned demobilization, for on 14 August 1947, British rule ended and the Dominions of India and Pakistan were born. The province which was home to most Indian soldiers, the Punjab, was tragically but inevitably divided. No sane person fantasizes that the British could have gone on ruling India for much longer; but the unseemly haste with which His Majesty's Government and the last Viceroy shed their responsibilities ensured that on Independence Day the whole civil administration of the Punjab, including the police, was on its way somewhere else, Moslems to Pakistan, Hindus and Sikhs to India. This resulted in massacres in which perhaps a million people died. The last task of the British-officered Indian Army was to set up the Punjab Boundary Force under the ebullient Welshman, General Pete Rees, to do what could be done to save life and property in the sundered province. Very little could be done. But although every man knew that his British Officers were counting the days to departure, and the regiments would soon be divided, discipline and esprit de corps held – just. There were a few exceptions, but in innumerable cases Moslem soldiers escorted Sikhs and Hindus to safety, and vice versa. However, the Boundary Force's task was impossible, and on both sides politicians and press denounced it and its commander as partial and incompetent. Not, of course, to their faces. Pandit Nehru said to Brigadier H. W. D. McDonald, 'I know you are doing your best, and I wish you luck in your difficult task.' But he would never have said that in public. After three weeks the force's responsibilities were handed over to India and Pakistan.

The Army was divided, roughly one third, the Moslems, to Pakistan, two thirds to India. The splitting up of the regiments was poignant beyond words. All over India Sikhs and Hindus were giving farewell parties to their departing Moslem comrades, seeing them off at the station with garlands round their necks and tears pouring down their faces; and in Pakistan, vice versa. Throughout, the emphasis was on the splitting perforce of a family, but the preservation of the Regiment. Various ceremonial parades were devised to that end, such as that which took place in Ahmednagar, in India, where the Scinde Horse and the Guides Cavalry were stationed. The Scinde Horse were allocated to India, the Guides to Pakistan, which meant that the Pathan squadron of the former and the Sikh squadron of the latter had to change regiments. On the appointed day the two squadrons paraded, face to face. Each man gave his regimental badge to his opposite number, thus symbolizing the handing over of the custody of the Regiment's traditions to the newcomer, and his welcome to the Regiment.

Once away from their regiments, those moving to the other dominion had a perilous journey. In some cases they could be escorted to the border by their former comrades. The Sikh squadron of the 19th Lancers, for instance, were escorted from Peshawur, through the Frontier Province seething with hatred for Sikhs, by the Punjabi Mussulman Squadron. But this was not always practicable. The Bombay Grenadiers had to fight their way through tribal lashkars from Thal to the Indus, the Pakistan police looking on, and lost eighty-seven killed or wounded. A party of Pathans of the Guides Cavalry, with a British Officer, set off by rail from Ahmednagar to Pakistan and were never seen or heard of again. And so with many more.

Throughout this book I have tried to focus the spotlight on individuals, regiments and battalions, rather than illuminate the whole. Let the spotlight now shine on the senior regiment of the Indian Army during the last weeks of its existence.

The Viceroy's Bodyguard, raised in 1773, consisted in 1939 of a lancer squadron, half-Sikh, half Punjabi Mussulman, employed mainly on ceremonial duties but nevertheless trained operational cavalry. They had a disappointing war. They became the Independent Reconnaissance Squadron of the 2nd Indian Airborne Division, and would have parachuted into Malaya but for the Japanese surrender. Every man had done his jumps and wore his parachute badge, but they had seen no fighting. In December 1945, they returned to Delhi to resume their proper role under the command of Lieutenant Colonel P. Massey, MC, Hodson's Horse, who had commanded a Baluch battalion in Burma. Its adjutant was Captain Hari Badhwar, 3rd Cavalry, who had behaved so heroically as a prisoner-of-war. They were to have three roles: ceremonial, internal security, and as a unit of the field army. Every man had to be both horseman and armoured car man.

Training – for the veterans re-training – in horsemanship was not easy, but in the autumn of 1946 they paraded on horseback, in scarlet, blue and gold, with white breeches and black Napoleon boots, on the occasion of the wedding of the Viceroy's, Lord Wavell's, daughter. Thereafter they were much in demand for ceremonial parades, for the nearer the time came for the British to leave India, the more important it seemed to put a cheerful face on it.

With Independence and the Punjab massacres, internal security suddenly replaced ceremonial as their main duty. Every Bodyguard patrol was composed of Sikhs *and* Mussulmans. For Massey it was a desperately anxious time, with two anxieties: that his men should remain true to one another, and that with the world disintegrating round them, discipline would be maintained. They did not fail.

'Communications in Delhi had broken down. The Bodyguard had, therefore, to furnish a jeep letter-service for the Viceroy's House. A Sikh and a Mussulman rode in the jeep. In a Mohamadan refugee camp Pathans clustered round and endeavoured to enlist the aid of the Mussulman in despatching his Sikh companion. This met with a spirited refusal. Shortly after, the jeep had to visit a Hindu food centre. Sikhs here suggested that the Mussulman should be killed, and drew their swords. The Sikh sowar pointed his Sten gun at his co-religionists and said, "You'll have to kill me before you touch him."

In Old Delhi pitched communal battles were being fought with 2-inch mortars and Brens. What was left of the Indian Army near Delhi, and the Police, were Hindu in fact and in sympathy. The only completely reliable force left in the Delhi area were a handful of British Officers and the Bodyguard.

The armoured car troops were employed in patrolling the streets. The remainder stood by and acted whenever rioting was most serious. Escorts were provided to collect and bring into refugee camps Mohamadans who lived in predominantly Hindu sections of the City. These escorts were usually under the command of the Sikh Risaldar Major.'

A mob of several hundred Sikhs and Hindus were seen chasing a group of grey-bearded Moslems and young children. 'One brave was shot by the Commandant's revolver in time to prevent him decapitating a small child who had tripped and fallen.'

Eventually Madrassi and Gurkha battalions, Hindu but detached from Punjabi communal passions, arrived and took over in the city, while the Bodyguard moved out into the countryside where Jats were massacring their Moslem neighbours.

'It was the time of the monsoon and wheels could not operate off the roads. The armoured cars patrolled the roads; the Horsed Troops would load their animals into lorries, drive along the road to a base and thence operate as cavalry across country.

The Punjabi Mussulmans must have longed for the comparative security of Pakistan. The Sikhs were faced with a more obvious problem. At times it would be unavoidable that they would be asked to act against their co-religionists. They never failed. And at no time was there the slightest hint of communal disharmony within the unit. The leadership of the VCOs at this time of crisis was truly magnificent. [Eventually, however,] the Commandant approached the Viceroy and pointed out that if more was to be asked of them, the Sikhs would be treated as outcasts in their own villages for having co-operated with Mussulmans instead of turning upon them and slaughtering them.'

So, last of all the regiments in the army, the Bodyguard was divided, the Sikhs remaining in India and the Mussulmans departing with appropriate leavetaking and ceremony to Pakistan. These friends and comrades could next meet only as enemies. What had taken two hundred years to build was demolished in a few weeks.

Let the last word be with Lieutenant General Sir Reginald Savory, who was Adjutant General in New Delhi on 13 August 1947. There was brought for his approval the draft Army Orders for the following day, concluding with a section about correct postal addresses after Independence.

'The draft was a model of efficient "staff duties". It struck me, however, as showing a lack of historical perspective. This would be the final order of the great British-Indian Army, and would signal the end of an era. It would be a pity if it dealt only with the minutiae of postal procedure. I took a red pencil, drew a line through the last section, and instead wrote simply, THIS IS THE LAST INDIAN ARMY ORDER.'

Select Bibliography

Bailey, Lieut. Col. F. M. *Mission to Tashkent.* 1946
Blacker, Lieut. Col. L. V. S. *On Secret Patrol in High Asia.* 1922
Barker, A. J. *The Neglected War.* (Mesopotamia.) 1967
Carmichael, P. *Mountain Battery.* 1983
Elliott, Major General J. G. *The Frontier, 1839–1947.* 1968
                      A Roll of Honour. 1965
Evans, General Sir G. and Anthony Brett-James *Imphal.* 1962
Greenhut, Jeffrey, 'The Imperial Reserve: The India Corps on the Western
    Front, 1914–15' in *Journal of Imperial and Commonwealth History,* Vol. XII, No
    1, Oct. 1983
Grimshaw, Capt. R. *Indian Cavalry Officer, 1914–15.* 1986
Jackson, Major Donovan *India's Army.* 1940
Leasor, James *The Boarding Party.* 1978
Lunt, Major General J. D. *Charge to Glory*
MacFetridge, Lieut. Col. C. H. T. 'The Light AA in the Withdrawal from
    Burma' in *The Journal of the Royal Artillery,* Vol. CIX, No 1, 1982
    with Major J. P. Warren *Tales of the Mountain Gunners.* 1973
MacKenzie, Compton *Eastern Epic.* 1951
Majdalany, F. *Cassino: Portrait of a Battle.* 1957
Mason, Philip *A Matter of Honour.* 1974
Moberly, Col. W. I. *Raj and Post-Raj.* 1985
Moorehead, Alan *Gallipoli.* 1967
Mosley, Leonard *Duel for Kilimanjaro.* 1963
Pockson, Lieut. Col. Maynard, 'Crossing the Rapido River' in *War Monthly,*
    No 76, Vol. 8, 1980
Rhodes, James K. *Gallipoli.* 1965
Slim, Field Marshal Viscount *Defeat into Victory.* 1956
Smeeton, Brig. M. R. *A Change of Jungle.* 1962
Tuker, General Sir Francis *Approach to Battle.* 1963
Turnbull, Patrick *The Battle of the Box.* 1979
Willcocks, Lieut. Gen. Sir. J. W. *With the Indians in France.* 1922

BRITISH OFFICIAL HISTORIES

Edmonds, J. E. *Military Operations in France and Belgium*
Aspinall-Oglander, C. F. *Military Operations in Gallipoli*
                     Military Operations in Palestine
Moberly, F. J. *The Mesopotamia Campaign*
Playfair, I. S. O. *History of the Second World War: Mediterranean and Middle East*

DIVISIONAL HISTORIES

Fourth Indian Division. G. R. Stephens. 1948
Ball of Fire. 5th Indian Division. Anthony Brett-James. 1951
Golden Arrow. 7th Indian Division
One More River. 8th Indian Division
History of the 17th Indian Division
Dagger Division. 19th Indian Division
A Happy Family. 20th Indian Division
Fighting Cock. 23rd Indian Division

REGIMENTAL HISTORIES

The Indian Sappers and Miners, 1914–39. Lieut. Col. E. W. C. Sandes. 1948
The Indian Engineers, 1929–47. Lieut. Col. E. W. C. Sandes. 1949
A Short History of the Corps of King George V's Own Bengal Sappers and Miners during World War I
A Brief History of the Corps of King George V's Own Bengal Sappers and Miners during World War II. G. Pearson. 1947
The History of Queen Victoria's Own Madras Sappers and Miners
A History of the 2nd Royal Lancers. Brig. E. W. D. Vaughan. 1951
Hodson's Horse. Major F. G. Cardew. 1928
The Poona Horse, Vol. II. H. C. Wylly. 1953
The Spirit of a Regiment: A History of the 19th KGO Lancers
The Central India Horse, Vol. II. A. A. Filose. 1956
The First Punjabis. Major Mohamad Ibrahim Qureshi
The Grenadiers: a tradition of valour (Bombay Grenadiers) Col. R. D. Palsokar, MC. 1980
A History of the Rajputana Rifles
The Fourth Battalion, the Duke of Connaught's Own, Tenth Baluch Regiment in the Great War. W. S. Thatcher
The History of the Frontier Force Regiment
The History of the 5th Battalion (Pathans) 14th Punjab Regiment (40th Pathans)
A History of the 1st (P.W.O.) Battalion, the Dogra Regiment
Historical Record of the 39th Garhwal Rifles
The 1st King George V's Own Gurkha Rifles
A History of the 2nd KEO Goorkha Rifles (The Sirmoor Regiment), Vol III. G. R. Stephens. 1950
A Regimental History of the 3rd QMO Gurkha Rifles, Vol. II. C. N. Barclay. 1953
A History of the 5th Royal Gurkha Rifles (Frontier Force). 1956
Historical Record of the 6th Gurkha Rifles. H. R. K. Gibbs. 1955

UNPUBLISHED SOURCES

An Account of Operations in Burma carried out by Probyn's Horse. Ed. Major B. H. Milne
An Account of Operations in Burma carried out by the Royal Decan Horse
The 6th DCO Lancers in Italy

Papers in the National Army Museum of Major C. J. L. Allanson, Capt. T. C. Catty, Lieut. Col. P. H. MacDwyer, Lieut. Gen. Sir R. A. Savory, Major R. S. Waters
Papers in the Ministry of Defence Library of Capt. W. G. Bagot-Chester
War Diary, A Squadron, 19th KGV's Own Lancers, 1945. Ed. Capt. A. B. Merriam

PAPERS, DIARIES, LETTERS, MEMOIRS IN PRIVATE POSSESSION

First World War

Captain R. Grimshaw
Lieut. Col. Sir Cyril Hancock
Brigadier D. S. E. McNeill

Between the wars

Major General G. J. Hamilton
Major J. A. Steward
Lieut. Col. L. G. P. Esmonde-White

Second World War

Major G. W. Acworth
Capt. A. G. Barron
Major P. G. Brooke
Lieut. Col. A. F. Chown
Brigadier H. E. Cubitt-Smith
Major R. Cuthill
Lieut. Col. R. A. A. Dawes
Major E. A. Dorman
Major J. E. H. Gait
Lieut. Col. A. F. Harper
Major P. Howarth

Lieut. Col. C. E. N. Hopkins-Husson
Sir Owain Jenkins
Capt. F. Joyner
Major R. B. Kennard
Major B. G. Kinloch
Capt. A. W. Lane
Major Lindsay Wince
Mr Philip Mason
Lieut. Col. P. Massey
Capt. A. B. Merriam
Lieut. Col. Brian Montgomery
Major General R. M. Rau
Major A. G. Raw
Lieut. Col. D. McV. Reynolds
Major W. N. Sample
Lieut. Col. R. A. Shebbeare
Lieut. Col. L. F. Steele
Major J. A. Steward
Capt. T. J. Thornton
Lieut. Col. S. C. H. Tighe
Lieut. Col. E. R. McM. Wright

PUBLICATIONS OF THE INDIAN GOVERNMENT

Operations in Waziristan, 1919–20
Operations on the North-West Frontier of India, 1921–35
Operations on the North-West Frontier of India, 1936–37
A Gurkha Brigade in Italy: the Story of the 43rd Gurkha Lorried Brigade

PUBLICATION OF THE INDIAN AND PAKISTAN GOVERNMENTS

Official History of the Indian Armed Forces in the Second World War: the Re-conquest of Burma

OTHER PUBLICATIONS OF HMSO

The Tiger Strikes
The Tiger Kills } Indian Divisions in North Africa and Italy
The Tiger Conquers

Chronology

1895 Amalgamation of Bengal, Bombay and Madras Armies into the Indian Army.
1903–09 Kitchener Commander-in-Chief, India.

FIRST WORLD WAR

	Western Front	Mesopotamia	Other Fronts
1914	13 Oct Indian Corps arrived Marseille 21 Oct Indian troops in action, Ypres	31 Oct Basra captured	2–5 Nov Fiasco at Tanga
1915	10 Mar Battle of Neuve Chapelle 24 Apr Second Battle of Ypres. German gas attacks 9 May Battle of Festubert	25 Nov Battle of Ctesiphon 3 Dec Kut invested	25 Apr First Gallipoli landings 7 Aug Suvla Bay landing. Battle of Sari Bair 19 Dec Gallipoli evacuated
1916		29 Apr Surrender at Kut	Feb Advance into German East Africa
1917	29 Nov–2 Dec Battle of Cambrai	1 Feb Battle of Hai Salient 23 Feb Battle of Shumran Bend 13 Mar Bagdad captured	
1918		26 Mar Battle of Khan Bagdadi 19–30 Oct Battle of Sharqat	19 Sep Allenby's offensive opens in Palestine 1 Oct Damascus captured

31 Oct 1918 Armistice with Turkey
11 Nov 1918 Armistice with Germany

6 May–8 Aug 1919 Third Afghan War
Dec 1918–May 1920 Operations in Waziristan
Apr–Oct 1930 Operations in Peshawur area
Feb–June 1935 Loe Agra operations
Aug–Sept 1935 Mohmand operations
Nov 1936–Aug 1947 Intermittent operations in Waziristan

SECOND WORLD WAR

Against Germans and Italians		*Against Japanese*	
13 Aug	11th Ind Inf Bde arrives in Egypt		1939
3 Sept	Outbreak of war with Germany		
17 June	Franco-German armistice		1940
11–18 Aug	Somaliland campaign		
Sept	5th Ind Div arrives Port Sudan		
9 Dec	Battle of Sidi Barani		
2 Feb–27 Mar	Battle of Keren		1941
24 Mar	Rommel attacks in Cyrenaica		
4–8 Apr	3rd Ind Motor Bde defends El Mechili		
6 Apr	Tobruk invested		
7 Apr	Capture of Massawa		
16 May	Duke of Aosta surrenders his army at Amba Alagi		
15–16 June	Operation Battleaxe		
Apr–May	Occupation of Iraq		
June–July	Occupation of Syria		
22 June	Germany attacks Russia		
July	Auchinleck takes over command of the Middle East		
Aug–Sep	Occupation of Persia		
18 Nov	Operation Crusader opens		
		7 Dec	Pearl Harbor. Japanese invade Malaya
9 Dec	Tobruk relieved		
24 Dec	Capture of Benghazi		

1942	21 Jan	Rommel attacks in Cyrenaica		
	28 Jan	Benghazi evacuated	31 Jan	Moulmein evacuated
			11 Feb	Surrender of Singapore
			23 Feb	Sittang bridge blown
			7 Mar	Rangoon evacuated
			10 May	Battle of Shwegyin Basin
	27 May	Rommel attacks in Western Desert. 3rd Ind Motor Bde at Bir Hakim	14–20 May	Retreat to Imphal
	5–6 June	Battle of the Cauldron		
	21 June	Tobruk surrendered		
	28 June	Mersa Matruh evacuated		
	1–28 Jul	First Battle of Alamein		
	8 Aug	Alexander takes over Middle East Command from Auchinleck		
	13 Aug	Montgomery assumes command of Eighth Army		
	23 Oct–4 Nov	Second Battle of Alamein		
	8 Nov	Anglo-American landings in North Africa		
			Dec 42–May 43	First Arakan campaign
1943	23 Jan	Capture of Tripoli	Mar–May	First Chindit operation
			9 Mar	Goa raid
	20–25 Mar	Battle of Mareth Line		
	5–7 Apr	Battle of Wadi Akarit		
	19–29 Apr	Battle of Enfidaville		
	6 May	Capture of Tunis		
	12 May	Surrender of Axis forces in North Africa		
	10 July	Allied landings in Sicily.		
	3 Sep	Armistice with Italy. Allied landings in south Italy		

9 Sep	Allied landing at Salerno		
19 Sep	8 Ind Div lands at Taranto		
20–30 Nov	Battle of R. Sangro	30 Nov	Advance into Arakan begins
8 Dec	'Impossible bridge' over R. Moro. 4th Ind Div arrives in Italy		

			1944
29–30 Jan	American attack at Cassino	4–24 Feb	Battle of the 'Admin Box'
16 Feb–24 Mar	4th Ind Div and NZ Div attack Cassino	5 Mar	Second Chindit operation begins
		6 Mar	Japanese begin 'March on Delhi'
		5–18 Apr	Kohima besieged
11–13 May	8th Ind Div cross R. Gari and break through Gustav Line		
16 May	Monte Cassino captured		
4 June	Allies enter Rome	June	Japanese withdraw from Assam
		22 June	Kohima–Imphal road open
Sept	Allies come up against Gothic Line		
Oct	4th Ind Div moves to Greece		
		3–4 Dec	Fourteenth Army crosses R. Chindwin

			1945
		14–15 Feb	R. Irrawaddy crossed at Nyangu
		1–2 Mar	Meiktila captured
		20 Mar	Mandalay captured
9 Apr	R. Senio crossed	22 Apr	Toungoo captured
23 Apr	R. Po crossed	1 May	Japanese evacuate Rangoon
3 May	German forces in Italy surrender	14 Aug	Japanese forces surrender
		Oct–Dec	Operations in Java

14/15 Aug 1947 Partition. Indian and Pakistan Independence.

303

Glossary of Vernacular and Foreign words

Allah ho Akbar!	God is great: Moslem warcry
Al Hamdulillah!	Praise be God! (Thank God)
Askari	African soldier
Ayo Gurkhali!	Gurkha warcry
Badmash	Rascal
Boxwallah	European merchant or shopkeeper
Bunniah	Shopkeeper
Bundobust	Arrangements, organization
Chaung (Burmese)	River-bed, generally dry except during the rains
Dah (Burmese)	Long, heavy chopping-knife
Darbar	Assembly or council
Dhal	Dried, split lentils, usually curried
Dis	Signallers' jargon for disconnected; out of order
Dumdum	Soft-nosed, expanding bullet
Hapana piga (pigeon Swahili)	Don't shoot
Huzoor	An honorific, rather more than Sir or Sahib
Jangian (Pushtu)	Warriors
Jawan	Young man; a term usually applied to Indian soldiers
Jiff	Japanese-inspired fifth column (Indian National Army)
Jirga (Pushtu)	Tribal assembly on the North-West Frontier
Jo Hukum	'Whatever the order': nickname of the Jodphur Lancers
Khassadar (Pushtu)	Irregular tribal levy on the North-West Frontier
Kukri	Gurkha chopping knife
Kwenda (pigeon Swahili)	Go away
Lascar	Indian merchant seaman
Lashkar (Pushtu)	Tribal army on the North-West Frontier
Malik (Pushtu)	Tribal headman on the North-West Frontier
Mām-bāp	Mother-and-father
Maro!	Strike! Kill!
Munshi	Language teacher
Narai	Col
Nullah	River-bed, generally dry except during the rains
Paltan	Infantry battalion or regiment
Panzer (German)	Armour; used, incorrectly, for 'tank'
Piffer	Punjab Irregular Frontier Force

304

Raja Ramchandraji ki Jai	Jat warcry
Safa	Turban
Sangar	Drystone wall, parapet or strongpoint
Sath Sri Akal!	Sikh warcry
Schutztruppe (German)	Storm-troops
Shikar	Hunting, shooting.
Shikari	A hunter, tracker
Shivaji Maharaj ki Jai	Mahratta warcry
Silladar	Irregular (cavalry)
Spandau (German)	Machine-gun
Syce	Groom
Tonga	Horse-drawn cab.
Tongawallah	Cab-driver
Umedwar	Hopeful; aspirant; used of recruits on a regimental waiting list
Wadi (Arabic)	River-bed, generally dry except during the rains
Waler	Australian-bred horse (Originally from New South Wales)
Yilderim (Turkish)	Lightning

Indian ranks and British equivalents

British	Indian Cavalry	Indian Other Arms
Private	Sowar (rider)	Sepoy, Rifleman, Sapper, Gunner
Lance Corporal	Acting Lance Daffadar	Lance Naik
Corporal	Lance Daffadar	Naik
Sergeant	Daffadar	Havildar
	Jemadar	Jemadar
	Ressaidar	
No British	(abolished 1919)	
Equivalents	Risaldar	Subadar
	Risaldar Major	Subadar Major
	Woordie Major	Jemadar Adjutant

Also Daffadar and Havildar Major, Quartermaster Daffadar and Havildar, etc.

Abbreviations

AA	Anti-aircraft	IEME	Indian Electrical and Mechanical Engineers
AT	Animal Transport		
BEF	British Expeditionary Force	INA	Indian National Army (raised by Japanese)
C-in-C	Commander-in-Chief		
CIH	Central India Horse	IOM	Indian Order of Merit
CO	Commanding Officer	KAR	King's African Rifles
CRA	Commanding Royal Artillery	KCIO	King's Commissioned Indian Officer
CRE	Commanding Royal Engineers	LAD	Light Aid Detachment
		OC	Officer Commanding
DF	Defensive Fire (artillery)	OP	Observation Post (artillery)
DQMG	Deputy Assistant Quarter Master General (colloquially, DQ)	PAIFORCE	Persia and Iraq Force
		PAVO	Prince Albert Victor's Own Cavalry
		PT	Physical Training
DWR	Duke of Wellington's Regiment	RA	Royal Artillery
		RAP	Regimental Aid Post
ECO	Emergency Commissioned Officer	RHQ	Regimental Headquarters
FID	Fuse instantaneous detonating	RIASC	Royal Indian Army Service Corps
FOO	Forward Observation Officer (artillery)	R/T	Radio Telephony
		RTR	Royal Tank Regiment
GS	General Service	SOS fire	Emergency fire suppor
HE	High Explosive	SP	Self-propelled (gun)
HLI	Highland Light Infantry	VCO	Viceroy's Commissioned Officer
IDSM	Indian Distinguished Service Medal		

Index

Figures in *italics* refer to illustration numbers

AFRIKA KORPS 156, 162, 169, 188, 221, 227; *see also* Rommel, Erwin

Afule, El 92, 95–7

Air-drop, supply by 245, 259–60, 268, 277

Air-power 188, 191, 211, 216, 222, 260

Alamein, El 187, 190, 221–3

Alexander, General Sir Harold 122; retreat from Burma 209; C-in-C Middle East 222; deputy to Eisenhower 228; in overall command Italy 245, 270

Ali Haidar, VC, Sepoy, 6/13 FF Rifles 273

Allanson, C. J. L., Major 1/6 GR 52–5, 64–6

Allenby, General Sir Edmund 91–2, 99

Amba Alagi, Italian surrender at 149

Arakan 216–7, *44*, 256–61, 286–8

Army, Indian: origins 9–10, *1, 2, 3, 4*; motivation and morale 9–10, 15–6, 31–2, 37, 42, 77, 79, 83, 138–9, 194–5, 215, 254–5, 277, 293–4; class composition 9, 11–2, 27–8, 116; languages 15; religions, attitude to 10–1; British Officers 7, 10, 15, 25–6, 43, 53, 116–9, 193; King's Commissioned Indian Officers 7, 117–8, 137; Indian Officers, Gurkha Officers, Viceroy's Commissioned Officers 24–5, 28, 36, 37, 53, 115, 117; recruiting 28, *27*; reserves 28, 43, 115; cavalry 26–7, *7, 8, 22, 24, 25*, 135; infantry 27; pioneers 29; artillery 29, *9*, 135, 216; Sappers & Miners 29; signals 29–30,

160–1; Indian State Forces 27; insulated from politics 11, 13, 120; reorganization by Roberts 13, by Kitchener 14, post-1918 115–6, pre-1939 134–6; N-W Frontier warfare 12, 13–4, 105–6, 120–2; major and minor roles 14, 135–6; aid to the civil power 120; frugality 139; cross-country mobility 139; before Pearl Harbor interest concentrated on Middle East 161; arms and equipment 26, 27, 29, 33–4, 115, 135, 160, 215–6, 227; numbers 1914–18 115; numbers 1939–45 293; partition 293–4; last Indian Army Order 296

Assam, operations in 261–8

Auchinleck, General Sir Claude 25, 122; Deputy Chief of General Staff 135–6; C-in-C Middle East 162, 165, 168, 190; empathy with Indian soldier 162; removed from command of Middle East Forces 222; C-in-C India 254

Auxiliary Force (India), AF(I) 117

Awal Nur, Havildar, Guides 102–3, *20, 21*

Ayub Khan, sepoy, 129 Baluchis 39–40; Jemadar 71

BADHWAR, HARI, Capt 3 Cavalry 194, 195, 294

Bagdad 76–7, 81, 87

Bagot-Chester, W. G., Capt 2/3 GR 38–9, 41, 42

Bailey, F. M., Lieut-Col 101–3, *20*

Barron, A. G., Capt 4/6 Rajputana Rifles 221–2, 227, 228

Basra 75, 79, 82 158

Battleaxe, operation 157

Bengal Army 9–10

Benghazi 169–74

Beresford-Peirse, N. H. de la P., Major General 141, 147

Bhagat, Premindrah Singh, VC, Lieut Bombay S & M 143–4

Bir Hacheim 184–7

Blaker, F. G., VC, Major 3/9 GR 269

Boucher, C. H., Brigadier 242

Brigades, Indian. Cavalry 1914–8: Secunderabad 45–6; Ambala 46–7; Mhow 48–9; 7th 87–8; 11th 87–8, 92, 94–5; 13th 92, 94, 97–8; 15th (Imperial Service) 92, 99

Cavalry 1939–45: 3rd Indian Motor Bde 150–6, 175–6, 185–7; 50th Indian Tank 286–8; 254th Indian Tank 278; 255th Indian Tank 277, 281–6

Infantry 1914–8: Garhwali 38–9, 41; Dehra Dun 41; 9th 81; 16th 75, 76; 17th 76; 18th 75, 76; 29th 50, 52, 53–5; 34th 89; 37th 83, 84

Infantry, N-W Frontier: Nowshera 122; Peshawur 122; Bannu 126–8, 128–30; Razmak 126–8, 132–3; Abbottabad 128

Infantry 1939–45: 5th 138–9, 146, 165, 168, 170, 172, 175, 221, 222–3, 225–7, 242, 245–6; 7th 138, 163, 168, 170, 172–4, 175, 225–7, 242, 244–5; 8th 192–3; 9th 143, 147–8, 163, 256, 258, 260; 10th 143; 11th 138–41, 143, 163, 165, 170, 172, 175, 188, 242; 13th 198; 16th 198, 199, 202, 204; 17th 231–3, 242, 247–51, 273;

19th 231, 232, 242, 247, 251, 273; 21st 231, 247, 251; 28th 193; 29th 143, 148; 33rd 256, 258; 43rd Gurkha Lorried 271, 273; 46th 198, 199, 202, 204; 48th 200, 202, 213, 283; 49th 291–2; 50th Parachute 263, 289; 63rd 283; 64th 286; 89th 256, 258; 98th 286; 99th 289; 114th 256, 258; 123rd 256, 266, 292; 161st 256, 263; Lushai 266, 279; 1st Burma 198; 2nd Burma 198, 199

Briggs, H. R., Brigadier 173–4; Major General 256, 258, 261

British units in Indian Brigades 10–11, 27, 31, 43–4, 139, 143

Bromhead, Sir B. D. G., Bart, Capt 34 Sikh Pioneers 113–4

Burma: separation from India 196; geography of 198; plans for defence of 198–9; attitude of inhabitants 199; retreat from 199–215, 43; recovery of 277–89

CAMBRAI, BATTLE OF 44–9

Cassells, R. A., Brigadier General 87–9; General, C-in-C India 135

Cassino 230, 243–51, 42

Catty, T. C., Capt 79, 80, 81, 83, 87

Chamberlayne, A., Lieut Col 2/76 Punjabis 111

Chindits 255, 268–9

Chindwin, river 212, 213–5, 277–8

Chown, A. F., Capt 1/12 FF Regt 247–51

Cobbe, Lieut General Sir Alexander, VC 82, 83, 87

Company, Honourable East India 9–11

Congress, Indian National 134, 137, 195, 215

Corps, 1914–8: Indian Corps on Western Front 32–40; I 75, 83, 87; III 78, 80, 82, 83; XXI 93; Desert Mounted Corps 91–3, 99 1939–45: III 192–4; IV 277, 279–81, 288–9; V 230; X 223, 224, 227; XIII 162–5, 190, 246–51; XV 256–61, 286–8; XXX 162–5, 223, 224; XXXIII 277–8, 280, 286, 288–9; Burcorps 209, 212

Cowan, Admiral Sir Walter 156, 185, 186

Crowdy, J. D., Lieut Col 2/5 RGR 110–1

Ctesiphon, battle of 77

Cubitt-Smith, H. E., Lieut Col 1/12 FF Regt 249

Cursetjee, H. M. M., Lieut IMS 90

Curzon, Viscount, Viceroy of India 13, 14

DAMASCUS 99–100, 158

Darwan Sing Negi, VC, Havildar 39 Garhwal Rifles 33, 13

Davidson, D. S., Capt 2 Lancers 95

Davson, H. J. H., Major 82 Punjabis 82, 83, 85

Dawes, R. A. A., Major 6 Lancers 273, 275–6

De Pass, F. A., VC, Lieut Poona Horse 36

Derajat Column 104–12

Dhargalkar, K. P., Capt 3 Cavalry 194–5

Divisions, Indian: Cavalry 1914–8: 4th 44–9, 92–7; 5th 44–9, 92, 94, 97–8 Infantry 1914–8: 3rd Lahore 32, 40–1, 80, 83; 6th 75, 76–8, 79–81; 7th Meerut 32, 40–1, 80, 83; 14th 80, 83, 84–6; 15th 87; 17th 87 Infantry 1939–45: 4th: Sidi Barani 138–41, Keren 143, 145–6, 147, Western Desert 157, 162–9, 170–4, 222–3, Tunisia 224–9, Italy 242, 243–6, Greece 271–2; 5th: East Africa 143, 147–9, Western Desert 172, 187, 188, 221, Arakan 256–61, Assam 263, 266, Burma 289, Java 292; 7th 256–61, 266, 277, 280, 281, 289;

8th 158, 159; Italy 230–42, 246–52, 253, 270, 271, 272–3; 9th 192–4; 10th 158, 159, 187, 189, 253, 270, 271, 273–5; 11th 192–4; 14th 216–7; 17th: retreat from Burma 98, 200–5, 208–9, 211, Assam 262–3, recovery of Burma 278, 281, 289; 19th 277, 278, 279, 280, 286; 20th 277, 278, 280, 286; 25th 286, 288; 26th 286; 1st Burma 198–200, 212–14

Doherty, F. J., Capt IMS 123, 124, 126

Durrani, Mahmoud Khan, GC, Capt 194

Dutt, S., Capt IMS 48

EAST AFRICA, German, 1914–18 67–74; Italian, 1939–41 142–9

Egerton, R. G., Major General 81, 84, 86

Eighth Army: Operation Crusader 162–9, 29, 37, 36; Ritchie takes command 165; withdrawal from Benghazi 170–4; Gazala position attacked 184, 187–8; tactical methods 175, 187–8, 222; withdrawal to El Alamein 188–90; first battle of El Alamein 190, 221; Montgomery takes command 222; lavish supplies of men and equipment in autumn of 1942 222; second battle of El Alamein 222–3; in Tunisia 224–9, 35; in Italy 230–53, 270–6; see also Auchinleck, Montgomery

Evans, G. C., Brigadier 258–9

FILOSE, A. A. E., Brigadier 176, 185–6

Fourteenth Army: Slim takes command 254; improving morale 254–6; operations in Assam 261–2, 268; recovery of Burma 277–8, 279–80, 44, 46, 47, 48, 49; race for Rangoon 288–9; see also Slim

Frontier, North-West 12, 13, 104–14, 120–33, *23*, *26*, *28*
GAIT, J. E. H., Lieut PAVO 152
Gallipoli 50–66, *14*, *15*
Gazelle Force 143, 144, 147
Gimson, W. A., Major Guides Cavalry and Tochi Scouts 128–9
Goa, raid on shipping in 217–9
Gobind Singh, VC, Lance Daffadar 2 Lancers 49; Risaldar 96, *11*
Godley, P. P., Lieut Col, 1/9 Royal Jat 214
Good, S. B., Major 5/12 FF Regt (Guides) 123–5
Grice, W. H., Lieut Col Calcutta Light Horse 218–9
Grimshaw, R., Capt Poona Horse 34–8
Guns, anti-tank 163, 188, 221, 222
HAI SALIENT 83–4
Hamilton, G. J., Lieut 5/12 FF Regt (Guides) 123–5
Hancock, C. P., Lieut 114 Mahrattas 83, 89–90
Hanna position 79, 80
Harper, A. F., Lieut Col R Deccan Horse and 3/9 GR 268–9, 293
Harper, T., Major 62 Punjabis 82, 86–7
Hassan Shah, Risaldar 9 Hodson's Horse, attached Sharif of Mecca's Forces 100
Hasted, W. F., Major General 278
Heath, L. M., Major General 143, 147, 149; Lieut General 192
Herdon, H., Lieut Col 55 (Coke's) Rifles 106
Hong Kong 191
Hopkins-Husson, C. E. N., Lieut 5/14 Punjab 195–6
Howarth, P. H., Capt Bengal S & M 249–50, 271
Hugh-Jones, N., Brigadier 202, 203–5
Hutton, Lieut General Sir Thomas 198, 208, 209

IBLANKE OPERATION 128–31
Indian National Army (INA) 194–5, 261, 267, 281, 289
Ingall, F. H. B., Lieut Col 6 Lancers 273, 275
Ipi, Fakir of 126, 128, 131, 132, 133
Iraq, occupation of, 1941 158
Irrawaddy, river 198, 212, 213, 277–81
Italy, campaign in: strategy of 230, 242–3, 270; Adriatic front 1943 230–2, 241–2; Cassino front 243–52; winter 1944–5 271–2, *38*, *39*, *40*; final advance 272–5, *41*
JAPAN, Japanese 136, 168, 192; tactical methods 193, 211, 217, 256, 258, 265; inclination to take administrative risks 260–1, 268; losses from sickness 255, 268; extraordinary courage 268, 282–4; treatment of prisoners 194–5, 209; co-operation after surrender 290–1
Java, operations in, 1945–6 291–2
Jones, J. K., Brigadier 202, 204, 206
KALBI MOHAMAD, Daffadar Guides 102–3, *20*, *21*
Kamal Ram, VC, Sepoy 3/8 Punjab 251, *50*
Kelly, P. J. V., Brigadier General 97, 98
Keren, battle of 145–9
Khaisora operation, 1936 126–8
Khan Bagdadi, battle of 87
Khuda Dad Khan, VC, Sepoy 129 Baluchis 33
Kibata, operation in 70–1
Kinloch, B. G., Capt 1/3 GR 202, 205–8
Kitchener, Field Marshal Lord, C-in-C India 14
Kohima 263–5
Kut-al-Amara 76, 77–8, 79–80, 81
LALBAHADUR THAPA VC, Subadar 1/2 GR 226

Lane, A. W., Capt Probyn's Horse 283–5
Lentaigne, W. D. A., Lieut Col 1/4 GR 202, 204
Lewis, H. V., Lieut 129 Baluchis 32, 38; Capt 71, 73
Lovett, O. de T., Brigadier 225, 244
MACANDREW, H. J. M., Major General 45, 92, 94
Macdonald, J. B., Lieut Col 1/19 Hyderabad 132–3
MacDwyer, P. H., Capt 3/11 Sikh 189–90, 252, 270–1
MacFetridge, C. H. T., Lieut 15 Mtn Bty 132–3; Capt 3 Light AA Bty 214, 215
MacNeill, D. S. E., Lieut Poona Horse 45
Malaya, campaign in 208–12
Massey, P., Lieut Col Hodson's Horse and Governor General's Bodyguard 294–5
Maude, General Sir Stanley 82, 83, 84, 87
Mechili, El 151–3, 174
Mesopotamian campaign 75–90, *16*, *17*
Messervy, F. W., Brigadier 143, 146–8; Major General 162–9, 170, 256, 258–61; Lieut General 277, 278
Meynell, G., VC, Capt 5/12 FF Regt (Guides) 123–4, 126
Mir Badshah, Jemadar 129 Baluchis 38, 73, 106
Mir Dast, VC, Jemadar attached 57 Rifles 42
Moberly, W. I., Major 3/12 FF Regt 242, 271
Mohmand operations, 1935 122–6
Molloy, G. M., Major Poona Horse 37
Montgomery, General Sir Bernard 25, 196; takes command of 8th Army 222; lack of enthusiasm for Indian Army 223; battle of El Alamein 222–3; decides

to use 4th Indian Div in Tunisia 224; battle of Wadi Akarit 227; tribute to 4th Indian Div 229; invades Sicily, Italy 230; leaves 8th Army 242

Morland Hughes, R. W., Major 1/5 RGR 240–1

Mountbatten, Admiral Lord Louis 277, 293

Mutiny of 1857 10, 11, 12, 5, 6

NAMDEO JADHAO, VC, Sepoy 1/5 Mahratta LI 273

Nazareth 92, 96–7

Nixon, General Sir John 75, 76, 81

ORGILL, R. C., Major Malerkotla S & M 205

PAKALITA SAR OPERATION, 1940 132–3

Palestine, campaign in, 1918 91–100, 18, 19

Parshotam Das, Capt 22 Mtn Arty Regt 195

Persia, operations in, 1914–8 101; occupation of, 1941 159

Peshawur, operations near, 1930 122

Pryde, B. R., Lieut 19 Lancers 287

Punjab Irregular Force, 'Piffers', FF 12, 13

RAU, R. M., Lieut Bombay S & M 279, 290–1

Raw, W. G., Lieut 3/11 Sikh 16–7

Rees, T. W., Capt 94; Brigadier 148; Major General 278, 286, 293

Reid, D. W., Lieut Col 3/5 Mahratta LI 147–8; Brigadier 190; Major General 270

Reynolds, D. McV., Capt 2 Royal Lancers 153, 156, 187

Richards, H. V., Colonel 263

Richpal Ram, VC, Subadar 4/6 Rajputana Rifles 146

Ritchie, General Sir Neil 165, 171, 172

Roberts, General Sir Frederick 13

Robinson, Lieut Col 6 Lancers 272

Rommel, General Erwin 150, 165, 168, 169, 170, 175, 189; see Afrika Korps

Russell, D., Major General 222, 230, 272

Russia 13, 14, 30, 101, 131–2, 137, 158–9

SALAITA HILL, battle of 68

Savory, R. A., Lieut 14 Sikhs 51–2, 55–6; Brigadier 141; Lieut General Sir Reginald 296

Scott, J. Bruce, Major General 198, 211, 214

Showers, L. C. J., Lieut Col 1/2 GR 229, 245

Shwegyin, battle of 214–5

Siam 192, 199, 290–1

Sidi Barani, battle of 139–41

Signallers 29–30, 160–1, 228, 267; see also Indian Signal Corps

Singapore 193, 194

Sittang River and bridge 200–8

Skeen, General Sir Andrew 106, 107–8, 134

Slim, W. J., Lieut 66; Lieut General retreat from Burma 209, 211, 212, 214, 215; General Sir William, takes command of 14th Army 254; tackles problems of communications, training and morale 254–6; deals with Japanese invasion of Assam 261–2, 268; recovery of Burma 277–80; race for Rangoon 288–9; see also 14th Army

Smeeton, M. R., Major Hodson's Horse 176, 185–6, 188; Lieut Col Probyn's Horse 281–3, 285–6, 289

Smyth, Major General Sir John, VC 199, 200, 205, 208

Sobha Chand, Capt 4/4 Bombay Grenadiers 281, 284

Sunnaiyat position 79, 81, 83, 85

Syria, occupation of 158

TANKS 44, 140, 157; in Western Desert 163, 175; comparison of British and German 157, 175; tactics 160, 163, 188; Japanese tanks in Malaya 193; British tanks in Assam and Burma, role of bunker-busting 208, 213, 256, 260, 277, 281, 283–4, 287, 288–9

Tanga 68

Thornton, T. J., Capt Bengal S & M 247, 250

Tobruk 151, 152, 156, 157, 162, 164, 168, 169, 188

Toogood, C. G., Lieut 1/2 GR 85, 86

Townshend, C. V. F., Major General 76–8, 79, 80, 81

Tuker, F. I. S., Major General 170; commands 4th Indian Div in withdrawal from Benghazi 170–2, 174; critical of 8th Army dispositions in Gazala position 175; prepares for pursuit after El Alamein 223; indignant at treatment of 4th Indian Div 223–4; at Wadi Akarit 225–7; attack on Tunis 229; in Italy, poor health 242; thoughts on Cassino 243–4, 246; invalided out of Italy 246

UNITS, BRITISH: 3rd Carbineers 266–7; 8th Hussars 46–8; Gloucestershire Hussars 98; 14/20th Hussars 273; 25th Dragoons 259; 7 RTR 140–1; 1st Field Regt, Royal Artillery 165; 2 Cameron Highlanders 140, 145, 188; 2 Highland Light Infantry 147, 148, 190; 2 West Yorks 148, 258, 259; 1 Royal Sussex 164, 225–6; 2 Duke of Wellington's 202–4, 207; South Lancs 280; 4 Royal West Kent 263–5; 1/5 Essex 242; 1 Royal Fusiliers 232, 241, 250–1; 2 Norfolk 84–6

Units, Indian (1922 designations shown; where relevant, pre-1922 designations shown in brackets)

Cavalry: Governor General's Bodyguard 294–6; 1st Skinner's Horse 10, 143, 144, 149; 2nd Royal Lancers (2nd Lancers) 48–9, 92, 95–7, 117, 150–6, 175–6, 187; 3rd Cavalry 191, 193, 194–5; 4th Hodson's Horse (9th Hodson's Horse) 92, 94, 99–100; 5th Probyn's Horse 127, 281–3, 284–6, 289; 6th Lancers 231, 241, 250–1, 252, 271, 272, 273, 275–6; 7th Light Cavalry 280, 289; 9th Royal Deccan Horse 281, 284; 10th Guides Cavalry FF 295; 11th PAVO Cavalry FF (23rd Cavalry) 87, 150–3, 174, 175–6, 185–6, 284, 289; 13th Lancers 135, 292; 14th Scinde Horse (Jacob's Horse) 92, 93, 135, 295; 16th Light Cavalry 284, 289; 17th Poona Horse (34th Poona Horse) 34–8, 45, 99–100; 18th Cavalry 150, 152, 156, 175–6, 185–6; 19th Lancers (18th and 19th Lancers) 48, 97–8, 287–8, 294; 21st Central India Horse 144, 162, 164, 168–9, 171, 173–4; 45th Cavalry 219–20

Sappers and Miners, general 29, 34, 69–70, 113–4, 174, 231; Bengal S & M 33, 84, 146–7, 149, 241, 247–50, 262, 271, 273, 275; Madras S & M 13, 29, 84, 146–7, 199–200, 280; Royal Bombay S & M 33, 84, 143–4, 146–7, 149, 241, 247–50, 262, 271, 273, 275, 280; Artillery, general 10–1; Mountain Artillery (the numbering is confusing because it changed so often. In this index, from 1922 onwards the 1927 numbers are given; but in the text, contemporary numbers are given, which may differ from these): 1st Royal (Kohat) Mountain Battery FF 50–1, 59; 2nd (Derajat) Mountain Battery FF 74, 213–4, 263–4; 3rd (Peshawur) Mountain Battery FF 210–1, 211–2; 4th (Hazara) Mountain Battery FF 193; 6th (Jacob's) Mountain Battery 50, 54; 7th (Bengal) Mountain Battery 107, 111, 130–1; 11th (Dehra Dun) Mountain Battery 263–4; 12th (Poonch) Mountain Battery 202–3, 211–2, 263–5; 15th (Jhelum) Mountain Battery 132–3; 19th (Maymo) Mountain Battery 130–3; 20th (Ambala) Mountain Battery 263; 24th Mountain Artillery Regt 259, 264–5; 1st Field Brigade 135; 2nd Field Regt 184–7; Anti-aircraft, general 216; 3rd Light AA Battery 208, 214–5

Infantry
1st Punjab Regt: 1/1st (62nd Punjabis) 82, 263; 2/1st (66th Punjabis) 77, 292; 3/1st (76th Punjabis) 111, 168; 5/1st (82nd Punjabis) 82–3, 85–6, 108
2nd Punjab Regt: 1/2nd 172, 275; 3/2nd 190
4th Bombay Grenadiers: 1/4th 287–8; 4/4th (109th Infantry) 106–7, 281–4; 5/4th (112th Infantry) 106–7
5th Mahratta Light Infantry: 1/5th (103rd Mahratta LI) 86, 106–7, 109–10, 273; 3/5th 147–8; 5/5th Royal (117th Mahrattas) 77; 10/5th (114th Mahrattas) 83, 89–90
6th Rajputana Rifles: 1/6th 141, 171, 175; 4/6th 146, 221–2, 227, 228, 245–6
7th Rajput Regt: 3/7th 126–7; 4/7th 141, 263–4; 5/7th 191; 6/7th 281–3, 290
8th Punjab Regt: 3/8th 240, 242, 251; 5/8th (93rd Punjabis) 81, 132–3
9th Jat Regt: 1/9th Royal 208, 214
10th Baluch Regt: 3/10th 221, 230; 4/10th (129th Baluchis) 32–3, 38, 39–40, 43, 67, 68, 70, 71–3, 148; 7/10th 200; 8/10th (130th Baluchis) 31
11th Sikh Regt: 1/11th (14th Sikhs) 30, 50, 51–2, 55–6, 258; 2/11th 130–1, 190–1; 3/11th (45th Sikhs) 83–4, 89–90; 4/11th (36th Sikhs) 83–4, 164, 165, 169, 175; 5/11th (47th Sikhs) 42, 193–4
12th Frontier Force Regt: 1/12th 241, 247–51; 3/12th 147–8, 230; 4/12th 202–5, 208; 5/12th (Guides) 94, 101, 102–3, 123–5
13th Frontier Force Rifles: 1/13th (55th Coke's Rifles) 106–7, 110–1, 192; 3/13th (57th Wilde's Rifles) 32, 33, 42, 110; 5/14th (58th Vaughan's Rifles) 35, 39; 6/13th Royal 148, 231, 273; 14/13th 255
14th Punjab Regt: 1/14th (19th Punjabis) 106–7; 2/14th 191; 3/14th 144, 145–6, 256; 4/14th (24th Punjabis) 77; 5/14th (40th Pathans) 39, 42, 68, 70, 73, 134, 195
15th Punjab Regt: 2/15th (26th Punjabis) 83; 3/15th 241
16th Punjab Regt: 4/16th 164, 168
17th Dogra Regt: 1/17th 266–7; 3/17th 192; 5/17th 208

18th Garhwal Rifles: 1/18th (1/39th Garhwal Rifles) 33, 39, 41; 2/18th (2/39th Garhwal Rifles) 39, 41

19th Hyderabad Regt: 1/19th 132–3

34th Sikh Pioneers 29, 108–9, 113–4, 116

Assam Regt 263–4, 286

1st Gurkha Rifles: 1/1st 81; 3/1st 267

2nd Goorkha Rifles: 1/2nd 84–6, 224, 225–7, 245; 2/2nd 34–5; 3/2nd 287–8

3rd Gurkha Rifles: 1/3rd 202–4, 205–8; 2/3rd 38–9, 40, 41, 42

4th Gurkha Rifles: 1/4th 202–5, 208; 2/4th 130–1

5th Royal Gurkha Rifles FF: 1/5th 50, 52, 240–1, 247, 250–2; 2/5th 110–1, 146, 202–4, 206, 213, 215, 262–3

6th Gurkha Rifles: 1/6th 50, 52–6, 65–6, 211; 2/6th 273

7th Gurkha Rifles: 1/7th 213, 214; 2/7th 77, 175; 3/7th 214

8th Gurkha Rifles: 2/8th 37–8; 4/8th 259, 261, 267

9th Gurkha Rifles: 1/9th 81, 245; 2/9th 84–6, 110–1; 3/9th 268–9, 292

10th Gurkha Rifles: 2/10th 50, 52, 271, 273

Indian Medical Service 48, 50, 79, 90, 165–6, 215, 254–5, 260, 264–5

Royal Indian Army Service Corps (RIASC) 138, 139, 149, 159, 215, 259

Indian Electrical and Mechanical Engineers (IEME) 280, 288

Indian Signal Corps 160–1, 267; *see also* Army, Indian, Signals

Indian States Forces:

Bikanir Camel Corps 67;
Jodhpur Lancers 92, 99;
Mysore Lancers 92–99;
Gwalior Lancers 258;
Faridkote S & M 68–9;
Sirmoor S & M 79;
Malerkotla S & M 204–5;
Jodhpur Sardar Light Infantry 230
Tochi Scouts (Civil Armed Forces) 126–7, 128–31

WATERS, R. S., Major 40th Pathans 39, 40

Wavell, General Sir Archibald 139, 142, 156–7, 162, 198, 208

Western Front, 1914–17 32–49, *10*, *12*

Wheeler, G. C., VC, Major 2/9 GR 85–6

Whitworth, D. E., Capt 2 Lancers 95–7

ZARDAD, HAVILDAR 129; Baluchis 72

Sources of Illustrations

Imperial War Museum, London 10, 11, 14, 15, 16, 17, 19, 29, 30, 31, 32, 33, 35–50; India Office Library, London 4, 7; National Army Museum, London 1, 2, 6, 9, 18, 26; Author's Collection 22, 23, 24, 34; F. M. Bailey *Mission to Tashkent* (1946) 20, 21; Courtesy Lance Cattermole and the Cavalry and Guards Club, London 25; Courtesy Hobhouse Ltd., London 3; Courtesy Parker Gallery, London 8, 13; Courtesy Royal Artillery Institution, Woolwich 28; Courtesy L. F. Steele 27; *The Graphic* April 1917, 12.

All maps and plans in the text drawn by M. L. Design (Martin Lubikowski): adapted from Charles Chenevix Trench, *The Frontier Scouts* pp. 113, 129; from Anthony Brett-James, *Ball of Fire* p. 145; from *The Tiger Kills* pp. 154–5; from G. R. Stephens, *Fourth Indian Division* pp. 166–7, 224, 244; from 1/3rd Gurkha Rifles regimental history p. 201; from Patrick Turnbull, *The Battle of the Box* p. 257; from *One More River* p. 274.